DESERTED
MEDIEVAL VILLAGES

DESERTED MEDIEVAL VILLAGES

STUDIES

edited by

MAURICE BERESFORD

*Professor of Economic History in the
University of Leeds*

and

JOHN G. HURST

*Inspector of Ancient Monuments, Ministry
of Public Building and Works and
Honorary Secretary of the Deserted Medieval
Village Research Group*

LUTTERWORTH PRESS · LONDON

First published 1971

Enquiries on matters arising from these *Studies* should be addressed to the authors of the chapters c/o Deserted Medieval Village Research Group, 67 Gloucester Crescent, London N.W.1. Attention is drawn to the explanation on p. 65 for possible delay in receiving a reply.

Enquiries concerning membership of the Research Group and access to its files should also be made at the same address *by post only*.

Telephone enquiries are not possible.

A Fieldwork Questionnaire setting out the most useful information for a local enquirer to collect is printed as Appendix II, pp. 313–17.

ISBN 0 7188 1373 1

Made and printed in Great Britain by
William Clowes & Sons, Limited, London, Beccles and Colchester

TO OUR PREDECESSORS

AND OUR SUCCESSORS

IN THESE STUDIES

Contents

PART ONE: ENGLAND

Chapter

PART TWO: SCOTLAND

PART THREE: WALES

PART FOUR: IRELAND

Acknowledgments

Apart from permission to reproduce plates and figures, noted separately below, the editors and authors would like to make these acknowledgments.

Prof. Beresford: Mrs. Mavis Batey for material on Nuneham Courtenay, in advance of publication; Mr. John Hopkins for communicating the map of Coombes; Mrs. Irene Poole for typing.

Dr. Butler: Mr. L. Alcock and Mr. H. Thomas for permission to use their plans (Fig. 40b, c, d and e) in advance of publication; those named in the captions for the other Figures in Chapter 9.

Dr. Glasscock: Mrs. Jennifer Lowry for help in the preparation of Fig. 42.

Mr. Hurst: Messrs. P. A. Barker, M. W. Barley, M. Biddle, L. A. S. Butler, R. T. Porter, P. A. Rahtz and J. T. Smith for comments on the draft of Chapters 2 and 3, and for suggestions incorporated: the responsibility for interpretation remains Mr. Hurst's; the excavators, museum curators and others who supplied information on excavations, often in advance of publication, or from museum records; without this help the compilation of the archaeological gazetteer and the interpretation of it in Chapter 2 would have been impossible; Mrs. Betty Ewins, Dr. John Sheail and Mr. Colin Treen for help in compiling and checking the archaeological gazetteer; Mrs. Betty Watt and Mrs. Wendy Golding for typing.

The publication of this book has been assisted by a grant from the British Academy.

Acknowledgments for Plates

1: The Hon. Lady Fairfax-Lucy (Warws. C.R.O., L6/1035); 2: Sir Richard Hamilton, Bart. (Warws. C.R.O., CR750/1); 3a: Dr. John Sheail; 3b and 4: Mr. R. W. Passmore (Church Farm, Coombe, Lancing); 5: Sheffield City Librarian (Fairbank Ms. WES 1L and CP 42/67–68); 6: Ministry of Defence (Air), Crown Copyright (R.A.F. CPE U.K. 1936/3492 of 18 January 1947); 7: Mr. G. Beresford; 8: Mrs. E. M. Minter; 9: Miss D. Dudley; 10–14: Ministry of Defence, Air Force Department, Crown Copyright Reserved, photographs by Dr. J. K. S. St. Joseph; 11–13, 16, 18–19 and 29–31: Dr. J. K. S. St. Joseph, Cambridge University Collection, copyright reserved; 15: Dr. N. McCord, University of Newcastle; 17 and 20: D.M.V.R.G.; 21: Estate Office, Dunrobin Castle; 22–23: Dr. H. Fairhurst; 24: Royal Commission on Ancient Monuments (Scotland), Crown Copyright; 25: School of Scottish Studies, Edinburgh; 26: National Museum of Antiquities, Edinburgh; 27: National Museum of Wales; 28: Royal Commission on Ancient Monuments, Wales, Crown Copyright.

Acknowledgments for Figures

Chapter 1

1, 2, 3, 11 and 12: Mr. B. Emmison, Graphic Artist, University of Leeds; 4: Miss Susan Williams after Dr. R. E. Glasscock, frontispiece to *Allison et al., 1966*; 5 and 9: Mr. Philip Sheail; 6: Mr. B. Emmison, after Warws. C.R.O., Willoughby de Broke Ms., Map no. 1; 7: Mr. B. Emmison, after a photograph taken in 1920 by Prof. A. C. Chibnall of the map then in the possession of Mr. G. Sheddon, East Cowes; 8: British Museum, from King's Top. Coll. XLII, 74; 10: Mr. and Mrs. Keith Batey after the original at Nuneham Park; 13: Dr. R. E. Glasscock, Dr. John Sheail, Mr. Philip Sheail and Mrs. Jennifer Lowry.

Chapter 2

14 and 19B: Mrs. E. M. Minter; 15: Mr. S. E. West; 16: Mr. P. V. Addyman; 17, 20D, 25, 27 and 30: D.M.V.R.G.; 18A and E: Mr. E. W. Holden; 18B–D, 20B, 24 and 28: Mr. and Mrs. J. G. Hurst; 19A: Miss D. Dudley; 19C: Prof. E. M. Jope; 20A: Mr. P. J. Fowler; 20C: Mr. P. T. Norfolk; 21A and 26: Mr. M. Biddle; 21B: Mr. P. A. Rahtz; 21C: Mr. F. H. Thompson; 21D: Mr. P. Savage; 22: Mr. J. W. G. Musty and Mr. D. Algar; 23: Mr. J. G. Hurst; 29: Mr. H. C. Jones. Figures 15, 16, 18B–E, 19B, 20B, 21A and D, 24, 26, 28 and 29 are Crown Copyright reserved. Figures 18–21 were redrawn by Mr. P. Ewence.

Chapter 7

31 and 32: Department of Archaeology, University of Glasgow; 33–35: Royal Commission on Ancient Monuments, Crown Copyright Reserved; 36: J. R. C. Hamilton, Crown Copyright Reserved.

List of Tables in the Text

List of Plates

xiii

List of Figures in the Text

xvi

Editors' Introduction

The study of the deserted medieval village impinges on many of the great themes of English economic history. Some of the desertions are connected with one of the commonest forms of disturbance to which pre-industrial economies were subject: the successive advance and retreat of population. Others were the result of another unsettling stimulus: a change in the relative profitability of different crops, and a consequent change in land-use; here the history of depopulation is closely tied to the history of prices, as Dr. P. J. Bowden has recently shown. Since these price-changes were induced by movements in wages and by the increasing demand of weavers for wool, the empty houses of the husbandmen are part of the long and unfinished history of the reaction of other parts of the economy to changes in manufacturing technology; and these in their turn were closely connected with the level of foreign demand for English exported cloth. And the dislocation that many of the depopulations caused to old-established ways of living is part of another long theme on English history, the conflict of economic interest between those who owned the land and those who worked on it.

The attention given to the subject by economic historians in the last 25 years may be said to have been crowned by the periods devoted to it at the International Economic History Society Conference at Munich in 1965. For that occasion French academic patronage made possible the publication in French of a long essay and bibliography reviewing the progress of the subject in England; and it was the stimulus for us to plan a longer review, bringing the subject up to date and also taking account of work in other parts of Britain. Such a review will also make it unnecessary to attempt the formidable task of bringing up to date *The Lost Villages of England* (1954), successive reprints of which have done no more than correct typographical errors. As far as possible the historical examples cited in Chapter 1 draw on evidences not available for, or not employed in *Lost Villages*.

Economic historians have not been the only specialists interested in the study of the deserted medieval village. Geographers, architectural historians and—above all—archaeologists have added to the liveliness of its study, and their necessary interdependence resulted in the foundation of the Deserted Medieval Village Research Group in 1952. The Group and its activities are rarely absent from any of the pages which follow, and some account is given of its origins and its programme of work. Its *Annual Report* has been issued to members in duplicated form and is not widely available in libraries, but the excavations and fieldwork which the *Reports* have recorded are the basis of the long analysis of the archaeological contribution to deserted village studies that forms Chapter 2.

In medieval village studies it is most desirable for the historian and the archaeologist to work in partnership since written evidences and archaeological evidences (including in this case fieldwork also) may each be available, occasionally overlapping and confirming each other but more commonly proving supplementary. Although for convenience archaeological and historical researches in England have been separately reviewed here, the smaller scale of each type of activity in Scotland, Wales and Ireland has made it possible for the authors of Chapters 7–12 to embrace both. For England the author of Chapter 1 returns in Chapter 4 to comment, from the historian's viewpoint on the conclusions reached by archaeologists and reviewed in Chapter 2.

This *Introduction* began by emphasising that the study of the deserted village, in whatever country, is fruitful only if related to the whole of the history of rural settlement and, indeed, of economic and social history in the broadest sense. In a utopia of polymaths and a cornucopia of research funds it might be possible for the studies and ambitions of the Research Group to range as widely as the whole of medieval settlement, the proper context of the deserted village. In the real world of research work carried on amid other responsibilities and with no paid staff, academic or secretarial, the range has had to be more modest and there are many local explorations still to be achieved, even in England. In other parts of Britain, as the authors of Chapters 7–12 make plain, the unachieved tasks are enormous.

The day may hopefully be near when methods of historical and archaeological inquiry pioneered in deserted village studies will be applied to the very much larger number of villages whose history, although locally highly varied, yet includes one feature denied to every settlement studied within these covers: that is, survival. If we ourselves concentrate for the present—and for some years to come—on that untypical and pathological representative of the medieval settlement, the total failure, it is in order to complete at some modest level a task that has already taken more than twenty years. If other hands turn to apply similar techniques to the study of the non-deserted settlements, they have our friendliest support. Historico- archaeological investigations are bound to be very limited where a village community is still flourishing, tilling the fields, and occupying the same house areas as its medieval predecessor. The dead cannot easily be sought among the living. In one field of study, however, there is hope and promise. The "shrunken" village is a phenomenon full of historical and archaeological interest. Its living portion resembles any normal English village, while its grass-covered houses and streets resemble the deserted sites. Its mysteries are open to the archaeologist without trespassing into cottage gardens and under cottage floors. For the historian the variety of causes and periods which could produce a shrunken village present a major challenge to the intelligent use of documentary evidence. And, it should be noted, the number of shrunken sites greatly exceeds the number of deserted sites. It is with confidence, therefore, that we dedicate this book to our successors.

Part One

ENGLAND

CHAPTER ONE

A Review of Historical Research (to 1968)

M. W. BERESFORD

INTRODUCTION

The Lost Villages of England, the god-child of Miss Margaret Stewart and Mr. J. T. Oliver of the Lutterworth Press, was commissioned in June 1949. At that time I had had a year's experience of fieldwork in Yorkshire but was still suffering from the shock of finding that a phenomenon which I, and all other commentators, had thought purely Midland was in fact equally visible in the fields of the northern plains and the Wolds. It was therefore a stimulus and a challenge to attempt a survey with the title "of England". A contract was signed in November 1951 and the typescript sent to the publishers in May 1953. It was longer than expected—an unhappy characteristic of my books—and therefore submitted to a publisher's reader for comment. Miss Gladys Scott Thompson, to whom the manuscript fell, was completely sceptical of its conclusions, she being bred in the old belief that depopulation was a Tudor phantasy, but the publishers had the courage of my convictions and in May 1954 the book was published. Pre-publication excitement had been heightened by the receipt of a postcard from another historian, bringing this advice:

> I feel impelled to advise you to consider whether or not you should really go ahead with such a book, and to weigh it very carefully as I myself have no desire to be drawn into further controversy, but my hand would be forced if the book maintained the argument I suspect.

His clairvoyant knowledge of the argument must have turned out to be inaccurate, for after 15 years the threatened exposure is still awaited.

In fact reviewers were in general too kind. It was a book with the usual complement of errors in text, footnotes and grid references; and no one noticed that Cornwall was completely missing from the gazetteer: for the very good reason that this page of the typescript fell down behind a piano without being noticed, and was found only when moving house in 1958. Mr. F. T. Wainwright was perfectly correct in saying in a review:

> It is easy to criticise arrangement, to point to over-hasty work, and to urge that the book should not have been written at this stage.[1]

[1] *Archaeol. News Letter*, v (1954), 76.

In a favourite phrase of Prof. Finberg, "one always writes too soon,"[2] but I have been fortunate in having had later opportunities to return to the subject of deserted villages. In 1957 my *History on the Ground* was able to consider six sites in a little more detail, and to print the whole of Thomas Clerke's plan of Whatborough in 1586 and part of the plan of Wormleighton in 1734[3] (see also Thorpe,[4] 1965). An unintended consequence of my second study was to cause a fellow-historian, who was writing a text book, to coalesce ideas from two of my chapters and thus to refer to the planted medieval town of Hedon as a "depopulated place". The irate Mayor of this borough threatened legal action and readers of the *Daily Express* were entertained by the commotion for a few days.

Prof. David Knowles' invitation to join Dr. St. Joseph in compiling an anthology of air photographs gave a further opportunity to describe sites not treated in *Lost Villages* and to publish thirteen new views (Beresford and St. Joseph, 1958).

Although *Lost Villages* is still a few years from its coming-of-age its general arguments may be said to have gained academic acceptance, and indeed to have been canonised by two recent authoritative studies of agrarian history, Prof. Postan's revised chapter in the *Cambridge Economic History of Europe* (1966) and Dr. Thirsk's in the *Agrarian History of England and Wales* (1967). The respectability of the subject in general may be said to have been crowned by the special sessions devoted to it at the International Economic History Conference at Munich in August 1965. For that occasion the patronage of the Sixth Section of the École Pratique des Hautes Études, Paris, produced in *Villages Désertés* a 615-page survey of the progress of research in the major European countries.[5] In it I attempted a review of the work achieved by English historians and archaeologists, and that review—revised and extended—has formed the basis of this chapter. In particular I have retained for the first nine sections a device employed in the French essay: to set at the head in italics a brief summary of points which I believe I made in *Lost Villages*, and then to follow with an assessment of work by others and myself in the intervening years. It thus has egocentric as well as self-critical passages; and, although I have tried to take account of all work known to me, there must be omissions which are due to that most subjective of academic traits, sheer ignorance. Fellow authors must not mistake this for indifference. They will also notice that I have acquiesced in the substitution of "deserted" for "lost" medieval villages, mainly under the influence of logical critics who argued that villages could not really be "lost" if I had found them.

I: EARLY DESERTION

Some considerable depopulation followed the Norman invasion of 1066, but there was rapid re-population of vills stated to be waste in Domesday Book (1086). The civil wars (1135–54) may have produced a similar impact and recovery. More depopulation —and this often permanent—was caused by the development of monastic-grange farming in the twelfth century. A few settlements may have been lost in war.

[2] H. P. R. Finberg, gen. ed., *The Agrarian History of England and Wales*, IV (1967), vii.

[3] Misdated 1724 in the caption to my Plate 9.

[4] Short-title references within brackets are to articles and books listed in the bibliography, pp. 213–26, below.

[5] It is unfortunate that this important volume carries no editor's name on its title page so that it is not easy to find in a library catalogue. The full title is given under *École Pratique* in the bibliography.

Of earlier desertions, those during the long centuries of Anglo-Saxon and Scandinavian colonisation, virtually nothing is yet known. In the period before the Norman Conquest no list of rural settlements was drawn up comparable to the list of *burhs* in the Burghal Hidage: or if one was drawn up, it has failed to survive. Common sense suggests that during the so-called Dark Ages there must have been sites chosen for early settlements that did not stand the test of time, as well as settlements destroyed in invasion and war but, without documentary evidence, the search for these is properly the task of the archaeologist [see pp. 76–144, below].

The classic sites of Saxon villages and cemeteries known to archaeologists lie mainly away from existing villages. These are clearly "desertions" but their discovery has been largely the result of chance factors such as gravel working or road construction.

Although the earliest documentary evidence for most deserted medieval villages continues to be Domesday Book (1086) it is now possible to adduce more examples of deserted villages recorded in Anglo-Saxon boundary charters of an earlier date. Thus ten Oxfordshire villages now deserted are named in charters dating from between 970 and 1005, and three Warwickshire desertions were of villages that occur in charters from the very beginning of the eighth century: Billesley Trussell (704); Weethley (708) and Milcote (710). Documents of this type, unfortunately, become progressively rarer as one moves north.

Apart from the research in progress by Mr. A. T. Lloyd (and unpublished) on the difficult subject of the New Forest depopulations, no further work has been done on individual villages known to have been devastated by the Norman Conquest and not repopulated. Such a site would be an excavator's treasure. The devastations of the civil war of 1135–54 has been little studied, for the period is poorly documented. In 1955 Sir Charles Clay published a remarkable confirmation charter for Ulceby on the Lincolnshire Wolds.[6] It was granted between 1163 and 1176 and it permitted Thornton Abbey to turn out sheep to graze in the fields of Ulceby to a reasonable number—*tot oves quot ibidem moderate habere*—until such time as the village should be repopulated and restored to life—*donec ipsa villa rehabitata et restituta fuerit*. The depopulation must have been during the late wars, for in both Domesday Book and the Lindsey Survey of 1115–18 there is no sign that the Norman Conquest emptied the vill. The anticipated repopulation must have taken place, for Ulceby is not a deserted village, but it is significant that the lord of Ulceby assumed that the best temporary garrison for an abandoned village was a flock of sheep. This was presumably the exact reaction of local landlords in later centuries where villagers retreated from marginal land, the light soils of the high Wolds.

Dr. R. A. Donkin has made important comments on the Cistercian factor in depopulation (Donkin, 1960, 1962, 1963 and 1964). He has shown that 44% of all known twelfth-century granges were built on land that was "waste" or largely waste in 1086, although the well-documented depopulations still remain. A critical account of the Yorkshire evidence will be found in Dr. C. P. S. Platt's unpublished University of Leeds thesis, *The Monastic Grange: a survey of the historical and archaeological evidence* (1965). The

[6] C. T. Clay, ed., *Early Yorkshire Charters*, x, Yorks. Archaeol. Soc. Rec. Series, extra series viii (1955), 58.

granters' charters did not always describe their vills in detail, and below the well-preserved earthworks of a grange such as Griff (Yorks., N.R., between Rievaulx and Helmsley) there may be those of a wasted Domesday vill or of a re-settled vill destroyed when it was given to the abbey in 1131. This fact adds to the importance of such sites for a research excavation, if one could be engineered.

Dr. Donkin has also emphasised that the well-known activity of the Cistercians as sheep farmers on their more remote estates should not lead to a belief that the granges were all pastoral, and that the Cistercians had the same motives as the enclosing graziers of the late fifteenth century. He writes:

> The typical grange was, I believe, a predominantly arable holding, although most had some pasture and played a part in the growing of wool. The great upland sheep walks were not as a rule described as granges in the 12th and 13th centuries. (Donkin, 1963, 187.)

In a short local study Mr. M. W. Barley has shown how the monks of Rufford (founded *c.* 1145) destroyed two Nottinghamshire villages, one of which had ten villein families in 1086 and the other, eleven as well as a church (Barley, 1957). The Cistercians did sometimes offer alternative accommodation if their grange was about to supplant a village. Mr. Barley suggests that Wellow grew in this way, and I have myself shown the shift of population at the founding of Byland Abbey (Beresford, 1957, 52–62).

Where monastic chartularies survive, there is a good chance that all such early depopulations will come to light eventually. The identification of non-monastic depopulations of this period is bound to suffer from the relative shortage of relevant documentation before the mid-thirteenth century, when the inquisitions *post mortem* and the reeves' accounts (p. 72, below) begin to be available. The feet of fines (P.R.O., class CP25) which take land transfers in some counties back to the end of the twelfth century, have not yet been systematically explored for deserted villages.

In the last decade of the thirteenth century, records of taxation of the laity begin to be available (P.R.O., class E179) and local record societies are moving ahead with their publication. Where they survive, these early lay subsidy rolls have been used in the Research Group's published county studies for two purposes: to indicate that a separate settlement worthy of the tax collector's attentions was still surviving; and to obtain some idea of the size of the settlement at that date, relative to its neighbours. Before 1377 the form of these documents does not permit any estimate of the absolute number of villagers.

The lay subsidy files were drawn upon for some of the counties analysed in *Lost Villages of England*, but these sources have been more thoroughly explored in the last ten years. Dr. R. E. Glasscock has transcribed and mapped all the payments made by the villages of England in 1334 (Glasscock, 1963, and subsequent unpublished work), and identified a number of additional desertions. The gazetteers that the Deserted Medieval Village Research Group aim to produce for each county must lean very heavily on the tax-lists and feudal surveys that begin with the Hundred Rolls of 1279 and continue with the lay taxation of 1296, 1307, 1327, 1332 and 1334.

The flimsy remains of an early, pre-plague depopulation were first observed on an air photograph (Beresford and St. Joseph, 1958, 112) and later identified by Dr. Allison as the former vill of Grenstein. It, and a second Norfolk vill with only early documentary references (*Turstanestuna* (Thuxton)) were excavated by Mr. Wade-Martins. It was vills of this sort that the tax collectors of 1316 categorised as *"parva et paupera"* (Shelswell, Oxon.), while at Langley in the same county they reported only four tenements remaining.

Four Norfolk vills—Pudding Norton, Testerton, Alethorpe and Little Ringstead—were assessed in 1334 at sums that were less than one fifth of those paid by their neighbours,[7] and it is not surprising that, when the church of Pudding Norton fell into disuse, "the fewness and the poverty of the parishioners" in 1401 were blamed on the barren soil.[8] Vacant holdings and uncultivated acres are a recurring feature of manorial surveys of the early fourteenth century, even in villages that now survive. They seem to be especially frequent on the high, dry chalklands of Lincolnshire and the East Riding of Yorkshire, and on the sands of the Breckland in Norfolk and Suffolk. Thirty-four places in Norfolk that were named in Domesday Book fail to appear in 1316 in the *Nomina Villarum* either because they were too small or because they were deserted (Allison, 1955, 122).

The reason for these early depopulations still remains mysterious. It would be logical and convenient to follow Prof. Postan's hypothesis that they were on marginal soil, reluctantly colonised in a period of population expansion, but soon disappointing the over-optimism of their settlers by poor crop yields. This explanation can be accepted most easily when the desertions lie close together on similar soils. In Norfolk, for example, Dr. Allison has shown that 31 of the 130 deserted villages had fewer than ten households in 1428 (Allison, 1955, 125). Taken together with the exceptional number of ruined churches in Norfolk and Suffolk, these figures suggest that some powerful local factor was diminishing settlement even before the Black Death. As Mr. J. Saltmarsh put it:

> It is probable that on marginal lands, colonised during the period of expanding demand and high prices in the earlier Middle Ages, whole villages were being abandoned. In the Brecklands of south-west Norfolk—marginal land in the Middle Ages, and marginal or sub-marginal still—I have visited five ruined churches in a single afternoon. Where their ruins could be dated, they were always of the thirteenth century and very small; the first tiny chapels built by the latest pioneer settlements of the High Middle Ages, never enlarged and early abandoned. (Saltmarsh, 1941–43, 24.)

But when an early desertion is found in the middle of a more prosperous county such as Oxfordshire, where only seven of the 101 deserted villages were reported[9] as having fewer than ten households in 1428, it will be necessary to pay close attention to its soil and situation, especially where adjoining parishes have every appearance of health. One might suspect a random factor such as fire or warfare, but it is difficult to envisage a well-sited village being deserted for long when there was general land-hunger and an expanding population. These depopulations must be set against the fact that the total population of England increased from about 1·1 million in 1086 to 3·3 million on the eve of the Black Death.[10]

[7] Calculated from figures in *Allison, 1955*, 127–29.   [8] *Cal. Pap. Letters*, V (1904), 474–75.
[9] *Feudal Aids . . . and Analogous Documents, 1284–1431*, V (1909), 201–02.
[10] J. C. Russell, *British Medieval Population* (Albuquerque, 1948), 146.

The more flimsy the houses of a village, the easier it would have been to rebuild after a fire or destruction in war. As to the fields, those who burned them were unintentionally assisting the crops by resting the soil and scattering ash.

The ease with which the vills of the lowlands were re-created between 1066 and 1086, and the subsequent prosperity of many upland vills that were waste in 1086, make an instructive lesson in the resilience of medieval settlement. The ravages of war, like the accident of fire, were always likely to afflict a village. After the civil war of 1135–54 there was internal warfare on more than one occasion, but only the Borders were continuously troubled. Here one might expect war to cause depopulation. In the early fourteenth century there were massive tax reliefs for villages damaged when the Scottish armies ranged as far south as York. The assessment of clerical wealth for taxation purposes made in 1291 was subject to wholesale revision downwards in 1318 to allow for the destruction wrought by the Scots, and in 1334, when the villages of the rest of the kingdom were re-assessed for lay taxation, it was not possible to value the counties of the northern border. Yet most of the places given heavy tax-reliefs are now normal villages. Clearly, other factors than war must have operated to produce the permanent desertions from this period.

II: THE BLACK DEATH

Some marginal settlements were already shrinking before the Black Death began in 1349, and after the Black Death there are a few well-documented cases of villages totally and irrevocably destroyed.

Authentic cases of Black Death depopulation were cited in *Lost Villages*, and an air photograph of one of these, Tusmore (Oxon.), has since been published (Beresford and St. Joseph, 1958, 114–15). In 1358 its lord was allowed to turn the fields into a park since every villein was dead, and the Exchequer was obliged to admit that there were no taxpayers left. In 1381 the poll-tax collectors made *nichil* returns for four Gloucestershire villages (Hilton and Rahtz, 1966, 84). The site of another Oxfordshire plague depopulation, *Tilgardesle*, still remains unlocated, a reminder that there is still much fieldwork to be done to trace sites that have been heavily ploughed in modern times or planted with woodland.

It will always be necessary to be so emphatic about the role of the Black Death for two reasons: firstly, it has been the most popular explanation of a deserted site in local folklore; and secondly, because there *was* an important way, to be discussed later, in which the long-term effect of the Black Death did deliver some villages into the hands of the would-be depopulators a century later, and weakened the resistance of many other villages. In this sense, the years following the Black Death were the "pre-history of enclosure" (Hilton, 1955).

Since it is so important to get the Black Death into the correct relation with the desertion of a particular village every effort is needed to establish the genuine Black Death destructions. The classic sequence for such a desertion would be three or more positive items, such as

    1086:   substantial recorded population in Domesday Book
    1316:   listed in the *Nomina Villarum*

1334:   paying a substantial amount to the village tax of that year
          followed by one or more of the negative items:
1352–5: high tax relief (from a fund provided by fines under the Statute of
          Labourers)
1377:   small number of heads taxed to the poll-tax
1428:   relieved from the parish tax.

In addition, the disappearance of a village name from tax rolls subsequent to 1355 would help to support the case for a plague depopulation; and the absence of prosecutions for enclosure in the sixteenth century would also lend support, at least in the Midlands. Fulbrook (Warws.) would seem to be one of these cases.   Half its tax quota was abated in 1352 and it was unable to pay the parish tax of 1428 since there were only four households.   In Berkshire three vills had abatements of more than 70% of their tax in 1352 and thereafter do not appear in the lists of taxed vills: Hodcot, Langley and Thrupp. It must be stressed, however, that the complete absence of any reference to a village in 1352–55 and 1377 is not significant: there are counties where documents from these classes do not happen to survive.

Lost Villages was too disdainful, I now feel, of records from the second and third poll-tax collections, taken in 1379 and 1381.   It is true that they were demonstrably evaded, compared with 1377 (Table I) but the importance of the poll-tax records in establishing village chronology is so great that one must clutch at any straw, and in those counties with virtually nothing from 1377, there may be (as for Gloucestershire) documents from 1379 or 1381 from which *minimal* populations can be established.   They also have one advantage over the receipts from 1377 in giving occupations of taxpayers; having moved away from the egalitarian fourpence-a-head of 1377, they also give some indication of differences in personal wealth: always remembering that those who evaded tax make up an unknown, invisible submerged proportion of the iceberg.

In counties where poll-tax receipts do survive, the argument of *Lost Villages* has not been undermined: plague depopulations were few, and the main utility of the poll-tax documents (on which Miss L. M. Midgley and I are working to produce a complete edition) is to prove that identifiable communities still existed in 1377–81, and to enable a further assessment of their size in relation to their neighbours.

In Leicestershire 37 of the 62 deserted villages have poll-tax receipts surviving. Some but not all of these data have been published, and Table I illustrates the usefulness of this source.   Prof. Hoskins' study had concluded that no more than eight Leicestershire depopulations could possibly be attributed to the plagues (Hoskins, 1946) and my own examination of the data suggests that the number is as few as three. Two of the three lowest scores in Table I are for places where a poll-tax receipt from 1377 is missing, and the next collection in 1379 was notoriously evaded, so that only Shoby may be accepted without question as being very small indeed with its 18 taxpayers, perhaps 27 souls.   But it cannot yet be called depopulated, and indeed it had not been much larger before the plague.   In 1334 its tax quota was less than half of the local average, so that it was already weak.   In the parish taxation of 1428 Shoby had fewer than ten households, but it struggled and struggled on, and was not finally extinguished until after 1450.

One very remarkable piece of evidence has been published by Prof. Hilton (Hilton

TABLE I

Number of taxpayers in 37 deserted villages of Leicestershire, 1377–81

Baggrave	38*	Noseley	75
Bittesby	21*	Potters Marston	26*
Bradgate	41	Poultney	54
Brentingby	53	Prestgrave	10*
Brooksby	39	Prestwold	59
Coton, Far	29	Quenby	27*
Eye Kettleby	40	Shoby	18
Foston	99	Stapleford	152
Frisby	39	Starmore	63
Gopsall	20*	Staunton Harold	69
Ingarsby	32	Stretton in le Field	21
Keythorpe	18*	Stretton Magna	21*
Knaptoft	35	Welby	75(?)
Lowesby	25*	Whatborough	22
Lubbesthorpe	26	Whittington	21
Misterton	49	Wiston	69
Newbold Saucy	29	Withcote	45
Newton, Cold	38	Wyfordby	44
Normanton Turville	49		

* Asterisks indicate data from the second and third collections of 1379 and 1381, when there was much evasion and under-assessment: e.g. the 41 heads in Bradgate in 1377 became 29, the 152 in Stapleford, 93.

and Rahtz, 1966, 83) showing that at the depopulated Upton (Gloucs.) in 1383–84 the village's tax quota was then being paid from the funds of the lord of the manor, the bishop of Worcester.

> Where we find the financial responsibility for the subsidy payment assumed by the lord, it could only mean that the lord has to pay either because of the villagers' poverty, or because they were no longer there. It was not until statutory tax exemptions of the 15th century that the burden of subsidy payment was officially lifted.

These exemptions, from 1433 onwards, were used in *Lost Villages* but since 1953 my confidence in the usefulness of the fifteenth-century tax reliefs has diminished. The methodical tabulation of tax abatements after 1433 has been continued in the Research Group's county publications but they often appear quite haphazard: a vill would receive a high rebate in one collection and then a low rebate, or none at all, in the next. The median abatement in Leicestershire and Norfolk for deserted villages was less than 20% (Beresford, 1965, Table 2). Much more research into the conventions of local reassessment is necessary.

III: DEPOPULATION AND SHEEP

The main force of depopulation was not felt until after c. 1450. The incentive was the demand for wool for the expanding English cloth industry, while the post-plague population had not recovered enough to increase the demand for corn. Pastoral farming was also tempting since it used a smaller labour force at a time when the bargaining power of labour was still high.

Nothing published since 1954 has shaken the contention—which goes back to John Hales' dictum[11] of 1549—that

the chief destruction of towns (i.e. townships) and decay of houses was before the beginning of the reign of King Henry VII (i.e. before 1485).

Hales, it will be remembered, had personal knowledge of the counties most affected and had bitter experience of the failure of the anti-depopulation legislation to punish enclosing graziers and effect re-conversion to arable. The failure rested on the unwillingness of successive Parliaments to look back further than 1488. As Dr. E. Kerridge has clearly shown (Kerridge, 1955) many of those accused were able to plead successfully that the alleged offences had taken place before the crucial date; Dr. Kerridge shows the great gap between the allegations made to Wolsey's itinerant commissioners and the facts later revealed in Chancery and Exchequer proceedings.

Possibly many of the decays and conversions presented by the inquisitions had been made before the statute of 4 Henry VII. (Kerridge, 1955, 221.)

Had Dr. Kerridge's otherwise detailed footnotes given the names of the villages concerned in the pleadings that he followed up, they would have strengthened his "possibly", for it cannot be a coincidence that the local juries time and again made allegations about villages that are now grassy earthworks. It would have been no use asking the judges to go out to the provinces and view the empty fields. Many a juror must have ground his teeth to hear that the judges had rejected allegations when he knew, as did Hales, that there were empty fields that in the memory of man had been peopled with villagers. It would not have been easy to convince him that the memory of living men was a span of time too long for Justice to take into her scales, nor that the depopulation of a village was any the less serious a social problem because it had taken its architects a long time to achieve.

This was the mood of indignation that runs through the comments of John Rous of Warwick, written *c.* 1486. No other contemporary list of depopulations has yet emerged in another county to match his, drawn from the experience of his own observations in the south Midlands. Most of his instances came from Warwickshire, and thus give the depopulations of that county the most firm date-limits of any, at least 75 falling between *c.* 1450 and 1520. In other counties the most generally available documents do not permit close dating for every village even after bringing in source-material not employed in *Lost Villages* (p. 70, below). The present state of knowledge for three Midland counties is set out in Table II.

One question arises from this pre-1488 dating which I did not ask in *Lost Villages*; and since no critic asked it, I will ask it here myself. Could this type of enclosure,

[11] E. Lamond, ed., *A Discourse of the Common Weal* (1929), lxiii: from B. M. Lans. Ms. 238.

economising in man-power just as much as the enclosures that troubled Wolsey and John Hales in the next century, take place without open warfare between the protagonists of arable and the protagonists of grass? Yes, if there were alternative holdings for a dispossessed husbandman. In the chronology of that crucial relationship—men to available land—the period before 1488 had a relative land surfeit, whereas the depopulations that aroused public opinion after 1488 were certainly taking place in a period when a Malthusian resurgence of population had brought back land-hunger, and with it not only a competition between one man and another for a piece of land but an aggregate competition between men and animals.

TABLE II

Probable periods of desertion in four Midland counties

	Northamptonshire %	Leicestershire %	Oxfordshire %	Warwickshire %
Period I (soon after 1086)	5	8	1	0
Period II (c. 1100– c. 1350)	1	8	8	0
Period III (c. 1350– c. 1450)	17	12	30	12
Period IV (c. 1450– c. 1700)	60	60	45	73
Period V (after c. 1700)	11	5	3	6
Totally uncertain	6	7	13	7
Total	82 villages	65 villages	101 villages	74 villages

In *Lost Villages* the changing relationship of wool prices to corn prices was put forward as a principal reason for the move from arable to pastoral farming, and the price-series employed was one published by Dr. Bowden (Bowden, 1952), drawing on material collected for his University of Leeds thesis (1952). That series went back no further than 1490, so that its principal value lay in showing the favourable conditions of pastoral profitability in the periods 1504–18 and 1537–48, each of which culminated in anti-enclosure legislation. It also showed how the long depression of cloth exports after 1550 led to more encouraging conditions for arable farming. Dr. Bowden's data survived the strictures of Mr. Wright[12] and Prof. Pollard[13] and they have now been extended back to 1450 and elaborated in the *Agrarian History of England* (Bowden, 1967, appendix A, 814–65). The figures dispel the doubts voiced by Prof. Gould (Gould, 1955, 108 fn.) whether there really was a rise in wool prices relative to corn in the crucial years before 1488.

In his commentary (Bowden, 1967, 593–697) Dr. Bowden set the movement in arable prices against two other series, livestock and animal products (*Ibid.*, Tables 23 and 24). He wrote (over):

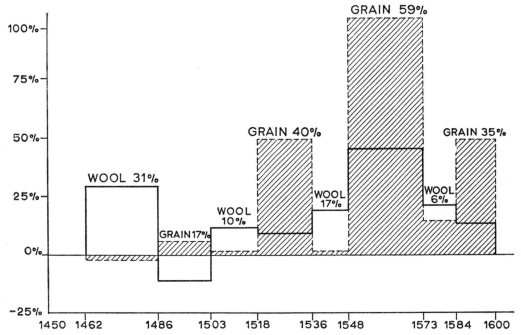

Fig. 1. Relative movements of grain and wool prices, by periods, 1450–1600

Wool is indicated by a firm line, grain by a broken line and emphasised by line-shading.

For each period the heights of each column represent the % increase in the annual average price of that commodity over the annual average for the previous period. The difference in heights indicates which commodity price rose the faster, and by how much: thus the price of wool rose 29% in 1462–86 compared with 1450–61; but that of grain fell by 2%; thus the *ascendancy* of wool prices can be measured by the index 31. In the next period, 1487–1503, grain prices rose but wool prices fell, an *ascendancy* index of 17 resulting. The ascendant crop and the ascendancy index are indicated at the top of each column.

Note: the alternating periods of ascendancy for each commodity; and that after 1503 *both* prices rose, but by markedly different amounts.

12 *Yorks. Bull. of Econ. and Soc. Research*, IV (1952), 110 and 124.   13 *Ibid.*, VII (1955), 156–61.

The urge towards increased wool production was very strongly felt in the years 1462–86 when the annual average price of wool was almost one-third higher than in the previous period. On the evidence of prices alone it seems possible to pinpoint these years as marking the most destructive phase in the sheep-enclosure movement.

Fig. 1 (above) takes six broad periods, the first of which is 1450–61, and shows by what percentage the average annual prices of wool and of wheat rose (or fell) compared with the previous period. Thus the average wool price in the crucial period 1462–86 was 29% higher than the wool price for 1450–61: but the average corn price was 2% lower in the second period. It will be seen that there were alternating periods:

1462–86	*wool* prices ahead	(*31 points lead*)
1487–1503	corn prices ahead	(*17 points lead*)
1504–18	*wool* prices ahead	(*10 points lead*)
1519–36	corn prices ahead	(*40 points lead*)
1537–48	*wool* prices ahead	(*17 points lead*);

and that in this reading of the evidence the governmental action discouraging pasture in 1488, 1517 and 1549 always came too late. Did governmental action nevertheless cause the swing back to arable profitability? Dr. Bowden thinks not. He sees the mechanism as triggered off not by government bans and bounties (which would have needed a long time to act even if they could have been efficiently administered) but by "the impersonal intervention of the weather", that is by runs of exceptionally good or bad grain harvests in western Europe with their important effect on purchasing power for goods that derived from sheep or cattle. Ironically, it was the good *grain* years that tempted conversion to grass: in 1549 the author of *The Discourse of the Commonweal*[14] recalled such a pair of years, 1536 and 1537, when the Husbandman and his neighbours recognised that "proffittes were but small by the plowes" so that they had

> turned ether part or all theire arable grounds into pasture, and therby have waxed verie Rich men.

Dr. Bowden also shows that 1504–18 and 1537–48 were periods when oxen and hide prices were showing even greater rises (relative to corn) than wool. Thus it may be possible to differentiate two enclosure movements: the first during the long period 1462–86, mainly for sheep; and then the two shorter periods, 1504–18 and 1537–48 for sheep *and* cattle.

In *Lost Villages*, seduced perhaps by the Tudor rhetoric on the theme of the devouring sheep, I certainly paid too little attention to the other grazing animals for which a man might want more pasture, although in doing justice to them I would not want to remove the sheep from pre-eminence. In particular, the evidence that Dr. Finch[15] and Prof. Stone[16] adduced for large numbers of cattle grazing the sites of villages is drawn

[14] E. Lamond, ed., *op. cit.*, 56.

[15] M. E. Finch, *The Wealth of Five Northamptonshire Families, 1540–1640*, Northants. Rec. Soc., XIX (1956), 42–47.

[16] "Discussion of sheep-farming in the sixteenth century has far too long been conducted on the erroneous assumption that sheep are perambulating empty woolly bags": L. Stone, *The Crisis of the Aristocracy, 1558–1641* (1965), 298. But Dr. Bowden (Bowden, 1967, 644) writes: "it is not until the latter half of the sixteenth century that evidence begins to accumulate of the growth of a market-orientated livestock fattening industry of any significance".

mainly from the later sixteenth century although I take the point (Thorpe, 1965, 101) that the draft bill of 1515 put butchers and tanners alongside graziers as the villains of the piece. But 1515, it must be said, was some distance from 1488, and by that time there was a rising population to make the demand for meat and hides (and grain) again buoyant. But it had not been ever thus when looms were breeding faster than men.

Legislation like that of 1533 to limit the size of sheep flocks, and that of 1536 to encourage graziers to keep milk kine, does not suggest that free market forces were turning graziers' minds to cattle; and in 1549 it was a sheep tax that was invented, not a tax on every four-footed grass-grazer (Beresford, 1953A and 1954A).

Part of the argument for price-movements as an incentive to conversion of arable rested on a farmer's sensitivity to wage-costs, which made up more of the expenses on an arable holding than the same area under a shepherd. In some ingenious calculations Dr. Bowden estimates that on an arable holding wages made up 36% of total expenses but only 11% for a sheep farm. His calculations also reinforce a point made by Dr. Finch and by Prof. Gould (Gould, 1955, 108 fn.) that there were considerable economies of scale in sheep-farming, and that greater profits per acre were made on the larger sheep-runs, thus tempting a landlord to engross holdings.

Becoming a sheep specialist was more tempting, the larger the holding; and indeed the amount of capital then necessary to stock it with sheep was larger than a small husbandman could face. Dr. Finch and Dr. Bowden have therefore helped to answer an awkward question: why did landlords choose to turn the *whole* of one or more of their villages to grass when they wanted more wool from it; why did they not convert a few acres to grass on *each* of their estates and thus avoid the opprobrium of total depopulation? The dispossessed husbandmen were the victims of two impersonal forces—the movement of product prices and the technical fact of economies of scale.

In the Dark Ages of our knowledge before 1488, with no government enquiries and no litigation to bring out names, dates and places, it is the more important to study manorial and estate records to elucidate the pre-history of enclosure, as Prof. Hilton has aptly styled the subject. His own study deals with two Warwickshire villages, Compton Verney and Kingston (Chesterton Parva), and the conversion of each to

> a comparatively sparsely populated village, where pastoral farming predominated. (Hilton, 1955, 684.)

Through evidence from manorial records he was able to demonstrate that the extinction of arable was virtually complete at Kingston by 1437 and at Compton Verney by 1461. It was not a simple case of vacant post-plague holdings falling into the hands of the seigneur. Surrenders between 1397 and 1401 at Compton Verney were by tenants still living. Nor was pastoral farming an imposition: surviving tenants were themselves increasing the area under grass, so that when the Verneys wanted to turn the two vills into a sheep-run a good deal of their work had already been done for them. Mrs. Spufford makes the same point about the peasants at Chippenham who, by swallowing up one another's holdings, halved the task of the lord of the manor when he sought to acquire holdings for the enlargement of his park (Spufford, 1965, 46). In all such manoeuvres the size of the village population at risk remains a topic of crucial significance (pp. 21–26 below).

3   15

The importance of the deserted village will not be diminished if its causation proves to be more complex than a simple act of landlord aggression. If its weakness in the face of a would-be grazier landlord depended on its absolute size at the time, then its history is at once involved in the difficult subject of the agrarian response to falling population (Postan, ed., 1966, 565–70 and 667–94); and since some villages were clearly more vulnerable than their neighbours, the local character of the response is emphasised the more.

And if, as at Whatborough, it was not its landlord, but the tenant on long lease who destroyed the village, the subject takes us to the central feature of fifteenth-century landlordism, an abdication from direct concern with the organisation of the demesne lands. It is this abdication which inevitably lessens the information set down in manorial records of the fifteenth century, compared with those of the fourteenth (pp. 72–73, below). Important, therefore, is any evidence for the place of grass among the open-field arable, a question raised first by Prof. Hoskins; for the degree of convertible husbandry; and particularly for the husbandry practices in those local economies where the sheep and the plough had long been complementary. Some combinations of sheep and plough, as in the Cotswolds, seem to have given immunity against wholesale conversion to pasture in the fifteenth century while others, as in the Wolds of Yorkshire and Lincolnshire, seem to have accelerated it. These topics must be on the agenda for local agrarian history.

It is now possible to see more clearly why the process of enclosure was long drawn out, and why the final depopulation might well concern only a few remaining tenants. In more than two-thirds of the proceedings against enclosers in years following the 1517 inquiry, the alleged depopulation involved only one house; in only twelve cases out of 482 (3%) was depopulation of ten or more houses alleged.

Prof. Hilton's study may again be quoted. He concluded:

> It seems likely that the drop in the number of tenants (i.e. after the Black Death), the tendency to the accumulation of holdings and the turn towards pasture farming also destroyed the cohesion of the medieval rural community. Given such conditions a vigorous landlord could carry these tendencies to their logical conclusion and become himself the final accumulator of all holdings, which he could then turn to pasture. (Hilton, 1955, 681.)

Since he wrote these words, the studies of two of his former students, Mr. C. Dyer and Mr. T. H. Lloyd, have further illuminated the dark period of "the prehistory of enclosure". These two studies show what use can be made of manorial accounts and court rolls where these chance to survive from a deserted village. Mr. Lloyd was concerned with Brookend (Oxon.) and Mr. Dyer with Hatton in Hampton Lucy (Warws.). Hatton displays a situation similar to that in Upton (Gloucs.), the lord of the manor forced to pay part of the villager's tax contribution himself as his tenants "absconded" in the 1380's (Dyer, 1968, 119); and the tithing man having to present in the manor court that "no tenants live there but it remains in the lord's hands as pasture".

A question frequently asked at public lectures on the theme of this book, is, where did the villagers from the deserted sites go? There is no new evidence since the publication of *Lost Villages*. The data about deserted village sizes and the spread-out chronology of their desertion make the single large-scale eviction, as described in some of the returns of 1517, not so typical as it once seemed; while evidence accumulates for considerable mobility among village populations in general in the centuries after the Black Death.   If an economy was accustomed to having villagers on the move, then it would not be so spectacularly disconcerted by the addition of the evicted to their number.   In any event, the decades when the migration from deserted sites was at its height were not devoid of alternative employment.   The very expansion of the textile industry that provoked conversion to grass necessitated an in-flow of labour.   Some of this was to rural industry not very far in miles from the countryside of abandoned sites, but some was to town employment.   In the towns there was work in the finishing processes of cloth-making and also much employment, some of it seasonal, in unskilled ancillary work in transport, handling, storing, and ship-loading.

It must be remembered that the period of the workless vagrant, when the greatest outcry arose to provoke State action in relief of the unemployed poor, was not the period of the main village depopulations but more than 50 years later.   By the time of the Elizabethan Poor Law the full pressure of population on land had been resumed and new employment opportunities on marginal land were limited; by this time, too, the broad cloth industry was in serious and long-term contraction and not able, either in town or countryside, to offer permanent work to outsiders and newcomers.   But in the second half of the fifteenth century, when the economy was most called upon to absorb the ex-husbandmen and their families, things were very different.   There was still an unoccupied margin for agriculturists and no troubles besetting the cloth industry.

The fact still remains, however, that we cannot go beyond such general statements as these, based on accepted views of economic change.   Names and faces are still elusive in a period before parish registers and when the collection of taxes was in such a form that no lists of names had to be returned to the Exchequer.   No doubt the vast un-calendared judicial records of the period will contain some autobiographical snippets among evidence and allegations in the course of litigation, but these will be casual, and I cannot myself envisage a documentary source from which systematic biographical information about the former village population will arise.

IV: DEPOPULATION ARRESTED

After 1488, sheep depopulations aroused much public hostility, and enclosers were driven to the defensive.   The type of enclosure that produced total depopulation became rarer after c. 1520 even though enclosure for improved arable farming continued, sometimes by force and sometimes by agreement.   The odium of an enclosure that totally depopulated a village was evoked by those who opposed these other enclosures.   This decline of depopulating enclosure can be explained in five ways: (i) government action and prosecutions, (ii) popular feeling and rioting, (iii) the recovery of the demand for corn and the rise in population, especially in industrial population, (iv) the depression in the cloth trade and therefore in wool prices after c. 1550, (v) the self-adjusting action, whereby the decreased area under corn reduced its supply and thereby assisted its relative price to rise.

The study of the main Tudor agrarian problem, land-hunger amid an inflation, has been carried forward by two local studies with more than local interest and by an important article on prices and rents.   The context of the enclosure troubles can now be studied in two excellent surveys, one a pamphlet, the other a chapter in a short book (Thirsk, 1959; Ramsey, 1963, 19–46). In addition, I have myself described two attacks on enclosures by the government (Beresford, 1953–54), and also shown how early seventeenth-century governments and public opinion began to accept two simple facts: that enclosure did not necessarily produce the depopulation of villages; and that Improvement was not the necessary enemy of Habitation (Beresford, 1961).

This essay in the Tawney *Festschrift* answered (as far as I could) two questions put to me publicly by Prof. Gould (Gould, 1955). In the course of his intervention he wrote:

> One cannot entirely avoid the suspicion that Mr. Beresford may have had another and less valid reason (than the fact that he was writing a history of deserted villages and not of the enclosure movement) for not mentioning the continuance in the Midland shires of enclosure and conversion at a high rate, for had he quite explicitly stated that fact, he would then have had to account for two apparent difficulties.

The "continuance" was in fact discussed (*Lost Villages*, 142–48) and the two "apparent difficulties" met. One question, according to Prof. Gould, that I had sidestepped was:

> why did the rate of village mortality decline while that of enclosure and conversion did not?

although something of the sting was taken from this rebuke by the admission on the next page that I had answered this question, "albeit in a rather haphazard and incidental way". The "continuance at a high rate", invoked by Prof. Gould, is a pure myth. I agree with Dr. Kerridge that precise quantification of total areas affected by enclosures at different periods is impossible—but one measurement is beyond doubt, as I pointed out in *Lost Villages* (p. 145):

> The average area in the thousand entries (from Prof. Gould's Lincolnshire document of 1607) is round about 13 acres and the average number of houses decayed about two per entry.

The "rate of enclosure and conversion" is therefore not relevant: however impressive the total number of villages affected may seem, the impact on any one village was trivial with such low averages as thirteen acres enclosed and two houses decayed. There was no question of deserted villages here and therefore no surprise that the "rate of village mortality" had declined while enclosure and conversion continued.

The second question which Prof. Gould considered that I had dodged was:

> why, if the "balance of advantage" . . . tilted heavily towards corn from the late sixteenth century, did such enclosures and conversion continue to take place at all? . . . There is no suggestion in his book that he knew the answer.

It was again a false homogeneity in the word "enclosure" that misled Prof. Gould. The encloser after *c.* 1550, with all the risks of coming up against the common informer, the anti-enclosure commissioners, and conciliar justice, certainly shared one aim with the depopulating grazier of earlier times: that is, the elimination of the open fields and the complete transformation of the landscape to hedged fields. But no more. The uses to which the enclosed fields were now to be put were those that matched the changed economic situation after 1550 when contracting cloth exports were taking the heart out of the demand for wool, and when grain and meat were being demanded by an expanding population, particularly that of the urban centres. Both grain and meat could most profitably be produced in enclosed fields, and it was Improvement for these purposes—arable, pastoral and pastoral-arable (as Polonius might have put it)— that Improvement took place. It was still the enemy of Habitation, in the sense that some reduction in the village labour-force was part of the cost of greater efficiency, but did not produce *total* depopulation.

Prof. Gould was certainly right, on the other hand, in emphasising a point not taken at all in *Lost Villages*, that transport costs overland were so high that only goods with a high value in proportion to their weight would be worth taking far: wool and fleeces were such a load, and there was therefore something like a national market and a uniform price for wool of the same quality. Corn, on the other hand (except in the worst harvest years) was not very valuable in relation to its weight, and therefore inland counties might not be so tempted by the increasing demand for food in such a distant market as London, thus keeping a higher proportion of grass in their new enclosures. One defender of the right of Midland graziers to convert from arable argued this way in 1607 and stressed that animals had an advantage when it came to transport costs by being able to come to London on their own four feet along the drove roads ("by drifte"):

> it weare more juste to gyve the free employeinge of their ground to suche Husbandrie as will reduce them to an equallitie of benefitt with the *Navigable* shires—which is by graseinge —to which their soyle is more fitte than other Counties, whearby the vent of suche theire Commodities shalbe more easie beinge by drifte and not by carriage.[17]

On the other hand there is a point not considered by Prof. Gould: the increase in the number of mouths, hungry for grain that they could not themselves grow, was not confined to London. There were expanding industrial areas inland, not all of them urbanised, and many of them not in the south-east. Was it not said, in the course of a plaint at Leicester about decay of tillage (*c.* 1650):

> the Countyes of Leicester and Northampton are as a Magazeene for Corne, both for the *North* and *West* (my italics).[18]

Another opponent of enclosure, Richard Sandes, wrote to Charles I:

> depopulated townes in the best naturall corne countryes which affore *supplyed ye wants of others every way* (my italics again) beinge in ye middle of ye land.[19]

If these later enclosures have an archaeological product, it is not the depopulated but the shrunken village. Thus an enclosure reported to Charles I's "commissioners for depopulation" at Farnborough (Warws.) had dispensed with thirteen houses. It was depopulation, but not total depopulation, and it made Farnborough a shrunken and not a deserted village.

A study of Chippenham (Cambs.) has excellently documented the two principal

[17] B.M., Lans. Ms. 487 f. 218.
[18] Helen Stocks and W. H. Stevenson, eds., *Records of the Borough of Leicester*, IV (1923) 396.
[19] P.R.O., SP16/206/69.

occasions in a village's history when its population could shrink without total depopulation. The first was the post-Black-Death period when the villagers fell in number from about 650 to about 300. Mrs. Spufford shows a jury surveying Chippenham in 1544 (when about 60 houses were still inhabited) and pausing to note 64 other crofts as "ten(emen)tes and cotageis and nowe clere decaied" (Spufford, 1965, 31). The houses of Chippenham were further reduced in number, but not totally depopulated, when Edward Russell, later Lord Orford, bought up most of the remaining copyholds in the village in 1696. The bottom part of the High Street and all of South Street went into his park, and a fine map of 1712 shows the line of streets and former house-garden merely by their surviving hedge-trees. Today the line of the two streets is still visible in air photographs but the outlines of one or two closes remain hedged (*Ibid.*, 47).

Lost Villages did not ignore the shrunken village with its house- and street-earthworks of exactly the same form as those visible at deserted village sites. Indeed there were eleven entries in the index under *Villages, shrunken,* and Plate 12 was devoted to the subject, showing Faxton and Cosford. But the author's own travels since 1953, the parallel observations of Mr. Hurst, and the aerial reconnaissances of Dr. St. Joseph have vastly multiplied the number of shrunken villages that are known. Another study describes three Derbyshire villages "shrunk almost to point of extinction" but surrounded by their ridge and furrow (Wightman, 1961). A short local survey (Allison *et al.*, 1966, 30) giving 22 examples in Northamptonshire concluded that

> if ever a complete survey is achieved, these shrunken villages will probably emerge as the commonest English earthwork of any type or period.

This was a bold prophecy but there is no reason to think that time will shatter it.

V: ANTECEDENTS OF DEPOPULATION

Although villages of all sizes were depopulated, the encloser's task was at all periods easiest in villages that were already smaller or poorer than their neighbours, and especially where the number of freeholders was small. This smallness and poverty, where it occurs, was not the result of the Black Death. There is every evidence that these vulnerable villages were small in the early fourteenth century.

Except in Romney Marsh (an area whose depopulation is still mysterious), it is rare to find a deserted village with other deserted villages on every side of it. For example, in Kineton Hundred of Warwickshire, where one village in four was deserted, there are still 54 survivors, and no Hundred in the Midlands had more than one third of its villages depopulated. This strange juxtaposition of deserted and surviving villages has to be explained. No broad geographical force can be invoked, since a deserted village and its neighbour shared similar soils, elevation and climate—and sometimes the same landlord.

Neither *climate* nor *weather* appeared in the index to *Lost Villages*. Deterioration in the weather, which can plausibly be said to have overtaken all western Europe in the late thirteenth century, would certainly be relevant to conditions on the highest and wettest marginal lands, such as Dartmoor or the Cheviots, discouraging advance and forcing a retreat. The heavier English clays might have been another such margin, and certainly grass is more tolerant of rain than is arable husbandry: although in such conditions cattle might do better than sheep, who are not at their happiest when their feet are too wet. The direct relevance of climatic change to the history of deserted villages is, however, bound to be minimal in view of the small proportion of depopulations that took place in the actual period of climatic deterioration, or—indeed—in the century following it. Indirectly, climatic deterioration might have helped to make the smaller villages smaller still, and thus to increase the number of potential victims of engrossing landlords in a later century. But the outstanding difficulty for a simple weather-change determinism is that deserted and non-deserted villages are found side by side all over the English countryside and—local as the English climate is—it would be rather difficult to imagine the raindrops being so locally selective. (The drowning of coastal towns and villages, such as Old Winchelsea and Broomhill in 1284, certainly destroyed medieval communities, but these depopulations are as irrelevant to the general argument about inland desertions as would be the continued erosion and destruction of coastal villages in Norfolk and Holderness.)

It is to two topics that any study of the morbid pathology of deserted villages must constantly return: the high proportion that were smaller than the local average; and the differences in the local intensity of depopulation. The second of these topics will be treated in section VI, below.

On the first topic, all further studies have confirmed the diagnosis of *Lost Villages*. In that book taxation records of the fourteenth century were drawn upon to show that as far back as 1334, long before the plagues, the villages that were to be the depopulators' victims were—on the average—poorer and smaller than the average village in the county. Its Tables 17 and 18 are now diagrammatised in Figs. 2 and 3.

One important fact about these comparisons was not sufficiently stressed. They only included data for villages that had separate tax assessments. Where two or more places were assessed together for one sum it is impossible to know what fraction of the total was attributed to each component vill, and such jointly-taxed vills had to be omitted from the calculations. The discovery of the contribution paid by the now-depopulated hamlet of Upton to the Blockley (Gloucs.) assessment is due to Prof. Hilton (Hilton and Rahtz, 1966, 83). But in most areas it was precisely the smaller vill that was likely to be allied to its neighbours for assessment purposes, and if these small vills could be included in Figs. II and III the bias towards smallness would be even more apparent.

This early weakness is visible not only in the Midland counties that were most investigated in 1517 and 1548, but also in the three Ridings of Yorkshire and in Lincolnshire. But these comparisons treat a whole county at a time. Are they unfair to deserted villages by failing to relate them to their immediate neighbours? It would seem not: if the Yorks. E.R. assessments are considered wapentake by wapentake, each area shows the same relative weakness. In Harthill the deserted villages were assessed at 74% of the sum paid by their neighbours, in Buckrose at 64%, in Howdenshire at 53%, in Holderness at 52%, and in Dickering at 46% (Beresford, 1952, 54).

In Norfolk Dr. Allison made an even more effective demonstration by extracting the assessments of the six villages that lay nearest to each deserted site. Data were available for 53 deserted villages, and in 1334 five of these were exceptional in exceeding or nearly equalling the wealth of their immediate neighbours. Holkham was assessed at

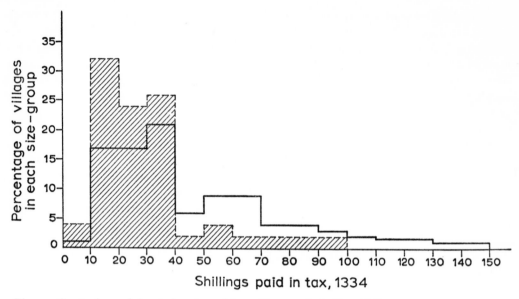

Fig. 2. Comparison of deserted and surviving villages: Yorkshire, E.R., taxed wealth in 1334

The deserted villages (shaded) then had assessments predominantly less than 40s., with over 30% paying less than 20s. The firm line shows the distribution of assessments for the whole county.

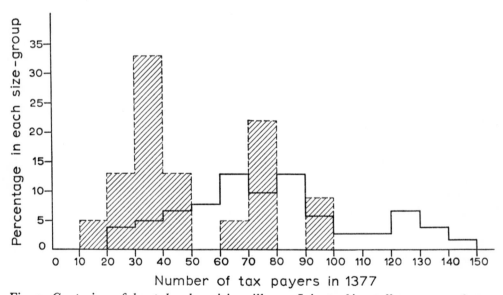

Fig. 3. Comparison of deserted and surviving villages: Leicestershire, poll-tax payers of 1377

The deserted villages (shaded) had taxpaying populations predominantly fewer than 50, with over 50% fewer than 40. The firm line shows the distribution for the whole county.

156% of the sum paid by the average of its six neighbours; Earlham at 140%; Coudham at 99%. (This list, it will be noted, includes a number of places not depopulated until the eighteenth century, being unviolated in the Middle Ages.) All the others were markedly less wealthy than their immediate neighbours, the extreme cases being Little Ringstead (19%), Alethorpe (18%), Testerton (10%) and Pudding Norton (5%). Just over 50% of these Norfolk deserted villages were paying less than half the tax that their neighbours paid (Allison, 1955, 127–9 and Table IV, p. 24 below).

TABLE III

Comparison of deserted villages in 1334 and 1377 with average of their counties

| | 1334 Village tax quotas | | 1377 Poll taxpayers | |
	County average, shillings	Average of deserted vills, shillings	County average	Average of deserted vills
Bucks.	74	44 (59%)	incomplete	
Cambs. (except fens)	110	72 (65%)	160	83 (52%)
Hunts.	96	57 (58%)		
Leics.	47	26 (55%)	99	59 (59%)
Lincs. Kesteven	79	38 (49%)		
Lindsey N.R.	73	18 (24%)		
Lindsey S.R.	60	30 (50%)	103	40 (39%)
Lindsey W.R.	57	36 (63%)	81	31 (38%)
Northants.	98	49 (50%)	140	64 (46%)
Notts.	23	27 (117%)		
Oxon.	76	45 (60%)	76	37 (49%)
Rutland	47	24 (50%)	99	68 (68%)
Yorks. E.R.	47	28 (58%)	100	48 (48%)
Yorks. N.R.	25	17 (68%)	62	34 (55%)
Yorks. W.R.	27	15 (55%)	67	33 (50%)

How much further back in time can this relative weakness be detected? The earliest lay subsidy accounts that are at all complete take us back no further than 1296. In a few Midland counties it is possible to go back to 1279 by noting the number of tenants in each vill in the Hundred Rolls. Table V shows the number of tenants in the

TABLE IV

53 Norfolk deserted villages: comparison with assessments of the six neighbours of each place, 1334

Assessment evidence	Number of deserted villages
Wealthier than average of six neighbours	2
90–99% of neighbours' assessments	3
81–90%	4
71–80%	3
61–70%	4
51–60%	7
41–50%	12
31–40%	5
21–30%	7
11–20%	4
1–10%	2
Total	53 (*no data available: 77*)

TABLE V

Numbers of tenants in 1279 in the nine Oxfordshire vills that were least wealthy in 1334

	Tax paid in 1334	Tenants in 1279
Cadwell	13s. 4d.	8
Chalford (in Aston Rowant)	18s. 11d.	16
Cutteslowe	8s. 0d.	no record*
Hardwick	6s. 0d.	no record*
Ludwell	15s. 4d.	20
Mongewell	18s. 2d.	22
Walcot	18s. 0d.	11
Widford	8s. 7d.	no record*
Willaston	15s. 0d.	19

* These vills must have been included with neighbours: Cutteslowe and Widford were treated as separate vills in 1377, with six and thirteen poll taxpayers respectively.

nine deserted villages of Oxfordshire that paid less than the small sum of 20s. in 1334. (The average Oxfordshire vill was paying 75s., and the average deserted vill 45s.)

Earlier than 1279 there are not sufficient data for general comparisons, except from Domesday Book. In 1086 Hardwick had one recorded tenant, Ludwell six, Mongewell twenty-three, Widford eleven, and Willaston nineteen; the other four places did not appear. Hardwick would thus seem to have been always small, and Widford to have suffered some disaster between 1086 and 1279. Ludwell seems to have enjoyed a normal increase in population, but to have suffered between 1279 and 1334. Mongewell and Willaston are remarkable in having the same number of tenants in 1086 and 1279: and no insignificant number at that. They, too, seem to have declined between 1279 and 1334, although Willaston still had about eight households in 1377; in 1428 Ludwell was returned as having fewer than ten.[20]

Table VI gives the recorded population (i.e. probably the number of households) in 1086 for 119 deserted villages from three Midland counties, although it must be remembered that there are no data for 1086 from a further 129 deserted villages in these

TABLE VI

Size in 1086 of vills later to be deserted; percentage of vills in each size-range

Recorded population	Northamptonshire	Oxfordshire	Leicestershire
1–10	48	42	39
11–20	43	38	36
21–30	8	11	19
31–40	0	7	3
41–50	0	2	0
51–60	0	0	3
Number of deserted vills with data	38	45	36
Total number of deserted vills	82	101	65

counties. (Some were yet to be founded; others had linked entries; others had no recorded population.) The published gazetteers for these counties show that it was not the smallest vills in 1086 that were always the first to disappear.[21] In Northamptonshire, for example, the smallest Domesday populations recorded were at Hothorpe, Hale, and Snorscomb, yet none of these had disappeared by 1350; conversely, among the

[20] Oxfordshire data from *Allison et al.*, 1965, 25–28.
[21] Table VI is based on data from D.M.V.R.G., 1963; and *Allison et al.*, 1965 and 1966.

seven earliest desertions in Leicestershire were vills with 24, 17, and 14 recorded population in 1086. Being large or small in 1086 was of less significance, apparently, than being small in 1296, 1301 or 1334.

How was this weakness (relative poverty or smallness of numbers) related to the depopulation? One can only surmise, since landlords did not open their hearts in public. In the first place, it must be emphasised that these less fortunate villages were not clustered together in one part of England or even in one part of a county. They lay most frequently in typical open-field districts of the arable lowlands, but even here the distribution map shows that they had neighbouring villages with normal population and normal tax quotas. How did these differences of size first come about?

For villages that were placed on poorer soils, near to land marginal for arable cultivation, the story would seem to be straightforward, and the low tax assessments must include some villages of this sort, unable to produce adequate food surpluses for the market. Such villages were doubly vulnerable if the balance of advantage swung in the fifteenth century away from arable farming. They had not been successful in grain-growing, and the alternative grass crop was a welcome temptation when the wool merchants beckoned. Some of their cornland would already have been abandoned, for the case of Ulceby (above, p. 5) showed that grass was the residual crop of despair on poor quality land, quite different from its place as a desired crop in a primitive rotation down in the better open-field areas. With smaller-than-average numbers in the village, the human obstacles to a complete conversion to grass were slighter; and the sheep already had a foot-hold.

More difficult to explain, in the present state of knowledge, is why abnormally small communities were also found all over the more fertile parts of the lowlands. We can reject at once the possibility that such villages were those that had been most cramped in the course of colonisation: their townships are not remarkable for the fewness of their acres, while their proximity to villages of normal size rules out most forms of geographical determinism. There must have been some important selective factor which is still undiscerned, and therefore conveniently labelled "random".

After this necessary emphasis on the tendency of fifteenth-century desertions to be concentrated in villages that were already smaller than normal in the early fourteenth century, it is necessary to re-emphasise two other points.

Firstly, it was not *absolutely* fatal for a village to be small, whether at the margin or on fertile soil. Many small villages survived. Secondly, the depopulations included villages whose population was far from ephemeral. Thus, while the first Leicestershire village (Hamilton) known to have been depopulated in the fifteenth century had only four families paying tax in 1381, the next two depopulations to occur, Ingarsby and Keythorpe, had about twelve and eighteen families respectively in 1337 and 1379 (Hoskins, 1946; D.M.V.R.G., 1963–64). In Warwickshire, where 22 deserted villages fall within the area that has a surviving record from the Hundred Rolls of 1279, ten then had more than 20 families, and six more had between twelve and 20 families. Insofar as three Black Death victims can be detected in this group, they were not the pygmies of 1279: they had 27, 20 and thirteen families.

It follows that a conjunction of depopulated and surviving villages within sight of each other occurs whether villages were small or whether villages were large. This apparently random local distribution was plausibly explained in 1954 by the hypothesis that landlord aggressiveness and tenants' security were both likely to vary considerably from village to village, independently of geographical position and (to a lesser extent) of size. It remains as much of a hypothesis, however, in 1968 as it did in 1954.

On the Continent, especially east of the Rhine, historians have produced many examples of depopulations brought about by another cause: the deliberate seignurial policy of re-grouping village populations by concentrating in one place the communities of two or three adjoining parishes. In England it is known that there were amalgamations of parishes in the fifteenth century but only on marginal land and after the retreat of population had made it economically impossible to maintain all the original churches. On the Continent, however, the amalgamations do not seem to have been desperate acts of salvage in bad times but acts of rationalisation at the height of seignurial affluence and social power. No similar evidence has yet emerged in England, although the most fertile ground for a search would seem to be in those parts of the west Midlands where churches stand isolated from any of the hamlets in their parish. Crucial would be the discovery of village-like earthworks alongside such a church, although isolated churches in regions of scattered, late-colonised settlement might well have been an original arrangement of convenience for the parishioners, and not the consequence of depopulation of a settlement (the "church-town") near the church. Occasionally the opposite can be observed.

There are also continental examples of village populations migrating to, or being coralled into, new fortified towns. I have had an opportunity of looking out for parallels in England since the plantation of new medieval towns was the research topic that I took up after 1954, but no evidence has emerged.

It is rare in any economy for every part to be contracting simultaneously, and there were certainly growth-points elsewhere in the English economy at all periods when villages were being depopulated. To these, such as London and the industrial towns, no doubt some medieval villagers successfully migrated when their village was depopulated. Prof. Carus-Wilson has shown how the cloth industry developed new settlement in the Stroud valley as well as in villages like Castle Combe.[22] But there is no evidence for planned removal of populations until squires of the eighteenth and nineteenth centuries built estate villages to house tenants whose houses they had pulled down, sometimes to clear the view in the park and sometimes in zeal for improved cottage dwellings on the best models of the sanitary reformers. Lord Anson is said to have re-housed the villagers of Shugborough (Staffs.) in an octagonal building with a central bakehouse, across the Trent from Shugborough Hall in Great Haywood. Milton Abbas (Dorset) was transplanted by Lord Milton to an adjoining valley. A new model village was built at Wimpole (Cambs.) in the 1840's. Harewood (Yorks. W.R.) was rebuilt at the park gates, and the immortalisation of the new village at Nuneham Courtnay (Oxon.) is separately treated in section VIII below.

It is clear that local variation in vulnerability to desertion is a major topic on the agenda of settlement studies. It will be an effective study only when all medieval settlement at the peak of colonisation has been recognised, so that the to-be-deserted

[22] E. M. Carus-Wilson, "Evidences of industrial growth on some fifteenth-century manors", *Econ. Hist. Rev.* 2nd. ser., XII (1959), 190–205.

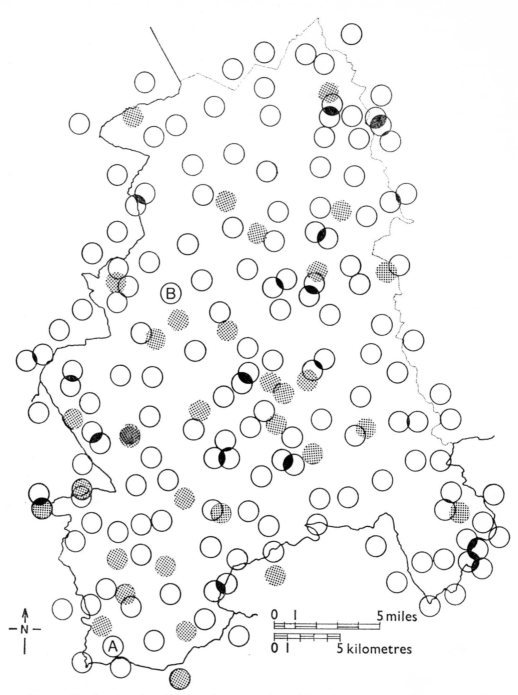

Fig. 4. Propinquity of settlements, deserted and surviving, in south-west Northamptonshire

Deserted villages as shaded circles, survivors as open circles. County boundary
as a firm line. *A* marks Aynho in the south, and *B* Badby in the north. For
commentary on the Figure see p. 29.

can be seen in the context of all their neighbours. One would then need, for example, to see whether desertion was more frequent in areas where settlements were densest, as tadpoles perish when a pond is overfull of frogspawn. Distribution maps of deserted and non-deserted settlements have been produced for areas where the study of desertion has been most actively pursued, north-east Oxfordshire and south-west Northampton-shire. The latter area, covering some 400 square miles, is shown on Fig. 4, with deserted settlements as shaded circles, and non-deserted villages as open circles. The radius of the circles, 0·1 inch, is half the average distance (for those districts) between a settlement (whether deserted or not) and its nearest neighbour (again, whether deserted or not). Thus the Figure indicates where desertion was frequent and where it was rare; but also, by observing closely the shaded overlapping of circles, it is possible to see whether the deserted sites are at all associated with "crowding" of the landscape. If circles overlap, a settlement stands at less than the average distance from its neighbour. In this sense, 42 (or 40%) of the 113 non-deserted villages were "crowded": but 18 (or 60%) of the 29 deserted villages were "crowded", and it will be noticed that proximity to villages over the county boundary has not been overlooked. Fourteen of the "crowded" deserted villages were jostled by non-deserted villages, but there were two instances (four villages in all) where a deserted village was jostled by another deserted village.

Borrowing from ecology, settlement geographers are developing more refined statistical techniques for measuring propinquities, and in time some of these may profitably be applied in areas where the totality of medieval settlement can be mapped. Alongside these studies, there will always be room for the study of the particular village and its group of neighbours, micro-geographical in character. And there will have to be archival study, closely concerned with tenurial differences between neighbour and neighbour. A model study of a complex area has recently been published by Mr. C. C. Taylor. Whiteparish (Wilts.) covers 6,000 acres, with two primary Saxon settlements and three others of "village" character, as well as several detached groups of farms in forest clearings. Yet all three of the secondary settlements, in addition to one of the two primary settlements, are now either totally deserted or marked only by a single farm. The fluidity of settlement in this area is emphasised further by the fact that many of the quasi-squatter cottages that were built on the surviving waste in the early nineteenth century have now gone, and only their abandoned gardens remain (Taylor, 1967).

VI: VULNERABILITY TO DEPOPULATION

Areas void of deserted villages, or with a very low density of depopulated places, can be explained by two forms of immunity. Villages were safe if they had first-quality cornland; and they were safe if their economy depended on other things than corn, especially if there was a great deal of surviving woodland or a scatter of small, early-enclosed fields. These were not attractive to graziers who wanted to graze 10,000 sheep in one continuous run of pastures, like those of John Spencer north of Wormleighton (Warws.)

I offered the late-surviving forest areas of Arden, Chiltern and Sherwood as examples of almost total immunity from depopulation, and Lancashire and Cheshire as counties whose economy already included a solid pastoral base. For first-quality arable I instanced the newly-reclaimed fields of the fenland around the Wash.

Dr. Thirsk's review[23] pointed out that the immunity of the Lincolnshire fenland rested also on its access to grass for cattle-grazing. This bonus of marshland grass enabled the parishes where the chalk Wolds meet the fen to be smaller in area and yet more densely populated than the parishes on the high chalk to the north of them. The villages were supported by a mixed economy in which ploughman and herdsman had come to terms: not a difficult task when both were the same person or in the same household.

The cow thus emerges as the defender of man, and I note that it was cast for the same role in the Midland counties in 1555. Parliament was then seeking to check further conversion of corn to grass, and it buttressed old-fashioned prohibitive statutes by a new measure, that forced everyone keeping sheep on enclosed pastures to have one milking cow for every 60 sheep. The extra cows and calves would provide meat, hides, milk and cheese, and so help to keep down the rising cost of victuals; they would also need more daily attention than sheep, and so assist in maintaining a village labour force. In general, therefore, a district with a cow economy was well protected against the depopulators.

The progress of local studies since 1954, reported below, pp. 68–69, has inevitably reduced the number of districts that can confidently be said to be void of deserted villages. Lancashire certainly has its desertions, and one of the most spectacular of the excavations has been at Hound Tor, high on Dartmoor, while Herefordshire and Worcestershire are succumbing to field-research. Nevertheless, this progress of local studies has not eliminated all the apparent regional differences noted in 1954. In *Lost Villages*, Chapter 7, "The Locale of Destruction", emphasised the local variations in the intensity of depopulation, and the linked head-notes to that chapter and Chapter 5, "The Occasions of Destruction", pointed to the difficulties of separating the questions, Time when and Place where. With the imperfections of documentation and the necessarily slow progress of excavation it is not always possible to have an answer to both questions. Thus the period of desertion may sometimes have to be inferred from the experience of a locale, with all the dangers of erroneous guilt by association.

Some counties had a small crop of deserted villages in 1954 simply because I had not been free to give them all the same attention. During my researches for *Lost Villages* (1944–53) I lived in two centres, first Rugby and then Leeds. In the former I was an amateur historian, exploring archives and the countryside in my spare time from wardening an adult education centre; and in the latter a young University lecturer, free—it is true—from the cares of administration but with much lecture-preparation to do, and limited University research funds to assist my travels. The parts of England most inaccessible from the Midlands and Yorkshire therefore had the least attention; and there were other barriers when a distant county also lacked a good county history or a volume of the *Victoria County History*. It appeared to Prof. Hilton (Hilton, 1955, 675) that the work in *Lost Villages* "mainly derives from Warwickshire investigations". This I resist. In fact my work on the three Ridings of Yorkshire and on Buckinghamshire was completed, and published, before *Lost Villages*; and its centre of gravity did lie a little further from Rugby than Prof. Hilton allowed (Beresford, 1951, 1952, 1953, 1953–54 and 1954).

[23] *Ag. Hist. Rev.*, III (1955), 52–54.

In years subsequent to 1954, largely in car journeys with Mr. Hurst, it was possible to make forays into some of the neglected areas, giving the increased number of sites indicated in Table VIII. The experience in Northumberland was particularly encouraging. It showed that inspection of maps and fieldwork could augment the number of known sites even in a county where excellent county histories were already available. The work of Mrs. Betty Grant, described below, also made available basic documentation for a county like Oxfordshire, then without its *V.C.H.*; or Berkshire with its *V.C.H.* compiled some time ago with little reference to topography and "visibles".

While *Lost Villages* was in the press Dr. Allison was completing his study of Norfolk (Allison, 1955), especially useful because it took up the problem posed by John Saltmarsh (Saltmarsh, 1941–43)—the multitude of ruined churches in Norfolk, particularly in Breckland. Norfolk was shown to have proportions of desertions as high as anywhere in the Midlands (Grimshoe Hundred, 31%; South Greenhoe Hundred, 21%; Smithden and Gallow Hundreds, 20%) although the chronology of desertion seemed to rule out massive sheep depopulations of the late fifteenth century; evictions there certainly were, but more commonly in the following century; and there was a considerable (but slow) retreat of settlement in the century following the Black Death. Although Dr. Allison's later work has thrown light on the local peculiarities of Norfolk field-systems, the county's settlement history still has many puzzles, some of them akin to the isolated churches of Suffolk and their large green-villages, a topic even less explored. It is hoped that Mr. Wade-Martins' intensive study of a small area of Norfolk for his Leicester University thesis will throw light in some of these dark corners.

My own Warwickshire study, published before *Lost Villages*, had attempted to marry the literary form of presentation that Prof. Hoskins had just employed for Leicestershire (Hoskins, 1946) to the terse gazetteer presentation employed in Canon Foster's pioneer study of Lincolnshire (Foster and Longley, 1924). My three studies of the Ridings of Yorkshire, and Dr. Allison's Norfolk study, all of which were under way while *Lost Villages* was being written, were cast in a similar form, which has also been followed for the Research Group's two county studies (see Table XIV, p. 68).

Of the counties neglected in 1954, two now have summary lists published. That for Berkshire was prepared in response to a request from local archaeologists and historians who needed a first indication of known and suspected sites; it is being followed up by the work of Mr. John Brooks for his University of Reading thesis. A summary list for Sussex, also prepared from the files of the D.M.V.R.G., was edited by Mr. E. Holden (Holden, 1962).

The *Transactions* of the Leicestershire Archaeological and Historical Society have been particularly kind to deserted village researches. It was here that Prof. Hoskins' pioneer essay appeared (Hoskins, 1946), and here that the Ordnance Survey's six experimental site-surveys were published (Hoskins, 1956). An invitation to the Research Group made it possible to compile and publish a Provisional County List in 1964 (D.M.V.R.G., 1963–64). In view of Prof. Hoskins' essay it would have been supererogatory to cast this in literary form, so that the opportunity was taken to publish an extensive tabulation of the quantitative data that various researchers, beginning with Prof. Hoskins himself, had collected. An alphabetical list of the 65 sites in the county

Extract from tabulation

	Mod. acres	Total teams D.B.	Popn. D.B.	(Nich.) 1279	SUBSIDIES			POLL TAX		
					1327	1332	Quota 1334	1377	later	(F'ham) families
32 NANEBY	200				3	4	5/6			
33 NEWBOLD FOLVILLE		5½	9							
34 NEWBOLD SAUCY					4	6	19/6	29		
35 NEWTON, COLD	1556	4½	11		9	8	29/3½	38		18
36 NORMANTON TURVILLE	1000			25	11	9	24/-	49		29
37 NOSELEY	880	8	28		10	10	63/-	75		
38 OTHORPE	300	4	14				Not sep. (8/-)			
39 POTTERS MARSTON	702	2	8		8	7	17/6		26	11
40 POULTNEY	208	4	18	28	12	12	35/4	54		29
41 PRESTGRAVE		2	6						10	5
42 PRESTWOLD	915	Not sep.	1 + Not sep.		6	8	23/-	59		

(8) Included in Subsidy with Slawston (quota 56s.)

32

VII

of Leicestershire data

Parish 1428	Relief 1445	S'sidy 1524	Bp's return Families		Hearth Tax 1670	Nichols Houses c.1800	Census			
			1563	1603			1801	highest	1901	1951
	18%		Not sep.			I				
						Nil				
	10%				9	3	Not sep.	(1841) 24	Not sep.	Not sep.
	15%	13+3	15	(with Lowesby) 25	15	15	101	(1881) 185	128	90
	17%		6		I	4	41	(1831) 55	(1871) 29	Not sep.
	22%	8	8		I		4	(1881) 70	57	51
						I	Not sep.			Not sep.
	26%				(1666) I		18	(1871) 21	21	44
	6%						Not sep.	(1841) 29	Not sep.	Not sep.
	22%	11+4	14		11		62	(1901 highest)	93	68

See KEY TO THE COLUMNS on page 34.

KEY TO THE COLUMNS OF TABLE VII

Modern acres: Area as given in *Census*, if civil parish is still counted as a separate unit.

Total teams, DB: Plough teams of 1086.

Population, DB: Recorded population of 1086.

(Nichols) 1279: Hundred Rolls as cited by Nichols from the incomplete returns.

Subsidies, 1327, 1332: Taxpayers recorded in the lay subsidies (E.179 in Public Record Office).

Quota, 1334: Shillings of tax paid in 1334 (E.179).

Poll Tax, 1377: Number of taxpayers, 1377 (E.179—*V.C.H., Leicestershire*, iii (1955), 163–5 is incomplete).

Poll Tax, later: Number of taxpayers, 1379 or 1381.

Poll Tax (Farnham), families: Families enumerated in Farnham's *Village Notes*, from his transcripts of 1379 and 1381 (E.179).

Parish, 1428: If recorded as having fewer than ten households (*Feudal Aids*, iii, 106–17).

Relief of 1445: Percentage relief allowed to impoverished vills: data from Nichols checked with original MSS at British Museum.

Subsidy, 1524: Number of taxpayers (E.179); document incomplete.

Bp's Returns, families: As printed in *V.C.H., Leics.*, iii (1955), 166–9.

Hearth Tax, 1670: As printed in *V.C.H., Leics.*, iii (1955), 170–2; including exempted houses; a few additions from 1666, excluding exemptions.

(Nichols) Houses, c. 1800: As in *Nichols's History*.

Census, 1801: As in *V.C.H., Leics.*, iii (1955), 179–203.

gave map references; an assessment of the archaeological clarity of each site; an evaluation of the quality of historical documentation available, on a five-point scale; and an indication of the period of desertion. The tabulation of data covered 21 vertical columns, mainly concerned with the tax assessments levied or the population recorded at different periods from 1086 to 1951. An extract forms Table VII.

Under the patronage of Prof. Finberg, then Head of the Department of English Local History at Leicester University, a more extended treatment was given to two further counties, Oxfordshire (Allison *et al.*, 1965) and Northamptonshire (*Ibid.*, 1966). The two counties were chosen to complement the work already done on the neighbouring Midland counties of Buckinghamshire, Leicestershire and Warwickshire; and if one takes into account Lincolnshire (Foster and Longley, 1924), Norfolk (Allison, 1955) and Yorkshire (Beresford, 1951, 1952, 1953 and 1954) a substantial part of the English lowlands is now covered. The two county studies published from Leicester were annotated gazetteers of the form that had been employed for Warwickshire, Yorkshire and Norfolk but with more emphasis on the quantitative data that had been exploited in the Leicestershire tabulation. Each was preceded by a long essay in which the local problems of the particular county were set out, together with some inter-county comparisons, and an account of research procedures followed.

The known sites now total 2,263 compared with 1,353 named in *Lost Villages*, and the improvements resulting from this subsequent work have been incorporated in Table VIII. There remain counties where work is still in progress. In the last ten years my own research has moved its centre of gravity from rural to urban history, so that I have not myself investigated those remaining counties where the score, as set in Table VIII, is implausibly small. Nor in latter years have Mr. Hurst and myself been able to con-

TABLE VIII

Number of deserted medieval villages at present (1968) known

Bedfordshire	18	Norfolk	148
Berkshire	43	Northamptonshire	82
Buckinghamshire	56	Northumberland	165
Cambridgeshire	17	Nottinghamshire	67
*Cheshire	4	Oxfordshire	103
*Cornwall	8	Rutland	13
*Cumberland	8	*Shropshire	9
Derbyshire	33	*Somerset	27
*Devonshire	15	Staffordshire	22
Dorset	42	*Suffolk	23
*Durham	29	*Surrey	5
*Essex	17	Sussex	41
Gloucestershire	67	Warwickshire	128
Hampshire:		*Westmorland	2
Mainland	91	Wiltshire	104
New Forest	33	*Worcestershire	7
Isle of Wight	32	Yorkshire:	
*Herefordshire	11	East Riding	129
Hertfordshire	44	North Riding	171
Huntingdonshire	18	West Riding	75
Kent	69		
*Lancashire	—		
Leicestershire	67		
Lincolnshire	220		
*Middlesex	—	Total	2,263

* Indicates counties where considerable local research remains to be done.

tinue to spare time for systematic fieldwork; our limited time has been devoted to maintaining the files of the Research Group (p. 65, below), compiling its *Annual Reports*, and producing the published county lists. In addition, as much information as possible has been supplied to local researchers.

The measure of work remaining to be done lies not only in those counties, such as Cumberland or Somerset, where virtually nothing has been done, but also in the problems of siting and dating that remain within counties which have had closer attention. In Oxfordshire the documents suggest 101 deserted villages but 11 of these have not even a conjectural siting. More damaging to complacency is the veil that documents so far studied cast around the actual date of desertion. For 13 of these 101 villages no conjecture is possible, and 48 others can only be placed in very wide chronological categories. In Northamptonshire 6% of the desertions are of totally uncertain date and another 24% can be placed in only wide categories. 15% of the 82 desertions in this county are still unlocated.

The potential for fruitful local research work has been increased by other developments: by the interest of medieval archaeologists (pp. 179–80, below); by the multiplication of county record offices and their acquisition of estate papers from county families (p. 69, below); by the aerial reconnaissances of Dr. J. K. S. St. Joseph (p. 74, below) and the transfer of the R.A.F. air photography library from its country seat at Medmenham to the Ministry of Housing and Local Government in Whitehall; and by the enthusiasm for local history and archaeology stimulated by W.E.A. and Extra-mural adult classes. Active research is currently known to be in progress in ten counties and it can confidently be anticipated that it will augment the numbers in Table VIII. Early news of the explorations in Staffordshire, Worcestershire, Shropshire and Herefordshire, for example, indicate abundant sites,[24] and the archaeological exploration of a relatively small area of Devon has produced a remarkable testimony to the intensity of medieval colonisation on the moorland (Linehan, 1966).

In Table VIII the counties where considerable work remains to be done are marked with an asterisk. With these reserved, it is possible to consider the important regional differences which are now visible. In *Lost Villages* the local differences were measured by calculating the proportion of villages in each area that had been taxed in the early fourteenth century but are now deserted (Beresford, 1954, Fig. 10, p. 224; Table 6, pp. 234–39). In the Midland counties, where that proportion was greatest, it is now necessary to raise the proportion a little higher. Thus in 1954 the deserted villages then identified in Oxfordshire gave a proportion of 11% but the more complete knowledge represented by the gazetteers published in 1965 gave a proportion of 25%; Northamptonshire, then 13%, should now read 18%.

These revisions, however, do not seem as though they will eliminate all inter-county differences. After all, there is a considerable difference between Oxfordshire's 25% on the one hand, and Northamptonshire's 18% and Leicestershire's 15% on the other. Table IX employs a measurement of local intensity not used in 1954, and here too there are significant differences between counties. This new measure divides the area of each county by the number of known desertions, giving a ratio of desertions per 10,000 acres. The results (for those counties where work has progressed reasonably far) are set out in order, and an important disparity of experience is revealed (Fig. 5). The leading position of the Isle of Wight evoked a stage whisper from Sir Mortimer Wheeler when a distribution map of sites was shown at a lecture: "My God, they've sunk the Isle of Wight". More historically, its leading position matches admirably the known fact that the first anti-depopulation statute, that of 1488, applied solely to the Isle.

Also outstanding, with ratios of over one per 10,000 acres are those counties whose fate induced later Tudor legislators to name them as most needing the protection of the law: in brief, the "Midland" counties, the arable counties of the high Middle Ages that were so vulnerable to the depopulators when the profitability of pastoral husbandry made itself so plain in the late fifteenth century (p. 13, above). These were also the

---

[24] A small area of the north-west has already yielded a promising harvest: W. Rollinson, "The lost villages and hamlets of Low Furness", *Trans. Cumb. and Westm. Ant. and Arch. Soc.*, new ser., LXIII (1963) 160-69.

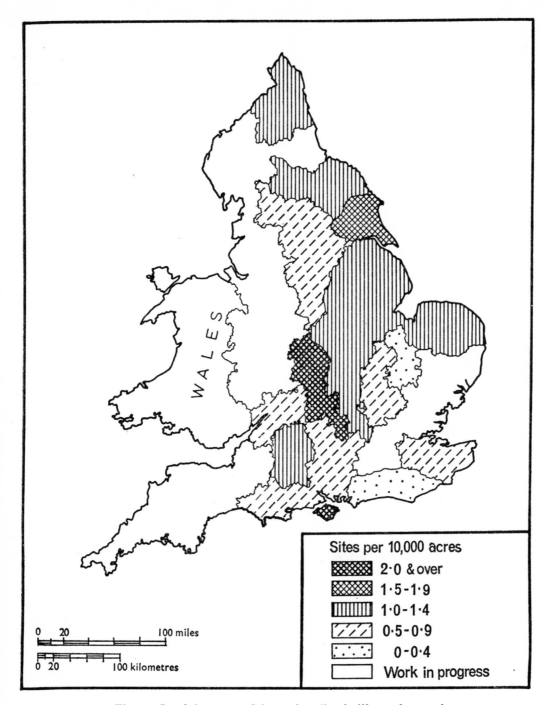

Fig. 5. Local frequency of deserted medieval villages, by counties
Based on Table IX, p. 39.   For counties where work is in progress, see Tables
VIII and XIV, pp. 35 and 68.

counties where the Commissioners for Depopulation went most frequently, from the initial inquiries of Wolsey in 1517 through to the money-raising inquiries[25] of Charles I in the 1630's when the total desertion of a village was more a memory than a current practice.   In particular, it will be noted that Northumberland ranks high in Table IX, despite the fact that a good deal of the county was always upland moor and therefore hardly comparable with the acres of the Midland calculations.[26]   If one excludes such areas of Northumberland (perhaps one half of the county) the ratio might rise from 1·3 to 2·6, although it must be remembered that even the Midland counties had their Forests of Arden, Rockingham, Sherwood and Wychwood—each almost devoid of deserted village sites.   For a strict comparison it would therefore be necessary to revise the acres that enter into the calculation of the Midland ratios.   Arden and other forests made up about one fifth of Warwickshire, and the county's adjusted ratio would then be 2·9 desertions per 10,000 acres.   Nevertheless the place of Northumberland and Durham among the Midland counties is not incongruous when it is recalled that depopulation in these two counties caused concern in the 1590's, and a preliminary re-conaissance in Durham suggests already that the 29 sites of Table VIII should be nearer 100.

Another problem is fundamental.   For there to have been a deserted village there must once have been a village or a substantial hamlet.   The compact array of houses at a recognisable centre (or centres) is the normal distribution for medieval rural populations.   Thus the name of a vill in the *Nomina Villarum* of 1316, or a Domesday Book place-name with a substantial number of tenants, should normally correspond with an existing village: if no modern village is to be seen on the map, there is a *prima facie* case for searching out a deserted site.   This pursuit would be in vain if the taxpayers of a vill entry or the villani numbered in Domesday Book had lived in houses that were peppered over the landscape, each in its own clearing.   Areas do remain where such a non-nucleated settlement pattern seems to have been a permanent local characteristic but it should be noted that such areas are constantly diminishing as research progresses.

Mr. C. C. Taylor's "forest-edge" Whiteparish (Wilts.) might once have seemed to be just the place where deserted village studies were quite irrelevant, for it was "forest" or "waste" vills, late-settled, that most often produced the non-nucleated type of settlement.   Yet his researches (Taylor, 1967), most strikingly summarised in his series of settlement maps, show that single, isolated modern farms stand where nucleated communities were once to be found; and other work in progress in the counties of the Welsh border, in Lancashire, and in the north-west, is making it annually more difficult to find extensive areas that can be ignored in deserted village searches in the belief that there were never medieval villages in that locality. And even Celtic Wales, as Dr. Butler's chapter shows, is now known to have had extensive nucleated settlement.   I have myself taken pleasure in showing from late thirteenth-century sources that Cornwall, another area often said to be village-less, was in fact peopled not by single farmsteads but by clusters; wherever one of these bigger clusters is reduced to one modern farm it seems quite proper to claim them as desertions in the local context.   One is not thereby

[25] For revenues from depopulation fines see P.R.O. C212/20.

[26] For a recent comment on Northumberland see R. A. Butlin, "Enclosure and Improvement in Northumberland in the Sixteenth century", *Arch. Aeliana*, 4th ser., XLV (1967), 149–60.

TABLE IX

Local intensity of depopulation per 10,000 acres

County	Number of known deserted villages per 10,000 acres (15 sq. miles)
Isle of Wight	3·1
Warwickshire	2·3
Oxfordshire	2·1
Yorkshire, E.R.	1·7
Leicestershire	1·4
Northamptonshire	1·4
Nottinghamshire	1·4
Lincolnshire	1·3
Northumberland	1·3
Rutland	1·3
Buckinghamshire	1·2
Wiltshire	1·2
Yorkshire, N.R.	1·2
Norfolk	1·0
Hampshire	0·9
Hertfordshire	0·9
Berkshire	0·8
Gloucestershire	0·8
Huntingdonshire	0·8
Dorset	0·7
Bedfordshire	0·6
Derbyshire	0·5
Durham	0·5
Kent	0·5
Yorkshire, W.R.	0·5

claiming that they were villages of the size encountered in the Midland plains but their desertion calls for explanation.   Its period is far from plainly discernable as yet.

Although some immunity for fen and forest villages still remains, the spread of areas of intense depopulation across the distribution map, especially to the south-west and to the border counties of the western Marches, takes the phenomenon of desertion not only further than was appreciated when *Lost Villages* was being written (Beresford, 1954, Table 5 and Fig. 9, pp. 220–21) but also beyond those counties where conversion to pasture and decay of houses of husbandry aroused the anxieties of Tudor legislators and publicists.   This extension of the infected area must be explained.

It is well known that even in the Midlands, the *locus classicus* for depopulation by conversion to grass, the legislation of 1488–89 (and even more the inquiries and prosecutions of 1517–18) caught only the last offenders (p. 11, above). One could therefore explain the empty townships and the visible village earthworks in a county where little or nothing emerged in 1517–18, by the fact that virtually all its conversion to pasture had taken place by 1488 (Kerridge, 1955, 221). Certainly this hypothesis would fit in with the known chronology of "ordinary" enclosure in these counties for improved arable (but without total depopulation) for it has long been clear that wide areas in the South-west, the west Midlands, and the chalk woodlands of the south and south-east had lost their open fields in a mysterious period before normal documentary sources for enclosure begin to apply.

In the absence of evidence for widespread complaints before 1488 we have to ask why these non-Midland areas could lose virtually all their open fields so peacefully; and why these areas of widespread ancient enclosure could also lose a proportion of their villages without protest. It is possible, though not wholly plausible, that *inter arma leges silent*, the silence here being that of the Law gagged during the clash of arms in the Wars of the Roses. But it is strange that nothing of this has so far emerged in any studies of the propaganda and counter-propaganda of the houses of York and Lancaster.

If that argument is discarded, the absence of protest may simply mean that, outside the Midlands, pre-1488 conversions to pasture took place in an economic climate where they were not considered a social evil, and therefore tolerable. In the majority of townships, where *total* depopulation did not result from conversion to pasture, men would tolerate enclosure of the arable because they had access to much more unexploited woodland, heath and pasture than in the more densely settled Midlands. Even in the minority of townships, where deserted villages do appear well before 1488, the peasants from the depopulated sites could find holdings without difficulty in the neighbouring townships or by assarting the wastes. Yet why here in the mid-fifteenth century, when in the late fifteenth and early sixteenth century, depopulated townships elsewhere were arraigned as the source of unemployment and vagrancy? The chief difference, surely, was the changed relationship of population to land.[27] Before *c.* 1470 the agrarian economy was still under the influence of the demographic contraction of the fourteenth century: relatively, as Prof. Postan has more than once shown, there was a land surfeit. Men and animals were not yet rivals. But by the 1480's the returning Malthusian pressures were making men truly rivals to sheep for the use of scarce resources at the very moment when the demand for wool was increasing fast, and to observers it would therefore seem that sheep were eating up men.

VII: VILLAGE SITES AFTER DESERTION

Although the visual characteristics of deserted village sites were described, there was very little study in Lost Villages *of the fate of village sites between their depopulation and the present day.*

What was the subsequent fate of a deserted village, its church, manor-house, houses

[27] The relation between population growth and resentment at enclosure is a leading theme of Thirsk, 1959.

and fields? Dilapidation of the church fabric and of the parsonage house may leave traces in subsequent litigation in the bishops' courts, particularly over tithes. But if the deserted village was the sole settlement in the parish, there would be little use for the church unless it became annexed as a private chapel or mausoleum to a manor house in which the depopulator continued to live. If a parish had several townships, and not all of them were deserted, then the church might continue in use, albeit curtailed in size. This happened in the parish of Wharram Percy (Yorks., E.R.) where, despite the depopulation of four of the five townships, the fifth, Thixendale, survived and had no other church than at Wharram. It was a long journey for the villagers of Thixendale, nearly three miles over the highest parts of the Wolds.

This church is above a mile from any town(ship) in the parish.[28]

reported the Parliamentary survey of 1650, and in 1743 the vicar reported to his bishop,

All my parishioners except one family live two Miles from the parish church.[29]

The fate of the actual houses of a village is a fairly straightforward story, belonging more to archaeology (Chapter 2, below) than to history, since their tumbled walls soon became overgrown and of no interest to subsequent generations. The fate of the fields, the prize for which husbandmen and graziers had come into conflict, is a more complex matter.

The practices of sheep husbandry did not demand that the whole township became one single field when arable husbandry was abandoned.

Different kinds of stock were carefully segregated in great closes, while frequent movement of animals from one part of the parish to another, or even from one parish to another, ensured that no pastures were overgrazed.

writes Prof. Thorpe of the Spencers' treatment of their pastures, very many acres of which had once been village arable fields (Thorpe, 1965, 106). All the estate plans drawn of deserted sites between 1550 and 1650 (the earliest available) show the townships divided into such closes. The well-known plan of Whatborough (Leics.) in 1586 (the whole of which was published in Beresford, 1957, pl. 11) shows the hedges thrown across the former open fields to create eight pasture closes; the plan of Compton Verney (Warws.) in 1736 shows more than 50 closes, the largest passing 70 acres and the average size just over 20 acres. The close that bore the actual village site was 34 acres.

Fields of this size did not prove incommodious in later centuries, and many deserted townships still have field patterns created at the depopulation. These often stand out on the six-inch O.S. map, partly by their unusual size and partly by their shapes. They do not have the straight-line hedges characteristic of later enclosures but their hedges and walls follow sinuous natural boundaries, taking no particular care to make fields of regular shape. At Wormleighton (Warws.) some of these "double ditches and double hedges" boundaries are still in use (Thorpe, 1964, 103–07 and 115; Figs. 9–10) although leasing of the pastures in the period between 1634 and 1734 has caused the larger closes to be subdivided. This undoubtedly happened elsewhere. The plan of Kingston

[28] *Trans. East Riding Archaeol. Soc.*, II (1894), 60.
[29] *Yorks. Archaeol. Soc. Rec. Series*, LXXV (1929), 216.

(Warws.) in 1697 shows that arable farming had come back to part at least of the township, and the duality is indicated by the names of the two fields where the village earthworks were sited, *Corne Towne* and *Grazing Towne* (Fig. 6). Yet even if there were second thoughts that brought the plough back to the fields of deserted villages, one thing is quite certain: the intermingled selions of open-field farming would not be restored with the plough, and the subsequent history of deserted village landscapes is generally one of hedged fields or enclosed parkland: an exception on the high chalk Wolds is described below, p. 43.

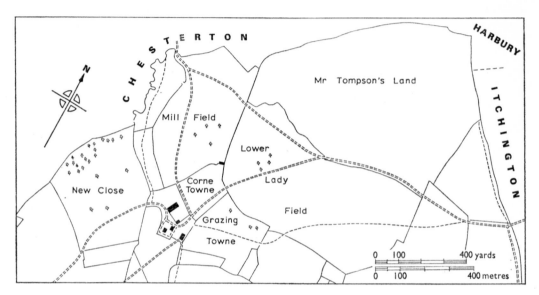

Fig. 6. Kingston, alias Chesterton Parva, Warws: Corne Towne and Grazing Towne, 1697

> The plough has returned to the village site. (Willoughby de Broke maps, no. 1, Shakespeare Birthplace Trust, Stratford upon Avon). A plan of *c.* 1750 in the same collection (no. 6) shows the Mill Field further divided. Note the great close to the north of the *Towne* fields, a typical product of an early enclosure and apt for development as a park if so required in later centuries.

At some sites the crofts of the former village houses were retained, being already hedged and ditched, and a skeleton of the village plan thus retained for posterity. Yet at Whatborough the plan of 1586 shows that the area of the village had simply been thrown into the largest of the new pasture closes, although remembered a century after the depopulation as "the place where the town of Whatborough stood". The lingering memory of a village could be preserved in the name *Town Field* given to the pasture close in which the earthworks lay.[30] Three Warwickshire estate plans follow Kingston (above) in having *Town Field* at the village site: Compton Verney, 1736; Charlecote,

---

[30] In the Byfield (Northants.) enclosure award of 1779 there were 20 fields of pasture, all old enclosures, that bore the name of "Trafford Grounds". The site of the deserted village of Trafford lay in one of these, "Old Town", that contained 23 acres.

1736 (Plate 1); and Walton Deyville, 1728 (Plate 2). Here, the croft banks had been ignored and the village site was simply part—but not the whole—of some close. Yet at East Layton (Co. Durham) a plan of 1608 shows empty garths, *the scyte of the howses*,[31] and old crofts stand out prominently in a plan of Chellington (Beds.).[32]

Many medieval villages had their crofts enveloped by a single boundary bank (probably the base for a fence) separating them from the open fields, the full circuit of the bank embracing all the village. This feature can still be seen in some surviving villages, such as Great Wolford (Warws.) and Wellow (Notts.), and it is a common feature of many deserted sites, often emphasised if there is surviving ridge and furrow from the open fields coming up to this bank but no further. Shilvington (Northumberland) has this feature marked very clearly. It was not often that these boundary banks were taken over as boundaries for the new closes. Unless the crofts were retained in use their perimeter bank was irrelevant to the needs of the graziers, and it followed the houses into decay under a grass shroud.

On the high chalk Wolds it has been shown (Harris, 1958) that large depopulated parishes were not at once cut up into fields. Dr. Harris estimated that at least 12,000 acres of these pastures and warrens were undivided by walls or hedges until the mid-eighteenth century. Arras, reduced to a single farm, was unhedged before 1770, and Dr. Harris' examples are drawn from other classic sites such as Riplingham, Holme Archiepiscopi, Eastburn, Cowlam, and Cottam. Some of these were late depopulations but the very lateness of the date emphasises the irrelevance of enclosed fields to the grazing and rabbit warren uses prevalent in the high chalklands at that time. Enclosed fields came only with Agricultural Improvement. Eastburn, for example, was reduced to three houses by 1671 and in 1698 the parish was one great sheep-walk, "not devided by Fences and ditches", and indeed there were none for another 150 years. Cottam was reduced to four houses in 1791 but was not completely hedged until the 1850's. In 1783 Cowlam, which had 14 houses as late as 1674, was a single farm of 1,900 acres, most of them used as a warren. Here, and at some other late-deserted Wold villages, there were vestigial open fields after the depopulation. The estate plan of Whitehill (Oxon.)[33] shows that in 1608 a disagreement between proprietors was enough to block the elimination of open fields even when the engrossing of holdings had reduced the proprietors to two, and something of this dogged conservatism must have occurred on the Wolds.

It is clear from Dr. Harris' study that on the Wolds a depopulation for sheep pastures did not produce in its first stage (which might last 300 years) a completely hedged landscape; and that the hedge came at the second stage when Improving eighteenth-century landlords were also bringing the hedges to other neighbouring and populous parishes on their estates.

> The initial depopulating enclosures having modified but not destroyed the old open landscape (Harris, 1958, p. 97.)

With the Improvers' hedges the ploughman returned to the pastures; the Sledmere

---

[31] Univ. of Durham, Dept. of Palaeography and Diplomatic, Baker Baker Ms. 72/249 and enclosure: see *Beresford, 1967*, 258.   [32] Beds. County Record Office X 1/79.
[33] Reproduced in J. G. L. Mowat, *Sixteen Old Maps . . . of Oxfordshire* (1888).

monument to the Improver, Sir Tatton Sykes, now looks out indifferently over the cornfields of deserted villages and the cornfields of ordinary villages. Modern cornfields at deserted village sites are not a contradiction in terms, for they are usually farmed, not from houses rebuilt at the village site, but from great, red-brick farmhouses built by the Improvers. There were no village farmhouses to take over when Cowlam was improved, and the 1,900 improved acres were farmed from a new house (*c.* 1783) that took the former parish church into its yard: in 1674 there had still been fourteen houses in the village.[34] At Cottam the new farmhouse stood on one side of the former street, and the plantations of its windbreak were set over the earthworks of crofts and over other streets from the village. Pockthorpe, Swaythorpe, Mowthorpe, and Burdale, all in the high Wolds, each consist of a single farmhouse situated at the village site. Most sites in the Wolds of Lincolnshire display the same pattern.

At Wharram Percy the first stage of Improvement, possibly in the 1770's, brought about one-third of the 941 acres of the township back to arable. The ploughman did not, however, return to the old village site, for the new farmhouse was built more than half a mile away. In a second Improvement, of 1808, another 532 acres were brought into three- and six-course husbandry and the farmhouse renovated.[35] The labour force necessary to keep these thousand-acre Wolds farms under the plough can be glimpsed in the Census returns, all under the single farm roof. At Wharram Percy Farm in 1841 there were nine resident labourers and in 1861 eleven, all unmarried and under 25 years of age, as well as two shepherds, a housekeeper and three female servants. The position was similar where the Improvers' farmhouses had been built at or near a deserted site: there was no re-erection of cottages along the grassy streets. At Raisthorpe in 1841 the single farm sheltered fifteen labourers; at Towthorpe nineteen labourers and five female servants were living in at the two farms in the township.[36]

The subsequent fate of village streets and roads was as various as that of the fields. Unless the village lay on some main thoroughfare its village street would silt up, become grass-covered, and then a "hollow way", once there was no community to come and go. The minor roads leading out over the open field furlongs would also be irrelevant to most of the needs of the graziers, especially if the landscape was re-aligned into closes. In extreme cases the village site lost all its access-routes but some of these would need to survive if there was a church continuing in use or if the herdsman of the flocks lived at the site. If the manor house continued to be the landowner's residence, at least one route would be preserved. Indeed, the location of a site can sometimes be determined by the confluence of unmetalled green lanes or footpaths at some point in open country, such as those converging on the river-crossing and former village of Trafford (Northants.). The former road-system converging on Walton (Northants.) includes the ancient track known locally as the Port Way. In 1600 the enclosure of Furtho, in the same county, caused the Northampton road to be diverted, the village removed to a new site and a new church provided for it. A century later the historian, John Bridges, detected the vestiges of the village alongside the course of the abandoned

[34] P.R.O. E179/205/522.

[35] Schedule to deed of July 9, 1808, Birdsall Estate Office, seen by kindness of Hon. Michael Willoughby.

[36] P.R.O. HO 107/1212/12–13.

road.   In our own day the deadend spurs of roads on the Downs above Warminster similarly point to the site of Imber, requisitioned by the War Office in 1943 and never released.

The relation of deserted sites to parkland is also complex.   There is one case, Tusmore (Oxon.), where it is certain that the park succeeded immediately on the village but this was an exceptional case, a Black Death depopulation (Beresford and St. Joseph, 1958, 112–14) with a royal licence in 1357 to create the park out of the abandoned fields.   Manorial lords, great and small, liked to have parks in the late fifteenth century, and no doubt these were sometimes fashioned out of unwanted agricultural land.   But there is no evidence, either documentary or topographical, for the grazier-depopulators of the late fifteenth century turning out their sheep into a decorative parkscape.   The estate-plan evidence, although a century later than the depopulation, is always of a utilitarian landscape of closes.   But soon after the middle of the sixteenth century on the smaller-scale county maps, such as those of Saxton, the country houses begin to be surrounded by symbols for park pales.

To create a park it was necessary to have privacy in the strict sense of the word. Village houses near a manor house were often considered to detract from its dignity, but to have a park in which tenants had rights of entry for common would have been quite impossible.   Its herbage had to be exclusive for hunting as well as for grazing.   Poacher as well as traveller had to be excluded by diverting rights of way that had once led to the villages.   A traveller coming south from Salisbury on the east bank of the Avon has twice to make a long curving circuit further east and then back again: in each case he is being taken round the pale of a former park, and in each park there is a deserted village: Barford and Standlynch.   If Shakespeare poached in Charlecote park, did he know that there was a deserted village site?   On the other side of the Warwickshire Avon was Welcombe, absorbed in the pastures of Stratford graziers, including Shakespeare's butcher father: but finishing up as a park, now the grounds of an hotel.

If an Elizabethan or Stuart landowner wanted to have a park, then a deserted site was doubly attractive: village houses and common rights had long disappeared, so that the obstacles here were minimal; and since many depopulating landlords had waxed fat on the profits of grazing, and risen in the world (as the Spencers and Knightleys rose), it was more than likely that many landowners would find that they already had a deserted village somewhere on the family estates, since their family fortunes often derived from a father or grandfather who had done well out of grazing in the time of the depopulations a generation or two earlier.   Their country house might even be a glorified extension or rebuilding of the manor house of such a village, the perfect centre for an emparking.

Thus, when the earthworks of a deserted village site are detected in a park or when a village church stands isolated along the gardens of some great country mansion, it must not be automatically assumed that the village has made way for the park.   Fifteenth- and sixteenth-century documentation will have to be scrutinised to see whether there was an intervening stage of sheep pastures.   This intervening stage is certainly visible, for example, at Compton Verney (Warws.) where estate plans[37] of 1736 and 1738 show the avenues, plantations, gardens and pools partly overlying the landscape of large

[37] Warwickshire County Record Office, Willoughby de Broke Estate Maps, nos. 3–4.

hedged closes and *grounds*, some as big as 70 acres.   One of these had the tell-tale name of *The townes*, and when the valley was dammed, the new artificial lake lapped at the edge of the church until Capability Brown moved it in 1772.   Yet Compton Verney, the documents make clear, had been deserted since the late fifteenth century (Hilton, 1955, 683).

With the village-less pastures as a ready-made base for a park, it was rarely necessary for a sixteenth- or seventeenth- century squire to incur odium by taking on the role of a depopulator.   Even in the eighteenth century, when Goldsmith's *Deserted Village* (1770) complained of men being evicted to make parkland, there was a good deal of re-housing elsewhere on the estate or building of estate-villages on new sites at the fringe of parks. Sometimes the squire would build a new church for this re-settlement and then appropriate the village church for his mausoleum.   If Mrs. Batey is correct in identifying Goldsmith's poetic deserted village with Nuneham Courtenay (Oxon.), then this is what happened there (p. 55, below).

It is not usually difficult to distinguish eighteenth- and nineteenth-century cases of removal or destruction of villages.   Estate, taxation, parochial, episcopal and even county records are likely to be available to show a village, there the one moment but gone the next.   The Hearth Taxes of 1662–89 are particularly important in proving the size and existence at that date of villages that were later to be taken for parkland.   Thus 100 houses were listed in 1673 at Milton Abbas (Dorset): it was more than a hundred years later that Joseph Damer, first baron Milton, began to plan the park that eventually resulted in the removal of every house (plans of 1771 and 1776: Beresford and St. Joseph 1958, fig. 40b; Beresford, 1957, fig. 19).   There were also substantial numbers of houses and hearths taxed in other villages that were later to be landscaped out of existence, such as Hinderskelfe (Yorks., N.R.), Nuneham Courtenay (Oxon.), Shugborough (Staffs.), Harewood (Yorks., W.R.) and Normanton (Rutland).   The emparking depopulation, it must also be noted, is typically a great enemy of archaeological evidence at the village site.   Apart from any area that has disappeared under the Great House itself, there are few country houses of that size which are not adjoined by extensive coachhouses and outbuildings, not to speak of shrubberies and other ornamental gardens.   Thus a comparison of the 1707 plan of Nuneham and the present Ordnance Survey map shows that the stables alone cover the sites of nine village houses and crofts. A surviving church in ornamental parkland may be the best pointer to the area where the former village houses stood but (as Nuneham itself shows) it was not impossible for a noble landscaper to come to an agreement with his bishop, and have not only a new, architecturally fashionable, church but also a new site for it so that its façade could fit in to the aesthetic of the park.

Great houses are not the only obscurantists: a single Victorian farmstead in an area such as the Yorkshire Wolds had outbuildings for farm animals and implements, together with fold yards, sufficient to cover up the major part of the area of a small village. Thus is it at Raisthorpe (Yorks., E.R.) where a site of great potential archaeological interest is quite obscured: for a deed of 1384 makes it plain that the ownership distribution of selions in the then open fields of this vill was by the regular pattern of *solskift*,[38] but

[38] *Yorkshire Deeds*, iv, Yorks. Archaeol. Soc. Rec. Ser., LXV (1924), no. 405.

it will now never be possible to examine the house pattern of the village to see whether it could have been the basis for the regular distribution of selions within each furlong.

The Hearth Tax is also useful in confirming evidence or suspicions that a village had already disappeared. Winterbourne Came (Dorset) was suggested in *Lost Villages* as a depopulated place, and the published Hearth Tax of 1662 indeed shows that it was reduced to two moderate-sized houses, one of eight hearths and one of five. Altogether Dorset had six townships that contained no more than two houses taxed in 1662.[39]

Since the Hearth Tax recorded the number of hearths in each house it is additionally useful in demonstrating what sort of houses were to be found in a deserted township two or three hundred years after its depopulation. Where there are a substantial number of one- and two-hearth houses in a township that has good-quality deserted village earthworks and well-documented depopulation in the fifteenth or sixteenth centuries, it is clear that resettlement for arable or for mixed husbandry had already begun in the 1660's. More commonly, the deserted village earthworks will be matched by Hearth Tax entries that consist of two or three houses only. Of these, one may be the parsonage, and this is easily checked since the Tax record gives the householder's name. The number of hearths in the remaining house or houses will at once reveal whether the occupier was squire or shepherd. At Tusmore (Oxon.) the only house had nineteen hearths, clearly the Squire's even if the name did not already identify him.[40] At Wharram Percy, on the other hand, the hearths were those of a shepherd's cottage and the parsonage house: the manor house was long decayed.[41] At Hardwick (Oxon.) the squire's house had twelve hearths, the rectory two and a cottage had one. There were no more, but from the outlook of those liable to the poor rate this was desirable loneliness. As the advertisement for the sale of Billesley (Warws.) put it in 1756, "there are only two houses in the parish and the taxes are trifling".[42]

After large-scale estate plans began to be made in the 1550's there is always a chance that one of these will record either an already-deserted site with some information about its previous condition; or a village that was yet to be depopulated, particularly the late emparkings. Some of these were known in 1954 (e.g. Hinderskelfe, Yorks. N.R.; Wotton Underwood, Bucks.) and to them can now be added: Milton Abbas (Dorset, 1771 and 1776, above); Overstone (Northants., 1671); Coombes (Sussex, 1677); Broxholme (Lincs., c. 1600) and West Burton (Notts.) (Plate 5), all surveyed while there were still houses in the village.[43] The queen of the pre-desertion plans, however, remains the sketch plan of Boarstall (Bucks.) drawn c. 1444, perhaps the earliest depiction of any English village.[44]

[39] C. A. F. Meekings, *Dorset Hearth Tax Assessments* (1951), I, 21–22, 41–43, 63–65, 83–84; Milton Abbas, 120.

[40] M. M. B. Weinstock, ed., *Hearth Tax Returns for Oxfordshire, 1665*, Oxon. Record Soc., XXI (1940), 205 and 207.

[41] P.R.O. E179/205/504, 514 and 522.

[42] *Birmingham Gazette*, May 24, 1756, cited by J. M. Martin, *Ag. Hist. Rev.*, XV (1967), 22.

[43] Overstone plan, Northants. Archives Committee, "Map ... belonging to Lord Fitzwalter"; Broxholme, Lincs. Archives Committee: and see *Beresford and St. Joseph, 1958*, figs. 9A and 9B; West Burton, Sheffield City Libraries, Fairbank Collection, Wes. I L: see *Holland, 1967*, 70.

[44] Reproduced in H. E. Salter and A. H. Cooke, eds., *The Boarstall Cartulary*, Oxford Hist. Soc., LXXXVIII (1930), and *V. C. H. Bucks.*, IV, 9.

Since 1954 a handful of large-scale estate plans has come to light where the site of a former village is indicated explicitly (as opposed to the *Town Field* indications mentioned above).[45] These are in the course of publication in successive volumes of *Medieval Archaeology*.   A plan of Fallowfield (Northumberland), preserved at Hatfield House, is three years older than the plan of Whatborough (Leics.), being drawn in 1583, and may be claimed as the earliest cartographic representation of a desertion.   Alongside *fallowe feelde towne* it shows dotted rectangles and explains them as *old howses foundacions*. (Beresford, 1966).   Whessoe (Durham) was surveyed in 1601 and the empty crofts and

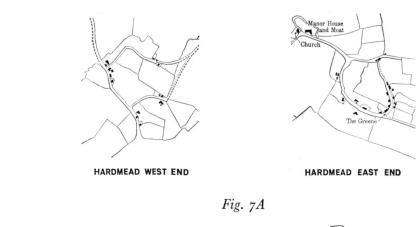

HARDMEAD WEST END   HARDMEAD EAST END

Fig. 7A

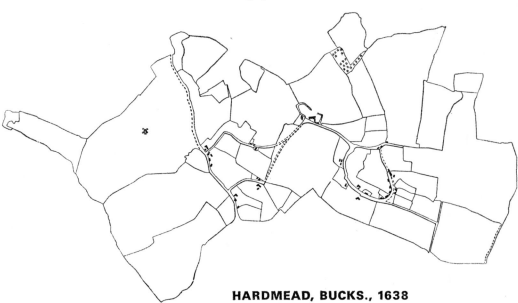

HARDMEAD, BUCKS., 1638

Fig. 7B

[45] Whessoe plan, P.R.O. Maps MR 396; East Layton, see fn. 31 above; Kirkby, Northants. Archives Committee, Finch-Hatton Ms. 272, ff. 5–7; Hardmead, copy seen by kindness of Prof. Chibnall.

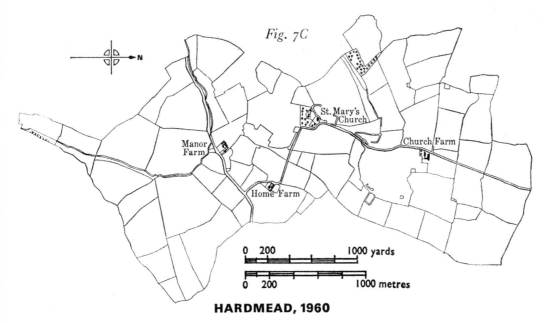

Fig. 7C

HARDMEAD, 1960

Fig. 7. Hardmead, Bucks., in 1638, partially deserted, and in 1960

Richard Bankes' map shows eighteen houses on the looped road at the East End; the Manor House, its moat and the church in a central position, but with no other houses adjoining; and a West End of twelve houses. (Figs. 7A and 7B). The parish is now worked from three farms (Fig. 7C), and a small group of council houses has recently been added.

former village green indicated. East Layton in the same county was surveyed in 1608 when the former village street was still in use as a highway, bordered only by *the scyte of the howses* (Beresford, 1967). Two plans of Kirby (Northants.) made in 1584 and 1587 show the vestiges of the village being submerged in the park and gardens of the Hall. A plan of Hardmead (Bucks.) (Fig. 7) shows the now-deserted village in semi-decay, consisting in 1638 of houses scattered around two distinct greens or "Ends" (the local term) more than half a mile apart. This same scattered pattern of "Ends" indicated by a web of former roads, is seen in the plan of Chellington (Beds.) in 1798, and is characteristic of the southern Midland plain.

A map with a desertion tacitly indicated by an isolated church is—remarkably—an early plan of London. Ralph Agas' plan of 1578 extends as far north as St. Pancras, and the Norman parish church (hidden today behind the railway arches north of St. Pancras and King's Cross stations) is shown surrounded by nothing but fields.

Direct description of the appearance of deserted sites in the period between Charles I and the Ordnance Survey maps is usually confined to the verbal, in the works of observant topographical historians like Sir William Dugdale and John Bridges. Writing *c.* 1720 (but not published until 1791), Bridges had the opportunity of describing such sites as Nobold (Northants.).

49

Throughout the whole of Old Nobold Close are many irregular banks and hollows, such as are usual in ruinous places, about which have been turned up walling stones and old hearthstones, as supposed from the marks they bore of fire. Round these heaps and hollows are partition banks and ditches, inclosing such extents of ground as are commonly allotted to the homesteads of cottages and farmhouses. Nearly the length of the close along the middle of it is a list or tract of ground, lower than the ground on both sides, which appears to have been raised by rubbish, supposed to have been the principal street.[46]

Sir William Dugdale had noted "depopulated places" in *The Antiquities of Warwickshire*, published in 1656, but without details of sites in the manner that Bridges adopted in the neighbouring county, description that could not be bettered until the availability of the ground- and air-photograph. Yet Dugdale pioneered another technique of recording *depopulated sites*, the use of a special symbol on the county maps which he himself drew to accompany *The Antiquities*. This symbol, a diamond with a heavy central dot, was also employed by Henry Beighton (Fig. 8), and for the maps illustrating the 1730 edition of the *Antiquities*.[47] The printed map had become complementary to printed history.

There are two other ways by which a scrutiny of a modern map can indicate that a settlement has disappeared. The most obvious is to search for exceptionally empty pieces of countryside. It was shown, for example (Beresford and St. Joseph, 1958, 75–8) that in the Midlands the villages lie very nearly one mile apart. If an area of infertile ground intervenes, this distance widens, but if in normal circumstances a village is not found with this frequency there is a *prima facie* case for further enquiry and fieldwork.

There may also be significance in the very shape of parish bounds in an area where a deserted site is suspected but has not been located. It is always worth while in these circumstances to take a large-scale map and work over the parish boundaries to see whether any parish has a projection or an appendage in which there is no settlement (or only a single farm), for the appendage shape is just what would result if, with the decay of one village, its parish area was added to that of a neighbour[48] (Fig. 9). (It need not be pointed out, perhaps, how unhistorical all geographical explanations of settlement distribution must be if they are based on the distribution of surviving settlements only.)

Plans of a different kind, but equally useful, published since 1954 are modern large-scale plans of village earthworks. Many of these accompany final or interim reports on excavations and are properly dealt with in Mr. Hurst's chapter (below) but special mention should be made of the seven plans drawn in the course of Ordnance Survey revision and published with a note by Prof. Hoskins (Hoskins, 1956); and the privately-produced plan of Pudding Norton in a Norfolk Research Committee *Bulletin* (Wade-Martins and Wade, 1967, 3). Small-scale county distribution maps by Dr. Glasscock were prepared as frontispieces for the Oxfordshire and Northamptonshire monographs (Allison *et al.*, 1965 and 1966).

[46] John Bridges, *History and Antiquities of Northamptonshire* (ed. of 1791), II, 23.

[47] P. D. A. Harvey and H. Thorpe, *The Printed Maps of Warwickshire, 1576–1900* (1959), 11–17.

[48] Villages with significant positions within the bounds of modern parishes include: Whatcombe, Berks. six-inch sheet O.S. XXVI NW; Holworth, Dorset LIV; Tiscott, Herts. XVII SW; Boughton, Hunts. XXI SE; Elkington, Northants. XXIII SW; Hesley, Notts. II SE; Armstalls, Oxon. XXXII SE; Hardwick, Rutland VI SW; Tolethorpe, Rutland VI SE; Bericote, Warws. XXXIII NE; Stoneythorpe, Warws. XL NE.

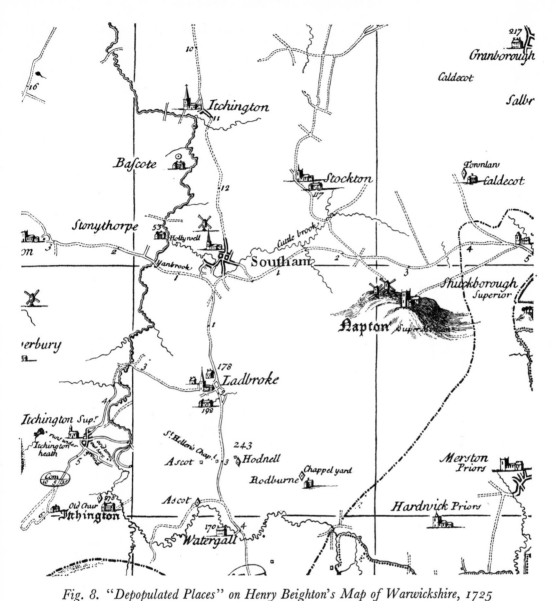

Fig. 8. "Depopulated Places" on Henry Beighton's Map of Warwickshire, 1725

"Depopulated places" were shown by a lozenge, an open diamond with a dot in its centre, following the example of Dugdale's own map. This extract from the southern section of the map (surveyed by 1725, printed 1728) shows such conventional signs at Lower Itchington, Chapel Ascote, Hodnell, Radbourn and Caldecote.

When a site is being sought on a map, it should be emphasised, perhaps more strongly than in *Lost Villages,* that a change of name for a village is not the same thing as a depopulation although both will result in names appearing in medieval tax lists but not on modern maps.   Here and there, villages have completely changed their names over the centuries, and—an allied complication—when there are two contiguous villages it is not unknown for the whole to be now known only by the name of one partner.   Similarly, what might be termed a "suburb" or outlier of a village can lose its separate rank and its name disappear from the map without this being evidence for depopulation.

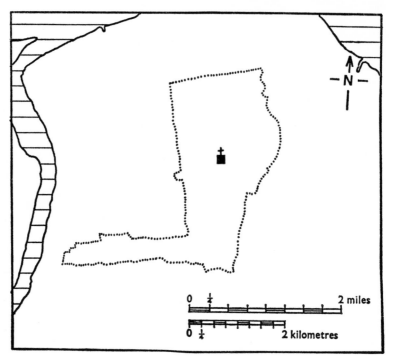

Fig. 9. Haythby in West Halton, Lincs.: The parish boundary as an indication of a lost township

The westward-projecting leg of the present parish indicates the area of the lost township of Haythby; the enclosure award names the 21 closes in this projection as *Hairby* (*Foster, 1920*, lxi); the village site lies near the rectangular bulge in the north of the township boundary.   The south-west corner of this Figure is at SE 860170.

The emptying of houses from a field left a village name suspended, as it were, in mid-air.   If there was a church in the village, the name would survive as a parish-name, even if an almost empty parish; and if the church decayed, as at Argam (Yorks. E.R.) then the name could survive as a civil parish.   If farm-building re-commenced in the eighteenth century (p. 44, above), the name would probably take root again at the new farm, even if that farm was situated a considerable way from the old village site (e.g. Goldicote, Warws.; Wharram Percy (p. 44, above); Coat, Oxon.).   A country house taking over the name of the village could also be built to fit into a parkscape but not at the village site (e.g. Compton Wynyates, Warws.).   The confusion thus caused in a search for a village site is obvious, and it may result in the search being abandoned as fruitless.

There are cases where the name of a deserted village has become attached to a farm in the next township, with even greater confusion for historical field-workers. If there was no farm by which the old village name could be preserved, it might leave its name in a field; if this was the field in which the village stood, all well and good, a divining rod for researchers: but sometimes it was a field in the *next* township, named after the (lost) township that it bordered, which preserved the deserted village name. Thus *Hunland* is a field-name in Full Sutton (Yorks., E.R.), preserving part of the name of the former village of Hundeburton in the adjoining parish of Stamford Bridge. There are also cases where the name has completely fallen into disuse, as at Butyate and Osgodby (Lincs.), Torpel (Northants.), and Aspley, Wike and Smercote (Warws.). The good-quality site now identified as Broadstone (Oxon.) was once thought to be one of the Chalfords until it was noticed that it lay outside the bounds of Over and Nether Chalford as drawn on a map of 1743.[49]

It should also be noted that a castle bearing a former village name does not always lead to the site (although there is a motte at Alstoe (Rutland); a fine, fortified manor house alongside South Cowton (Yorks., N.R.); and defences at Kilpeck which embrace the whole village). The siting of the castle would be related to military strategy, and this consideration could dictate a position different from that of the medieval village of the same name as the castle.

VIII: GOLDSMITH'S *DESERTED VILLAGE*

In Goldsmith's poem, The Deserted Village, published in 1770, the noun and the adjective were immortally joined together. Yet Dr. Johnson and other contemporaries were sceptical that the events in the poem existed elsewhere than in the poet's imagination. Goldsmith was insistent, but did not identify the location of his "Auburn".

Since the eighteenth-century emparking enclosures paid at least lip service to the rights of property-owners, however small their holdings, there was no way in which the hostility of the law could be invoked against a well-conducted enclosure. And if a new estate village was provided for the deserving tenantry, as it often was, then tears had to be shed only for the undeserving; and if their going relieved the poor rate, there were not many to weep. Goldsmith was exceptional in his compassion, perhaps remembering his native Ireland as well as England.

> ... the man of wealth and pride
> Takes up a space that many poor supplied;
> Space for his lake, his park's extended bounds,
> Space for his horses, equipage and hounds.
> The robe that wraps his limbs in silken sloth
> Has robbed the neighbouring fields of half their growth.

Others were less troubled. On the obelisk overlooking Castle Howard (Yorks., N.R.) and the site of Hinderskelfe village, Charles, third earl of Carlisle, had inscribed:

[49] Mowat, *op. cit.* in f.n. 33, nos. 9–14.

If to perfection these plantations rise
If they agreeably might earn surprise,
This faithful pillar will their age declare
As long as time these characters shall spare.
Here, then, with kind remembrance read his name
Who for posterity performed the same:
Charles, the Third Earl of Carlisle.
Begun 1702.   Finished 1731.

Nearly a century later a similar approval was expressed for an emparking depopulation which properly belongs to North Britain, although the international importance of the site makes it desirable to rescue the comment from obscurity.   Between 1805 and 1807 the earl of Mansfield removed the village and church of Scone, Perthshire, from beside his new Palace.   In 1807 the approving but anonymous author of some local historical and architectural notes wrote:

> he has bought up the adjacent village and grounds annexed . . . and erected a new and handsome village at a proper distance from the palace. In a word, everything which fortune, taste, and patriotism, can effect has been called forth to complete the embellishment of this spot, so highly favoured by nature.[50]

But by the early-nineteenth century there were those who were more critical of the landed interest and its policies.   A very Goldsmithian viewpoint was expressed by one celebrated landscape engineer who was very familiar with parks, parkscapes and parkowners.   Humphrey Repton wrote:

> I have, on several occasions, ventured to condemn as false taste that fatal rage for destroying villages or depopulating a country, under the idea of its being necessary to the importance of a mansion. . . .   As a number of labourers constitutes one of the requisites of grandeur, comfortable habitations for its poor dependants ought to be provided.[51]

This attitude inspired an unusual illustration in *The Builder*, showing Victorian rural labourers watching sorrowfully while a country-house is being built, presumably over the site of their village since the engraving is entitled, "The Deserted Village".   What country-house the artist had in mind I have not been able to discover.

In January 1968 Mrs. Mavis Batey drew my attention to evidence which, taken together, makes it very likely that Goldsmith's *Deserted Village* of "sweet Auburn" can be identified as Nuneham Courtenay, Oxfordshire.   No previous identification had been credible, although I had pointed out myself the odd coincidence that a village washed away by the sea on the east coast of Yorkshire was also called Auburn.   Bartholomew's *Gazetteer* has no place of this name except Aubourn, six miles south-west of Lincoln. The Irish Tourist Board has given official approval to the claim that Goldsmith was referring to his native village in Ireland, and the district is appropriately sign-posted; indeed, in the spring before receiving Mrs. Batey's first letter I had myself paused like a pilgrim at the heap of stones said to be the inn of Auburn.

Mrs. Batey has published the evidence in full in *Oxoniensia*, but in advance of pub-

[50] Anon., *Sconiana* (Edinburgh, 1808), 13–14; J. Urquhart, *Historical sketches of Scone* (Perth, 1883), 83 and 104; there is an inventory of the former village in the (*First*) *Statistical Account* (1796).

[51] H. Repton, *The Art of Landscape Gardening*, ed. J. Nolen (1907), 173–74.

lication she kindly gave me permission to draw upon her notes. In 1927 Mr. R. S. Crane published a number of fugitive essays contributed by Goldsmith to the London press. It was known that Goldsmith's method of composition was first to sketch a poem in the form of a prose narrative, and the extracts below are from "The Revolution in Low Life", published in *Lloyd's Evening Post* in June 1762. The parallels with *The Deserted Village* are so striking that Mr. Crane was convinced that this essay was in fact the preliminary prose sketch.

> I spent part of last summer (i.e. 1761) in a little village, distant about fifty miles from town, consisting of near an hundred houses. . . . They were shortly to leave this abode of felicity, of which they and their ancestors had been in possession time immemorial, and they had received orders to search for a new habitation. I was informed that a Merchant of immense fortune in London, who had lately purchased the estate on which they lived, intended to lay the whole out in a seat of pleasure for himself. I staid 'till the day on which they were compelled to remove . . . their neat gardens and well cultivated fields were left to desolation . . . I am informed that nothing is more common than such revolutions.[52]

Goldsmith went on to compare the situation with that in Rome before the decline, the 'barren splendour' of great gardens of pleasure!

Indeed "distant about fifty miles from town" was Newnham or Nuneham Courtenay, a village on a bluff overlooking the Thames and within sight of Oxford spires. The first condition of identity with Auburn is therefore met. What had been happening at Nuneham in the summer of 1761? The removal of the village to make the first Earl Harcourt's park had begun in 1760 with the buildings that lay on the slope between church and river where the gardens were planned around a new, Palladian house, completed in 1760. In the summer of 1761 the main evacuation of houses from around the village green was in train, exactly when Goldsmith came upon the scene. By chance, the diary of the Rev. James Newton, then rector of Nuneham, has survived for the period April 1761 to April 1762. The bishop had agreed to an exchange of the glebe in 1760 so that there could be a new site for the rectory and the old site be submerged in the park. The diary shows that he had moved into his new rectory in the summer of 1759 and was planting his garden for the first time in the spring of 1761. In May 1761 he visited a parishioner in the new village that Lord Harcourt had built outside the park on the turnpike road, and four days later he baptised the first child to be born there.[53] In June 1761 there was a village fete, and these were probably the celebrations mentioned at the beginning of Goldsmith's poem. The church still stood, although the churchyard had been incorporated in the flower garden of the House. In September the rector took away gravestones to pave his new garden. It was not until the summer of 1762, after Goldsmith's visit, that Lord Harcourt began to plan the demolition of the now-isolated medieval parish church and the erection of a quasi-classical temple nearby where it could be incorporated in a scenic vista, and it is significant that Goldsmith made no charges of desecrating the church at Auburn.

It is also a remarkable coincidence, if Nuneham is not Auburn, that the poet Laureate, William Whitehead, a former tutor and close friend of the Harcourts, wrote a poem in defence of the transfer of Nuneham to its new site. In "The Removal of the

[52] R. S. Crane, ed., *New Essays by Oliver Goldsmith* (Chicago, 1927), 116–19.
[53] Glebe exchange, Oxford Diocesan Papers 2197 no. 8; diary, Bodleian Library, Ms. Eng. Misc. e. 251.

Village at Nuneham" he relates how a "solitary widowed thing" remained in the classical parkscape, giving it an authentic but unintended Arcadian touch, for the landowner had, according to Whitehead, taken pity on her pleadings and allowed her to stay when the others were removed.

The careful matrons of the plain
Had left their cots without a sigh
Well pleased to house their little train
In happier mansions warm and dry;
While Mopsa still with lingering pace
And many a look and many a tear

Oft tried in vain to quit the place . . .
This Harcourt heard with pitying ear
And midst the enchanting scene he planned,
Indulgent to her humble prayer,
Allowed her clay-built cot to stand.

The historical Muse normally lives a solitary life these days, remote from her sisters, especially Poetry, and it is a pleasure when reality and imagination can occasionally meet as they seem to do at Auburn and Nuneham. Mrs. Batey's communication enlivened the academic year in which this chapter has been under way, and has been crowned by her discovery of Robert Smith's plan[54] of Nuneham, made in 1707, a corroboration for Goldsmith's thesis of which the poet was unaware (Figs. 10–11).

Deserted Villages, it may be added, continue into our own day. Snap, Wilts., was destroyed in 1913 and critics were countered with a slander suit (Smith, 1960), a hazard which Goldsmith escaped. Faxton, Northants., has been finally deserted since 1945 and its excavation by Dr. Butler has shown remarkable promptitude in getting off the mark smartly.[55] In 1943 Imber (Wilts.) was taken over in order to give scope for more realistic training in street fighting than normal villages offered the War Office. Although the church, protected by a thirteen-strand barbed-wire fence, is re-opened for the former villagers once a year, the death of the village has recently been underlined by the omission of its name from the quarter-inch Ordnance Survey map. However, an Association for the Restoration of Imber exists. Troops also make mock havoc on another deserted village site, although here things had been eased for the War Office by earlier events. In the Stanford Battle Range (Norfolk) the tank tracks plough past the ruins of Sturston Hall and the site of the church: however, there have been no villagers since 1597 when Edmund Jermyn, lord of Sturston, evicted the last householders (Allison, 1955, 136 and 158). No Association for the Restoration of Sturston is recorded.

IX: FIELDWORK AND SITE QUALITY

My initial stimulus to study deserted villages was the chance discovery of a Leicestershire site. Sites in the county gazetteers of Lost Villages *were listed irrespective of their visible quality, and indeed many of them had not been visited. Even now, after determined fieldwork, there are villages known from documents but without sites located on the ground; and a small number of sites observed on the ground or from the air but to which no village name can be given. The visual quality of sites varies considerably even within the same district.*

[54] Bodleian Library. (E) c17:49 (105); original now at Nuneham Park: Mavis Batey, "Nuneham Courtenay: an Oxfordshire 18th-century deserted village", *Oxoniensia* xxxiii (1968), 108–24.
[55] See *Gazetteer* no. 147, below, p. 159.

The clarity of earthworks at a site will depend to some extent on its age, for the sheer passage of time can obliterate, particularly on light and friable soils. For the local studies of Leicestershire, Northamptonshire and Oxfordshire Mr. Hurst visited every one of the sites that could be located in order to report on its quality of preservation. This was to serve three ends: to save a reader who wished to see a good quality site from wasting his time; to indicate to local researchers where it had still proved impossible to locate a village; and to assist the Research Group in its selection of first-quality sites in the various natural regions of England so that a minimal preservation scheme could be submitted to the Ancient Monuments Board (Appendix, p. 303).

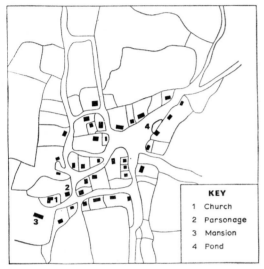

KEY	
1	Church
2	Parsonage
3	Mansion
4	Pond

Fig. 10. Nuneham Courtenay. Copy of 1707 estate map

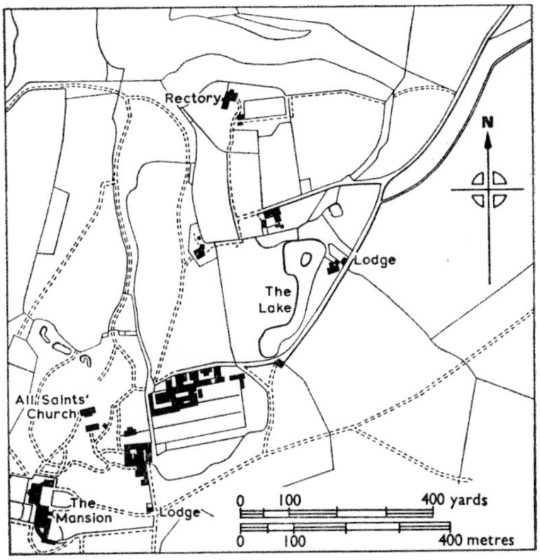

Fig. 11. Nuneham Courtenay in 1968

Note the extensive stables, greenhouses and other outbuildings north-east of *The Mansion*. The Rectory stands where it was re-built in 1760; in 1762 the church was also re-sited. Goldsmith's visit to his 'Auburn' was in 1761. (The Harcourts' new village stands on the main road, outside the area of this map.)

A five-point scale was devised, using the symbols A*, A, B, C and D, as explained in Table XIII, p. 64, below. Four supplementary terms were employed, P, G, CM and EM, to indicate the character of the surface. A query mark and the letter U indicated the barrier of ignorance where it existed, and COV the common experience of finding a large modern farm or country-house and gardens covering enough ground to make it impossible to detect any remains of the village. It will be noticed that two other symbols, RES (i.e. re-settled) and REB (i.e. re-built) make allowance for later settlement changes. A RES site is one such as Wormleighton, where John Spencer I built a new village soon after 1506 on the hill above the depopulated site (Thorpe, 1964, 97–107). Many Black Death depopulations are known to have been re-settled almost immediately. Padworth (Berks.) and Clothall (Herts.) are two examples. Only archaeological excavation could determine whether at such re-settlements the newcomers occupied

57

the houses of their dead predecessors of whether they fearfully avoided them. In the latter case there should be the remains of an older village alongside the new, but these are so similar to the earthworks of a shrunken village that there is bound to be confusion at the fieldwork stage.

A REB site is likely to be produced by the spread of building in the last two centuries, particularly near large towns. One can therefore have a site like St. Pancras (Middlesex) built over, both disguising its identity as a former deserted medieval village and removing any chance of inspecting the village earthworks. Suburbs of Coventry have likewise re-peopled deserted villages, and the New Town developments projected for the Milton Keynes area will do the same on a grand scale. The post-war New Town of Peterlee (Co. Durham) has enveloped the site of Yoden but it is to be preserved as an open space with the intention of marking out the lines of the former village for the information of visitors. I myself live in one of the Leeds suburban houses that in the 1930's brought back habitation to within sight of the isolated Norman church of Adel (Yorks., W.R.).

Table X summarises the visible quality of sites in Leicestershire, Northamptonshire and Oxfordshire at the time of Mr. Hurst's inspection. The proportions in the three counties are not very different, but it should be noted that these grassy shires have been very susceptible to the blandishments of the ploughing-up subsidy, and anyone making an inspection to-day would certainly have to demote sites in each county.

TABLE X

Visible quality of sites, three Midland counties

	Visual quality of sites (for code see p. 64)						
	A* %	A %	B %	C %	D %	U %	Total number
Leicestershire	5	18	18	33	8	17	65
Northamptonshire	—	18	25	35	8	15	82
Oxfordshire	2	12	28	32	16	11	101

Table XI attempts to relate the visible quality to the period of desertion. The most disappointing visible quality is, not unexpectedly, possessed by those sites that have been destroyed longest, yet the best sites are not, as might have been expected, the most recent destructions but those from the period 1450–1700. There is an explanation of the paradox, for the more recent depopulations are mostly emparkings and the combination of landscape gardening and ornamental gardening, not to speak of stables and outbuildings, can be a very effective concealment.

TABLE XI

Visible quality of sites of different periods of desertion, Northamptonshire

Period of desertion	Visual quality of sites (for code see p. 64)						
	A*	A	B	C	D	U	Total number
In Domesday Book only	—	—	—	—	—	4	4
c. 1100–*c.* 1350	—	—	—	—	—	1	1
c. 1350–*c.* 1450	—	3	2	2	—	3	10
c. 1450–*c.* 1700	—	5	11	11	3	4	34
After *c.* 1700	—	1	1	4	3	—	9
Unknown period	—	6	6	11	1	—	24
Total	0	15	20	28	7	12	82

Visits to sites in other counties are not completed, and Tables cannot be presented for all parts of England, but it is clear that for the country as a whole the clarity of present-day earthworks depends primarily on the character of local soils and the proximity of suitable stone for building. In regions of light soils, especially since in England such soils are often far from easily-worked stone quarries, there are two reasons why so little can be discerned on the surface. The light soils more easily settle and are more easily levelled by later ploughing while the village houses, likely to contain very little stonework, will leave virtually no surface impression. The inspection of sites in all parts of the country which has been carried out for the Research Group (principally by Mr. Hurst) has indicated that even in areas of heavier, clay soils, where the imprint of medieval streets, croft boundaries and village boundary-banks can be very clear indeed, a timber house will have left little for the eye to detect except the raised platforms on which it stood. In recent years archaeological techniques have begun to decipher such structures (p. 95, below) but the difficulty in identifying the position of houses within the crofts has not made clay-timber sites the first choice for excavators with limited funds and time.

The sites with the best surface-remains of houses are those where local building stone was available and being employed for house-building just before the desertion, whether the granite boulders of Hound Tor (Devon), the Cotswold limestone of Upton (Gloucs.) or the walls of houses at Wharram Percy (Yorks., E.R.) composed of chalk blocks that excavation has shown to come from shallow quarries which villagers had dug in every croft. If the list of top-quality sites recommended to foreign visitors in *Villages Désertés* is studied, it will be seen that they lie in a very limited number of counties: Cornwall (2); Devon (11); Dorset (1); Durham (5); Gloucestershire (2); Lincolnshire (3); Northumberland (4); Nottinghamshire (1); Oxfordshire (3); Rutland (1); Warwickshire (1);

TABLE XII
Sites with best visible remains of houses

Cornwall	Garrow
—	Trewortha
Devon	Badgworthy
—	Blackaton
—	Bolt Head
—	Challacombe
—	Cordonford, Little
—	Cripdon
—	Ford
—	Hayne
—	Hound Tor
—	Rowden, North
—	Rowden, South
Dorset	Ringstead
Durham	Embleton
—	Garmondsway
—	Hartburn, West
—	Swainston
—	Walworth
Gloucestershire	Norton, Lower
—	Upton
Lincolnshire	Aunby
—	Gainsthorpe
—	Riseholme
Northumberland	Middleton, South
—	Ogle
—	Welton
—	Whelpington, West
Nottinghamshire	Keighton
Oxfordshire	Bainton
—	Broadstone
—	Walcot
Rutland	Pickworth
Warwickshire	Brookhampton
Wiltshire	Gomeldon
Yorkshire, East Riding	Argam
—	Cottam
—	Cowlam
—	Givendale, Little
—	Riplingham
—	Towthorpe
—	Wharram Percy

Wiltshire (1); and Yorkshire, E.R. (7). The list is clearly biased against the counties with light soils, and towards granite.

The mid-nineteenth-century Tithe Award for Astwick (Northants.) has the significant field-name *Stoneheap Ground* at the village site, and the only field in the township not then under the plough was this field with its stubborn remains of stone house-foundations. Elsewhere in the stone counties there have been sites preserved (at least until very recently) because the ploughs were deterred by the large pieces of building stone under the surface. Clay sites were more likely to be ploughed over and disappear from view, although some very deep hollow-ways and high croft-banks at clay sites have been known to unseat tractor drivers.

On heavy clay soils the best visible remains leading to the location of the actual village site are not the earthworks of houses, streets or crofts but the ridge and furrow of the former open-fields. When the arable selions of the open fields went over to grass at the depopulation and remained unploughed for generations, their high-backed ridges are as effectively preserved as any grass-covered house-wall, especially in the heavy soils. Although much ridge and furrow has been ploughed up in recent years, there is an excellent record of it in the post-war R.A.F. air photographs and in the earlier surveys of Dr. St. Joseph. Even after ploughing and sowing, the heavier soils still bear crop-marks and earth-marks in the long, reversed-S bands. Since these open-field selions came up to the boundary bank of the village but were then replaced by the hedged crofts—as every village plan shows—there is a strong chance of detecting a village site by following the ridge and furrow and observing whether it encircles an area that lacks ridging. Such islands may reveal the village site even when there are no earthworks of streets and houses (Fig. 12). The ridge and furrow surrounding the site of Water Eaton (Oxon.) has been recently studied (Sutton, 1964–65, 111); the excavation reports on Upton (Gloucs.) and West Whelpington (Northumberland) include surveys of ridge and furrow beyond the village boundary bank; a study of open fields in the Peak District has also related ridge and furrow to deserted village sites (Wightman, 1961, 117).

There are several interesting sites where there is ridge and furrow of characteristic medieval appearance and dimensions within the banks of former house-crofts. Is this arable cultivation within the crofts during the lifetime of the village, or some vestigial selions from the open fields that had been enclosed when the houses in that part of the village were first erected? Cestersover and Radbourn (Warws.), Sunderlandwick (Yorks., E.R.) and Cawthorn (Yorks., N.R.) have these features.

Anyone first approaching the search for deserted village sites would be wise to begin with the well-attested and well-defined sites in his locality, for there is an infinite gradation of clarity from A* to near-U, and experience of the characteristic earthworks is the best aid to further explorations, remembering always that the type of earthworks will vary with the basic soil conditions (*stone* or *clay*) differentiated above.

The different seasons of the year bring their rewards and penalties. The ripening corn of late summer makes it a good season for crop-marks but these are a bonus more likely to be enjoyed by the air photographer: on the ground it is the season of maximum hedge-growth, defiant brambles, agressive nettles and other obstacles to entry and vision. In this season even a good-quality grass site can be confusing to an inexperi-

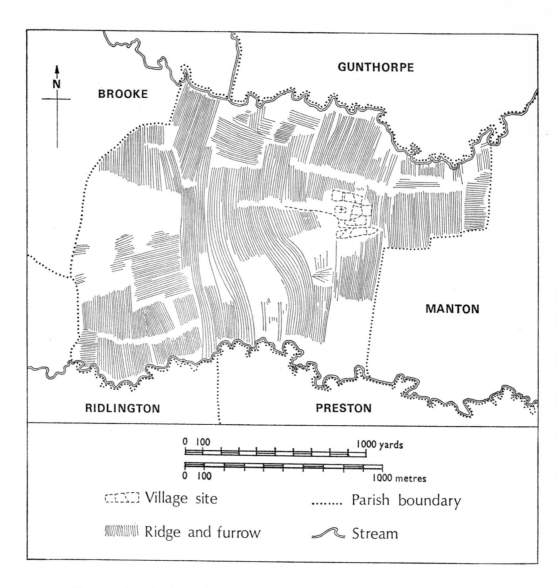

Fig. 12. Martinsthorpe, Rutland: village site and surrounding ridge and furrow

enced eye if the field is not closely grazed. With rank grass-growth, the small differences in level that mark the inside and outside of a house-earthwork or the line of croft walls will be evened out. Only buried walls very near the surface will discourage the growth of normal grasses and bear a cover of other flowering plants. Circles of nettles at this season may sometimes crown the place where the hearth-floors lie under the grass.

The best season is undoubtedly spring, when hedges have not become opaque and fields can still be appraised from the roadside; and when grass is short. Winter has its own advantages particularly on days when a hoar frost outlines differences in the depth of soil-cover over buried walls and when melting snow responds to differential heat-retaining properties in soils with buried features.

Even so, there are bound to be disappointments for the field-worker. He may find that an A-quality site has been bulldozed, and although the surface may only have been skimmed and the top-layers of building stone from the houses scattered around the surface, for him the site has lost its detail, whatever deeper archaeological soundings may still make of it.

In 1954 it was not appreciated how fatal to the preservation of sites would be the agricultural policy of successive British governments in both *Stop* and *Go* moods. The re-conversion to arable that Tudor legislators failed to achieve was induced almost overnight by the ploughing-up subsidy, and John Hales has been born again in the person of successive Ministers of Agriculture who have wooed the plough and the bulldozer. In the face of these, official archaeological preservationism has been able to do little, and sites are disappearing at an alarming rate.

Thus the lost Holme (Beds., TL 197429) was brought to light by Dr. Glasscock's work in the county taxation assessments. Its site was not visited. It had documentation going back to the 22 households of 1086, and was important in its locality since Bedfordshire has few sites of good visual quality: yet when Dr. St. Joseph photographed the site in 1967 it had just been ploughed away (Plate 16).

If he does not encounter the bulldozer, the field-worker may find new buildings covering a site; a new rural factory; or something military and so secret that he hurriedly stows away his large-scale plan, binoculars, camera and other apparatus of legitimate fieldwork, and flees before the shadow of the Official Secrets Act and M.I.5. Or it may simply be that the farmer's wife is converting the former grave-yard of a church into a rockery. All these things happen. *Teste meipso.*

Or, in scorn, he may find that a site has been wrongly reported as a medieval village. A large manorial complex and the buildings of a monastic grange can yield surface features not unlike those of a small village: for example the exact nature of the sites near Sysonby, Leics. (Beresford and St. Joseph, 1958, Fig. 110), remains to be determined; there is a similar puzzle near Knaptoft (Leics.). One should not be put off by local claims that a site is really Roman, prehistoric, or a monastery: after all, the Ordnance Survey has not been free from these fancies. Dunstall and Somerby (Lincs.) first appeared on the Ordnance Survey plans as "Roman", Lubbesthorpe and Shoby (Leics.) as "monastic", and the road system of East Lilling (Yorks., N.R.) as "moats" despite the fact that the complex pattern could not be water-holding earthworks. And at some sites there is a genuine problem of disentangling earthworks of different periods: there are Roman features in and among the medieval village earthworks at Thornton-le-Street (Yorks., N.R.), Widford, and Wilcote (Oxon.), Bocolt (Hants.) and Wood-yates (Dorset). At Arram and at Riplingham (Yorks., E.R.) there are prehistoric companions to the medieval village. And was it not at Wharram Percy that a small trial trench dug across the banks of the manor complex at the north end of the village had not gone far before it hit on an Iron Age burial?

6

And there are the problems. Two very puzzling sets of "village" earthworks lie across the stream from the undoubted site of Quarrendon (Bucks.). Has the village twice migrated before finally settling down on the hillside where the church and manor house clearly identify the latest site? Or are these unidentified hamlets of Quarrendon, each as large in area as the parent village yet without trace in documents so far studied?

TABLE XIII

Code indicating visible quality of sites

A*	Excellent. (Very good pattern of roads and crofts with house-sites visible, e.g. Wharram Percy, Yorks., E.R.)
A	Very good. (Pattern of roads and crofts, but no house-sites visible, e.g. Hamilton, Leics., Quarrendon, Bucks.)
B	Medium. (Good street or streets but otherwise confused earthworks, e.g. East Tanfield, Yorks., N.R.)
C	Poor. (Vague bumps making no certain pattern; or church ruins without visible earthworks, e.g. Stoke Mandeville, Bucks.)
D	Nothing to see at all at known site (e.g. Grove in Great Tew, Oxon.)
(P)D	Nothing to see but site under plough or crop, so may have been destroyed (e.g. Aston Mullins, Bucks.)
P	Now ploughed
G	Now grass
CM	Crop-marks
EM	Earth-marks
COV	Sufficiently large modern farm or country-house and gardens to have obliterated a suspected site
RES	Re-settled before Industrial Revolution (*c.* 1800)
REB	Re-settled, *c.* 1800–1918
?	Site not precisely located
U	Neither documents nor tradition indicate location of village

X: THE WORK OF THE DESERTED MEDIEVAL VILLAGE RESEARCH GROUP (D.M.V.R.G.)

The Group was founded in August 1952 by Mr. Hurst, Prof. H. C. Darby, Mr. G. C. Dunning, Mr. J. Golson, the late Prof. (then Dr.) W. A. Singleton and myself. Its first meeting was held, appropriately, at the site of a deserted village. The founding fathers thus comprised three archaeologists, an architectural historian, an economic historian and an historical geographer. These six circularised a wider group of specialists—some amateurs, and some professionals—and were gratified by the support for a combined effort to push forward the study of deserted villages, from which different specialists might be expected to gain, and to which different specialisms could contribute.

The Group has no official status, is not supported by public funds, and is not attached to any academic or government body. Its members have never yet all been seen together in the same room, but their expertise is available to the smaller number of members who are concerned at any one time with deserted village studies. In turn, they value the information that is circulated to members in the duplicated *Annual Reports.*

It was agreed to hold an Annual Meeting in London, to circulate an *Annual Report* of members' work, and (if funds allowed) to initiate work. A London address was made available for enquiries and information, and the dossiers described below began to be built up there. Foreign scholars working on the subject were contacted, and where possible their publications were obtained. Details of the Group's own publications and subscription terms are available from the Honorary Secretary, D.M.V.R.G., c/o 67 Gloucester Crescent, London N.W.1.

It was at first hoped that the Group's work would attract the financial support of an educational, archaeological or charitable trust on a scale that would allow one or more full-time research workers to examine historical source materials or to carry out trial excavations. These hopes were disappointed, and the only grant obtained between 1953 and 1963 was one of £500 from the Pilgrim Trust which enabled filing cabinets to be purchased and a small collection of air photographs made. Subsequently an anonymous donor contributed annual sums for the out-of-pocket expenses of volunteers who were assisting with filing and correspondence, and in 1964 the British Academy made a grant towards the cost of the Oxfordshire and Northamptonshire monographs, the forthcoming Wharram Percy *Area 10 Excavation Report* and the present volume.

The Group has no funds for carrying out research excavations but those organised by Mr. Hurst and myself (and financed by the profits of site-catering) at Wharram Percy have been latterly carried out in the Group's name. Since 1966 the Group has administered *ad hoc* grants from the Ministry of Public Building and Works for two short emergency excavations each year, carried out at sites threatened by development. Ministry funds are not available for research excavations on unthreatened sites, a situation which always seems incredible to foreign visitors with properly endowed State archaeological services.

With these limited resources of money, and depending on what leisure time Mr. Hurst and I could spare, the Group's first aim was to build up a central file on deserted sites. As many sites as possible would be visited by Mr. Hurst, and reports would also be sought from local correspondents, particularly in those counties that had been sketchily treated in *Lost Villages.* It was hoped to build up dossiers with the following data as a minimum:

(i) National Grid map reference; one-inch O.S. sheet number.

(ii) Six-inch O.S. map reference.

(iii) The data from the standard documentary sources, i.e. 1086, 1296–1334, 1316, 1377–81, 1428, 1436–45, 1517–18, 1524, 1563–1603, 1662–89 and 1801–61.

(iv) A sketch plan drawn in the field, showing the condition of the site when inspected, the crops and any significant environmental features, e.g. ridge-and-furrow; the presence or absence of water.

(v) R.A.F. vertical air photographs of the site and, for selected places, of the complete parish.

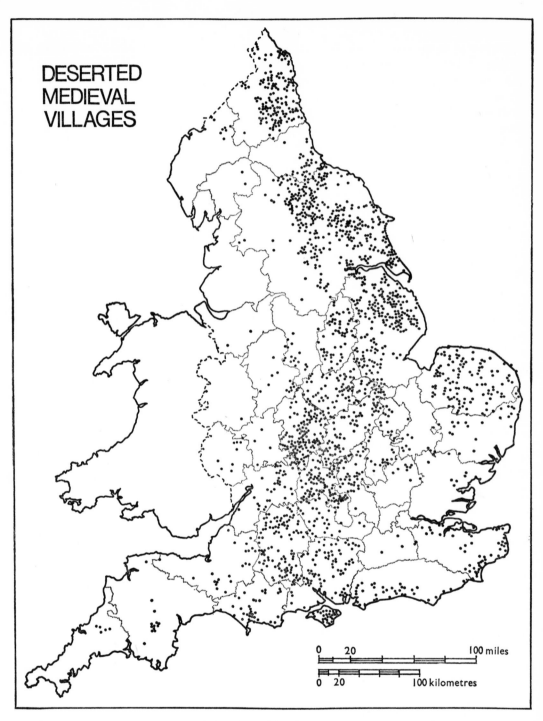

DESERTED
MEDIEVAL
VILLAGES

0   20   100 miles

0   20   100 kilometres

Fig. 13. Distribution map of sites located by the D.M.V.R.G. up to the end of 1968
The map is based on the information in the county gazetteers, Chapter 5.

(vi) Dr. St. Joseph's oblique air photographs of the site.
(vii) Any printed references to the site.

It was hoped that *Lists* could then be issued to the public that would set out for each county the deserted villages and give (a) map references, (b) an indication of the quality of the historical documentation available, (c) an indication of the nature and visual quality of the remains of the village, and (d) the period when the village was deserted, if sufficient evidence were available. The reduction of this information to list form was to be facilitated by sets of standard abbreviations for (b), (c) and (d).

Mr. Hurst and I, aided by a small group of volunteers (largely students of University College, London) began to work on these *Lists* during evenings when I found myself in London. The Group at first hoped that a distribution map could be prepared for the whole of England, rather on the lines of the O.S. Period Maps, embodying the principal data from the *Lists*. But this project proved too large for the small number of active members of the Group, none of whom was free to do research except after working hours, and all of whom had other research projects under way. No funds for professional secretarial help were available. In these circumstances even an assembly of map, air photograph and documentary evidence for each of 2,000 sites was recognised as at least a ten-year task, and no national distribution map with any validity could be offered for publication until this basic work was completed. It was decided to concentrate effort on a final revision of the *Lists* for Midland counties, and the preparation of a pilot distribution map for one county. The progress of work is indicated in Table XIV and Fig. 13.

At this stage, through the good offices of Prof. H. C. Darby, Vice-Chairman of the D.M.V.R.G., Mrs. Betty Grant was appointed to a research fellowship at University College, London, and commissioned to search the main printed and P.R.O. sources for twelve Midland counties, to tabulate the results, and to prepare a dossier on each place. Although the fellowship was not a permanent endowment, Mrs. Grant's work during 1959 and 1960 demonstrated how much progress could be made by a full-time research worker proceeding methodically through the main documentary sources. The data which she assembled were extensively drawn upon for the Northamptonshire and Oxfordshire studies, for the published tabulation of Leicestershire sites and for the less elaborate list for Berkshire.

Working from a fixed centre, with expeditions to London in vacations, I myself made very little use of County Record Offices in *Lost Villages*, and only a small number of estate offices were visited, principally in Yorkshire and the Midlands. But London is far from monopolising useful source material. It was the Holkham estate archives that provided plans and surveys which greatly helped Dr. Allison in preparing his gazetteer of Norfolk desertions. The full story of the Whatborough enclosure only emerged from the papers that remain with the landlords, All Souls' College, Oxford. The earls of Northumberland had many deserted sites on their estates, and the archives at Alnwick and Petworth are invaluable for the study of northern depopulations on the Percy estates. The Harewood muniments, that have recently passed to the keeping of the Leeds City Archives, revealed the location of three deserted villages on the estate as well as a map

67

TABLE XIV

Progress of English county lists

County	Year of latest revision	Number of sites on revised list	Relevant publications
Bedfordshire	1960	18	
Berkshire	1960	43	*Beresford and Hurst, 1962*, 92–97
Buckinghamshire	1957	56	*Beresford, 1953–4*, 26–28
			Annual Report, 1957, Appendix C
Cambridgeshire	1955	17	
Cheshire	1955	4	
Cornwall	1955	8	*Dudley and Minter, 1962–3*, 282–283
Cumberland	1963	8	
Derbyshire	1955	33	
Devonshire	1963	15	*Linehan, 1966*, 124
Dorset	1961	42	
Durham	1960	29	*Dobson, 1962*, 187
Essex	1955	17	
Gloucestershire	1962	67	*Annual Report*, 1959, Appendix C
Hampshire	1966	91 ⎫	*Annual Report*, 1961, Appendix A
New Forest	1959	33 ⎬	*Annual Report*, 1966, Appendix A
Isle of Wight	1966	32 ⎭	
Herefordshire	1955	11	
Hertfordshire	1959	44	*Munby, 1961*, 11–16
			Rutherford-Davies, 1964, 11–12
Huntingdonshire	1955	18	
Kent	1955	69	
Lancashire	—	—	
Leicestershire	1961	67	*Hoskins, 1946*, 67–107
			D.M.V.R.G., 1963–4, 24-33
Lincolnshire	1967	220	*Foster and Longley, 1924*, xlvii–xc
			Annual Report, 1967, Appendix
Middlesex	—	—	
Norfolk	1955	148	*Allison, 1955*, 116–162
Northamptonshire	1963	82	*Allison et al., 1966*
Northumberland	1963	165	*Annual Report*, 1963, Appendix C

County	Year of latest revision	Number of sites on revised list	Relevant publications
Nottinghamshire	1962	67	*Phillimore, 1884*, 66–88
			Phillimore, 1894, 128–135, 150–
			152 and 161–168
Oxfordshire	1964	103	*Allison et al., 1965*
Rutland	1958	13	*Hoskins, 1963*, 49–52
Shropshire	1955	9	
Somerset	1962	27	
Staffordshire	1955	22	
Suffolk	1962	23	
Surrey	1955	5	
Sussex	1960	41	*Holden, 1962*, 321–325
Warwickshire	1958	128	*Beresford, 1950*, 49–106
			Annual Report, 1958, Appendix B
Westmorland	1954	2	
Wiltshire	1961	104	*Annual Report*, 1961, Appendix B
Worcestershire	1958	7	
Yorkshire:			
East Riding	1959	129	*Beresford, 1951*, 474–491
			Beresford, 1952, 44–70
North Riding	1960	171	*Beresford, 1951*, 474–491
			Beresford, 1954, 280–309
West Riding	1956	75	*Beresford, 1951*, 474–491
			Beresford, 1953, 215–240
Total		2,263	

showing the removal of part of the village of Harewood itself.   Progress in local pursuit of desertions in records of this kind will depend on the speed with which hard-pressed and under-staffed archivists can achieve the lists and indexes that open the way for historians.

Since 1954 the Record Offices have greatly increased their collections of estate records, by gift or loan, and knowledge of their contents is increasingly facilitated by the duplicated *Lists* of the National Register of Archives, which also deal with collections still in private hands.   Since Mrs. Grant and Mr. Dodd (see p. 71, below) were also tied to one centre, London, their work was not able to extend to County Record Offices but the first task of anyone pursuing a serious local study would be to remedy our deficiency.   If the study of Northamptonshire (Allison *et al.*, 1966) could have waited for someone to endow research in the county itself, the gazetteer would not have omitted the interesting site of the potters' village on the edge of three parishes in the forest at Lyveden, discovered by Dr. St. Joseph and excavated by Mr. J. M. Steane (Steane, 1967). The last proof of the village's existence is a record of ten tenants attending a manor court in 1403, and this document is in the Northamptonshire Record Office.[56] The name of the village did not appear in the P.R.O. records examined by Mrs. Grant.

Certain documentary sources had been under-employed in *Lost Villages*, and others ignored. Although tax assessments in the P.R.O. class E179 had been much used, the main reliance had been on those made between 1290 and the mid-fifteenth century, after which even the abatements to the villages quotas became conventionalised and immutable. Too little use was made of the assessments resulting from the revision of the basis of lay taxation in 1524 which Dr. J. Sheail has analysed for his London Ph.D. thesis[57] (1968). Although this tax in turn became stereotyped, the first assessments of 1524 and 1525 do enable important distinctions to be made between normal villages and those already reduced to one, two or three households. Their date is near enough to the proceedings of 1517–18 for them to confirm whether a village had been truly depopulated in 1500 and to isolate those depopulations that took place after 1525. Thus, while at Knaptoft (Leics.), which was depopulated in 1500, only two names appear in the assessment; there were nineteen at Foston (Leics.) which was not enclosed and depopulated until 1622; while at Stapleford (Leics.), a late emparking-enclosure, there were 25. At Stowell (Gloucs.) on the other hand, where there had been at least ten households in 1381, there was only one taxpayer in 1524.

Dr. Thirsk has provided a useful survey of population data between 1500 and 1760 (Thirsk, 1959A) and it must be confessed that the Chantry Certificates of 1547, the Muster Rolls, and the Protestation Returns of 1641–42 have not yet been exploited by the Group's researches. The bishops' returns of parishioners and communicants in 1563 and 1603 were known in 1954 and were tabulated by Mrs. Grant, although the documents have not survived from all parts of the country. They, like the lay subsidy assessments of 1524–25, serve to point out the parishes that had been virtually emptied of parishioners or to indicate where villages, later to be deserted, were still flourishing. Higham Gobion (Beds.) had two families in 1563 and Fleet Marston (Bucks.) the same number. In 1563 nineteen Lincolnshire parishes were reported to have no more than one family each. In contrast, Foston and Stapleford (Leics., see above) still had 32 and 35 families respectively.[58]

The last comprehensive counting of houses in England before the Census of 1801 was in connection with the Hearth Tax, levied between 1662 and 1689. Some instances of its utilisation for establishing the population of a village and the nature of the houses remaining at a site after its depopulation have been given above (p. 47).

The printed *Census* from 1801 tabulates the total number of houses and persons,

---

[56] The so-called "poll tax" printed by Mr. Steane at p. 36 from P.R.O. E179/155/31 is not in fact a poll-tax document but probably a subsidy list of 27 persons taxed in *Parva Lyvedon* at a date lying between 1296 and 1334.

[57] J. B. D. Sheail, "1524 Lay Subsidy Returns", unpublished Ph.D. thesis, University of London (1968).

[58] The 1563 and 1603 returns are in B.M. Harl. Mss. 594, 595 and 618.

township by township, even when there was only one house, as at Alethorpe (Norfolk) and Hodnell, Warws.[59]   The *Census* does not indicate where the houses were located in a township.   A deserted site that had remained deserted even though Improvement had brought farms back to the periphery of the township (above, p. 44) will thus have a deceptive populousness in these *Census* volumes.   It is only in 1841, when the unpublished enumerators' returns, house by house, become available, that it is possible to establish where the population was in fact living.   The printed totals for Wharram Percy in 1851, for example, give the illusion that the site had been re-populated.   In fact, apart from one farm, the large population recorded on Census night is shown by the unpublished enumerations to be housed in the huts of contractors who were building the railway tunnel for the Malton and Driffield Railway Company.[60]   But the earlier *Census* volumes do offer one useful tool to the student of topographical history. In them the component townships (or in the south, *tithings*) of parishes are methodically set out; and the parishes are grouped within the old and now-disused administrative units, the *Hundreds*.   Since all earlier taxation assessments were made and filed by *Hundreds* this is a very convenient indicator of where to look for the tax records of a particular village or township.

An opportunity to assess the major gaps in the Group's collection of documentary information came when Mr. E. E. Dodd generously offered in 1961, to put part of his retirement leisure at the disposal of the Group.   It seemed that the most profitable use of his time, remembering Mrs. Grant's experience, would be to work methodically over all the documents in one particular source rather than pursue a small number of village names through a large number of catalogues.   Certain sources were rejected for immediate action even though it was known that interesting topographical information had come to light when scholars had used them in local instances.   Thus, the names of small and now-lost forest vills occur in those parts of the Forest Eyre rolls that record the limits of jurisdiction (Shaw in Alton, Wilts., Puthall, Wilts., North Standen, Berks., 1257–70), but it was not thought that further information would be useful in proportion to the effort that would be required to master such bulky rolls.   In particular it would expedite work if a documentary source could be used that already had its printed indexes.   A source such as the *Feet of Fines*, where there had been a good deal of publication *in extenso* by various societies, was also given second place in favour of materials either unpublished or treated only in calendar summary.

The topographical and demographic data collected by Mr. Dodd would contribute to knowledge in three ways: they would establish a minimum size and a *terminus post quem* for a village; and they would indicate minor topographical features of the village that might then be sought in fieldwork at the site or appear in the course of excavation. Much new evidence for the date and circumstances of the actual depopulation was not expected from the particular sources selected: sources useful for this purpose had been discussed in *Lost Villages*, chapter 9.   Mr. Dodd's first searches were in the six volumes of the *Calendar of Ancient Deeds*.

In *Lost Villages* the inquisitions *post mortem*, surveys of assets in the manors of deceased tenants-in-chief of the Crown, had provided two pages of evidence for Wharram Percy

[59] *Enumeration Abstract for 1811* (1812), 211 and 348.
[60] P.R.O. HO 107/2369.

(1367–1457) but little else. Mr. Dodd worked in this source between January 1962 and the autumn of 1963. He extracted references from the index of the printed *Calendars* for every place named in the Group's county lists, and then read through the documents themselves, making notes under standardised headings. These work-sheets are available in the Research Group's files. In January 1966 Mr. Dodd resumed his voluntary work and moved over from the Public Record Office to the Manuscript Room of the British Museum and followed the same process for documents in the class, Additional Manuscripts, and in all the groups of Charters and Rolls. Having completed this task he returned to the P.R.O. for a third alphabetical pilgrimage, this time through the indexes to the accounts of medieval manors preserved in the classes SC6 and DL29.

Some examples from the more than a thousand work-sheets compiled by Mr. Dodd, and now in the files of the Research Group, may be given.

The accounts of the manorial reeves (P.R.O., SC6 and DL29) are principally useful for their evidence that a village was still grain-producing at a particular time. Thus sales of grain are recorded by the reeves of Hampton Wafer (Herefords.) in 1321, Aston Mullins and Caldecote (Bucks.) in 1340, and Eaton Hastings (Berks.) in 1354–55. Sales of grain and a flow of villein rents occur in accounts from Halse (Northants.) from 1322 to 1447. The accounts generally give total sums for rents paid by villagers without enumerating the houses but occasionally numbers are recorded: thus, there were at least 18 villeins and 17 cottars at Alnham (Northumberland) in 1314; 39 messuages, as well as one "completely collapsed" at Colston Basset (Notts.) in 1456–57; 15 messuages at Ascott (Oxon.) in 1468; and messuages, tofts and crofts at Budbrooke (Warws.) in 1480–81.[61]

At Compton Verney (for which see also Hilton, 1955) the I.P.M. of 1297–98 reveals alongside the manor house, its gardens and dovecote, the houses of three free tenants, ten villeins, ten cottagers and one other messuage. The convergence of different lines of research is exemplified by Prestgrave (Leics.). Scrutiny of R.A.F. aerial photographs had indicated the location of the site; there was an I.P.M. of 1301–02 at the P.R.O., a court roll of a decade earlier at the British Museum and rentals from the early fourteenth century to 1467 were also at the British Museum. The earlier rentals give the names of open-field furlongs while that of 1467 has a croft ominously called *Shepecote Yard*. A rental of Weston (Leics.), *t.* Edward III, lists 22 messuages, thus putting its depopulation between 1327 and 1344, for Prof. Hoskins had already shown that the monks of Merevale had converted it into a grange by 1344. A rental of the same period indicates 14 messuages at Welby (Leics.). Reeves' accounts of Shifford (Oxon.) in 1380 confirm the evidence of the poll tax of 1377 that the village was still a lively com-

---

[61] Hampton Wafer, P.R.O. SC6/1145/6
  Aston Mullins, SC6/759/9 and 1120/10
  Caldecote, SC6/1119/3 and 1120/10
  Eaton Hastings, SC6/748/7
  Halse, SC6/1147/18; also 948/3 and 1108/3
  Alnham, SC6/950/1
  Colston Basset, SC6/954/11
  Ascot, SC6/1093/11; DL29/655/10599
  Budbrooke, DL29/642/10421 and 645/10464.

munity but accounts and court rolls of various dates between 1458 and 1467 are full of references to messuages "ruinous and not repaired". Rentals of Kingston (Warws.) from 1386 to 1434 list 14 messuages and a dovecote: a document from the Warwickshire Record Office (Hilton, 1955, 682) had already shown that the village was almost all enclosed for pasture by 1437. In Tattenhoe (Bucks.) court-roll entries allow messuages to be seen in relation to each other and to streets; and there is similarly much topographical detail of open field selions in series of charters such as those for Aleby (Lincs.) in the thirteenth century or Bramcote (Warws.), 1262–1390. There is an unusually early description of open-field land at Papley (Northants.), 1208, and at Hothorpe (Northants.) there is the celebrated charter, first noticed by Prof. Sir Frank Stenton, recording that the village church had been built on land granted by the lord but assisted by gifts made by the villagers, "homines mei de Huttorp"; other charters describe their common arable and common pasture in the mid-thirteenth century.[62]

XI: OTHER DEVELOPMENTS 1954–68

Apart from the work sponsored by the D.M.V.R.G. itself, the study of deserted villages has been facilitated by several other developments of the last ten years. The revision of the one-inch Ordnance Survey maps and the republication of the six-inch maps on sheets with National Grid boundaries gave Mr. C. W. Phillips and the staff of the Archaeological Branch of the O.S. the opportunity of inserting (as "antiquities") those deserted villages whose earthworks are particularly clear.[63]

In the course of the revision of the National Map, trial surveys were carried out on seven Leicestershire sites (Hoskins, 1956) but the labour necessary to plan the complex earthworks of a typical deserted site proved too expensive for the venture to be extended. On the revised one-inch and two-and-a-half inch O.S. maps the village earthworks are usually marked conventionally. The O.S. publication, *Field Archaeology: Notes for Beginners* (revised edition, 1964), has also drawn attention to the deserted village sites.

Even though excavations have usually been confined to a small area of any given village, many excavation reports have included surveys of the earthworks of the whole site, and sometimes of the medieval field systems accompanying them (e.g. Upton by P. A. Rahtz in Hilton and Rahtz, 1966, 87; Wade-Martins and Wade, 1967, 3).

[62] Compton Verney, P.R.O. C133/83/9
  Prestgrave, P.R.O. C133/105/1; B.M. Add. Roll 41558(ii); 41569; 41557–58; 41613
  Weston, B.M. Add. Ms. 37671, f. 61
  Welby, B.M. Add. Ms. 37671, f. 62–63; P.R.O. C133/73/11
  Shifford, B.M. Harl. Roll K41 and L1 sqq.
  Kingston, B.M. Eg. Roll 2106–8; also Eg. Ch. 1777–88
  Tattenhoe, B.M. Add. Roll 53962; also many charters, Add. Ch. 53802 sqq.
  Aleby, B.M. Harl. Ch. 43–45, 47–48, 50–52, 57: many references within these divisions of the
    charters
  Bramcote, Add. Ch. 17360–1; 17373; 17377–80; 17382
  Papley, Add. Ch. 6014
  Hothorpe B.M. Add. Ch. 22012.
[63] Although, as noted in *Lost Villages*, early editions of the six-inch O.S. map for Yorkshire carried quite elaborate surveys of sites, it is rare to find additions until the post-1945 revisions. An exception is Bardolfeston, Dorset, surveyed in the six-inch revision of 1902.

The use of air photography for the detection of lost villages and the elucidation of their earthworks goes back to O.G.S. Crawford's photograph of Gainsthorpe (Lincs.), taken in 1925. A number of illustrations in *Lost Villages* and in other authors' monographs were drawn from the R.A.F. collection of air photographs, then stored at Medmenham but now available to accredited research workers at the Ministry of Housing and Local Government, Whitehall, London, S.W.1. These photographs were taken in all seasons and at all times of day: the majority are verticals. They therefore vary enormously in their utility for identification of sites and surrounding ridge-and-furrow but their availability was the biggest stimulus to the first extension of my enquiry beyond Warwickshire and Yorkshire. Good unpublished examples are Embleton (Co. Durham), Baggrave (Leics.), Coton (Warws.), Downtown (Northants.) and Gt. Kelk (Yorks., E.R.).

More specifically useful in the investigations of the last decade have been the photographs taken in the course of his reconnaissances by Dr. St. Joseph, then Curator (now Director) in Aerial Photography at the University of Cambridge. His photographs have now an unintended historical value in that many were taken before the ploughing-up of grassland began its destructive work. Historians are also in Dr. St. Joseph's debt for bringing to light more than 100 new sites that conventional historical research and ground fieldwork had not discovered. One such is Newbold, Northamptonshire (St. Joseph ed., 1965, Plate 64). A few examples from this vast collection were published by us (Beresford and St. Joseph, 1957) and many others have been used to illustrate articles by other authors, cited in the bibliography, but the research potential of the collection for this and cognate medieval studies is almost inexhaustible. Dr. St. Joseph's oblique angle of vision admirably displays the topography of deserted sites.

Apart from the books and articles specifically devoted to deserted villages, our study has been aided by the progress since 1954 of four publications. These are:

(i) *The Victoria History of the Counties of England.* The pre-war tradition of a parish-by-parish history has been followed, but with a much greater attention to field-work, topography and the use of map evidence. The reproach levelled against the older volumes that failed to note whether a parish was deserted or not, can no longer be made. *Wiltshire* and *Leicestershire* have included general surveys of the agrarian history of the county as well as a tabulation of poll-tax and other population data. Oxfordshire, Staffordshire and Gloucestershire are progressing in the new mode.

(ii) *The Domesday Geography of England.* Professor H. C. Darby and his collaborators, as a preliminary to their maps, had to decide on the location of every place-name in Domesday Book, and necessarily to note when no village of that name survives. These instances are commented upon, with examples, in the text of each county of the *Geography* and data for all the "lost" places has been made available to the D.M.V.R.G.

(iii) *The English Place-Name Society.* The county volumes (the 43rd of which appeared in 1967) are indispensable in the elucidation of past topographies. For each township they give the past forms of all major and many minor place-names, together with documentary references. Not only are these useful for the history of deserted places but they often indicate the earliest occurrence of a place-name; and they greatly facilitate the identification of places that have obsolete spellings in tax lists.

(iv) *The Royal Commission on Historical Monuments.* The county *Inventories* list all surviving earthworks and buildings of historical character. Pre-war volumes sometimes surveyed village sites, but more often ignored them. The work now in progress is of much more thorough order, and in the course of the work in Dorset the Commission's field staff have already discovered several unsuspected sites. Careful surveys are in course of publication.

Publications of local historical and archaeological Societies have found room for excavation reports and for articles on local deserted villages that are listed in the Bibliography. With deserted villages so widespread, almost every Record publication not devoted to a single place or to modern archives is likely to have some information about one or more deserted places, before or after depopulation. There may be instanced the recent volumes of *Calendars of Inquisitions Post Mortem* and Sir Charles Clay's *Early Yorkshire Charters*.

ENVOI: BEYOND BRITAIN

If important causes of desertion were universal factors such as population contraction, the relative prices of corn and wool or the expansion of cloth production, it might well be asked whether the deserted village has appeared beyond Britain on the mainland of Europe.

For an interim answer one can turn to the account of work in progress that was published in Paris in 1965.[64] The importance of work in different countries, especially in archaeology, should not be measured by the number of pages there devoted to each country: Scandinavia was particularly badly served by its authors. In the briefest outline one may say that research on the continent has certainly not failed to produce deserted villages. The distribution maps for Spain, Sardinia, Greece and parts of Italy in *Villages Désertés* are quite astonishing. As to causation, clearly the pull of a cloth industry demanding wool was more felt in some countries than others, but perhaps nowhere as much as here in England. This was not the only difference between England and the Continent: there was much more marginal land in Europe, available for occupation in the thirteenth-century clearances but then rejected with the contraction of population; there was more physical devastation in the wars, civil and international, of the early modern period; there was probably more panic flight from villages to the safety of towns; there was certainly deliberate rationalising of estates by feudal landowners; and also engrossing of holdings by wealthy landowners in the seventeenth century (that is, the English phenomenon of decay of houses of husbandry but without conversion of arable to pasture). At this stage no more can be said. It is hoped that Mr. Hurst may edit a second volume of *Deserted Medieval Villages: Studies* devoted to the progress of historical and archaeological researches beyond Britain.

[64] For full title of *Villages Désertés* see *École Pratique* in bibliography.

CHAPTER TWO

A Review of Archaeological Research
(to 1968)

J. G. HURST

INTRODUCTION

The origins of medieval archaeology

Until the late 1930's medieval archaeology was almost entirely concerned with the study of the remains of those buildings erected by the wealthier sectors of the population: principally churches, abbeys. castles and manor houses. Most investigations were carried out by antiquarians who concentrated on ecclesiastical subjects, or by architects whose main interest in medieval buildings was a one-period plan rather than an attempt at scientific excavation to determine building sequences or to obtain dating material. There were a few notable exceptions during the first outburst of archaeological excavation in the middle of the nineteenth century but, as with prehistoric archaeology, it was General Pitt-Rivers who first attempted the meticulous excavation of medieval sites in the 1880's.[1] Unfortunately this was not followed up for more than forty years until the 1930's when, following the transformation of prehistoric and Roman archaeological methods of excavation by Sir Mortimer Wheeler, it was suggested not only that more accurate work should be organised for the medieval period[2] but that this should concern itself with the medieval peasant and his way of life, a study which had previously been almost entirely left to historians.[3]

Little work was done on Anglo-Saxon peasant houses before excavation by Mr. E. T. Leeds at Sutton Courtenay between 1921 and 1937 (Leeds, 1923, 1927 and 1947). There were several earlier excavations on deserted medieval village sites (hereafter D.M.V.) but the real breakthrough came in the 1930's with Lady Fox's excavations at sites on Gelligaer Common in Glamorgan[4] and the excavation at Great Beere (site 35,[5]

---

[1] A. L.-F. Pitt-Rivers, "Excavations at Caesar's Camp near Folkestone", *Archaeologia*, XLVII (1883), 429–65, and Id., *King John's House Tollard Royal, Wilts.* (1890).

[2] *Report 38th Congress of Archaeol. Soc., Earthwork Comm. First Report* (1930), 36.

[3] Lecture by C. F. C. Hawkes on Oct. 29, 1937, *Univ. London, Inst. of Archaeol., Rep.* 1 (1937), 47–69.

[4] See *Fox, 1937* and *1939*.

[5] Such references lead a reader to the gazetteer of excavated sites in Chapter 3, pp. 149–68, and (Jope, 1958) etc., refers to the bibliography in Chapter 6, pp. 213–26.

Jope, 1958).   This decade saw the formation of medieval archaeology as we know it today, with the pioneer work by Dr. G. C. Dunning on the classification of medieval pottery,[6] the work on medieval paving tiles[7] and small finds[8] by Mr. J. B. Ward-Perkins, and the important town excavation on the site for the Bodleian extension in Oxford carried out by Dr. R. L. S. Bruce-Mitford.[9]   It was not only in Britain that this new interest in medieval archaeology was aroused.   At the same time in Germany Prof. P. Grimm was conducting his classic excavation at Hohenrode, in the Harz, the first major excavation of a D.M.V. in Europe (Grimm, 1939).   Slightly later Prof. A. Steensberg was starting his major series of excavations in Denmark (Steensberg, 1952). Unfortunately the Second World War intervened and set the study of medieval archaeology back ten years.

The formation of the D.M.V.R.G.

It was not until 1948 after Dr. Bruce-Mitford's call for the study of medieval archaeology, and especially that of the medieval village,[10] that the subject was taken up by the post-war generation.   On the historical side, the pioneer work in the 1940's by Prof. W. G. Hoskins (Hoskins, 1946) and Prof. M. W. Beresford (Beresford, 1950) made apparent the vastness of the problem of D.M.V.s even at the time when other economic historians were saying that it hardly existed (Beresford, 1954C, 79).   Without the many hundreds of D.M.V. sites which preserved, fossilised under grass, the remains of peasant houses and the whole medieval layout, the archaeological investigation of the peasant way of life would have been almost impossible.   On village sites still occupied the medieval remains are either buried under surviving houses and buildings or disturbed and destroyed by constant gardening activities over the centuries.   Only in very few cases can such sites provide information important enough to make excavation worthwhile and then usually only over a very limited area.[11]

A portent of collaboration and cross-fertilisation of ideas was a meeting in Cambridge, followed by a tour of Leicestershire sites, in June 1948 by a party which included Messrs M. W. Beresford, T. A. M. Bishop, J. G. D. Clark, K. D. M. Dauncey, W. G. Hoskins, E. Miller, M. M. Postan, J. Saltmarsh and A. Steensberg.   This was followed by a series of limited excavations with rather inconclusive results, limited by the historians' lack of archaeological experience or training, and even more by their ignorance of the very great complexity of village sites and the very flimsy remains that they would find.[12]   In the same year I went up to Cambridge to study prehistoric archaeo-

---

[6] In an important series of appendices to excavation reports.   Unfortunately no list is published but see *Med. Archaeol.*, VI–VII (1962–63), 135–36.

[7] J. B. Ward-Perkins, "English Medieval Embossed Tiles", *Archaeol. Journ.*, XCIV (1937), 128–53. See also L. Haberly, *English Paving Tiles* (1937).

[8] *Medieval Catalogue*, London Museum Catalogues, VII (1940), 3rd Imp. 1967.

[9] R. L. S. Bruce-Mitford, "The Archaeology of the Site of the Bodleian Extension in Broad Street, Oxford", *Oxoniensia*, IV (1939), 89–146.

[10] R. L. S. Bruce-Mitford, "Medieval Archaeology", *Archaeol. News Letter*, I, no. 6 (1948), 4.   See also renewed appeal by C. F. C. Hawkes "Anglo-Danish Lincolnshire and the Deserted Villages of the Wolds", *Archaeol. Journ.*, CIII (1946), 100–101.

[11] Sites 80, 105, 221, 226, 231, 245 and 248.

[12] Sites 99, 151, 238, 261, 287 and 290.

logy and, in 1950, became interested in medieval archaeology, starting the excavations on the medieval manor at Northolt (site 128, Hurst, 1961). These are still in progress, although at the time I had no idea that there was a Saxon and early-medieval village underneath the manor preserved in a different way from the normal deserted village site. It was Mr. J. Golson[13] who first suggested to me that deserted medieval villages would provide the kind of evidence which was needed if we were to understand how the ordinary people lived in the medieval countryside. He had himself been introduced to the subject by Prof. M. M. Postan following the 1948 tour of D.M.V.s and Mr. Golson changed from the History to the Archaeological Tripos in 1949. It was during 1951 that our interest in deserted villages became fully formed. In the spring of 1952 Mr. Golson went to Denmark to excavate with Professor Steensberg while I visited Professor Beresford's excavations at Wharram Percy (site 274) that June and, immediately following this, the Deserted Medieval Village Research Group (hereafter D.M.V.R.G.) and the subsequent organised collaboration of historians, archaeologists, geographers and architects was born. From then on progress was fast, and many other excavations took place on deserted village sites during the nineteen-fifties.

Without funds for private research, many of these were emergency excavations, conducted by the Ancient Monuments Inspectorate of the then Ministry of Works on threatened sites, of which there has been an increasing number since the war; owing to the great increase in the bulldozing and ploughing up of old pasture, the building of houses, factories and roads, and quarrying. As village sites are usually large, covering an area of anything up to twenty-five to thirty acres, official funds have never been available for a full excavation, especially as time is usually limited between notice of a threat and the actual destruction of a site. It has, therefore, been Ministry policy to excavate a single house site on a few selected sites each year. In this way, with the advice of the D.M.V.R.G., a series of house plans from different parts of the country has now been collected.

D.M.V. excavations

Meanwhile other bodies have started large-scale excavations with the aim of excavating a considerable area over a long period of time, although lack of funds restricts most of these excavations to a short season each summer, so that excavation is painfully slow by continental standards. For example, twenty years of excavation at Wharram Percy represent only about twelve months' actual work. Excavations are scattered over the country, and so give a very satisfactory coverage of different types of village site, although they all lie in areas where the peasant houses were built of stone, and one of the greatest needs now is for a large scale excavation of a D.M.V. with timber-buildings at all periods. Such stone sites have been found at Hound Tor on Dartmoor, Devon (Mrs. E. M. Minter, site 38); at Upton on the Cotswolds in Gloucestershire (Mr. P. A. Rahtz and Prof. R. H. Hilton for Birmingham University, site 67); at Gomeldon in Wiltshire, just north of Salisbury, on the chalk (Mr. J. W. G. Musty and Mr. D. J. Algar for the Salisbury Archaeological Research Committee, site 244); at Wharram Percy, on the chalk of the Yorkshire Wolds (by the author for the D.M.V.R.G.,

---

[13] Now at the Research School of Pacific Studies, Australian National University, Canberra.

site 274); and at West Whelpington in Northumberland (Dr. M. G. Jarrett for the Ministry of Public Building and Works, site 162). This last is the only emergency excavation which can continue each year since the threat is a gradually advancing quarry.

All these excavations in their different ways have added to our knowledge of the medieval peasant and his way of life. They have also shown that there can be no easy answer to any of the questions which may be asked about medieval peasant house types and other aspects of medieval life. This applies to all aspects of medieval archaeology and is not confined to house types and village life alone, as can be seen from the present difficulties in the study of medieval pottery.[14] Nevertheless this seems an appropriate moment, sixteen years after the formation of the D.M.V.R.G., to review the present position and to try to assess the results of the many excavations which have taken place during this period. Some of the trends currently suggested by the evidence may be modified or refuted by future work since there is still so much to be done. I have therefore tried to record the present state of knowledge on different aspects of the medieval village and at the same time to draw attention to the major gaps in the information, hoping thereby to encourage others to fill them in and to stimulate others to take up controversial points.

Links with vernacular architecture

During the past fifteen years there has been increasing collaboration between medieval archaeologists studying the medieval peasant-house and students of surviving vernacular architecture, but there is room for much greater interchange of information between the two. The main problem at the moment is that the results of medieval excavation and the study of vernacular buildings seems to show two quite different worlds. This is hardly surprising since the roughly constructed medieval peasant-house nowhere survives, and existing vernacular buildings of the medieval period belonged to those much higher up in the social scale, the homes of the emerging yeomen freehold farmers rather than peasant villeins, much less cottars. There are numerous surviving houses from the sixteenth century onwards, the product of the "Great Rebuilding" of 1570–1640, which made a fundamental change from the medieval type of peasant-house (Hoskins, 1953). Most D.M.V.s were deserted before this crucial period of change, so that only in rare cases such as West Whelpington (site 162, Jarrett, 1962) is the change from medieval to post-medieval building to be seen from excavation. Even here the sixteenth- and seventeenth-century peasant-houses seem less substantial than surviving examples. It is not clear whether this is due to local poverty in the north or whether, as in the medieval period, surviving cottages belong somewhere above the bottom of the social scale. The D.M.V.R.G. have, therefore, advised the Ministry of Public Building and Works to continue its excavations at West Whelpington over a number of years, and there is a strong case for more later desertions to be investigated, to provide a better link with surviving buildings.

Archaeologists are on very dangerous ground when they use recent vernacular parallels to try to interpret the ruined foundations and post-holes, found during excavation, as houses with walls and roofs. The archaeological traces may also not show the

---

[14] J. G. Hurst, "White Castle and the Dating of Medieval Pottery", *Med. Archaeol.*, VI–VII (1962–63), 135–55.

substantial nature of the superstructure above (site 210). It is essential to try to put the flesh on the dry bones of an excavation, but there are many pitfalls in the argument from recent vernacular analogies, and the best that can be done is to suggest general possibilities. In the reverse way, many students of vernacular architecture tend to assume that the complications of their buildings were developments of the sixteenth or seventeenth centuries although archaeological evidence has shown that such features go back at least to the thirteenth century and reflect the range of standards within a village rather than an improvement in living conditions over a period of time.

Some features, such as the stone or brick chimney and the second storey, are confirmed as developments in peasant-houses from the sixteenth century onwards. In the medieval period solid clay canopies have been found in many areas which might be regarded as peasant copies of stone chimneys in medieval castles but not, as has recently been suggested, as a late "native response to the novelty of chimney flues"[15] following the sixteenth-century introduction of the stone chimney to slightly better class peasant-houses. Peasant houses had no upper floors as such, though there may well have been half-lofts and other similar devices. Likewise, although medieval peasant-houses are only one room deep and the square house is a post-medieval development, there was constant use of outshuts to increase the space available. On the other hand it is quite clear that there were three-roomed long-houses from at least the thirteenth century onwards, so that these houses cannot be used to show increasing privacy over a period of time but demonstrate all these variations in use at the same time. In fact many so-called late developments, such as staggered entrances, can be found in thirteenth-century peasant-houses. Of far greater importance was the change from the badly-built short-lived house to the more substantial buildings which still survive today: a subject which needs a great deal of work. It is hoped therefore that some of the facts and suggestions given below will lead to a greater co-ordination of the evidence from excavation and surviving buildings and enable us to build up a coherent picture of the development of the peasant-house which clearly should not end abruptly about 1500 but which should be followed on right to the present day.

Early excavations 1840–1900

The honour of carrying out the first excavation on a D.M.V. site goes to the Rev. Dr. J. Wilson who carried out excavations at Woodperry in the early 1840's (site 182); although the main emphasis was on the church and Roman remains, Dr. Wilson was fully aware of the D.M.V. and records medieval foundations, pottery and small finds, many of them illustrated. It is of interest to see this work taking place in the notable decade during which there was such an upsurge of field-archaeology with the formation of the British Archaeological Association, the Archaeological Institute and the start of many local societies. Another small and early medieval excavation was at Smallacombe (site 29). The earliest record of the excavation of Saxon sunken-huts was in 1857–58 when Mr. S. Stone recorded finds from three gravel pits in Oxfordshire (sites 179, 180 and 183). As was first pointed out by Mr. Leeds (Leeds, 1922, 189), Mr. Stone was aware of the nature of the site as he wrote "From appearances I am led to infer that around this spot were the dwelling-places of the people whose burying-ground was

[15] E. E. Evans, *Irish Folkways* (1957), 63.

situated close by" (Stone, 1857, 99). Mr. Leeds was critical of Mr. Stone's view that the sunken-hut "had been used in the manufacture of the things found in it" (Stone, 1858, 215), but it is in fact in line with our present interpretation of sunken-huts as working or industrial buildings. Of even more interest is Mr. Stone's statement that "I thereupon wrote to the Rev. Dr. Wilson, President of Trinity College, Oxford, informing him of the discovery which had been made; who, with characteristic liberality and that zeal in promoting archaeological research for which he is distinguished, at once placed the necessary funds in my hands, requesting me to pursue the investigation as far as time and other circumstances would permit." (Stone, 1858, 215–6.) This was the same Dr. Wilson who excavated at Woodperry so the first recorded excavations on both Saxon villages and a D.M.V. are firmly linked with his name.

An even more remarkable passage in Mr. Stone's report, which unfortunately does not include any plans, though these and models were clearly made, concerns the early recognition of crop-marks which makes one realise that many techniques have a long history. He writes "from the shallowness of the soil, and its inability to retain moisture for any length of time, lying as it does upon a bed of gravel, which acts as a most effectual drain, the crops of corn, or clover, or whatever else may chance to have been planted, are so quickly affected by drought, that a few successive days of dry sunny weather in summer are sufficient to show the situation and extent of every excavation underneath the soil as clearly as though a plan had been prepared and drawn upon paper" (Stone, 1857, 99–100). As early as 1719 Dr. W. Stukeley had observed differential growth of grass and crops over buildings and streets of several Roman towns,[16] but Mr. Stone is the earliest person to have recorded crop-marks over the pits and ditches of a prehistoric and Anglo-Saxon domestic site. Besides watching the gravel pits, Mr. Stone excavated an area 20 m. square at Stanton Harcourt (site 180) with Dr. Wilson's money. Unfortunately nothing developed from these promising beginnings and no further Anglo-Saxon huts are recorded until 1882 when features were recorded during ironstone-working at Woolsthorpe (site 126). After this no more work is recorded until 1921 when Mr. Leeds began his classic work at Sutton Courtenay (site 6; Leeds, 1922, 1927 and 1947). For the medieval period there was a similar gap from the mid-nineteenth century till Mrs. R. Burdon's work at Yoden in 1884 (site 52). This remarkable surge of activity in the mid-century applied to medieval pottery as well as structures. Early volumes of the *Journal of the British Archaeological Association*, and the *Archaeological Journal*, had frequent references to, and illustrations of, medieval pottery. This early interest in medieval archaeology seems to have been lost in the third quarter of the nineteenth century, possibly with the growth of interest in prehistoric archaeology and other topics. Dr. L. A. S. Butler has suggested to me that the growth of the Cambridge Ecclesiological Society may have diverted interest from archaeological to architectural aspects. The history of this rise and fall is a subject which badly needs further study. The 1880's was the decade in which General Pitt-Rivers was mainly active but his medieval work was confined to other types of site.[17] The first excavation of a D.M.V. site on any scale, together with what seems to have been the first archaeological

[16] W. Stukeley, *Itinerarium Curiosum* (1724). I am indebted to Dr. St. Joseph for this reference and for others to nineteenth-century observations of crop-marks on other Roman sites.

[17] *Op. cit.* in note 1.

survey,[18] was carried out between 1891–92 by the Rev. S. Baring-Gould at Trewortha (site 32, Baring–Gould, 1892–93). His work was made easy by the fact that sites on Bodmin Moor are often still plainly visible, and the soil cover thin, so that much could be accomplished without extensive excavation. His plan and description are a model for the time, though his interpretation was often odd, which is hardly surprising since he was a pioneer with little previous work upon which to base his conclusions.

Excavations 1900–1939

During the first decade of the twentieth century there were two publications of importance, one in 1908 the other in 1907. The more significant of these was the book *Earthwork of England* in which Mr. A. H. Allcroft describes for the first time the typical features of a midland-county D.M.V. site and includes a plan of Crow Close, Bingham, Nottinghamshire (Allcroft, 1908, 551–53) and mentions excavations at Cublington (site 12). In 1907 appeared the account of Whimpton (site 168): with a plan of the earthworks and a record of some excavation. In 1906 there were excavations at Claxby (site 108) and in 1909 at Mallows Cotton (site 146), and Morgan's Hill (site 247). In 1910 followed the publication of the second excavation of any consequence, at Hullasey (site 63). Here three buildings and a chapel were uncovered but little attention was paid to the finds. In 1911 came excavations at Holcombe, where one building was excavated (site 195). Then the First World War intervened and it was 25 years before any further serious excavation took place on another D.M.V. site. There were excavations on church-sites in 1913 (site 225); in 1929 (site 249) and in 1933 (site 158), but no work was done on the medieval peasant-house in England until the late 1930's, except for a single building excavated in 1930 at Bury Walls (site 189).

Sir Cyril and Lady Fox were already carrying out their pioneer work in south Wales[19] but in England nothing happened until 1936–8 which saw three excavations, at Great Beere (site 35, Jope, 1958), at Seacourt (site 5, Bruce-Mitford, 1940), and at Sennington (site 65). If the war had not intervened there might have been a breakthrough in the study of the medieval peasant house fifteen years before it actually happened. At Beere, Prof. Jope completely excavated for the first time in England a classic three-roomed long-house, showing that this was not a purely Celtic house-type. At Seacourt and Sennington trial excavations showed the great promise of both sites but further investigation was prevented by the war although in the former case excavation was to be continued in 1958 (site 5A, Biddle, 1961–62).

The investigation of the Anglo-Saxon house continued much more slowly and nothing more was done until the period between the wars when Mr. Leeds recorded 33 sunken-huts at Sutton Courtenay (site 6, Leeds, 1923, 1927, 1947). During the same period Mr. C. F. Tebbutt excavated a series of sunken-huts of the later Saxon period at St. Neots (site 86). Mr. T. C. Lethbridge, another important pioneer of medieval archaeology in the 1930's,[20] excavated two sunken-huts (sites 21 and 213) while another

[18] There were earlier plans of deserted villages by the Ordnance Survey in the 1850's. *cf.* p. 73.

[19] See bibliography, p. 272.

[20] Especially his recognition during the 1930's of Late Saxon glazed pottery, against constant opposition, and his work with Mr. Tebbutt on moated and castle sites in Cambridgeshire and Huntingdonshire. *cf.* Burwell Castle, *Proc. Cambs. Antiq. Soc.*, xxxvi (1936), 121–33; Flambards Manor, *ibid.*, xxxv (1935), 101–3; Paxton, *ibid.*, 97–105; and Southoe, *ibid.*, xxxviii (1938), 158–63.

was excavated by Mrs. O'Neil (site 60). Evidence for Anglo-Saxon sunken-huts was obtained from seventeen other sites during the 1920's and 30's.[21] This was largely due to gravel-working during which the dark fill of the sunken-huts was easily recognised. No post-hole buildings were recorded during this period and it is unfortunate that so little of this work, especially the indomitable work of Mr. G. Wyman Abbott, has ever been published. There was therefore far more work done during the inter-war period on the Anglo-Saxon house but this was largely due to chance discovery rather than planned excavation.

Excavations 1939–1959

During the Second World War, and immediately afterwards, there were five small excavations on various D.M.V. sites[22] but none of these produced any satisfactory plans of houses. In 1947 and 1948 Prof. Hoskins and Prof. Beresford started their excavations and trenches were dug on six sites;[23] between 1948 and 1952 thirteen other small excavations took place,[24] but again with very little result and the subject might have died again due to the unsatisfactory nature of the results of these excavations and the feeling that excavations on medieval village sites were not productive enough to be worthwhile. It was, therefore, lucky that the D.M.V.R.G. was founded at this time and various archaeologists came forward to show that by open-area excavation, rather than trial trenches, it was possible to sort out the complexities of D.M.V. sites and obtain house plans from even the most unpromising sites.

It was Dr. G. Bersu who first demonstrated the possibilities of medieval open-area excavation in Britain with his excavations at Vowlam (Isle of Man) which produced a complex series of superimposed Viking structures on different alignments (Bersu, 1949). This technique was first used on a D.M.V. in England at Wharram Percy (site 274) by Mr. Golson and myself in the summer of 1953 during the first D.M.V.R.G. season on the site. This was followed by the emergency excavations on threatened sites by the Ministry of Works.[25] At the same time eleven local groups attempted small scale excavations following the increasing popularity of medieval archaeology. But as most of these were still using trenching techniques, many of the results were very poor and produced few plans of buildings.[26]

During the second half of the 1950's the Ministry of Works continued its policy of excavating single house sites on threatened D.M.V.s and useful plans were obtained at four sites.[27] At Seacourt (site 5), where Dr. Bruce-Mitford had already shown the importance of the site before the war (Bruce-Mitford, 1940), Mr. M. Biddle excavated several house-sites and recorded in outline most of the village plan as the site was being bulldozed for a road (Fig. 26, p. 121) (Biddle, 1961–62). A similar survey made at

[21] Sites 4, 81, 83, 84, 91, 104, 125, 127, 138, 144, 153, 171, 174, 178, 228, 233 and 259.
[22] Sites 90, 102, 163, 276 and 283.
[23] Sites 99, 238, 274, 281, 287 and 290.
[24] Sites 49, 71, 108A, 137, 152, 167, 193, 218, 236, 246, 260, 270 and 272.
[25] Sites 157, 192, 196 and 263.
[26] Sites 117, 136, 166, 169, 182A, 195, 222, 240, 257, 275 and 289.
[27] Sites 121, 151, 162 and 268.

Babingley (site 129), showed that a great deal of information on stone (but not timber) building could be obtained by simply watching the destruction of a site (Hurst, 1961A). In 1958 the Dorset Archaeological Society excavated a house site at Holworth (site 45, Rahtz, 1959), and in 1959 a long-house at Garrow was excavated (site 23, Dudley and Minter, 1962–63), but most of the small private excavations of this period were still not able to produce substantial results.[28]

Anglo-Saxon post-war excavations

After the war there was an increase in work on Anglo-Saxon sunken-huts and many sites were watched or excavated. There were two large excavations in Yorkshire (sites 277 and 284) but the traces of structures were very hard to work out. Several sunken-huts were excavated on two other sites (118 and 172) but most work was more of a recording nature in advance of various threats. In the south-west Prof. A. C. Thomas's work at Gwithian (site 25) produced an important sequence while for the later period a courtyard farm was excavated at Mawgan Porth (site 28). Excavations by Dr. B. Hope-Taylor at Old Windsor (site 9) also produced a long sequence of structures, unfortunately still not published. The first timber buildings were located at Mucking in 1955 (site 56, Barton, 1960) and Sedgeford in 1958 (site 139); in 1960 Mr. P. V. Addyman excavated the first extensive settlement of the middle-Saxon period at Maxey (site 150, Addyman, 1964). During the last few years several more sites have been investigated on varying scales but the large scale excavations at Mucking (site 56A), and West Stow (site 210A) are the most important for the Pagan period. At the former a very early settlement of the early fifth century is being uncovered but so far all the huts are sunken. At West Stow there is a possibility of excavating the whole settlement and so far 34 sunken-huts have been excavated but only three buildings located. Excavations at Eynsham in 1968 (site 175) have produced buildings and associated sunken-huts for the first time in the area. The problems of these discoveries, and related work on the continent, are discussed later (p. 100). At Witton (site 142) several sunken-huts have been excavated while single sunken-huts have been excavated at Puddlehill (site 3, Matthews, 1962), Erringham (site 223), Upton (Northampton-shire) (site 156) and Fladbury (site 256). Later buildings have been excavated at Buckden (site 77), Eaton Socon (site 78, Addyman, 1965) and St. Neots (site 86A).

Medieval excavations 1960–68

It was in 1960 that a major development came with the second long-term planned excavation, similar to that in progress at Wharram Percy (site 274), aimed at investigating a large part of a site and not just a single house or toft. This was with the first season of the Birmingham University excavation at Upton (site 67) initiated by Prof. Hilton and directed first by Mr. J. S. Wacher and since 1961 by Mr. Rahtz for a season each summer (Rahtz and Hilton, 1966). This was followed in 1961 by Mrs. Minter's project for the complete excavation of a Dartmoor site at Hound Tor (site 38), and in 1963 by Mr. Musty's programme of extensive excavation at Gomeldon (site 244). These four excavations are still in progress and their wide scope has added tremendously

[28] Sites 33, 72, 88, 111, 120, 124, 176, 280 and 288.

to our knowledge though other smaller excavations in the past five years have given us other important house plans from different parts of the country.[29]   This great increase in the production of complete house plans by local amateur groups to supplement those obtained by larger bodies and the Ministry of Public Building and Works[30] has been a most encouraging development, and it is much to be hoped that no more small trial trenches will be cut across D.M.V. sites.   The only excuse for such work would be at sites in process of being destroyed where some record of the date range of the site and information about building materials is better than no evidence at all.   Even in these cases, many workers have shown that much better results can be obtained by making a survey of the whole levelled area, collecting pottery for dating from each croft, and plotting any foundations and boundaries observed.   This was successfully done at Seacourt and Babingley as previously described (sites 5A and 129).   Such work will not necessarily give the early history of the site since early timber buildings will not be visible, and it is possible that the earliest pottery will not be disturbed.   Nevertheless in most cases it is the last opportunity to record the plan of the village as it was in its final period.   In special cases it may also be possible to draw fundamental conclusions as to the history and development of the whole village, as was done so remarkably at Wawne (site 273).

Methods of excavation

Many of the earlier excavations, and unfortunately many post-war ones, have been unsatisfactory because of the poor techniques of excavation used.   It is now realised that medieval village sites are very complex since the houses are likely to have been re-built or repaired at least once every generation over many hundreds of years.   The foundations of the houses were also very insubstantial and the remarkable cleanliness of the medieval peasant house, which was quite unexpected, means that very thin occu-pation levels remain with very little of the build-up that is found on Roman sites or on other medieval sites such as towns and castles.   A whole sequence of up to ten periods or more might thus be represented by less than 0·3 m. of deposit.   Mr. Biddle has demonstrated a very similar state of affairs on a town site at Winchester in his excava-tion of cottages on the Brook Street site.[31]   For this reason the trench or grid system, evolved for the excavation of major masonry buildings or sites with complex stratifica-tion in depth, is not applicable to a village site.   Only the large scale area excavation of each period in its entirety, before going down to the next level, will give a true picture of the remains.

It has been demonstrated on many sites that trial trenches, far from being informa-tive, very often give little information and they can be disastrous if larger scale work is envisaged later, since many important features, which cannot be observed in a narrow trench, are destroyed and the relationship of features to each other is cut away; the out-

[29] Sites 27, 30, 37, 39, 40, 50, 173, 187 and 241.
[30] Sites 31, 134, 141, 147 and 188.
[31] Interim reports by M. Biddle, *Antiq. Journ.*, XLIV (1964), 196–202; XLV (1965), 243–49; XLVI (1966), 313–19; XLVII (1967), 259–66; XLVIII (1968), 250–84.   For discussion in detail of the reasons for and methods of open-area excavation see M. Biddle and Berthe Kjølbye-Biddle, "Metres, Areas and Robbing", *World Archaeol.*, 1 (1969), 208–19.

lines and complex rebuildings of medieval peasant-houses are such that even if substantial stone foundations are visible it is not possible to plan a building by simple cross-trenches.

The grid or box system is equally disastrous for various reasons.   As the deposits are often very thin the sections show nothing of the sequence of floors or walls which are sometimes not visible at all in a section.   With the very slight changes in appearance from one level to another, and the uneven alignment of the walls of buildings, it is often impossible to relate the features in one box to those in another since they change in the baulk.   At Wharram Percy (site 274) in 1953 I was not yet fully convinced by the open-area method of excavation and I tried to combine the two systems by opening up a large area 23 by 12 m. but leaving two control baulks across the site (Hurst, 1956, 272, Pl. XLV).   The result was disastrous, for not only did the sections show very little of the ten superimposed periods which were later worked out (and therefore failed to serve their main purpose), but in both cases the baulks were found to cover important structures which it was impossible to relate to the main plans when the baulks were later taken down.   As a result of this experience each toft is now excavated as a complete unit with no long-term baulks.

This method of open-area excavation, which has been in use on the Continent for many years, is now used on most major village excavations in England but prehistorians and Romanists have been slower to see its potential.   On the medieval side, open-area excavation has been applied also on many manor sites and notably in a series of excavations since 1962 by Mr. Biddle at Winchester with great success on a town layout of streets, houses and churches very similar in their complexity and flimsy nature to many medieval peasant-houses.   There are still unfortunately far too many small trial excavations by local groups on village sites which, through lack of resources or the necessary knowledge to deal with such complex sites, do more harm than good.   No one should embark lightly on the excavation of a village site which is not threatened unless they can open up a large enough area to obtain significant results.   Many earlier trial excavations cannot be fully understood or re-interpreted due to the lack of data.   In particular, excavations which simply uncover a house site without taking into account its immediate surroundings are very unsatisfactory.   For example if a single building only is excavated it is quite impossible, unless the whole toft has been stripped, to tell whether it was a genuine long-house standing by itself or part of a larger farm-complex.   Partial excavation of a house simply to obtain the dimensions is worse since it is often impossible to tell where the doors, hearth and other important features were.

Methods used at Wharram Percy

Methods of open-area excavation differ from site to site and have been adapted and improved by many excavators.   The methods used at Wharram Percy (site 274) by the D.M.V.R.G. have been evolved over fifteen years from those used for the past twenty-five years by Prof. Steensberg of Copenhagen in his important excavations of village sites in Denmark.   Mr. Golson excavated with Prof. Steensberg at Store Valby in 1952 to learn their methods, and I spent six weeks in 1960 at Borup Ris to gain more experience, and to exchange information on the development and modifications of the method in both countries.   Prof. Steensberg's methods were adapted from those originally developed by Prof. G. Hatt on his important series of excavations of Iron Age settlement sites in Denmark in the 1930's[32] and we owe a great deal to both Prof. Hatt and Prof. Steensberg for their pioneer work in evolving this method of excavation.

Between 1950 and 1952 Prof. Beresford excavated several house-sites at Wharram Percy by simply digging along walls to obtain the plan of the latest period. The full complexity of the building sequences was not fully appreciated. In 1952 I joined Prof. Beresford and a trial-trench located a complex sequence, demonstrating that there was far more to be found than the walls which lay under the visible earthworks. The site therefore looked very promising for a trial of the new methods of excavation. The area to be excavated was divided into 5 ft. (1·52 m.) squares and a contour survey made. The turf was then removed and the humus cleared to expose a general rubble level (A1.) This was planned and a counter survey again made at 2½ ft. (0·76 m.) intervals. Wharram Percy lies on chalk, and the later buildings were mainly constructed of chalk, so that the initial appearance was of general chalk rubble. In the second stage (A2) all small stones which were obviously not part of a wall were removed, leaving in place all stones larger than 0·15 m. across which might be part of walls in situ, tumble or just odd stones lying about. Every stone was plotted and levels taken with the aim of making as complete a record as possible, for at that stage only a limited number of clear wall lines were apparent, and special evidence might otherwise have been lost if all stones were not fully recorded. The plotting of the smaller spreads of stone was much more difficult and a laborious task to draw in detail. Here recent developments in photogrammetry will be crucial in enabling not only a much fuller record to be made but also in enabling the recording to be much more objective. This point is of the greatest importance: it is not sufficient to plan in detail the obvious wall lines while only sketching in all other features when at a lower level the exact position of each stone may turn out to be crucial in understanding a structure.

The third and most difficult stage (A3) was to remove all stones which seemed to be tumble or random stones and so expose the actual walls themselves. This was often a very complex operation where there was no firm wall line of dressed stones or the walls had been robbed, and there was a danger of removing, as tumble, stones which were in fact part of the walls. But, if the A2 level was fully recorded, all would not be lost if some wall was accidentally removed since missing parts could be reconstructed afterwards when the complex pattern was better understood. By this stage on Area 10 at Wharram it was quite clear not only that there was a very complex series of buildings but that earlier periods were on quite different alignments. This is another reason why the box is difficult, for even if the grid was laid out at right angles to the visible remains, once lower and earlier structures are found on a different alignment their sections will often be oblique.

The excavation was then continued by the gradual removal of all walls, since if the levels underneath were to be understood it was not possible to leave the later periods *in situ*. This was doubly important at Wharram where the earlier periods were of timber and the only hope of understanding them was to see the whole site cleared to one level with all the stone removed. Level-naming procedure will vary from site to site,

[32] G. Hatt, "Nørre Fjand, an Early Iron Age Village Site in West Jutland", *Archaeol. Kunsthist. Skr. Kong. Danske Viden. Sel.*, II, no. 2 (1957).

but at Wharram the lower stone buildings on different alignments were planned and recorded as B numbers while the timber sequence was given C numbers. This makes reference much easier since it is clear that C2 will be one of the timber buildings while one might have to think twice to remember what level 8 was.

Sections and baulks

In the early years at Wharram, as previously mentioned, two control baulks were left to provide the basic cross sections. When the second area (Area 6) was started in 1961 there were no permanent baulks left but nevertheless a number of basic control sections were still obtained, a level at a time, by a method suggested by Mr. Rahtz. The A1 level was taken down leaving a number of baulks. The sections were then drawn in the normal way and the baulks finally removed to expose the whole site at the A1 level. When the next layer was peeled off, baulks were again left at the same places and recorded in the same manner, being added on to the bottoms of the sections previously drawn. The baulks were then removed as before to expose the full area excavated without any obstructions. It is by this method possible to have the best of both worlds: to have visible sections, and to see each level in its entirety.

Of course the sections need not be confined to the basic ones in the baulks which will continue down in the same place season by season regardless of the features encountered. Other sections can be cut across features in any direction desired without being constricted by rectangular boxes. When deep deposits are encountered, such as banks, ditches and pits, these are of course sectioned in the usual manner and it may be necessary to leave certain control sections standing. This has been found necessary by Mr. Biddle in his complex excavation of the Minster site at Winchester where he carried out an open-area excavation in conjunction with leaving a number of baulks standing for periods of the excavation. The method can therefore be adapted for many types of site whether the deposits are shallow or deep. By far the greatest benefit is the much greater flexibility which this method makes possible while the ability to see exposed at one time the level in its entirety is crucial to the understanding of complex flimsy medieval structures.

The recording of finds

In view of the complexity of these sites the recording of the finds is a difficult problem. It is no longer sufficient to record them by layers and their relation to visible structures or features. At any one moment there may well be as yet unrecognised features with which the material should be associated. It is therefore important that all finds should be precisely pinpointed: at Wharram in the early years all finds were carefully plotted three-dimensionally, and in Area 10 over 6,000 such measurements were made. This was following the Danish practice where it not only helped to date walls and other features but floor levels, which were not visible to the excavators, were worked out from scatters of finds separated by sterile layers. In the event this proved unsuccessful at Wharram since the plotting of the finds failed to produce any indication of previously existing floor levels, and it is now realised that at Wharram there was hardly any build-up in the houses: in fact the opposite was the case, with floors being so thoroughly swept that even earlier levels were cut away. For the dating of the walls and other features the pottery sequence is such in the East Riding of Yorkshire that the Staxton ware cooking pots, which formed the bulk of the finds, had a date range of over 200 years so that sherds could not be used to differentiate periods of rebuilding as close as 25 years apart. The system has therefore been modified and all small-finds and insignificant sherds are bagged according to the level and the 5 ft. (1·52 m.) grid square. Only significant or datable finds are fully recorded three-dimensionally. Nevertheless the original work was of value as it demonstrated many facts which in those early days were imperfectly understood and there may well be other sites where a fuller recording might be necessary. The methods and developments at Wharram have been cited in order to bring out some of the problems and to show that no method is perfect, and that there should be modifications made to suit each individual site, otherwise area excavation will be in danger of becoming as hidebound and restricted as the old trench and grid systems.[33]

I. BUILDING CONSTRUCTION

Anglo-Saxon buildings

Very few buildings of the Anglo-Saxon period have been excavated, so that it is difficult to determine the origin of the various types of medieval peasant-house, especially the different forms of plan. It is, however, easier to discuss the question of building construction. With certain exceptions in the south-west and Lincolnshire (sites 115 and 118), it can be stated that every peasant-house in England from the end of the Roman period in the fifth century until the twelfth or thirteenth century was built of either wood, turf or unbaked earth.[34] It is in fact possible to go further and say that this also applies to most manor houses,[35] and apparently to many palaces as well as is shown by the excavations at Yeavering and Cheddar.[36] It seems that it was only in ecclesiastical buildings[37] and some defensive works[38] that there was any substantial use of stone before the Norman conquest. Thereafter, however, there was an increasing use of stone in manor houses and other buildings though this was not apparent in peasant-house building before the late twelfth century.

Later disturbance rarely allows traces of Anglo-Saxon domestic buildings to survive under existing villages. The best chance might therefore be thought to be in D.M.V.

[33] For fuller details of the problems encountered at Wharram Percy see report on Area 10, *Soc. Med. Archaeol. Monograph*, forthcoming.

[34] As used by *Clifton-Taylor*, 1962, 272–79. This is not a very satisfactory term but nothing else has been proposed which covers mud, cob, pulverised chalk, wichert, pisé de terre and clay lump. See *Williams-Ellis et al.* (1919).

[35] The only stone Anglo-Saxon domestic buildings so far excavated were at Old Windsor but it is difficult to assess the nature of these until the publication of the report. For interim report see *Med. Archaeol.*, II (1958), 183–85.

[36] For Yeavering there is only an unillustrated interim report in *Med. Archaeol.*, I (1957), 148–49. For Cheddar there is a fully illustrated interim report, P. A. Rahtz, "The Saxon and Medieval Palaces at Cheddar, Somerset—an Interim Report of Excavations 1960–62", *Med. Archaeol.*, VI–VII (1962–63), 53–66, with seven plans of buildings.

[37] H. M. and Joan Taylor, *Anglo-Saxon Architecture* (1965).

[38] Mainly the stone walls defending Saxon *burhs*, e.g. South Cadbury, Wareham and Hereford. But see also the stone structure in the bank of the Saxon thegn's hall at Sulgrave, Northamptonshire, *Current Archaeol.*, II (1969), 19–22.

sites where the documentary evidence shows that the site was occupied before the conquest. Unfortunately although many D.M.V.s show traces of early medieval timber buildings underneath later medieval structures it is very rarely possible to determine the exact nature of the building from only odd stake-holes, post-holes or foundation-slots. The evidence for Saxon peasant-houses must therefore come from settlement sites which were abandoned early or which were covered by later structures where the ground was built up rather than dug away. Far more of these sites, unoccupied since Anglo-Saxon times, have been located than is often realised. 108 examples are listed in the gazetteer Chapter 3, though most of the plans are of stereotyped sunken-huts. There are very few substantial timber buildings known so there is not sufficient evidence to discuss regional variations or other details. The large number of these apparently deserted sites, at a time when settlement should have been expanding, suggests a major shift in many village sites during the late Saxon period. This is a phenomenon that we do not understand but Mr. Biddle has suggested to me that this might explain the apparent lack of early settlement evidence from many of our surviving villages.

Sunken-huts

There were two main types of Anglo-Saxon timber buildings: *Grubenhäuser* or sunken-huts, and buildings on the normal ground surface which have left traces of post-holes, stake-holes or foundation-slots. Sunken-huts are by far the most common find simply because they are much easier to see. This is not necessarily because they were the more common building type in Saxon times (see further discussion on p. 100). They take the form of a rectangular pit, dug into the ground, which may vary in depth from 0·2 m. to 1 m. or more. The average size was quite small, about 3 m. by 2 m., though there were exceptionally large ones such as that at Upton (Northamptonshire, site 156) which was 9 m. by 4·5 m. There was usually a single large post in the centre of each short side which presumably supported a ridge-piece. There is very often nothing else remaining so that it is difficult to reconstruct the walls. Some sites had rows of stake-holes round the edge which may be either vertical or sloping, suggesting a flimsy tent-like building. Other sunken-huts with more posts, either at the corners or along the sides, may be reconstructed as more substantial buildings. Recent excavations by Mr. S. E. West at West Stow (site 210), on a sunken-hut which had burnt down, suggest that many examples which have left slight traces of their walling may in face have been quite substantial timber structures resting on a series of sill-beams placed on the ground without disturbing the soil at all. This shows the difficulties of reconstructing the walls, much less the roofs, of timber peasant-houses from post-holes and slots; but the task must nevertheless be attempted, however hazardous.

Timber walls

Timber buildings of the Anglo-Saxon period were usually constructed of spaced uprights placed into separate post-holes or continuous foundation-trenches. No peasant-house so far excavated had the closely set vertical timbers of the Northumbrian royal palace at Yeavering or the late Saxon church at Greensted, Essex. The natural development from what must have been a very insubstantial structure of individual posts in uneven lines (site 78), which it would be very difficult to frame with a wall-plate under the roof, was to fix the posts into a horizontal timber sill-beam in a foundation-slot. This was not necessarily a chronological development, as can be seen by the use of both methods at Maxey in the same building (site 150, Addyman, 1964, Fig. 4). The use at West Stow of sill-beams laid directly on the ground, leaving no archaeological trace, may well explain lines of post-holes which have no wall parallel to them. It is difficult to distinguish foundation-slots with horizontal sill-beams in them from trenches into which vertical spaced posts were placed. On many sites the post impressions cannot be differentiated from the infilling round the posts, especially if the posts were withdrawn before they rotted. Mr. Barker has dramatically demonstrated at Hen Domen Castle, Montgomeryshire, and at Wroxeter, Shropshire many of the problems of excavating slight traces of timber buildings.[39]

Turf walls

The best evidence for continuity from late Saxon to medieval times comes from Hound Tor (site 38), where Mrs. Minter uncovered a complex series of buildings, (Fig. 14), going back in time from the thirteenth century to about the ninth century, though the earliest periods are not closely dated. Here the walls consisted of turf lined on the inside with wattle hurdling, leaving a complex series of stake-holes showing the frequent rebuilding of the houses. Very little is known about the life of such structures and in view of the lack of dating material from the earliest periods it cannot be said whether they may go back to the ninth or only to the tenth century. It might be argued that these houses would last five, ten, fifteen or twenty years and this makes a very great difference in any sum worked out to determine the date of the earliest of the turf and stakehole buildings should be assigned. Other work in the south-west has shown that this type of walling was used over a large part of the area (sites 30, 31, 39 and 40). There is also important evidence from the Isle of Man (Gelling, 1962–63). There is as yet little excavated evidence for turf walls in the medieval period outside the south-west though it is clear from documentary evidence that this was not unknown, for example in the fenland areas of eastern England.[40]

Cob walls

Several examples have been found of other types of unbaked earth construction notably the semi-wet mixes of mud (mixed with lime and straw) and cob (mixed with chalk) (Williams Ellis *et al.*, 1919). Clay-lump (unfired clay blocks) was much used in East Anglia[41] but it cannot easily be distinguished from cob in an excavation. There are excavated examples of cob walls[42] from most of the areas where it still survives as the characteristic vernacular wall material (Clifton-Taylor, 1962, 272–79).

---

[39] P. A. Barker, "Some Aspects of the Excavation of Complex Timber Buildings", *World Archaeol.*, I (1969), 220–35.

[40] W. B. Stonehouse, *History of the Isle of Axholme* (1839), 233.

[41] Lt.-Col. S. E. Glendenning, "Local Materials and Craftsmanship in Norfolk Buildings", *South Eastern Naturalist and Antiquary*, LIII (1948), 15–25.

[42] Sites 11, 30, 42, 80, 120, 134, 141 and 147.

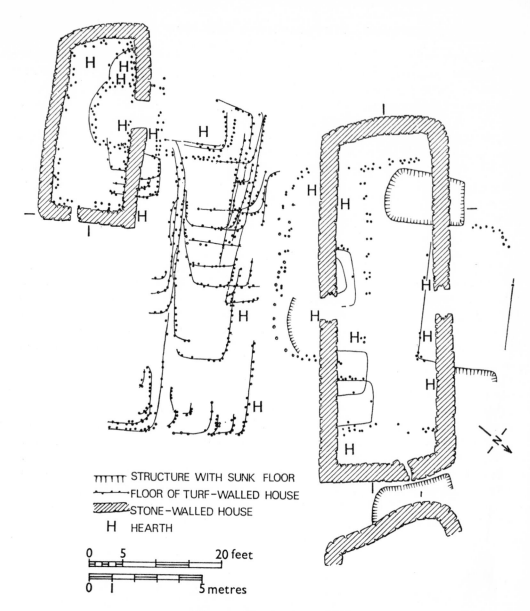

STRUCTURE WITH SUNK FLOOR
FLOOR OF TURF-WALLED HOUSE
STONE-WALLED HOUSE
H   HEARTH

0   5   20 feet

0   I   5 metres

Fig. 14. Hound Tor I, Devon

Plan of excavated areas 1 and 2 showing the succession from late Saxon sunken-huts, through a complex series of superimposed turf-walled buildings to the stone-walled buildings of the thirteenth century.   Building 2 on the left and building 1 on the right (see pl. 8).   There is a fundamental change in the alignment of the turf-walled buildings through 90 degrees from north–south to east–west as well as changes in building positions, see pp. 91 and 124.

Medieval timber walls

There are remains of timber-walled medieval peasant buildings of many types from most parts of the country but, because of disturbance from later stone buildings, in very few cases has more than the odd post-hole or slot been found. It can therefore only be said that the techniques of timber-wall construction vary widely and it is difficult to suggest any chronological or regional development when, for example at Seacourt (site 5A), the same building had some walls of individual posts and others with the foundation-slot for a continuous timber-sill (Fig 21A, Biddle, 1961–62, 97). Where plans have been preserved there is often the appearance of very rough alignments, which would make a wall-plate impractical, and very few matched or spaced uprights to support a carpentered framed roof.

The change from timber to stone walls

One of the most important results of recent excavation has been to demonstrate the remarkable change which took place in the building materials used for the medieval peasant-house during the late twelfth and thirteenth centuries. At this time in almost all stone-producing areas buildings with timber walls were being replaced by walls built of stone.[43] It does not happen at exactly the same time all over the country but the trend becomes more marked during the thirteenth century. It seems to happen first in the south and south-west then, later in the thirteenth century, in the north. The reasons for this change are imperfectly understood and it is a problem which the economic historian should try to help explain.

It may be assumed that houses of Saxon and early-medieval date were built of timber, for at this time there would be plenty of wood available and especially during the early centuries the very action of clearing woodland for agriculture would produce building materials. This would follow on into the post-conquest period in those areas where waste land still had to be cleared. The time would come though when all major timber would be cleared or villagers would have to travel further and further from the settlement to obtain wood. With the decrease in the supply there might be increasing manorial restrictions on tree felling. In areas such as the chalk, where the stone had to be quarried, it is hardly surprising that timber was used as long as possible but in areas such as Dartmoor, where there must always have been abundant surface stone, it is surprising that it was not used earlier, especially since the process of clearing the ground for agriculture must have necessitated the removal of large quantities of stone. In the south-west, where the houses were never of timber but of turf, the changeover may have taken place due to the shortage of satisfactory turf, for with the expansion of cultivation peasants would have to travel further and further to collect turf as those in other areas would have to do for wood. Unlike rotted wood, turf could be reused, but not indefinitely. There may, therefore, have been many social and economic factors involved in this change from timber, turf or unbaked earth walls to stone contruction. The further investigation of this phenomenon will be one of the major tasks of the next few years, trying to work out the timetable of the change in different areas. It is of considerable interest that this same change was occurring also in other parts of Europe

[43] Sites 5A, 30, 31, 38, 39, 40, 45, 67, 111, 117, 121, 147, 157, 192, 227, 231, 244, 268 and 274.

about the same time, for example in the Harz area of Germany (Grimm, 1939). This could argue better for a technological reason than social or economic factors.

Stone walls

The stone used for peasant building was always that close to hand since villagers would not have the resources to carry the stone several miles from a different source. In those villages where peasant-houses have exotic stones incorporated in their walls, these have presumably been robbed from other more substantial buildings such as churches and manor houses which would be often built of stone from a greater distance. This is so at Wharram Percy (site 274) where most of the building-stone was the rough natural chalk quarried in the individual tofts (or back-yards) but there was also a scattering of sandstone which must have travelled at least three or four miles. Many of these stones were dressed and had complex mouldings showing that they must have come from some demolished part of the church or manor house.

It is of considerable interest that the use of building materials in post-medieval vernacular building is very similar to that in the earliest thirteenth-century peasant buildings. For example in the chalk areas, the buildings in Yorkshire and Lincolnshire were always built of chalk[44] not flint, while in Sussex, Wiltshire and Dorset they are mainly built of flint,[45] thus demonstrating the continuity of building methods. The use of lime mortar in medieval peasant building is very rare and is usually a sign that the structure being excavated is manorial or ecclesiastical and not a peasant-house. The use of clay-bonding for the stones is on the other hand very common.[46] Cases of completely dry-stone walling are very hard to prove since in many cases there may have been a clay mortar which has washed out or been replaced by humus through worm action. In almost all cases the stone walls are laid straight on the ground; the digging of foundation-trenches is very rare (site 67). The walls vary in width between 0·6 m. and 0·9 m. but it is often impossible to demonstrate to what height the walls originally were built.

In most cases with walls of this width it may be assumed that they went up to their full height in stone. Where walls have collapsed or been rebuilt, the surplus stone has usually been removed, so that it is difficult to deduce from the volume of rubble the original height of the walls. Where walls have been completely robbed away the resulting robber-trenches are very difficult to work out in view of the very flimsy state of the succeeding walls and the complex series of walls which often cover and underlie them. The spoil from robber-trenches also sometimes leaves confusing patterns on the ground which are mistaken for the plans of buildings, so it is by no means safe to try to plan even the last period of a village from the visible earthworks alone.

Although bricks were in use in many areas of eastern England from the twelfth

[44] Sites 108, 110, 124, 258, 262, 268, 269, 270, 271 and 274.
[45] Sites 10, 45, 47, 221, 222, 224, 227 and 230.
[46] Sites 35, 50, 51, 67, 186, 258, 268, 269, 271 and 274. See discussion of recent survivals of this practice in the East Riding of Yorkshire, T. C. M. Brewster, "Excavations at Weaverthorpe", *Yorks. Archaeol. Journ.*, forthcoming.

century onwards[47] there is no evidence for their use in peasant-houses before Tudor times.

Timber walls on stone foundations

In some stone areas there is evidence for a late medieval change from solid stone houses to half-timbered houses on dwarf stone walls (site 274). This is by no means a regional or strictly chronological change since at Wharram Percy (site 274) in the fifteenth century some houses were still built of stone while others were of timber. These dwarf stone wall foundations for half-timbered buildings were usually between 0·3 m. and 0·45 m. wide. They were often only two courses or so high and in some cases have flat tops for a timber-sill, though in many others they are roughly finished off. This late medieval trend away from stone to timber building occurs in more substantial buildings such as manor houses and has been attributed to the improved carpentry techniques then available. This is not so likely to be the reason for the change in village housing where there is little evidence for timber-framing of any substantial kind, although it might be the response to the changes in upper class building just as the earlier change from timber to stone might alternatively be regarded as the peasant response to the lordly twelfth-century stone manor houses. A more likely reason is the economic decline of the fourteenth and fifteenth centuries, with the possible greater availability of timber on waste land previously cultivated. On the other hand well-to-do peasants would now be able to purchase timber or make assarts in newly released royal or seigneurial forest.

The surviving evidence for ridge and furrow at Wharram Percy shows that almost the whole 1459 acres (590 ha.) of the township were cultivated at some time during the economic expansion of the twelfth and thirteenth centuries. Later there is documentary evidence of waste land and one wonders how much the scrub returned to provide again a more plentiful supply of timber for building purposes. This was unlikely to be very substantial and may well explain the very flimsy nature of late medieval peasant building, which was not necessarily due to the poverty of the individual peasant but to the stunted re-afforestation of waste parts of the parish. This would depend a great deal on the effect of animals in preventing natural regeneration and especially on the assumed increasing use of this land, no longer ploughed, but for sheep.

Non-stone areas

In the clay areas to the south-east and north-west of the stone belt the change from timber to stone construction would not be possible. The examination of sites on the ground and from the air clearly shows in these areas the flat tofts with no signs of house foundations (Pls. 10 and 11), in marked contrast to the areas of abundant stone where the ruined stone foundations are clearly visible as substantial earthworks (Pls. 13, 14 and 15). It is unfortunate that the excavation of these clay sites has been neglected because they

[47] J. S. Gardner, "Coggeshall Abbey and its Early Brickwork", *Journ. Brit. Archaeol. Assoc.*, 3rd ser., XVIII (1955), 19–32. For general discussion of bricks see N. Lloyd, *A History of English Brickwork from Medieval Times to the End of the Georgian Period* (1925, 2nd ed. 1934).

are much more difficult. Early excavations on these sites had most unpromising results (sites 190 and 240). The main problem is that with no visible traces on the ground
it may be a long and costly business even to find the house before it can be excavated.
On the stone sites it is quite easy to lay out a square and excavate the house, thereby
producing spectacular results at once.

Recent excavations at Thuxton (site 141), Grenstein (site 134), Faxton (site 147) and
Barton Blount (site 34) by the D.M.V.R.G. for the Ministry of Works, specifically
chosen to investigate this problem, have had most important results. They have shown
that it is possible to locate very flimsy structures of cob and timber often leaving very
little trace. At Thuxton for example, house-sites were visible as negative areas surrounded by pebble courtyards. At Barton Blount for the first time in England a
D.M.V. site has been found with a complex sequence of timber buildings (Pl. 7)
which were never replaced by either stone buildings or timber buildings raised up on
stone foundations. Preliminary work in 1968 on three tofts has produced not only a
sequence of different buildings from the twelfth to the fourteenth centuries but also
some fundamental changes in house position and alignment for the first time in the
Midlands. It is hoped that further excavation will be possible on this site which is just
the kind of site that the D.M.V.R.G. have been searching for, since excavations with a
similar object started at Faxton had the opposite result to that expected. It had been
supposed that in these clay areas the peasant-houses would always have been of timber
or unbaked earths and that the change from timber to stone would not be reflected
there. At Faxton, however, there was a change from timber and cob houses built
straight on the ground to timber and cob houses built on a dwarf stone foundation,
though no traces were visible on the surface. In this case although the village site had no
stone outcrops, it was available only about half a mile away. There would always be a
wide variety of surface stones collected from the boulder clay which would suffice for the
dwarf-walls. Other sites have been excavated where no stone foundations were visible
on the surface but stone was found. This makes it very difficult to classify sites by examining the earthworks alone (sites 17 and 192).

It is therefore possible that there will be three types of site: in areas of abundant
stone, where there was a thirteenth-century change from timber to stone construction;
in areas of clay, etc., with no quarried stone supply for many miles, where the construction would continue in timber, turf or unbaked earths throughout the medieval
period; and thirdly in areas where there might be stone nearby, not in sufficient quantities to make it possible for the peasant to build solidly of stone, but enough to enable
him to lift his timber or cob building off the ground on a stone foundation. There is
no doubt that this change, from timber or cob put directly into or on to the ground to
timber or cob walls raised up on dwarf-walls, was an important improvement since it
would protect the timber and cob and keep it dry, thus lengthening the life of the building. It is for this reason that much vernacular timber architecture surviving from the
medieval period is preserved. The same does not seem to have happened with the
roughly-built peasant buildings which still seem to have lasted little longer than a
generation after the introduction of this important improvement. This must surely
suggest that they were not built of well-carpentered timbers as the houses of their more
prosperous neighbours which have survived till this day.

Wall infilling

It may be assumed that the wall infilling of most timber peasant building was of wattle and daub. Fragments of daub, often bearing the impressions of the wattles, have been found on several excavations, but not on very many since the number of houses excavated which were burnt down, and therefore likely to preserve large quantities, is very few (sites 37, 50, 78 and 187). This is perhaps surprising in view of the insubstantial nature of the houses and the open fire which must have been the main feature of every house. Where daub is found there is also the possibility that it may be the remains of ovens or fire canopies.

Entrances

The positions of doorways are usually clear as gaps in the timber or stone foundations, though actual thresholds are rare. The discovery of socket-stones[48] or iron hanging-pivots[49] on many sites together with the common occurrence of keys,[50] padlocks,[51] hinges and latches suggests that, poorly built as the houses were, they had solid wooden doors rather than insubstantial wattle hurdles, mat[52] or sacking hangings. Door studs are rare but are found on a few sites (site 5 and 67). It is almost impossible to obtain any information on windows from the archaeological record. There are small hinges and latches, possibly from shutters or else from furniture. There is no evidence for glazed windows in any peasant-house before Tudor times (site 162) and small wooden shutters may be assumed. Some peasant-houses seem to have one wall much less substantial than the other three, and it might be suggested that this was to make it easier to insert a door and windows leaving the gables and one side solid. There is evidence for the building or the addition of porches, especially in the higher villages in the south-west from the thirteenth century onwards[53] so this is by no means a late development as has been suggested.

Partitions and furniture

The internal arrangement of buildings is often obscure, for if walls leave little trace the partitions were even more ephemeral. The clue is sometimes given by changes in floor level (site 227A, building 11) or in the composition of the floor in different parts of the building (site 74). Internal post or stake-holes may often be interpreted as partitions but may also represent furniture of various kinds (site 227, building 3), though these may very well have often been combined as in the Welsh house till recent times (Peate, 1940, 104). In the south-west, especially Cornwall, the furniture was made of stone from the thirteenth century onwards and took the form of benches, beds, mangers, wall recesses and cupboards (sites 23 and 32) often in the thickness of the wall. In Devon,

---

[48] Sites 27, 31, 35, 50, 67, 160 and 274. See also: Dartmoor Exploration Committee twelfth report, *Trans. Devon Assoc.* LXVII (1935), 127–29; R. H. Worth, *Dartmoor* (1953), 356 and 404; C. F. Innocent, *The Development of English Building Construction* (1916).

[49] Sites 5A, 35, 45, 50 and 67.

[50] Sites 5A, 20, 45, 121, 192, 227 and 274. There was a lock-plate at Upton, site 67A.

[51] Sites 5A, 67 and 240.

[52] A. T. Lucas, "Wattle and Straw Mat Doors in Ireland", *Arctica*, XI (1955), 16–35.

[53] Sites 27, 31, 38, 188 and 274.

where stone is just as plentiful, furniture seems to have been mainly of timber, remains of which are rarely found except in exceptional cases such as Dinna Clerks (site 37) which was burnt down leaving many fragments of wooden structures.   The only other archaeological traces of furniture are the metal fittings such as chest handles, hasps, keys and decorative studs which are reasonably common.[54]   This suggests that most peasant-houses had at least some basic items of fairly sophisticated furniture.   That a certain amount of carpentry was carried out is shown by the finding of chisels, gouges and other woodworking tools.[55]

Heating and cooking

The central hearth was universal in the medieval period and comprised either a fire lit directly on the floor, producing only a burnt area on excavation,[56] or a solid stone hearth often constructed in the south-west of a single large stone or elsewhere a number of smaller stones[57] or tiles.   Other hearths were constructed of clay with a stone surround.[58]   In the south-west vertical fire-backs (sites 23 and 32) have been found similar to those known in Wales.[59]   Other houses have a firepit[60] instead of, or additional to, the main central hearth, and this may have been used for the storage of ashes or for baking.   Other pits which contain no traces of fire may have been for various storage purposes as is shown by the remarkable example of Dinna Clerks where there was a complete cooking pot, presumably used for water storage, sunk in the floor near the hearth.   Various types of post-hole and stake-hole are found associated with hearths. These were often used for supporting the spit or other accoutrements of cooking but Mrs. Minter has demonstrated in the south-west that they were also often the supports for clay chimney canopies which seem to be a feature of Devon and Cornwall[61] and may well be represented on other sites but unrecognised.   The remains, consisting of a layer of burnt clay over a hearth or by the side of it, have often been interpreted as a later period clay hearth.   Several sites, especially in the south of England, have clay ovens in the corner of the room[62] either in addition to the central hearth or in some cases instead of it.   They are however by no means common, whereas in central Europe the oven and stove were usual throughout the medieval period and later, as evidenced by the remains of ovens and stove tiles.   The examination of charcoal from burnt areas can be useful in determining the type of wood burnt and its size.   Unfortunately few excavators seem to have collected samples or had them analysed.[63] Remarkably, coal is found in several medieval peasant-houses,[64] often in cases like Wharram Percy as much as 100 km. from the nearest seams.   This presents many

[54] Sites 5A, 45, 67 and 192.
[55] Sites 5A, 50, 67 and 227.
[56] Sites 5A, 38, 40, 50, 160, 226, 227, 231, 273 and 274.
[57] Sites 27, 30, 31, 32, 35, 36, 38, 39, 40, 50, 67, 72, 176, 177, 192, 241, 257, 270 and 274.
[58] Sites 5A and 151.
[59] I. C. Peate, "The Double-ended Firedog", *Antiquity*, XVI (1942), 64–70.
[60] Sites 30, 38, 40, 117, 227 and 254.
[61] Sites 27, 31, 35, 38, 39, 40 and 188.
[62] Sites 5, 32, 67, 227 and 244.
[63] Sites 5 various; 36 oak; 227 poplar.
[64] Sites 5A, 50, 51, 67, 227 and 274.

problems of cost and transport which cannot as yet be explained. Odd pieces are more common and it is possible that small quantities were brought in for specialist purposes rather than normal heating.

Floors

Floors were either of clay,[65] stone,[66] cobbles[67] or covered with stone flags:[68] on only two sites, except for West Stow (see p. 103), has there been strong evidence for timber floors. At St. Neots (site 86A) there were parallel foundation-slots which must have supported a timber floor, while at Muscott (site 151), one of the buildings had four parallel rows of small post-holes. For many peasant-houses the excavator finds no floor at all since it was scoured away by the constant sweeping of the housewife. In some cases this has produced such a U-shaped depression, helped also by constant wear, that the foundations of the house have been undermined.[69] In general very few peasant-houses have any accumulated rubbish on their floors, and the general impression all over the country is of houses swept clean with the rubbish deposited in the yard. This is a most important point as it explains why medieval village sites have such thin deposits and why there is no thick build-up of accumulated rubbish leading to well stratified levels. This evidence must clearly affect very strongly our views about the dirtiness of the medieval peasant as still presented in history books. It also means that phosphate analysis, which would show the sites of yards if the rubbish was dumped there, is not likely to locate the house-sites, except by plotting the negative areas. It was for this same reason that early excavations of peasant-houses in wooded areas were so unsuccessful. After trial trenching had located areas rich in finds, these were opened up only to produce rubbish deposits, while the house-sites themselves must have been in the largely barren areas between (site 240).

Roof construction

While it is very difficult to be sure about the wall construction from the foundations found by archaeological excavation, it is almost impossible to reconstruct the roofs from the slight traces usually found. It is very unusual to find, as at Gomeldon (site 244), post-holes reasonably spaced for a carpentered truss roof. In fact it must be assumed that many of the peasant-houses must have been roofed by quite flimsy, roughly-cut branches. The much quoted illustrations of the Strata Florida[70] farmhouse may in fact give a very good picture of what one of these unstable medieval uncarpentered roofs was like. Though in this case the building was originally of good quality. It is unlikely that the peasant would be able to obtain large enough timbers or have the resources to cut them if he did, but it may be one of the main reasons for the short life of the medieval peasant-houses. If they had well-carpentered roofs they would surely

---

[65] Sites 72, 80, 121, 151, 176, 192, 268 and 289.
[66] Sites 11 and 74 chalk; 254 flint; 45 gravel; 198 limestone chips and 67 and 186 pitched stones.
[67] Sites 45, 186, 226, 268 and 273.
[68] Sites 50, 107, 121, 159, 160, 162 192 and 195.
[69] e.g. the last period of house 6 at Wharram Percy (site 274A).
[70] S. W. Williams, "An Ancient Welsh Farm-House", *Archaeol. Cambrensis* (1899). 320–25. Quoted and republished in *Peate*, 1940, 139–41 and Figs. 32–36.

have lasted much longer than they did. The cause of the constant rebuildings could have been the decaying roof as well as collapsing walls especially if the thatching or wall-infilling was of poor quality so as not to fully waterproof the structures. It may be that this flimsy construction was intentional, with the idea that in each generation the son taking over from his father would rebuild his house anew.

The only evidence for roof construction again comes from the burnt down sunken-hut at West Stow (site 210A) and the house at Dinna Clerks (site 37) where the remains demonstrate a structure of oak rafters with hazel twigs twined between them. In view of the almost complete absence of tiles from excavated sites, thatch or turf roofs may be assumed to have been universal. On the few sites where clay,[71] stone or slate tiles[72] are found these are very few in number so they can hardly have been completely tiled. It may be that some peasant-houses had a limited covering around the hole in the roof to let the smoke out, thereby giving some protection to this area against the dangers of fire. There may also have been tiles along the wall tops to stop the rain percolating through, or the wind from lifting, the thatch. At Seacourt (site 5A) ridge tiles were found. These were presumably used because the ridge is a difficult place to make water tight. No attempt will therefore be made here to describe the various possible roof types since the archaeological evidence is insufficient. It is hoped that this may be attempted at some future date in a joint paper with Mr. J. T. Smith.

II. BUILDING PLANS AND USES

Anglo-Saxon buildings and sunken-huts

Although there have been very few recent excavations of Anglo-Saxon village sites, it has been demonstrated from earlier work that the *Grubenhaus* or sunken-hut is the most common type of building. Excavations on the Continent have shown that this was the same over large parts of Europe[73] but that on most sites there were also larger buildings at ground level. Until recently these had not been discovered in this country but they are now known from several sites. It has been suggested that, as was the case with the so-called prehistoric pit-dwellings which have now been reinterpreted as storage-pits associated with substantial timber structures which were not previously recognised, the Anglo-Saxon actually lived in large houses at ground level while the sunken-huts were used for weaving or for other industrial activities, not being lived in at all (Radford, 1957). Recent work has, however, suggested that the pendulum has swung too far, for at West Stow (site 210) and Mucking (site 56A) where the complete or large-scale excavation of two pagan Anglo-Saxon villages is in progress, by far the largest number of structures are sunken-huts. The only pre-war large scale excavation of a Saxon village was at Sutton Courtenay (site 6, Leeds, 1923, 1927 and 1947) where Mr. Leeds found 33 sunken-huts and no larger buildings were recognised. Since the results of recent

---

[71] Sites 5A, 45 and 227.

[72] Sites 30, 45 and 227.

[73] W. U. Guyan, "Die frühmittelalterliche Siedlung von Osterfingen", *Zeitschrift für schweizerische Archäologie Kunstgeschichte*, XI (1950), 206–12 and "Einige Karten zur Verbreitung der Grubenhäuser in Mitteleuropa im ersten nachchristlichen Jahrtausend", *Jahrbuch der schweizerischen Gesellschaft für Urgeschichte*, XLII (1952), 174–97.

work on the Continent he has been much criticised for having missed the large timber buildings which it has been supposed must have been in the gaps between. At West Stow, however, a pattern of 34 sunken-huts has so far been excavated but only three buildings have been located and these are quite small compared with continental

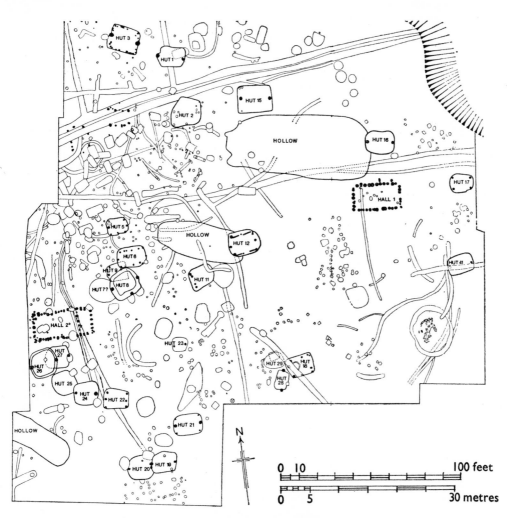

Fig. 15. West Stow, Suffolk

Plan of part of the pagan Saxon settlement showing sunken-huts, with only two larger buildings, and a number of pits and ditches, see p. 101.

buildings, only about 10 m. long (Fig. 15). Although Mr. West has shown that many of the huts were used for weaving and other processes connected with wool, it is hard to believe that there were only three living-houses in this part of the village with so many associated working-huts. The same applies at Mucking where a pattern of sunken-huts is visible on the air photography, 68 having so far been excavated. No certain houses have been located at all on this part of the site although the dating of many post-hole features is uncertain due to the complexity of earlier remains of the Iron Age and Roman periods. At the Linford site (site 56), adjoining Mucking and of the same early fifth century date, Mr. Barton did find at least one house, though unfortunately its length was uncertain since it was quarried away, together with another smaller weaving shed nearby. The whole question has been further complicated by the discovery at Eynsham (site 175) of five sunken-huts associated with three buildings. Prof. Jope was unable to locate any buildings when he investigated the nearby site of Cassington (site 172) and he had argued that Mr. Leeds may not have missed buildings at Sutton Courtenay. There is clearly no simple answer to this problem and it is difficult to draw

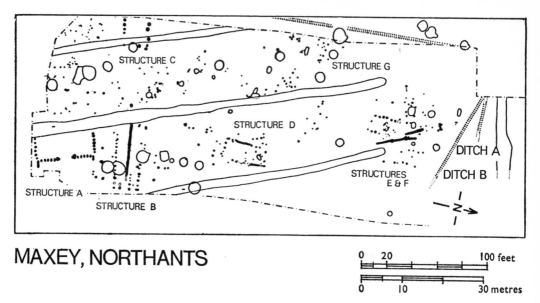

MAXEY, NORTHANTS

0   20   100 feet

0   10   30 metres

Fig. 16. Maxey, Northamptonshire

Plan of the middle Saxon settlement with post-holes defining timber buildings, various types of pit between and overlaid by the furrows of the medieval field system, see p. 102.

firm conclusions from earlier excavations; although nearly 100 sites have produced evidence for sunken-huts one can never be sure whether larger buildings were missed, especially as so much of the evidence was only recorded during gravel-working.

At Maxey (site 150) in the middle-Saxon period, seven buildings excavated were post-hole structures and five possible sunken-huts were located (Fig. 16). At the late-Saxon village of St. Neots eight sunken-huts were excavated in 1929 (site 56) but when Mr. Addyman returned in 1958 to an adjoining site (site 56A) he found a row of large buildings with no sunken-huts at all. Excavations at the middle- and late-Saxon site of Old Windsor (site 9) produced important results with associated large buildings and sunken-huts, but full assessment of this site must await publication of the report.

Since only these seven Saxon settlements have been excavated on a large scale, and are not only of various dates, the fifth to the tenth century, but are also in different parts of England, it is too early to attempt a solution to the problem. From the present evidence at Mucking, West Stow and Sutton Courtenay it might be suggested that there were very few large houses and that the poorer peasants must have lived in sunken-huts. At Maxey and St. Neots there were certainly groups of substantial buildings and at St. Neots the sunken-huts were grouped behind them. As only part of the site was excavated at Maxey there might well have been more sunken-huts on another part of the site, i.e. not mixed in with the other houses. This could either be interpreted as separate working-huts going with the houses but separated from them or the houses of the poorer peasants segregated from those of the more prosperous ones.

Only the complete excavation of several village sites of different dates and periods can give us the answer. Because of the costs involved this is likely to be a long time ahead. Unfortunately due to gravel-working the complete plan of Mucking/Linford can never be obtained, but there will in due course be a complete plan of West Stow which may provide crucial evidence if a single large house, or a group of houses, is found on one part of the site. On the Continent, although there have been a large number of excavations of the Migration period, later village excavations on any scale, such as that at Warendorf,[74] are very rare. In the later Saxon period at Tilleda, in the Harz, Prof. Grimm has shown that there were both sunken-huts and above-ground buildings in use and he suggests that both types were inhabited.[75] Sunken-huts continued until the twelfth century[76] into the thirteenth–fourteenth centuries,[77] or even till recently in Somerset and Ireland,[78] but there are only isolated examples of this. The type also disappeared on the continent in the thirteenth century (Grimm, 1939). Sunken-huts on village sites may be related to the cellars, first found on Anglo-Saxon town sites, which of course continued throughout the medieval period, usually built of stone as vaulted storerooms. This suggests another possible use for sunken huts and the important evidence obtained at West Stow for a timber-floor over the sunken part raises other interesting possibilities for those sunken-huts which apparently have no features actually in the bottom. The industrial use of many of these sunken-huts is often shown by the large quantities of ash found in them and by the clay loom-weights and post-holes for vertical looms found in others (Radford, 1957).

There are too few excavated Saxon timber houses as yet to attempt any classification but it can be said that neither at Hound Tor (site 38) nor at Maxey was there any evidence for the medieval type of long-house. This is surprising as aisled buildings, with

[74] W. Winkelmann, "Eine Westfälische Siedlung des 8 Jahrhunderts bei Warendorf, Kr. Warendorf", *Germania*, XXXII (1954), 189–213 and "Die Ausgrabungen in der Frühmittelalterlichen Siedlung bei Warendorf (Westfalen)", *Neue Ausgrabungen in Deutschland* (1958), 492–517.

[75] P. Grimm, "The Royal Palace at Tilleda, Excavations from 1935–66", *Med. Archaeol.*, XII (1968), 91–96.

[76] Sites 18 and 80.

[77] Sites 226, 244 and 274.

[78] H. Laver, "Ancient Type of Huts at Athelney", *Proc. Som. Archaeol. Soc.*, LV (1909), 175–89, reproduced in *Colvin* (1958), 79; C. O. Danachair, "Semi-Underground Habitations", *Journ. Galway Archaeol. and Hist. Soc.*, XXVI (1954–56), 75–80 and "Some Notes on Traditional House Types in County Kildare", *Journ. Kildare Archaeol. Soc.*, XIV (1966–67), 234–46.

humans and animals under the same roof, had a long life on the Continent, going back to the Bronze Age (Hurst, 1965), and it is strange that it is not represented in any Anglo-Saxon house so far excavated in lowland Britain, though there are early examples of long-houses at Jarlshof[79] and Mawgan Porth (site 28) which are hard to fit into the main development of the medieval peasant-house. The problem must therefore remain for the moment, with the long-house apparently becoming common from the twelfth century onwards. Recent comparison of the pottery from Mucking with that from Feddersen Wierde in north-west Germany[80] suggests that it is so similar there must be links between the abandonment of Feddersen Wierde c. 400 and the start of Mucking at the same date. The main stumbling block though is that the inhabitants of these north-west German sites had a cattle economy and lived in long-houses, while those at Mucking, and many other English sites like West Stow, had a sheep economy and had a preponderance of sunken-huts. It may therefore be that we are asking the wrong questions and the different house types may be due to different economic rather than cultural conditions. Though it is hard to see how the change could be so sudden and complete from Feddersen Wierde to Mucking and West Stow.

Medieval house plan types

There have been excavations on more medieval than Anglo-Saxon peasant-house sites, so it is easier to draw conclusions, although there is still a great deal to do and future work may modify the conclusions presented below. Although 209 excavations have taken place on 186 sites only 90 of these produced buildings and many of these are difficult to interpret due to incomplete or poor excavation. Single building plans have been recorded from 56 sites and 35 have produced plans of several houses, enabling comment to be made on the general layout of the medieval village (see Table XVI, p. 147). There are many variations in house plan (see Figs. 17–21) and it may in time be possible to draw distribution maps of regional types and chronological variations but at the moment the excavations are too widely scattered for this to be possible. The houses so far excavated may be divided into three main groups (Fig. 17), first defined in Hurst, 1965.

A. At the lower end of the social scale was the hut of the cottar or bordar who had no land of his own. This was the *cot* which was either a small one-roomed house about 5 m. by 3·5 m. or a larger two-roomed house about 10 m. by 4 m.

B. The medieval villein would have lived in a *long-house*. This would have at one end a living-part, often divided into two rooms, with a byre at the other end usually separated from the living-part by a cross-passage but always with access between the two without going outside. These long-houses varied greatly in size from small two-roomed buildings little bigger than the larger cots, about 10 m. by 4 m., to a more nor-

[79] J. R. C. Hamilton, *Excavations at Jarlshof* (1956).

[80] W. Haarnagel, "Die Ergebnisse der Grabung auf der Wurt Feddersen Wierde bei Bremerhaven in den Jahren von 1955–1957", *Neue Ausgrabungen in Deutschland* (1958), 215–28; "Zur Grabung auf der Feddersen Wierde, 1955–9", *Germania*, XXXIX (1961), 42–69 and "Die Ergebnisse der Grabung Feddersen Wierde in Jahre 1961", *Germania*, XLI (1963), 280–317. For English summary see Helen Parker, "Feddersen Wierde and Vallhagar: a Contrast in Settlements", *Med. Archaeol.*, IX (1965), 1–10.

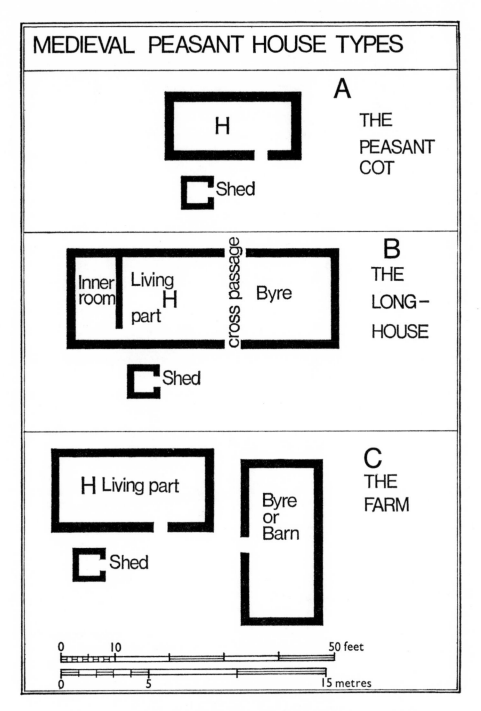

MEDIEVAL PEASANT HOUSE TYPES

A
THE PEASANT COT

H

Shed

B
THE LONG-HOUSE

Inner room | Living part H | cross passage | Byre

Shed

C
THE FARM

H Living part

Byre or Barn

Shed

0   10   50 feet

0   5   15 metres

Fig. 17. Medieval peasant-house types
(A) The peasant cot, (B) the long-house, (C) the farm, see p. 104.

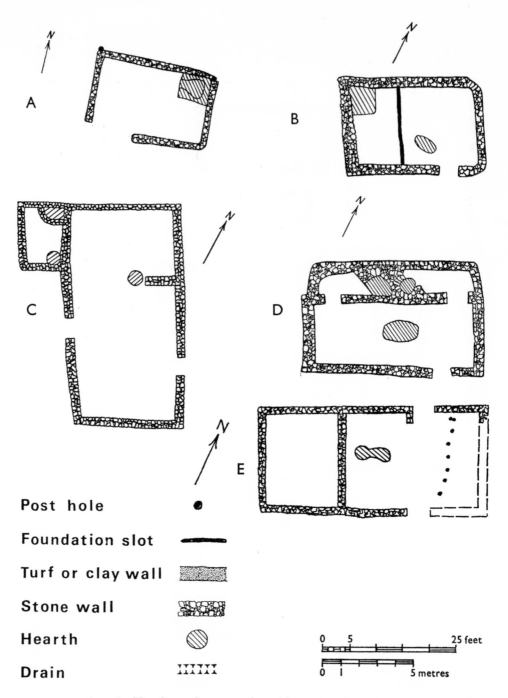

A

B

C

D

E

Post hole

Foundation slot

Turf or clay wall

Stone wall

Hearth

Drain

0   5   25 feet

0   I   5 metres

Fig. 18. Hangleton, Sussex, various thirteenth-century house plans

(A) Building 3, single-roomed cot; (B) Building 11, double-roomed cot;
(C) Building 12, long-house at right angles to slope, with staggered entrance and
outshut; (D) Building 10, single-roomed house with long outshut; (E) Building 1,
three-roomed long-house parallel to the slope, see p. 104.

mal size of up to 15 m. in length, but there are many examples which are as long as 25 or 30 m.

C. The third main type of peasant-house was the *farm* in which the byre or barn was separated from the main living-house and placed in a distinct building, usually at right angles to the other, forming the basis of a rectangular courtyard. This would be the home of the most prosperous villagers especially the emerging yeoman farmers who were acquiring their freeholds during the later medieval period.

The long-house

A most important result of medieval excavation since the war has been to demonstrate that the long-house, which was at one time thought to be a Celtic house-type, because of its survival in Wales and other highland areas, was common, being found on 27 sites (Figs. 19–20) over large areas of England. Examples have now been excavated in south-west England, all across southern England as far as Sussex (site 227), in the west Midlands (site 187, where there is also good medieval documentary evidence (Field, 1965)), in Northamptonshire (site 157), in Yorkshire (site 274), and further north (site 51). The main gaps at the moment are the central Midlands, East Anglia and Kent although very few excavations have as yet taken place in these areas. The earliest authenticated examples, with the exceptions already listed (see p. 104, above), are in the south-west where Mrs. Minter suggests that they developed out of, or replaced, earlier simple structures in the twelfth century. On most sites where the earliest complete plans are late twelfth or thirteenth century they are already fully developed with three rooms. Although many long-houses have earlier timber buildings underneath them their plan is almost always too uncertain either to give the dimensions of the timber building or the purposes to which various parts of it were put.

The farm

Farm complexes have been found in many areas from the thirteenth century onwards (Site 5A, Fig. 21A), and excavations at Hangleton (site 227 where long-houses and farms were in use side by side) show that these were not regional variations in plan but more a question of the prosperity of peasants who seem to have tried to make a break with the long-house by emphasising the distinction between the living and farm accommodation, not only by putting them in separate buildings, but also by putting them at right angles to each other. Farms have been recognised on 11 D.M.V. sites. There have been 22 excavations on isolated farms as opposed to 112 excavations on D.M.V.s and 52 excavations on shrunken or surviving villages (see Table XVI, p. 148). In many of these the buildings have been long-houses not farm complexes. With the latter a certain amount of copying of the manorial complex, with its building round a courtyard, may also be suggested. Excavations at Gomeldon (site 244) and Upton (site 67) are crucial since here the actual process of change from the long-house to the farm has been found by excavation. At Gomeldon in at least two cases long-houses were changed into courtyard farms, Fig. 22. The change from long-house to farm did not take place at the same time all over the country as is shown by the case of Wharram Percy where, when the village was destroyed in the early sixteenth century, all the houses were long-houses,

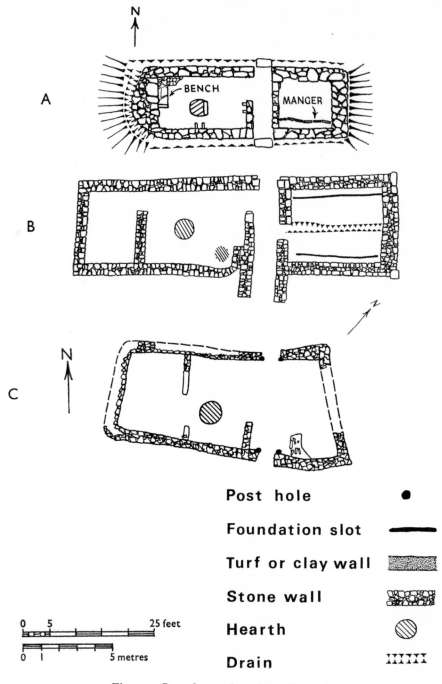

Fig. 19. Long-house plans from the south-west

(A) Garrow, Cornwall, small two-roomed long-house; (B) Treworld, Cornwall and (C) Great Beere, Devon, three-roomed long-houses, A and B with mangers, see p. 107 and Plate 9.

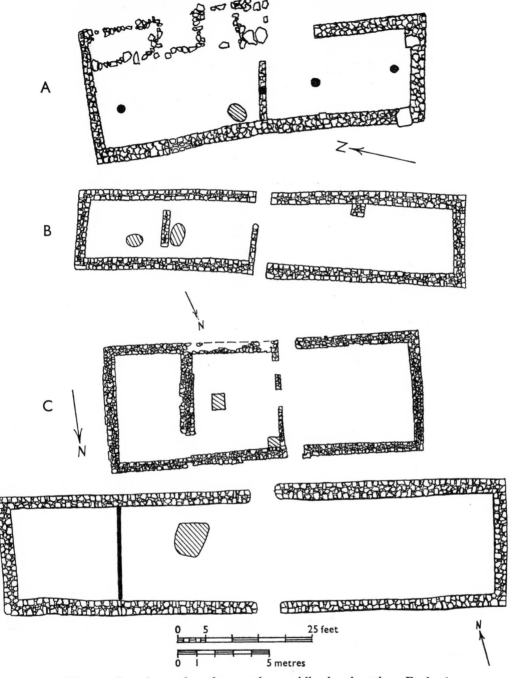

Fig. 20. Long-house plans from southern, midland and northern England
(A) Wroughton, Wiltshire, with outshut; (B) Wythemail, Northamptonshire,
three-roomed long-house with hearths in both upper rooms; (C) Riplingham,
Yorkshire East Riding and (D) Wharram Percy, Yorkshire East Riding, three-
roomed long-houses, see p. 107.

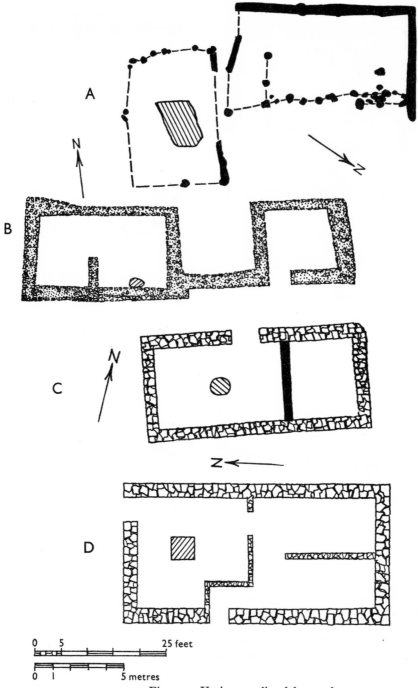

Fig. 21. Various medieval house plans

(A) Seacourt, Berkshire, Area 5, timber-built farm complex with farm building at right angles to the living-house; (B) Holworth, Dorset, long-house or farm on the same alignment; (C) Riseholme, Lincolnshire, two-roomed house; (D) Muscott, Northamptonshire, two-roomed house with baffle entrance, see p. 107. For key see Fig. 19, p. 108.

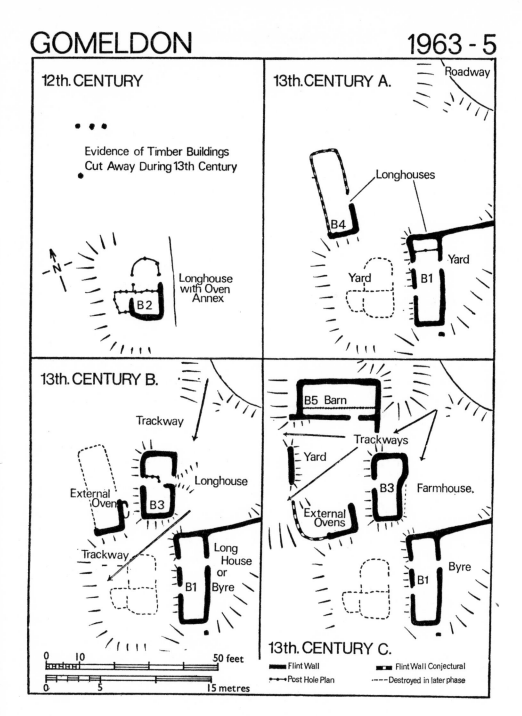

GOMELDON
1963 - 5

12th. CENTURY

Evidence of Timber Buildings Cut Away During 13th Century

N

Longhouse with Oven Annex

B2

13th. CENTURY A.

Roadway

Longhouses

B4

Yard

Yard

B1

13th. CENTURY B.

Trackway

Longhouse

External Oven

B3

Trackway

Long House or Byre

B1

B5 Barn

Trackways

Yard

B3

Farmhouse.

External Ovens

Byre

B1

13th. CENTURY C.

0   10   50 feet

0   5   15 metres

███ Flint Wall   ▬▬ Flint Wall Conjectural
•—• Post Hole Plan   ---- Destroyed in later phase

Fig. 22. Gomeldon, Wiltshire
Plans showing the development from long-house to farm, see p. 107.

9

as is clear from the plan, except a courtyard farm in the manorial enclosure which may be interpreted as the demesne farm or the bailiff's property (Fig. 25).

By the middle of the sixteenth century courtyard farms were appearing in the East Riding of Yorkshire as is shown by the earthworks at Duggleby and Towthorpe, quite close to Wharram: Towthorpe was deserted by about 1600 so these buildings should be sixteenth century in date.   One must suppose that over most of lowland England the long-house had disappeared by the middle of the sixteenth century, as Mr. M. W. Barley has demonstrated, so that by the time Tudor inventories become available no long-houses are recorded (Barley, 1961).   It may be supposed that most of the last survivors in lowland England were swept away during the Great Elizabethan Rebuilding which must have so transformed the peasant-house in the Midlands (Hoskins, 1953).

Use of the term long-house

In modern times the term long-house was first used for the house with the byre under the same roof by Dr. I. C. Peate in the 1930's when he was making his study of the Welsh house.[81]   Since that date the word has been widely used but recently there have been several attempts to change it to byre-house or some other similar alternative.[82]   I think that in view of the fact that this has been an accepted word in the literature for over thirty years it should be retained.[83]   It is also fully descriptive since the crucial fact is that the living-part of the house and the various farming activities are all under one long roof.   The term byre-house confines the usage to houses which have cattle at the lower end but the archaeological evidence suggests that this would be unduly restrictive. Long-house is a term used fairly widely over the world to describe various types of house but if the term long-house is understood to describe a type of medieval peasant-house there can be no confusion in its context.   Finally, Dr. Peate used the term long-house simply because this was the word used by the Welsh people who described their houses to him.[84]   He therefore thought that the word long-house might have been what medieval people themselves called this house-type.   This view has been fully vindicated by documentary evidence from Worcestershire where at least one house with cattle at the lower end was called *longa domus* (Field, 1965, 115).   It is not suggested that every such building was called a long-house in medieval times or that each time *longa domus* occurs in documents a long-house should be inferred, but it does seem more satisfactory to use as the name for our house-type a word that was in current usage in the medieval period rather than coin a new one unnecessarily.

I have suggested that the term long-house is preferable to byre-house since the latter places too narrow a restriction on the use of the building.   The use of the third, or

[81] The term long-house was first used by Sir Cyril and Aileen Fox in "Forts and Farms on Margam Mountain", *Antiquity*, VIII (1934), 409–10 but it was not defined in its present sense till a lecture by Dr. I. C. Peate given to the British Association in Blackpool in 1936.   I. C. Peate, "Some Welsh Houses", *Antiquity*, x (1936), 448–59.   Reaffirmed in Peate, 1940, 60 and 65.

[82] P. Smith, "The Long-house and the Laithe-house", in *Culture and Environment*, ed. I. LL. Foster and L. Alcock (1963), 439–44.

[83] As has also been suggested by S. R. Jones and J. T. Smith "The Houses of Breconshire: Part I. The Builth District", *Brycheiniog*, IX (1963), 5.

[84] I. C. Peate, "The Welsh Long-House: A Brief Re-appraisal", in *Culture and Environment*, ed. I. LL. Foster and L. Alcock (1963), 440.

lower room, beyond the cross-passage is often as difficult to determine from the archaeological evidence as is the type of roof construction. Only in cases where there are actual mangers (Plate 9), animal pens or some form of drain in position can one be sure that animals were in fact housed in this room. On many excavations the third room has no such evidence but at the same time the wide entrance is a good reason for suggesting that it housed cattle. In other cases it is difficult to tell either way and it is quite possible that this was a basic house-type which was adapted to differing farming needs. A peasant might have few animals or require to store grain or other farm equipment. This third room would therefore be invaluable for all such purposes, as in fact Sir Cyril Fox suggested (Fox and Raglan, 1953, 105). Mr. Rahtz has suggested at Upton that his third room was used for some process in the making of cloth and yet the house plan is a typical long-house. It seems illogical to exclude cases where the housing of animals cannot be proved when the plan is so similar. I suggest that all houses, where the third room is used for housing animals or for some other farm purpose, should be termed a long-house. This is important, for Mr. Barley has suggested that the third room may have been used to house an extended family (Barley, 1961, 13); this would not therefore be a long-house. There are certainly documentary references to two families living under the same roof (Colvin, 1958, 92) but in no excavated long-house is there any evidence for this. If the third room was used for living a hearth would be essential and this has never been found so far. Much more likely is that the father or son might build himself a new house in the same toft but under a different roof as Mr. Rahtz has suggested to explain the Upton (site 67) sequence. There are other possible archaeological evidences of this where there are two living-houses in the same enclosure (sites 50, 141 and 244).

Hall-house and long-house

I am unable to understand the distinction suggested by Sir Cyril Fox between the hall-house, with its cross-passage inside the living-room, and the long-house, with its cross-passage outside the living-room, thus suggesting evolution along different lines from a common ancestor (Fox and Raglan, 1953, 104). This division may be true in the Welsh vernacular architecture that he was studying but if so this is a post-medieval evolution which has no bearing on the position in the medieval period. Many thirteenth-century long-houses have no major wall at all either side of the cross-passage although various types of partition were often used. Even here some of the posts might have been used for tethering rather than solid walls. There is no evidence for such a firm division and the same applies to the earliest excavated manor houses. I would therefore suggest that the only difference between the hall-house and the long-house, in their earliest phases, is that in the former the third room was used for domestic purposes with the farm activities, if any, already relegated to separate buildings, while in the latter the third room was used for various farm purposes, usually, but by no means always, for housing animals. The branching out from one stock therefore happened much later than Sir Cyril Fox imagined.

Vernacular architecture and excavation

Students of vernacular architecture are far too inclined to base their theories on evidence which only goes back to the Tudor period. It must, of course, be readily admitted that fifteen years ago nothing else was possible, but now a reassessment of the evidence is necessary taking into account the large number of peasant-house excavations which are now taking place. Many other examples may be quoted besides those already referred to (see p. 80) if various features of excavated long-houses are discussed. There is no question of the long-house plan developing from a simple form in the thirteenth century to a more developed one in the post-medieval period. Already by the thirteenth century are found both two and three-roomed long-houses so the inner room cannot be regarded as increasing privacy in the late medieval period. There are long-houses which are quite open, with timber partitions or solid stone walls between house and byre already by the thirteenth century. Also at this early date are staggered entrances, separate byre entrances, and hearths at the junction of the living-room and the inner room so as to heat both at the same time. In fact most of the possible improvements were already current in the thirteenth century with the exception of a proper stone chimney (though clay canopies were in use), and a full upper floor, though there were almost certainly half-lofts for storage and possibly for the children to sleep as well. These are difficult to prove from the archaeological evidence. These differences should be interpreted as due to the differing status or prosperity of the peasant, rather than as having a chronological significance.

The use of the inner room, off the living-room, in both the long-house and the two-roomed cot, is more difficult to determine than the third room where there is sometimes clear evidence for animals. In many examples there is no evidence of its function. The two most likely uses were as an inner sleeping room or as a pantry and dairy. There is very rarely heating in this room, but such cases could result from two families sharing the house, or they could be kitchens. The best evidence for an inner room comes from Dinna Clerks (site 37) which was left in a hurry as it burnt down. Complete pots and a cistern were found suggesting use as a pantry or dairy, as in many surviving examples, though one feels that as with so many arguments this room could have served a dual purpose and we may be too subtle in trying to pin down a single use for each room.

Building size

It has recently been suggested that peasant houses were laid out and built according to fixed geometric rules.[85] Whatever may be the case in more recent periods this is unlikely to have been true of the Anglo-Saxon or medieval peasant-houses. Excavated buildings show endless examples of walls not built straight, nor at right angles or parallel to each other. While there is a tendency for buildings to be built on the double-square principle, if there were two bays,[86] and in multiples thereof if they were longer, the actual measurements were very likely governed by the timber available for roofing in different areas. In fact many peasant houses were narrower than half their length, presumably because the materials to span a greater width were not available. The length also varied very greatly and although a pattern may emerge when more work has

[85] J. M. Jenkins, "Ground Rules of Welsh Houses, A Primary Analysis", *Folklife*, v (1967), 65–91.
[86] A. C. Thomas, "Post-Roman Rectangular House Plans in the South-West", *Proc. West Corn. Field Club*, ii (1956–61), 156–62.

been done there does not seem to be any fixed length suggesting a bay unit, either in the same area or even the same site where buildings of many different sizes were constructed.

The actual width of peasant buildings with unsupported roofs varied between 3 m. and 6 m., which was about the limit which could be spanned without a central row of posts or aisles. Houses wider than 6 m. must have belonged to a higher social scale than most peasants were able to aspire to. The most common width falls between 4 and 5 m. The length of peasant buildings differs very considerably between about 4·5 m. and as much as 30 m. but by far the greatest number of excavated examples are between 8 and 15 m. comprising two or three rooms (Figs. 17–22).

Ancillary buildings

Besides the main living buildings, barns and byres, there were often other out-buildings in the peasant toft or backyard.[87] Very little is known about these since so many excavators have simply uncovered a single house without attempting to place it in its context in its toft. Where tofts have been stripped it has often not been possible to work out the plans of these small outbuildings. At a time when the peasant houses themselves were so insubstantial as to leave very little trace it may well be imagined how little evidence remains for these outbuildings. On many sites a small building about 2 m. square seems to be typical of most tofts, whether they contain a cot, long-house or farm (Fig. 17). These could have served many purposes, one of which, for example, in the south-west was the peat store. Others may have been pigsties or for various forms of storage.

One very important structure was the corn-drying kiln. These are best known from the south-west and throughout the highland zone[88] but are likely to have been very common not only on the higher marginal land where the crops would have been difficult to dry out naturally, but also in many other areas with the climatic deterioration of the fourteenth and fifteenth centuries (sites 5A and 147). These structures were also used for drying peas, beans, flax and hay. The plan of these kilns were in the form of a circular oven with a long flue leading to a stoke-hole. They were very similar to pottery kilns except that the flue was usually longer. Sometimes they seem to have been outside or under a very flimsy covering but at Hound Tor, for example, they were massive struc-tures set in pairs in substantial buildings. These more than anything else show the extensive arable cultivation of this part of Dartmoor which must have been very margi-nal at 335 m. above sea level even with the climatic optimum of the twelfth and thir-teenth centuries.

Other activities were carried out not in separate rooms or outbuildings but in *out-shuts* attached to the main living building. These sometimes took the form of a long narrow room or aisle (Fig. 18D) under the same roof-line[89] or a rectangular attachment to part of the house (Fig. 18C) which might either be under the same roof or have a separate one.[90] Many of these contained ovens, presumably for baking.

[87] Sites 5A, 23, 35, 134, 141, 147 and 274.
[88] Sir Lindsay Scott, "Corn-drying Kilns", *Antiquity*, xxv (1951), 196–208.
[89] Sites 5A, 51, 134, 195 and 227.
[90] Sites 5A, 38, 40, 162, 198, 227 and 244.

Disposal of rubbish

The disposal of rubbish varies very much from site to site. As has already been said, most medieval peasant-houses were kept swept clean and the rubbish must have been thrown or dumped in the toft where there are often the most finds of pottery and other small finds. What happened to it next is a serious problem since, unlike the Roman period, when the manure was spread on the fields, as is clear from the ubiquitous scatter of Roman pot sherds on any ploughed field within a considerable radius of any Roman settlement, medieval sherds are rarely found outside the actual boundaries of the village itself.[91] To solve this problem far more work is required of the kind now being carried out by Mr. P. Wade-Martins in Norfolk. He is plotting finds from village sites and their surroundings, which seem to show that there was rubbish disposal, in this area at least, on the fields immediately adjoining the village. Rubbish was not often buried, as is shown by the absence of rubbish pits or cesspits on many village sites. Only at Upton (site 67) were they remarkably large, similar to those found on town sites. It is possible that they had an industrial purpose in this case. In the same way there is little evidence for underground storage-pits which were such a feature of the prehistoric period and which continued well into the Saxon period.

It must, therefore, be supposed that the rubbish was either dumped into hollows or there was a village rubbish dump which in many cases has not been found. At Wharram Percy (site 274), curiously enough, the chalk quarries were not used as rubbish pits as most of them do not contain any black soil or more then a few odd sherds. But after they were backfilled with small unusable rubble the hollows left were filled with rubbish. The main rubbish dump may have been along the hillside on which the village was built and there may well be other similar disposal points on other village sites.

Quarries

A striking feature of the tofts at Wharram Percy (site 274) was the network of building-stone quarries which honeycombed the chalk. They were all small individual quarries, the normal medieval industrial practice, as can be seen from the remains of the large stone quarries at Barnack (Beresford and St. Joseph, 1958, Fig. 97). There was no large face worked as in modern times but a hole was dug about 2 m. across and varying from 2 m. to 5 m. in depth, depending on the amount of stone required. If more was required at once, a second quarry pit would then be sunk about 0·5 m. away from the first leaving a narrow bridge between the two so that the sides would be secure. The unwanted stone would then be backfilled right away into the first quarry thereby saving any double action. At Wharram, as each toft lay on chalk, the peasant was able simply to dig in his back garden to obtain his building material. It is therefore perhaps even more surprising that he did not attempt this before the thirteenth century but went to the trouble of collecting timber. In other villages various forms of quarry are visible on different parts of the village site though the larger disturbances are more likely to have been for building materials for the church or manor house if these were constructed of local stone.

[91] P. J. Fowler, J. W. G. Musty and C. C. Taylor, "Some Earthwork Enclosures in Wiltshire", *Wilts. Archaeol. Mag.*, LX (1965), 67.

One major problem of the interpretation of the plans of D.M.V.s is the presence not only of medieval quarries but also of later ones for stone, clay, sand or gravel. This goes far beyond the simple robbing of walls for stone. D.M.V. sites were natural places to be used as quarries throughout the post-medieval period since they must often have been rough ground, which without modern machinery could not be levelled or put to any useful purpose except grazing. These later quarries, except where they clearly cut through medieval features, which even here could be earlier medieval structures destroyed in the last years of the village, are very difficult to distinguish from medieval operations. From the large numbers of documents complaining about people digging illicit holes some of the most unlikely disturbances might well be medieval in date. Only excavation can solve this difficult problem which makes the planning of so many sites very difficult. The best evidence for the eighteenth and nineteenth century date of this type of digging was obtained at Clopton (site 20, Alexander, 1968).

III. THE CHANGING VILLAGE PLAN

Lack of Anglo-Saxon village earthworks

Anglo-Saxon villages consisted of timber buildings which have left only marks in the ground. They had no substantial earthworks which could survive to the present day. This is why the sites are so hard to find. They can only be discovered by quarrying, ploughing or other disturbances which bring the remains to light (Figs. 15–16). Their plan may be discerned by aerial photography in the right conditions. In the few villages excavated on a large scale there is very little evidence for property divisions many of which had hedges or fences with shallow drainage gullies (Figs. 23–24). This pattern continues on into the medieval period until the thirteenth-century change from timber to stone houses.

Medieval village earthworks

At this time the first substantial village earthworks were constructed. These were most common in the Midland clay lands where each *toft* (back-yard) or *croft* (back-garden or paddock) was built up as a platform surrounded by a ditch which was often of quite large size (Plates 10–11). In stone or well-drained areas, tofts were not built up but were defined by substantial walls or hedged and fenced banks (Fig. 25). This development of earthworks in medieval times is demonstrated not only on D.M.V. sites where traces of timber buildings are visible on the old ground surface beneath but on many other sites where remains of Saxon or early medieval peasant buildings are preserved under later earthworks (Hurst and Hurst, 1967). In all these cases the traces of timber buildings are surrounded by small drainage ditches rarely more than 0·6 m. wide and 0·6 m. deep (Figs. 23–24).

The reasons for this change are hard to understand. The fact that it mainly occurs on clay sites, and not on well-drained chalk sites, suggests that it was not an attempt simply to copy the substantial moats of the upper classes which were significantly also starting at this same period in the later thirteenth century. It is hard to see the peasant taking so much trouble and time in what must have been a major project, and then building a very flimsy house on top. It may well be that these raised tofts were not built

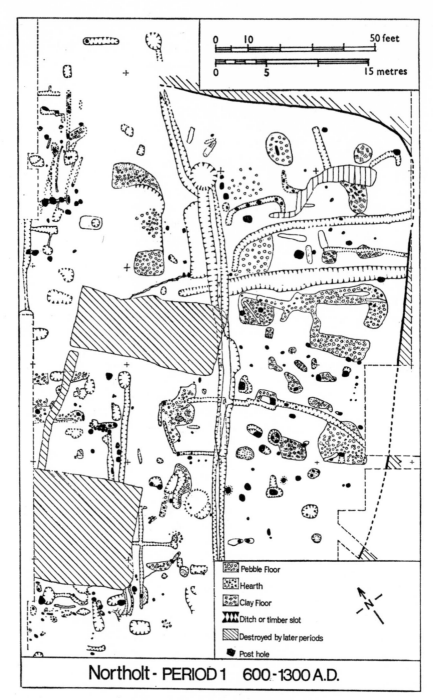

Within the figure:

50 feet

0   10

0   5

15 metres

Pebble Floor

Hearth

Clay Floor

Ditch or timber slot

Destroyed by later periods

Post hole

N

Northolt - PERIOD 1   600 - 1300 A.D.

Fig. 23. Northolt, Middlesex

Eighth- to thirteenth-century complex sequence of timber buildings, surrounded
by small drainage ditches, and sealed by fourteenth-century moat (see p. 117).
Compare with Fig. 24, where the periods have been differentiated and with
Plate 7, for a photograph of a similar type of site.

MILTON, HAMPSHIRE
Interpretation plan

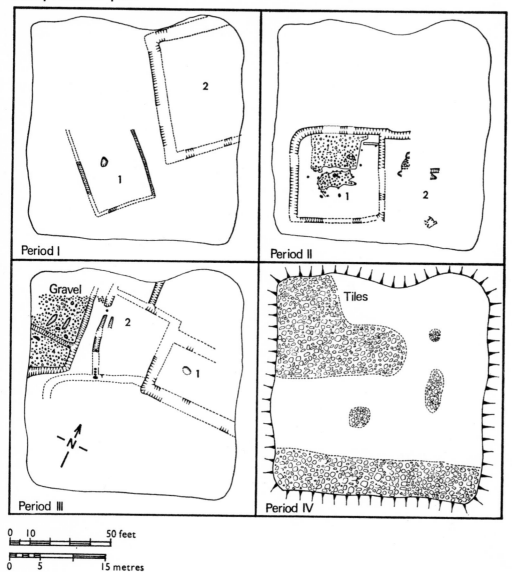

Period I

Period II

Gravel

Period III

Tiles

Period IV

0 10   50 feet

0   5   15 metres

Fig. 24. Milton, Hampshire
Eleventh- to thirteenth-century superimposed lay-outs on different alignments
sealed by fourteenth-century moat (see p. 124).   Interpretation separating the
various periods: I–III, small boundary ditches (see p. 117); period IV fourteenth-
century moat.

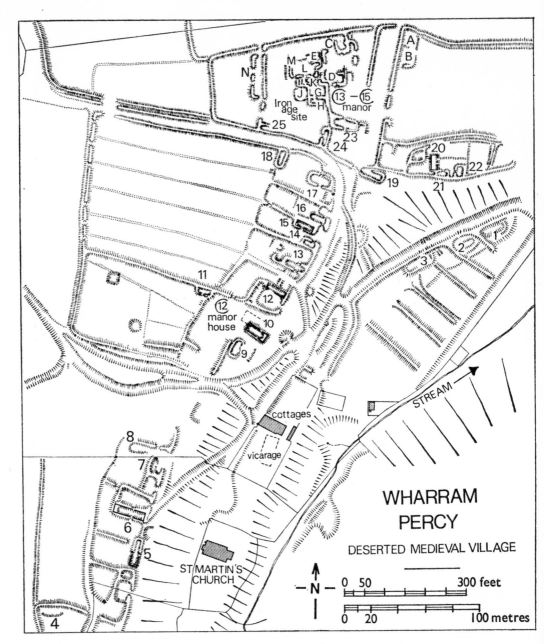

Fig. 25. Wharram Percy, Yorkshire East Riding

Plan of the village showing the early extent of the settlement (4–8) with the twelfth-century manor house and boundary bank; to the north the thirteenth-century planned extension of the village (12–18) with the new site for the manorial complex (A–N and 19–25), see p. 127.

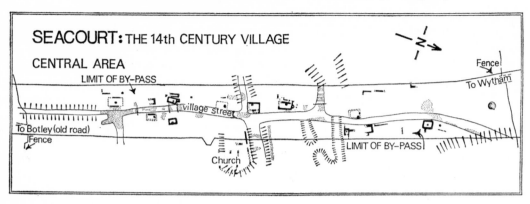

Fig. 26. Seacourt, Berkshire

Plan of village recorded during scraping for a new road. It was possible to plan most of the fourteenth-century stone-built structures and their relationship to the village street, but not the earlier timber buildings which were only recovered by excavation, see p. 83, Fig. 21A.

as a single operation but gradually accumulated over the later medieval period as the large ditches and sunken roads were cleaned out and constantly re-cut with the resultant spoil heaped up to form the raised tofts. This process of constant re-cutting of ditches and the raising of levels is best demonstrated at Holworth (site 45).

If this was the case, the question must be asked why deep ditches were not cut in the late Saxon and early medieval period.

Climatic change

Although it is not fashionable to attribute such fundamental changes to climate it is very striking that in the period of supposed climatic optimum during the massive land clearance of the eleventh and twelfth centuries, peasant-houses were built on the old ground surface, only surrounded by shallow gullies on land which was quite low lying and is now often waterlogged, while as soon as we get suggestions of the deteriorating climate of the later thirteenth and fourteenth centuries[92] these raised platforms were constructed with clear evidence for very frequent re-cuttings and clearing out. It is hard to avoid the conclusion that these platforms were an attempt to meet the worsening conditions and the increasing wetness.

This may not necessarily have been fully intentional since the clearing out and re-cutting of ditches and the digging out of the muddy roads would have provided soil which would have to be put somewhere. It would soon be realised that, by building

[92] H. H. Lamb, *The Changing Climate* (1966) and A. Steensberg, "Archaeological Dating of the Climatic Change in North Europe about A.D. 1300", *Nature*, CLXVII (1951), 672–74.

up the tofts, living conditions and drainage were much improved. It has been suggested that the same development occurred with manor houses since all early examples so far found have been on the original ground surface, again only surrounded by small drainage ditches except at the social level of the castle with its defensive ditches. It was not until the end of the thirteenth century that moats became common, and where they were dug the spoil from the ditches was often heaped up inside to form a raised platform (Hurst and Hurst, 1967). In the early period very few tofts were cobbled but this became increasingly common in the later medieval period.[93] This can hardly be entirely due to rising standards of living which would require less muddy yards. But on the other hand even in the period of climatic optimum conditions must have been very sticky on clay sites in winter.

Changes in house alignments

The gradual evolution of the raised toft during the medieval period raises the whole question of changing layouts, a very important aspect of the development of the village, as has been shown by many recent excavations. It has already been pointed out that the peasant-houses were very flimsy and were unlikely to last more than a generation without either repair or even complete rebuilding. It is a very striking fact that on many village sites rebuilding took place once a generation on completely new foundations and often on a new alignment. The first classic demonstration of this in Britain was at Vowlam (Isle of Man) where Dr. Bersu excavated six superimposed Viking buildings on different alignments (Bersu, 1949). In England many examples have now been found[94] but these changes are best demonstrated at Wharram Percy (site 274) (Fig. 27), where the houses were turned through an angle of 90° in the fourteenth and fifteenth centuries.

At Wharram Area 10 the period B houses were sideways on to the village street and each new house was built on quite a new site with slight changes of alignment. Yet the fifteenth-century houses were turned round completely to be gable end to the street and, although each house was basically on the same site in the last three periods, each one was built on a new foundation slightly offset from the one before (Pl. 17).

This is very hard to understand, since it would seem natural to re-use the earlier stone foundations rather than go to all the extra work of rebuilding the walls from scratch, and often in such a way that one face of the wall was on the earlier foundation, thus giving it support, while the other face was only on soil and must have collapsed very soon, making the house even more flimsy than was necessary.

On Area 6, where the same stone house continued throughout the fifteenth century on the same basic site (though it was completely rebuilt once, making it narrower and so doing away with the necessity for a central row of posts to hold up the roof), in its later phases 1·5 m. to 3 m. lengths of wall were rebuilt on the same general line as they collapsed or became dangerous. This suggests that the later Area 10 houses were so poorly built that any rebuilding entailed complete replacement, while the roof on the Area 6 building was much more substantial and perhaps properly carpentered so that the repairs were carried out in sections, leaving the roof intact. This would fit in well with

[93] Sites 11, 88, 141, 157 and 273.
[94] Sites 30, 34, 38, 70, 78, 147, 157 and 274.

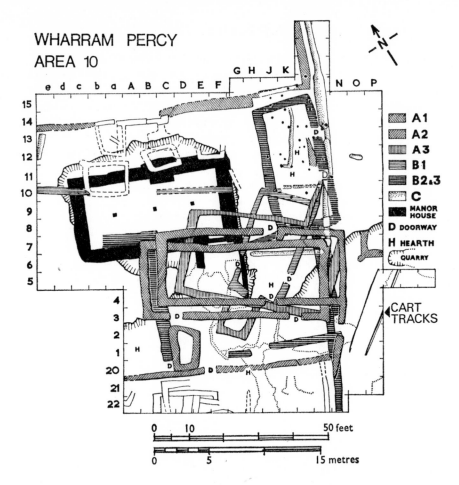

Fig. 27. Wharram Percy, Yorkshire East Riding

Plan of Area 10 showing the complex sequence of superimposed periods on different alignments. The late twelfth-century Percy Manor house and chalk quarries were replaced by two thirteenth-century houses oriented north–south (B2–3). In the fourteenth century these were replaced by a single house (B1.) while in the fifteenth century the long-houses were built east–west on quite a different alignment (A1–3), see pp. 122 and 124 and Plate 17.

our supposition from the plan that the peasant in the long-house 10 which was 15 m. long was less prosperous than his neighbour in the latter years of the village's life in the long-house 6 which was 30 m. long (Fig. 20D).

At Hangleton (site 227A), the development of building 9 not only changed from a structure sideways on to the road to one gable end on to the street in a series of slight changes of alignment, but the house gradually moved from the back of the toft, away from the street, to the front (Fig. 28) (Hurst and Hurst, 1964, 98, Fig. 3). Change of alignment was not, however, confined to the period of stone or stone foundation building. It is clearly seen in the late Saxon and early medieval changes at Hound Tor and Milton.

At Hound Tor (site 38) the turf houses were built on a slightly different site each time, though on the same general alignment (Fig. 14). This may be interpreted as the cutting back of the thick turf walls as the retaining hurdles rotted and collapsed and new hurdles were inserted further back. Here also there was a sudden complete change in alignment through 90°. In this case the change was from houses built parallel to the contour to houses built up and down the slope. Mrs. Minter has suggested that this may be connected with the introduction of the long-house, which would need a slope for drainage.

At Milton (site 70, Hurst and Hurst, 1967, 53, Fig. 3) the early timber buildings gradually changed their alignment through three periods (Fig. 24). At Eaton Socon (site 78, Addyman, 1965, 46, Fig. 7) there was a possible late Saxon change in alignment through 90°. On three different tofts at Faxton (site 147) the change was from siting parallel to the contours to a building at right angles up and down the slope as at Hound Tor. At Tresmorn (site 30) there was a fundamental change in alignment from the early timber buildings to the later stone ones, while at Barton Blount (site 34), which had timber buildings throughout, there were the same changes through 90°. There are as yet too few examples of these changes in alignment for the reason to be understood, though examples from all periods all over the country show that it was not a chronological or a regional feature. The alignments do not always change for the same reason, such as change from north-south to east-west, or from sideways to the street to gable end on. There is however, on most sloping sites, a tendency for the change to be from parallel to the slope to up-and-down, so giving much better drainage whether the building was a long-house or not. At Wythemail (site 157) there was a change from a building parallel to the slope to a long-house at right angles. This was later replaced by another long-house parallel to the slope again. This was because a road was cut across the site necessitating a change in alignment. These changes may therefore have been for many different reasons.

Major changes in village plan

These changes in alignment were not confined to actual house sites but affected the whole toft pattern and the fundamental layout of the village. At Wharram Percy (site 274) Area 10 comprised two tofts in the late thirteenth century, each containing a single peasant-house (Fig. 27). These were both dwelling-houses, since each had a hearth. In the fourteenth century these were amalgamated into one toft with a single house on the same alignment parallel to the street and set midway between the two earlier houses. Later this house was turned round through 90° to be gable end to the street. It cannot be suggested that these changes in alignment were due to the increasing scarcity of land since it was at the time when the houses were closest together that they were sideways to the street. When they were turned round there must have been large gaps between them. That this was not just a single example in one part of the village is shown by the recent excavations on Area 6 at Wharram (site 274a). Here exactly the same thing occurred and not only were two houses in the fourteenth century replaced by a single house in the fifteenth century but the toft boundaries on either side were on very different alignments suggesting not a simple amalgamation of tofts but a more fundamental change in the whole area.

Similar changes can be seen at Hangleton (site 227A) where in the thirteenth century there were four peasant houses of various sizes all set very closely together in their individual crofts. In the fourteenth century these were all demolished to be replaced by a single farm (Fig. 28) which not only obliterated all the earlier buildings but had its eastern boundary bank running straight down the middle of house 12, instead of about 3 m. further east where the earlier bank could have been utilised (Hurst and Hurst, 1964, 96, Fig. 1). We can surely see here very clearly the archaeological evi-

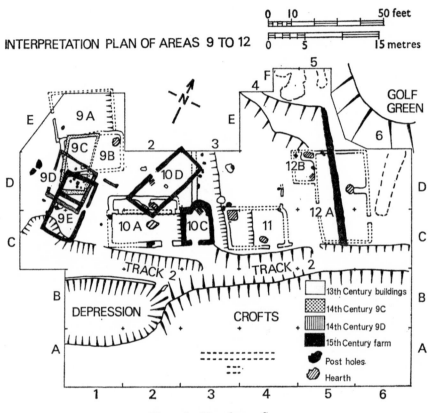

Fig. 28. Hangleton, Sussex

Plan of part of the village showing four close-set crofts in the thirteenth century (9–12) succeeded by a single farm (in solid black) in the fifteenth century, see p. 125; various rebuilds of area 9 on different sites and alignments can also be seen (9A–E), see p. 123.

dence for the contraction of these villages in the late medieval period of decline following the decimation of the population by the fourteenth-century plagues.

A much more fundamental change is shown by the survey carried out by Mr. H. C. Jones at Wawne (site 273) while it was being bulldozed. In the twelfth and thirteenth centuries there were about twelve peasant-houses set in a rectangular area in one part of the village, which was at that time very extensive. These were arranged in a very haphazard fashion as though they had been built and added to over the years as the village gradually expanded (Fig. 29). In the fourteenth century, however, all these houses were destroyed and a completely new layout was constructed some distance to the south with sixteen houses all laid out in a row parallel to the street. This must surely have been a planned redevelopment by the lord of the manor and it is tempting to

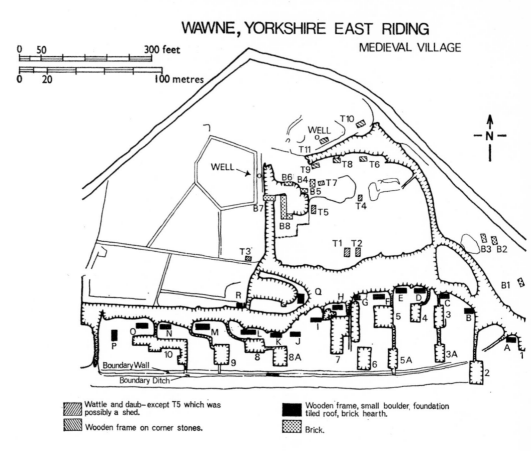

WAWNE, YORKSHIRE EAST RIDING
MEDIEVAL VILLAGE

Wattle and daub– except T5 which was possibly a shed.

Wooden frame on corner stones.

Wooden frame, small boulder foundation tiled roof, brick hearth.

Brick.

Fig. 29. Wawne, Yorkshire East Riding

Plan of bulldozed village showing the twelfth- to fourteenth-century haphazard layout of timber buildings (T.1–11), succeeded by a completely new regular lay-out of fourteenth- and fifteenth-century buildings on stone foundations (A–R), with a shrinkage to two brick post-medieval farms (B1–3 and B4–8), see p. 125.

associate this with a completely new start in this part of the village following the Black Death. It is hard to give the exact date archaeologically but the first site produced mainly decorated sandy wares which are datable to the late thirteenth and early fourteenth centuries while the new block produced only Humber wares of the later fourteenth and fifteenth centuries.

An examination of the plan of Wharram Percy (Fig. 25) shows a very similar state of affairs, suggested by the visible earthworks but to be fully proved by excavation. Firstly there is no evidence for Anglo-Saxon structures on the top of the hill. These were all in the valley bottom near the church and it may be assumed that the whole Saxon village was on the terrace above the stream on which the Saxon church was originally built. The village then expanded in the twelfth century up on to the hill to the west with a fairly haphazard group of houses built in rectangular tofts. Before this happened the area was open field as is suggested by a boundary ditch on the edge of the plateau very similar to that defining the limit of the ridge and furrow to the east of the valley. This ditch contained only two sherds of pottery and it is therefore inconceivable that it was the boundary ditch of a house in use on the plateau at the time it was open.

Towards the end of the twelfth century the Percy family built their massive manor house leaving an open area or village-green between them and the village. The major bank round the enclosure associated with the manor may have been the limit of the village at this time though this has not yet been proved archaeologically. In the thirteenth century the manor house was abandoned and the area used as quarries. Then, later in the century, a large new manor house was built at the far end of the present earthworks to the north. In between was imposed another very clear example of planning with the tofts of regular size and the houses placed within them all gable end to the street. There can be little doubt that this area was first occupied when the new manor house was built on a block of open-field strips which was presumably replaced by further clearance further away from the village. The resultant plan was therefore similar to that of the twelfth-century village, though on a larger scale, with village, manor house and boundary bank, the manor being separated from the village by a street.

We can therefore see here the expansion of settlement as the village population grew in its peak period of prosperity. In view of the toft changes, however, we should not identify the visible layout with the thirteenth-century settlement of this area, which may have contained almost twice as many houses, parallel to the street or not. The present layout, however, is very clearly planned as a unit and might be equated with the acquisition of the manor by the Hilton family in the early fifteenth century, to which period presumably dates the manor as we see it today, a complex series of buildings round courtyards. With the late fourteenth-century decline, many of the tofts may have been decayed and the lord therefore decided to replan this whole part of the village with a regular layout, and it may well be that it was he who decreed that henceforth all houses should be gable end to the street. A similar change of plan has been demonstrated at Holworth (site 45) where the present regular plan of a street with rectangular crofts on either side is defined by ditches, one of which cuts through a twelfth century house. Further excavation is required to confirm that this is not a single boundary change but the regular layout, like those at Wharram and Wawne, does suggest a thirteenth-century replanning of the whole village.

Changes in site of manor and church

Wharram Percy (site 274) also demonstrates another most important fact: that the site of a medieval manor may have been changed. We do not know where the Anglo-Saxon manor was but it may be assumed to have been near the church. The manor

house was then moved in the twelfth century up on to the hill at the north end of the
then village, and again moved several hundred yards further north in the thirteenth
century (Fig. 25). There were, then, at this early date two attempts by lords to separate
themselves from the peasant-houses which in many villages must have been clustered
round the manor house; this separation is not usually thought of as common until the
emparkings of the eighteenth century. That the sites of manor houses were by no
means static is shown by other sites such as Northolt (site 128, Hurst, 1961) where the
late thirteenth-century manor house was built on an entirely new site (the earlier one is
not known), over the nucleus of the Saxon and early medieval village which must have
been moved down the hill to its present position. We therefore have here not the rebuilding on a virgin site but the deliberate destruction of what must have been the
major part of the village, perhaps as many as twenty houses or more, to construct the
moat. This may be compared with the eleventh-century clearance of town houses by
William the Conqueror to make way for some of his castles.[95] The moat at Northolt
cut away a great deal but the build-up inside for the manor house sealed the remains of
the timber houses of the early village in a way that is most unusual, though more early
settlements are now being found under similar medieval building activities both in the
country[96] and in the towns.[97]

The remarkable picture that emerges is very different from that in towns, where at
Canterbury[98] and Oxford[99] documentary evidence suggests the type of continuity of
early property divisions that is confirmed by recent documentary research and excavation at Winchester.[100] Recent excavations at Lydford, Devon, have shown remarkable
continuity even in unusual kinks in property lines unchanged since the Anglo-Saxon
period.[101] The medieval village seems to have been constantly changing. It was not
simply the rebuilding and realignment of peasant-houses and possible amalgamation
or other changes between individual tofts, but the complete replanning and laying out of
whole sections of villages.

It might be thought that the site of the church would be static, especially in view of
its burial yard but there are at least two examples of churches moving and there may in
fact have been quite a number. At Eaton Socon (site 78, Addyman, 1967) the twelfth-
century castle was built not only over the Late Saxon village but also over the Saxon
church and churchyard. The village was then rebuilt on quite a different site with a

[95] e.g. Archaeological evidence at Northampton, Norwich and Oxford. Domesday Book records
destruction of houses to make way for castles at Wallingford, Shrewsbury and Lincoln. E. M. Jope,
"Late Saxon Pits under Oxford Castle Mound: Excavations in 1952", *Oxoniensia*, XVII–XVIII (1952–53),
79.

[96] Sites 70 and 74.

[97] J. G. Hurst, "Excavations at Barn Road, Norwich, 1954–5", *Norfolk Archaeol.*, XXXIII (1963),
131–32 and in 1968 at Hereford also under the medieval defences, *Current Archaeol.*, I (1968), 242–46.

[98] W. Urry, *Canterbury Under the Angevin Kings* (1967).

[99] H. E. Salter, *Medieval Oxford*, Oxford Hist. Soc., C (1936); *Map of Medieval Oxford* (1934); *Survey
of Oxford*, Ed. W. A. Pantin, Vol. I, Oxford Hist. Soc., new ser., XIV (1960).

[100] M. Biddle, Interim reports *op. cit.* in note 31, p. 85.

[101] P. V. Addyman, Interim note in *Med. Archaeol.*, XII (1968), 155. Full report *Royal Archaeol.
Inst. Monograph* forthcoming.

new church.   At Potterne (site 248, Davey, 1964) a new church was built in the twelfth century on a fresh site again from the Saxon one which remained an open space in this case, as the site was not needed for a different purpose.

In the twelfth century many new churches and chapels were built and excavations have demonstrated that in several cases[102] these were not built on virgin land but, like castles and manor houses, were placed on the sites of peasant-houses which had to be cleared away to make room for them.   We therefore see the Late Saxon and early medieval village as being in a continual state of flux with very substantial replanning of house, manor and church-sites, as well as castles, giving no regard to the previous layout.   It could be argued that sites such as Eaton Socon were cleared for strategic reasons in the siting of the new castle.   This could not apply, however, to the siting of manors or churches.   Dr. Butler has suggested to me that this can be related to the concept of *eigenkirchen* whereby the church, equally with the houses of the village, was the property of the lord and disposable at his will; changes may also reflect transfer of ownership and the combining of previously separate lordships or manors.   All this has been quite unexpected since settlement historians and geographers have expected that the present plan of a village, which maps have often shown goes back unchanged to the sixteenth century,[103] reflects the original Anglo-Saxon settlement.   Geographers have attempted to explain the green villages in terms of events at the time of the original settlement[104] perhaps in early Saxon times, when we may now regard most of them as the result of improving landlords often in the late medieval period.   It is therefore clear that such views must now be suspect until far more excavation is done.   Unfortunately, as we have seen, this will be a very slow process and in the next generation we are not likely to see many large-scale excavations of village sites completed.

A great deal could, however, be accomplished by the studying of plans and aerial photographs of D.M.V.s which, in the light of our new knowledge, can suggest all kinds of changes which may have occurred although they cannot be dated.   The expansion of many Lincolnshire villages can be seen in a quite remarkable way in the fine series of photographs taken by Dr. J. K. S. St. Joseph (Plates 18 and 19).   Planning is often visible with groups of rectangular tofts laid out in areas.   This is clearly planning similar to that at Wharram Percy and should be associated with the population expansion of the twelfth and thirteenth centuries.   At Bardolfeston, Dorset, a plan made by the Royal Commission on Historical Monuments shows a remarkable sequence with an early village comprising a series of rectangular crofts, presumably containing timber buildings, overlaid by a single-street village on a quite different alignment with well preserved stone houses on either side.   We have here a clear demonstration on the ground of one of these fundamental changes in planning; a careful examination of other sites should produce the same type of evidence.   There is much work still to be done, for these possibilities have only very recently been recognised.   So while the study of present plans of villages or of the earthworks of D.M.V.s is dangerous without confirmatory excavation,

---

[102] Sites 20, 75, 87, 90 and 218.

[103] Beresford and St. Joseph, 1958, 7–17.

[104] H. Thorpe, "The Green Villages of County Durham", *Trans. Inst. Brit. Geog.*, xv (1949), 155–80 and "The Green Village as a Distinctive Form of Settlement on the North European Plain", *Soc. Belge d'Études Géog.*, xxx (1961), 93–134.

many useful hypotheses could be formulated by local amateur groups who have not the experience or the resources to excavate.

This pattern of change in the medieval village makes it difficult to draw firm conclusions about village plans either from excavations or the examination of earthworks. For very few surviving villages can we take the picture back before the earliest Tudor maps since later disturbances will in most cases have destroyed the evidence for changes in plan. There should however be some examination of surviving village-greens or other open spaces to see if they have always been open. No intensive study has been made but there are many so-called greens which show clear traces of earlier buildings on them, and it would be important to determine if these are medieval or later so that the planning of the green or other feature could be dated.

It is possible to work out plans of D.M.V.s in different areas at different points in time by planning earthworks in villages which were deserted in different periods. This is almost impossible for early desertions but, with the appearance of substantial village earthworks from the thirteenth century onwards, typical village plans of the fourteenth-century marginal retreat, fifteenth-century sheep depopulations and eighteenth-century emparkings can be obtained. One danger, however, arising from the expansion and contraction of settlement suggested by the historical evidence and demonstrated on such sites as Wawne (site 273), is that one cannot assume that when the village was deserted it was covering the whole area of its visible earthworks. In fact two blocks of house sites might be successive, as at Wawne, so a simple count of tofts cannot show us the number of houses inhabited in any one period. For example at Faxton (site 147), where all the earthworks look basically similar, different parts of the village were deserted at different dates and the most prominent earthworks are not necessarily the latest.

In the earlier periods it would be much easier for fundamental changes in village plan to be made than in later centuries, because of the slight earthworks before the thirteenth century. Where as at Wharram Percy there was no development of toft platforms in the late period, changes in toft boundaries could more easily be made. On the other hand, the increasing depth of sunken roads meant that changes would have to be within their existing framework. More work requires to be done on Midland Clay sites where substantial raised platforms divided by deep ditches would again suggest permanence. It would be fairly easy to amalgamate two tofts (as happened at Faxton, site 147, crofts 1 and 2), but not nearly so easy to replan the whole village. This may well be why very few Midland sites show evidence of a regular grid layout. We might assume, despite the grid plans of Alfredian towns at the end of the ninth century, that most early villages would grow up in a fairly haphazard way, or at best with a general layout in rows as at Sutton Courtenay (site 6) without any exact regimentation of the tofts and house positions.

Most Midland sites show a general rectangular network of sunken roads often pursuing a fairly sinuous course between a general rectangular layout of tofts made more irregular by these curving roads. On the other hand there clearly was some planning in regular street plans such as that at Baggrave, Leicestershire (Hoskins, 1956, 118), which has high raised platforms on either side of a wide sunken street. Recent excavations at Faxton have shown that an area of four tofts remained basically the same over quite a long period but that when the ditches between the tofts were recut they were on slightly different lines without any basic replanning.

A medieval village in which most of the villagers were tenants could easily be replanned on the order of the lord. This would be very difficult in a town where the freeholders of individual burgage plots could successfully block any improvement scheme in the days before compulsory purchase. It does not however explain why seigneurs went to such trouble and presumably expense. The laying out of the completely new blocks at Wharram or Wawne and the apparent complete new planning of Bardolfeston must have been major communal efforts. It would be valuable to inquire what type of landowner was involved in some of these major changes and to see if he was trying to emulate the regular planning shown in the new *bastides*[105] which they would see when they went to market. Or were in fact some of these replanned villages on estates of kings or lay and ecclesiastical lords who were planning towns? Mr. Biddle for example has suggested that the Abbot of Ramsey might have been fortifying his villages *c.* 1140.[106] This type of activity could lead to fundamental replanning or the concentration of a scattered settlement into a restricted area.

In view of these problems and changes it is premature to attempt to list village forms and suggest whether they are the result of regional or cultural differences, though this should be attempted in the future. There are in this section far more suggestions for research than in the earlier ones on excavation. This shows how much the emphasis has been on the actual peasant-house itself. More excavators are now trying to examine the houses in the wider context of the tofts in which they are situated but very few have attempted to study the whole village plan and its morphology, much less go beyond into the open fields and try to work out the complex events which must have taken place here as well. In very few cases, out of nearly 200 sites excavated, has there been any attempt to place the village in its complete setting of fields by survey and the examination of aerial photographs,[107] a subject that will be discussed further in the next chapter.

IV. GENERAL ECONOMIC DEVELOPMENT

The manor

It is not the place here to attempt a history of the development of the manor house, but clearly the peasant-houses cannot be studied in isolation and the development of the manor site is of the greatest importance in understanding the history of the rest of the village. In its simplest terms the excavation of a manor house can demonstrate the changing living standards of the lord of the village which ought to have influence on the village as a whole. If the lord is prosperous and has many properties, if he is poor with only one manor, if the village is divided between two or more resident lords, or if the village belongs to a more powerful class altogether with the possibility of no resident lord but only a steward or bailiff: all this may be reflected in the development of the village

[105] M. W. Beresford, *New Towns of the Middle Ages* (1967).

[106] M. Biddle, "The Excavation of a Motte and Bailey Castle at Therfield, Hertfordshire", *J. Brit. Archaeol. Assoc.*, 3rd ser., xxvii (1964), 67–68.

[107] Sites 67, 141, 147, 157, 162 and 274. Surveys have also been made by the D.M.V.R.G. at Cestersover, Warws. and Martinsthorpe, Rutland (see Fig. 12).

plan. Much of this would be apparent in the historical evidence but only archaeology can demonstrate the physical consequences with, for example, a new family coming into the village completely changing the site of the manor house. Excavation of the manor house will show the development of the manorial house type from the early hall, usually almost by itself, through the larger thirteenth- and fourteenth-century complexes with attached solar and kitchen block, to the larger courtyard plans of the late medieval period.[108] All these changes are likely to have influence right down the social scale as has already been suggested, with the emerging yeoman farmer trying to copy at least some of the ways of upper classes in the development of his courtyard farm.

A study of the plan and changes in the farm buildings within the manorial compound or moat will also have considerable significance not only in assessing the prosperity of the village but in giving clues as to the actual economy and the emphasis on different farming activities. The foundations of the large barn at Wharram Percy, over 30 m. long (Fig. 25, building N), for example, must show considerable prosperity for the time when this was built. The main difficulty is that with funds for research as they are at present, and as they are likely to be in the foreseeable future, the prospect of any large scale excavation of an associated manor and village site is most unlikely. The D.M.V.R.G. has been concentrating on the examination of peasant houses and tofts on village sites. These are complex enough and, with only a short season possible each year, it may take many years to excavate a single house-site. At Wharram Percy two house complexes have now been excavated and it is possible that the time has now come to study the late manor house and its associated remains since these must throw light on the decline of the village in its later years after its greatest period of expansion. A further intricacy here, however, is the fact that underneath the manor house there are the remains of a very extensive Iron Age settlement which although of very considerable interest archaeologically, has no bearing on the medieval village as it is several hundred mètres from the Saxon nucleus and there is as yet no firm evidence for Roman structures which might give a chance of proving the continuity of settlement in the valley.

The church

A most important further research project at Wharram Percy (site 274A) has been the investigation of the parish church. The partly ruined fabric itself shows a very great complexity of building sequences. As the covering plaster has been removed inside many straight joints and other changes, such as blocked windows, are visible, showing how much evidence is lost in many parish churches where none of these features is observable except during periods of repair. The excavation of the church, however, has shown an even more complicated story, starting with the discovery of an early stone church, which may be pre-Danish (Fig. 30). Even if it is in fact tenth century (as only further excavation will show) there are two eighth-century *sceattas* from the church-yard at least proving settlement at that period even if there was no church or preaching cross there. In the Norman period there was a massive rebuilding of the church (Pl. 20) and in the later twelfth and early thirteenth centuries aisles and side chapels were

---

[108] There is unfortunately as yet no synthesis of Manor House excavation but see Margaret Wood, *The English Medieval House* (1956).

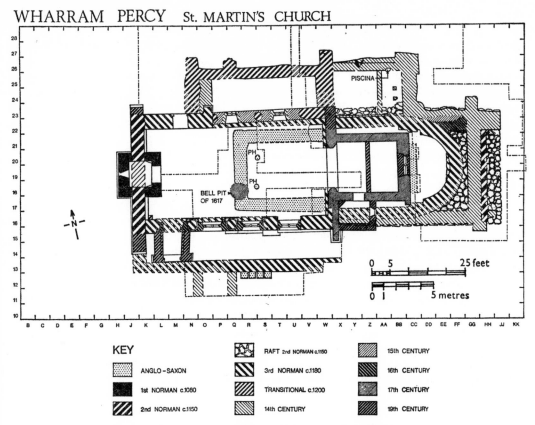

KEY

ANGLO-SAXON

1st NORMAN c.1080

2nd NORMAN c.1150

RAFT 2nd NORMAN c.1150

3rd NORMAN c.1180

TRANSITIONAL c.1200

14th CENTURY

15th CENTURY

16th CENTURY

17th CENTURY

19th CENTURY

Fig. 30. Wharram Percy, Yorkshire East Riding

Plan of the parish church showing the expansion from the small Saxon church to the large medieval church with nave, chancel (see Plate 20), north and south aisles, and chapels at the peak of the prosperity of the village in the fourteenth century. In the fifteenth and sixteenth centuries the aisles and chapels were pulled down and in the seventeenth century the chancel was halved in size after the desertion of four of the five townships in the parish, see p. 132.

built. These clearly reflect the greatest expansion of the parish which then comprised five different townships. In the late medieval period the church was reduced. The aisles and chapels were gradually demolished and the chancel halved, leaving by Tudor times only the Norman nave with a truncated chancel. The decay and desertion of Wharram Percy and three of its attendant settlements is therefore clearly demonstrated: the standing remains and the buried foundations reflect the growth, expansion and contraction of the village. It is hoped that the Ministry of Public Building and Works will take the site into guardianship and preserve both the earthworks and the remains of the church since the site should make a very satisfactory demonstration of the development of a medieval village, something that cannot be done in any surviving village with its modern additions and changes. Twenty-two churches and chapels have been excavated on D.M.V. sites:[109] for example, Mr. Biddle has shown the similar considerable complexity of the parish church at Cuddington (site 214). But, as with manor houses, it is difficult to excavate further on any one site, and where churches have been excavated it has often meant that nothing else has been done so that the church and its development remain out of context. This constant change in a church is just as likely on town sites as in villages as Mr. Biddle has also shown at Winchester where St. Mary's church, on the Brooks site, went through at least twelve phases between 1275 and 1470, not counting possible earlier Saxon periods not yet excavated.[110]

Medieval population

The only way to obtain some idea of what the medieval peasant was really like is by the examination of burials. There are representations in illuminated manuscripts which give information on dress, hair styles and general appearance but these cannot give us the exact height, while other evidence, such as suits of armour, has suggested erroneously that the medieval population was short. To get useful results a large statistical sample is essential and this is usually difficult to obtain, for unlike the Continent, where the complete excavation of medieval churches with all their burials has become commonplace since the war,[111] conditions in England make this rarely possible. There have been cases in the City of London and in other cities where church sites have been excavated before development but most of these contain sequences of burials at least up until the nineteenth century so that, not only have earlier burials been much disturbed, but it is often impossible to date the discoveries except by a very wide margin.[112]

As with so many other subjects it is therefore only in the churchyard of a D.M.V. that it is possible to excavate a large sample of the medieval peasant population uncontaminated by later burials or disturbance. This has so far only been done on three sites on a large scale, but, as the results from these excavations will take up to five years to evaluate, we must await the result before accumulating more material. At Clopton (site 20) 110 burials were lifted and are in process of study by Dr. D. Hughes. At Cuddington (site 214) 100 skeletons, sealed by Henry VIII's palace of Nonsuch were excavated, while at Wharram Percy (site 274A) the largest group has been uncovered. Nearly 300 burials were recovered from a section of the northern part of the churchyard. These two groups are being studied by Mr. D. R. Brothwell.[113] The Wharram Percy group will be of great value in understanding the biology of the medieval inhabitants of north-east England. It will be possible to compare this peasant population with the

---

[109] Sites 12, 17, 20, 62, 63, 75, 87, 90, 94, 96, 122, 158, 182, 214, 217, 218, 219, 225, 245, 248, 249, 274 and 285.

[110] M. Biddle, "Excavations at Winchester 1967: Seventh Interim Report", *Antiq. Journ.*, XLIX, (1969), 305 and Fig. 2.

[111] Many examples especially in Germany and the Low Countries. cf. *Kirche und Burg*, Kunst und Altertum am Rheim, VIII (1962) and especially G. P. Fehring, "Frühmittelalterliche Kirchenbauten unter St. Dionysius zu Esslingen am Neckar", *Germania*, XLIV (1966), 354–74; with its remarkable photographs of the complete excavation of a standing church.

[112] W. F. Grimes, *The Excavation of Roman and Medieval London* (1968).

[113] I am grateful to Mr. D. R. Brothwell for supplying this interim report on work so far, in advance of its full publication.

urban groups from nearby Scarborough and then with data from other periods and places. By such temporal and spatial comparisons a picture of the morphological, genetic and disease differences which occurred in earlier British peoples will be slowly built up.

The Wharram Percy skeletons

Preliminary results from a study of the Wharram Percy material suggest that, in terms of body size and shape, they appear to have been a fairly robust community with a mean stature for males of 1·68 m. which is much larger than had been previously assumed. As in many medieval groups from other types of site, brachycephaly was common and this contrasts sharply with the Anglo-Saxons. The reason for this marked change within a matter of a few centuries is still a complete puzzle but the finding of this same trait in an isolated village population does suggest that the changes were not due to the possible bias of town and monastic sites where the many Norman monks, merchants and others may have mixed with the earlier populations. This is one of the most important results and requires further study before anything but extremely tentative explanations can be put forward.

Signs of disease are not uncommon in early British skeletons and these have been noted in detail in the Wharram Percy bones. In particular rheumatic disease (osteoarthritis) was common, not only in the vertebral column, but in certain other joints. Dental troubles were the rule rather than the exception, the provisional frequency for dental caries being 8·1% of all teeth examined. This frequency is far less than for modern Britons, but more than total British Neolithic, Bronze Age, Iron Age and Anglo-Saxon figures. Surprisingly there is evidence that this medieval percentage was less than that for the Romano-Britons on the present evidence. One of the more important results of Mr. Brothwell's excavation has been the recovery of gall and bladder stones. These are often missed by excavators and it is clear that a considerable amount of extra information can be obtained if the burials are excavated and lifted by a trained physical anthropologist.

The Wharram Percy churchyard excavation has in addition confirmed that the average depth of medieval peasant burial was about 0·6 m. as had been suspected from other excavations. There was no evidence for clearance of earlier burials to a charnel house. Burials were always laid out east-west, and it must be assumed that there were markers of wood to help the orderly arrangement of the cemetery. Later burials were then cut into the earlier ones but it is hard to estimate the length of time before an area was used for a second time. Up to four levels of burials were found on the eastern part of the site where the sloping hillside had been built up.

Extent of cultivation

Modern economic developments, especially the great changeover from grass to arable in many parts of the country where whole areas had been grazed since the late medieval desertions, have meant that fewer and fewer sites of D.M.V.s are preserved intact. Sites are being destroyed at an increasing rate (Pl. 16) and the D.M.V.R.G. has drawn up a memorandum suggesting that 60 sites should be preserved and that a number of these should be taken into guardianship by the Ministry of Public Building and Works.[114]   Only in this way can future generations study them.   We are very lucky in this country that the study of D.M.V.s started just as the destruction was getting under way, since abroad most of this levelling has already taken place and there are very few D.M.V.s in the rest of Europe which are visible as earthworks.   This process of destruction applies even more to the areas surrounding the villages, many of which only survive as islands of grass in a sea of arable completely out of context.   There is in fact no medieval village surviving or deserted in lowland England where the complete earthworks of the village and its associated fields can be seen.   It is only in marginal areas like Dartmoor[115] that the evidence is still intact although even here destruction is increasing apace.

We are fortunate to have the R.A.F. vertical air photographs which were taken for the whole country during the 1940's.   They are of varying quality but for most areas the whole medieval landscape can be observed with its ridge and furrow in a way that now, only twenty years after, is no longer possible.   Where the surface marks of cultivation of the medieval fields have already been destroyed they are often still visible as crop or soil marks, and at a few sites a complete plan has been made of the whole parish to demonstrate the extent of cultivation (Fig. 12 and note 107).   These show that every possible part of the area has been under the plough at some time, though not necessarily all at once.   This evidence demonstrates very clearly the tremendous expansion of settlement and the pressure on land in the century before the fourteenth-century plagues.   The plotting of larger areas of ridge and furrow on a smaller scale has been attempted by geographers in various counties[116] but there has been hardly any excavation.   This is something which is badly needed but we just do not yet know how much this may help in elucidating some of the problems of medieval ploughing and how ridge and furrow was produced and operated.   There are only a few cases so far known where thirteenth-century ridge and furrow is fossilised without any later disturbance. In most cases although the association of the ridge and furrow with D.M.V. earthworks makes it almost certain that this is medieval, and has not been changed since the fifteenth century, this cannot be proved definitely to the satisfaction of Dr. E. Kerridge and his school.   At Whatborough the Elizabethan surveyor demonstrated that the land around the D.M.V. had once been arable open field and witnesses in the law suit stated that "the greatest parte of Whadborowe lyeth by ridge and furrowe" (Beresford, 1957, 116).   At West Stow (site 210A) there is a large area of ridge and furrow which overlies the Saxon village site, demonstrating a change of settlement site, as was the case at Maxey (site 150), but here the ridge and furrow was destroyed by later ploughing. At West Stow the whole area was covered by a sand-blow in the fourteenth century, further evidence of changing climatic conditions at this difficult period, completely sealing and preserving the ridge and furrow.   A section of this is now in process of ex-

---

[114] See Appendix I, pp. 303–310.

[115] For example Challacombe, Devon, with over 400 acres of medieval lynchets, A. H. Shorter, "Hut Circles and Ancient Fields near Challacombe, Dartmoor", *Proc. Devon Archaeol. Explor. Soc.*, IV (1951), 102–05.

[116] W. R. Mead, "Ridge and Furrow in Buckinghamshire", *Geog. Journ.*, CXX (1954), 34–42 and N. Harrison, W. R. Mead and D. Pannett, "A Midland Ridge and Furrow Map", *Geog. Journ.*, CXXXI (1965), 366–69.

cavation and this may lead to important results. In particular it is hoped to locate the headland and see how this was linked or fitted in with the ridges. There are several cases where ridge and furrow is clearly medieval since it is sealed by datable features (Beresford and St. Joseph, 1958, Figs. 24 and 98). Since then there have been further examples such as Mr. P. A. Barker's discovery that the castle of Hen Domen, in Montgomeryshire, which was built in 1070, was placed on ridge and furrow which continues under the outer bank. This is so far the earliest demonstrable example. Archaeology therefore has much to offer in the further elucidation of this vexed subject and in time more clear Saxon evidence may be forthcoming. There is already the evidence from Gwithian for a narrow type of ridge and furrow cultivation in the Dark Ages[117] and there must be other examples. It can however already be said that ridge and furrow is pre-Conquest but not how much further back it may go. Where ridge and furrow has been found cutting across earlier sites the furrows seem to be fixed in one position suggesting that once formed there was little change, unlike the village plan itself.

From the actual village sites too, from excavated buildings and small finds, there is much to be learnt about the economy. The finding of corn-drying ovens, even if one did not have the fields, is clear evidence at sites such as Hound Tor (site 38) for extensive arable cultivation on Dartmoor at the peak of the medieval expansion in the thirteenth century. The interpretation of barns for grain storage, however, is a more difficult matter, for unless they are burnt down and remains of charred grain survive it can never be quite certain what was stored there. In cases like Muscott (site 151), where there was a raised floor, the most likely explanation is a granary. From the peasant houses themselves the best evidences for arable cultivation are the numerous remains of hand querns for grinding corn. It could be argued that other substances were ground, or that grain purchased from other manors was being imported into an entirely pastoral or industrial community, but querns are so common that in most rural cases one must assume actual arable cultivation, which is of course almost always supported by other evidence such as ridge and furrow. One thing which is clear is that the manorial embargo on the individual grinding of flour, which should have been done at the manorial mill only, was either not by any means universal or was not very successfully enforced, as is in fact suggested by the documentary evidence.[118]

Finds of large iron objects such as ploughshares are very rare and therefore provide little evidence for plough types in different areas. Other parts of plough fittings are doubtless found but it is very difficult to distinguish them from objects belonging to other farm implements and carts or even door fittings. There are finds rarely of scythes, more commonly of sickles, but these could be used just as well for grass as other crops.

Animals

On most sites, after pottery the most common finds are animal bones. It should, therefore, be possible to say a great deal about the animals kept and eaten in the medieval period.[119] Unfortunately the bones found are often very fragmentary and

[117] P. J. Fowler and A. C. Thomas, "Arable Fields of the Pre-Norman Period at Gwithian", *Cornish Archaeol.*, 1 (1962), 61–84.
[118] H. S. Bennett, *Life on the English Manor* (1937), 130.
[119] I am indebted to Dr. M. L. Ryder for his advice on this section.

scattered or do not survive in the acid soil (e.g. in the south-west); it is therefore difficult to obtain sufficient examples or complete specimens for measurement, and it is also
only recently that bone specialists have worked out the techniques to give a fuller
account of the implications of the finds.   For this reason many excavation reports consist only of a series of bone lists which have little value for economic history.   In the few
instances where there have been adequate reports an important conclusion has been the
suggestion that most of the stock was not killed off each winter.[120]   It seems to have
been possible to keep most of them alive through the winter.   The age at which sheep
were killed seems to vary considerably.   At Wharram[121] the main bulk was apparently
slaughtered at two years while at Upton[122] sheep were kept longer so that their main
purpose could have been for wool rather than meat.   Most cattle, it seems, were killed
at two years and it has been suggested that the cattle, although fewer in number, would
have provided a larger proportion of the diet than sheep as each would have more meat
suitable for eating.[123]   Some cattle were kept till a greater age.   These were presumably the draught animals for ploughing.   Most pigs were killed at about eighteen
months for meat, the fewer older ones presumably being kept for breeding.   In general,
most of the domestic animals of each species were small in size.   On some sites which
were clearly fully arable, as is shown by the complete coverage of the parish by ridge and
furrow, there is a very large proportion of sheep, see Table XV, which suggests that the
economy can never have been entirely arable and that more sheep must have been kept
than could be grazed on the fallow field.   In the earlier period this suggests infield-
outfield cultivation with the more distant or marginal lands being ploughed only occasionally, with sheep run over them a lot of the time, at least on the chalk or limestone
uplands.   We have very little evidence so far from Midland Clay sites.   In the later
medieval period, on sites such as Wharram, it suggests a gradual change from arable to
sheep which is confirmed by documentary evidence for waste.   This may well mean
that the late fifteenth-century change from arable to pasture was not so sudden as
might have been thought but was a gradual process linked with the retreat from the
marginal land and the increasing demand for wool for the rising cloth industry.   Other
animals included domestic fowl, goose, dog, cat and some rabbit remains.   Wild animals are very rare on village sites; this is more likely to be due to their absence in areas
fully cleared of forest, or lack of spare time, rather than any restrictions placed on hunting.   In fact hunting arrows are fairly common.[124]

Typical proportions of food livestock from those sites where a statistical analysis is
possible are shown on Table XV.   There are only two Saxon sites with significant results so far (Cassington and Maxey).   Maxey is not much help since the proportions of
sheep and cattle were almost equal.   At Cassington there was an unexpectedly large

[120] This has also recently been demonstrated for the prehistoric period, E. S. Higgs and J. P. White,
"Autumn Killing", *Antiquity*, xxxvii (1963), 282–89.

[121] Interim report in M. L. Ryder, "Livestock Remains from Four Medieval Sites in Yorkshire",
Agric. Hist. Rev., ix (1961), 105–10.   Full report in *Soc. Med. Archaeol.   Monograph* on Wharram
Percy, forthcoming.

[122] S. Yealland and E. S. Higgs, "The Economy", in *Hilton and Rahtz*, 1966, 139–43.

[123] *Ibid.*; *Addyman*, 1964, 69; Interim reports on Gomeldon by R. Harcourt (references under Site
244).

[124] Sites 5A, 67, 150, 182, 227, 244, 257, 268 and 289.

amount of cattle since it is now thought that many of these early settlements were based on a sheep economy. It is hoped that this will be clarified by work on major groups from sites like West Stow (site 210) which is now in progress. It will be seen that on all the other village sites, with the exception of Seacourt (site 5A), sheep predominate. Data from three other sites are also added to the table so that these results can be compared with those from monastic and town sites. At Pontefract the proportions are

TABLE XV

Percentage of bones of animals used as food found at various excavations

Site number	Site name	Sheep	Ox	Pig
SAXON VILLAGES				
150	Maxey[a]	43	44	13
172	Cassington[b]	14	52	34
MEDIEVAL VILLAGES				
67	Upton[c]	78	18	4
244	Gomeldon[d]	77	14	9
186	Martinsthorpe[e]	73	20	7
274	Wharram Percy[f]	61	31	8
5A	Seacourt[g]	41	46	13
MONASTIC SITES				
Yorks.	Pontefract[h]	47	34	19
Yorks.	Kirkstall[i]	5	92	3
MEDIEVAL TOWN				
York	Petergate[j]	32	57	11

[a] D. Seddon, D. Calvorcoressi and C. Cooper, with E. S. Higgs, "The Fauna", in *Addyman*, 1964, 69–71.

[b] Figures by Margaret Jope quoted by *Wilson*, 1962.

[c] Yealland and Higgs, *op. cit.* in note 122.

[d] Figures for 1964, other years similar, by R. Harcourt in stencilled annual interim reports (references under Site 244).

[e] Miss J. E. King, in *Wacher*, 1963–64, 17.

[f] Figures from Area 10, M. L. Ryder, *op. cit.*, in note 121.

[g] Margaret Jope in *Biddle*, 1961–62, 197–201.

[h] M. L. Ryder, "Animal Remains" in C. V. Bellamy, "Pontefract Priory Excavations", *Pub. Thoresby Soc.*, XLIX (1965), 132–36.

[i] M. L. Ryder, "The Animal Remains found at Kirkstall Abbey", *Agric. Hist. Rev.*, VII (1959), 1–5.

[j] M. L. Ryder, "The Animal Remains from Petergate, York", *Yorks. Archaeol. Journ.*, forthcoming.

similar to village sites, but at Kirkstall material from the kitchen shows a vast preponderance of cattle, though this figure clearly represents the animals eaten rather than
the numbers kept.   The York figures also show quite a large ratio of cattle to sheep.
We therefore badly need more figures of this kind before firm conclusions can be drawn.
Extensive work is now in progress with new methods and it is hoped there will be a
major breakthrough in the study of this subject in the next five years, helped by the
large quantities of bones now being produced from many sites all over the country.   In
this study bones from village sites are likely to give much better evidence as to the proportions of different animals kept than do the more specialist groups from town, manor
or monastic sites.

Animal bones are not, however, the only archaeological traces of the presence of
animals.   Besides byres with their drains and mangers, metal objects suggest animal
presence but not of course numbers.   Horseshoes are a common find[125] as are spurs[126]
which might be thought surprising in peasant-house excavations.   Stirrups are much
more rare, with only one so far recorded (site 50).   The whole question of horses and
their use in the medieval peasant economy is one which requires much more study.
The high proportion of horse bones on some sites, as much as 20% in some levels at
Wharram Percy, is hard to explain, even taking into account the large numbers of
horse bones resulting from the burial of a single animal.   Harness is difficult to distinguish from furniture and door fittings but is definitely present at some sites.[127]   Small
bells from cattle, sheep or packhorses are fairly common and there is now no doubt of
the medieval age of those without the initials which are so typical of the seventeenth and
eighteenth centuries.[128]

Iron-working

Metal small-finds of iron or bronze are the next most common find after pottery and
bone and this raises the question of local iron-working in the medieval village.   Fragments of iron slag are common on many house-sites though there are often single examples rather than large groups.   It has been said that this implies evidence of iron
smelting but the slag from this basic process has often not been fully differentiated from
that produced by the reworking of iron.   To what extent iron-working was carried out
by a single smith in each village, by travelling tinkers or by individual villagers themselves is a subject about which very little is known.   This is not helped by the fact that
iron-working hearths were very small flimsy affairs not leaving much trace and therefore
examples may have been missed.   Only at Braggington (site 188) so far has clear evidence for iron-working been found in a peasant house on a village site.   It may be that
other examples have not been recognised but certainly no massive smithy with industrial remains similar to those often found on manorial and monastic sites has been
located.   This may mean that this important activity was confined to the manorial
complex.   Of other industrial activities little trace has been found though Mr. Rahtz
suggests that the lower end of his long-house at Upton (site 67A) was used for fulling.

[125] Sites 5A, 18, 27, 50, 52, 67, 121, 227, 244, 268, 274 and 279.
[126] Sites 5A, 45, 50, 121, 147, 159, 192, 227 and 268.
[127] Sites 5A, 50 and 227.
[128] Sites 5A, 67, 147 and 226.

Each village would have its windmill[129] or watermill[130] but few have been excavated and none of these has been linked with excavated village sites.

Pottery

The large bulk of small finds from the peasant-houses are more humdrum items of household utensils or minutiae of dress. Pottery is by far the most common object found and the stratified sherds form the basic dating evidence for most village sites. Unfortunately pottery is so little studied in many areas that the coarse wares cannot be closely dated. It is also now realised that many types of ware were made over a very long period, especially the fabrics, so that the body fragments, without datable features of rims or decoration, may date to any time within a period of 100 years or more.[131] This makes it impossible to date precisely the many rebuildings since there is no hope of dating pottery as closely as 25 years. It is therefore only possible to suggest that each period is of roughly the same length, which might not be correct: some buildings could have lasted twice as long as others. Most coarse unglazed cooking vessels had a distribution of not more than about 30 km. and were therefore very regionalised. Highly decorated glazed jugs in the thirteenth and fourteenth centuries often had a much wider market, travelling anything up to 160 km. or more.[132] In some cases if seaborne trade was possible, as with the products of the Scarborough kilns, the pots could travel 500 km. up into Scotland and down to Sussex.[133] It is by no means uncommon to find good quality glazed jugs in peasant-houses and the proportion of these if often no different from those in a manor house. The average on most sites is about 10% but on village sites the proportions vary from 3% at Holworth (site 45) to 13% at Upton (site 67). This is likely to depend to some extent on the prosperity of the individual peasant whose house is being excavated but even on a large prosperous manor there was sometimes only 2% of highly glazed pottery (Hurst, 1961, 276) so these figures must be viewed with caution. Highly decorated glazed jugs would be obtained either from travelling potters selling their wares or, more likely, by the peasants attending the regular markets and fairs of the district where these wares would be sold. It is possible that every peasant would aim to possess one of these fine jugs in the same way that, in the nineteenth century, one might expect to find a Staffordshire figure on the mantlepiece of each cottage. In fact, although we now regard these jugs as rather fine examples of individual craftsmen potters, it may well be that we should regard them in the medieval period as similar to the plaster animals and other trivia purchased or won

---

[129] M. Posnansky, "The Lamport Post Mill", *Journ. Northants. Nat. Hist. Field Club*, XXXIII (1956), 66–79, with bibliography of earlier excavations and references and S. V. Pearce, "A Medieval Windmill, Honey Hill, Dogsthorpe", *Proc. Cambs. Antiq. Soc.*, LIX (1966), 95–104.

[130] The only medieval watermill fully excavated is by Mr. P. Mayes at the Knights Templars site of South Witham, Lincolnshire. Interim note and plan in *Med. Archaeol.*, XI (1967), 275 and Fig. 77. B. Hope-Taylor excavated an impressive middle Saxon watermill at Old Windsor (site 9).

[131] J. G. Hurst, "White Castle and the Dating of Medieval Pottery", *Med. Archaeol.*, VI–VII (1962–63), 135–55.

[132] E. M. Jope, "Whittington Court Roman Villa", *Trans. Bristol and Gloucs. Archaeol. Soc.*, LXXI (1952), 71–75 and Fig. 11.

[133] G. C. Dunning, "Report on Scarborough Ware Found at Kildrummy Castle", *Proc. Soc. Antiq. Scot.*, XCVI (1962–63), 233–36.

at present-day fairs. Certainly good quality glazed pottery was not at the peak of the social scale where more precious metal vessels would have been in daily use at manorial, monastic and royal tables.

Many medieval pottery kilns have been excavated[134] but often the work is restricted in surviving towns or villages. As with so many other topics it is only on D.M.V. sites that there is a good chance of excavating a kiln not disturbed by any later features. More important though is the possibility of expanding the excavation to include not just the kiln but the potters' workshop, house and in fact the whole industrial complex. Four such sites have been investigated, at Potters Marston (site 102) the kiln only was excavated but at Olney Hyde (site 15) a whole toft was cleared. Unfortunately the site had been too badly ploughed for many structures besides the kiln to be interpreted. At Lyveden (site 49a), however, the remains were better preserved and a major excavation is now in progress to study an industrial pottery site in detail. Already two kilns and a potter's workshop have been excavated. In 1968 a pottery kiln was excavated at Knighton, Isle of Wight (not included in the Gazetteer).

Trade

Decorated pottery does confirm that the medieval village economy was by no means closed. Historians now realise this and manorial self-sufficiency is no longer a dogma in textbooks, but it is important that archaeology confirms the wide contacts which the medieval villager had either by going himself to fairs and markets or by buying from travelling merchants and pedlars. It makes one realise that he was not perhaps so cut off in an isolated valley like Wharram Percy or Upton. In fact the idea of isolation is often over-emphasised for us by the lack of tarmac roads to many D.M.V.s. Besides the pottery which he obtained from long distances, other items brought in might include sea fish from quite a considerable distance. This was clearly a necessity due to the Friday rule for eating fish, but the needs should normally have been satisfied by the local fishpond of which there would usually be one in each village. Finds of cod bones at Wharram Percy have shown that even the humble peasant was eating sea fish as well, at least 30 km. from the coast. Coal has been found on many village sites (see p. 98) not only near to where coal might outcrop, and therefore be easily collected, but at Wharram Percy where the nearest coal would have to come at least 100 km. from the West Riding. The high cost of carting stone, which made even the building of castles and abbeys a difficult business unless there was a convenient waterway, makes it very hard to understand the economics of transporting coal overland to Wharram. It can hardly have been for ordinary domestic consumption and the frequent finding of coal fragments with slag suggests some industrial process. But it would surely have been more economical to make the iron tools nearer to coal and iron supplies rather than transport the bulky raw materials. The most remarkable trading of all, however, was the vast trade in lava quern stones from the Eifel region of the Rhineland.[135] This hard stone

---

[134] J. W. G. Musty, The Medieval Pottery Industry in Great Britain, unpublished M.A. thesis, University of Bristol (1966).

[135] F. Hörter, F. X. Michels and J. Röder, "Die Geschichte der Basaltlave-Industrie von Mayen und Niedermendig", *Jahrbuch für Geschichte und Kultur des Mittelrheins*, II–III (1950–51), 1–32 and VI–VII (1954–55), 7–32.

was eminently suited for this purpose, and was in fact traded over a very long period of prehistory and the Roman period, and especially in Anglo-Saxon and medieval times[136] when there are few sites which do not produce at least a few fragments. It is the very great weight of these quern stones, many of which were 0·6 m. across, which makes the mind boggle at the transport problems involved. They would be of the right size to travel on pack-animals, so no carts or even roads would be necessary, but the cost of bringing them from Germany, even though the major part would be by sea, must have been large and one wonders how the medieval peasant could afford it. Other similar finds include Devon slate[137] and Purbeck marble mortars which also travelled quite large distances.[138] The problem of schist whetstones[139] and whether they came from France or Scotland[140] is complicated by the fact that the schist may have been collected as glacial erratics.

Household activities

Minutiae of dress, especially buckles,[141] are common finds as are knives[142] and other simple household objects and implements. Other activities in the home and the presence of sheep and wool are demonstrated by the finding of spindle whorls,[143] bone weaving tools, thread pickers as a feature of Anglo-Saxon sites,[144] and shears.[145] For the actual loom itself there is no evidence in the medieval period after the introduction of the horizontal type. In the Anglo-Saxon period the vertical loom was in use and the two characteristic post-holes are a feature of several sunken-huts. The warp was, however, held by a series of clay loomweights. These may be divided into three types[146] and are amongst the commonest Anglo-Saxon domestic finds. In fact they are found from 35 sites in addition to many of those in the gazetteer showing clear evidence of settlement, but they are often found without associated structures. Sewing is indicated by the discovery of needles, thimbles and scissors. In fact by gradually accumulating the small bits of evidence from many excavations it is possible to build up a very reasonable picture of daily life to supplement and expand what we already

[136] For discussion see *Hurst*, 1961, 279 and *Holden*, 1963, 156–57 with documentary references to their importation. For terminology see M. Biddle, *The Journ. Brit. Archaeol. Assoc.*, XXVII (1964), 82.

[137] E. M. Jope and G. C. Dunning, "The Use of Blue Slate for Roofing in Medieval England", *Antiq. Journ.*, XXXIV (1954), 209–17; E. W. Holden, "Slate Roofing in Medieval Sussex", *Sussex Archaeol. Coll.*, CIII (1965), 67–78; J. W. Murray, "The Origin of Some Medieval Roofing Slates from Sussex", *Ibid.*, 79–82.

[138] E.g. to Seacourt in Berkshire, *Biddle*, 1961–62; for sea trade see G. C. Dunning, "Medieval Pottery and Stone Mortars Imported to Aardenburg from England and France", *Berich. Rijksdienst Oudheidkundig Bodemonderzook*, XV–XVI (1965–66), 205–07 and Fig. 13, Map.

[139] G. C. Dunning, "Whetstones", in Kathleen M. Kenyon, *Excavations at the Jewry Wall Site, Leicester*, Soc. Antiq. Res. Rep. XV (1948), 230–32, with list and map.

[140] June E. Morey and K. C. Dunham, "A Petrographical Study of Medieval Hones from Yorkshire", *Proc. Yorks. Geol. Soc.* XXIX (1953), 141–48.

[141] Sites 5A, 50, 52, 67, 117, 121, 159, 192, 227, 270 and 274.

[142] Sites 5A, 6, 35, 50, 100, 121, 147, 150, 227, 268, 270 and 274.

[143] Sites 21, 35, 45, 50, 67, 100, 150, 192, 227 and 274.

[144] Sites 5A, 6, 56, 100, 150, 205, 210 and 284. Identified in *Dunning*, 1952, 50.

[145] e.g. Maxey, site 150.

[146] J. G. Hurst, "Middle Saxon Pottery", *Med. Archaeol.*, III (1959), 23–25 and Fig. 6.

know from the documentary evidence.   All the items so far described are those which last, but one must also consider the objects made of wood, leather, and basketry which very rarely survive.   Charred wooden vessels are sometimes found (site 37) but no substantial waterlogged deposit has so far been found in a village site which might produce other perishable items.   In the Anglo-Saxon period there are grain impressions in pots (Wilson, 1962).   Examples of charred grain are found occasionally.   At Wharram Percy these were mainly barley, as might be expected on an upland site.   The actual material used for thatch can also be determined from burnt remains.

Ecology

   To build up an adequate picture of the medieval ecology, however, pollen analysis is necessary.   Unfortunately on none of the sites so far excavated has this been done and where it would have been possible the conditions have not been conducive to the survival of pollen.   There is an urgent need to find a site where this might be possible, to fill out the picture and tell us the types of plants and trees which were growing in the medieval period with some idea of their frequency.   The results of such a study could tell us a great deal about the landscape and the flora present at different times.   The prehistoric period has been fully worked out for many areas but in England this has not been carried forward for the medieval period.   Many problems such as the extent of the return to wild vegetation following the end of Roman rule and the areas and speed of the Saxon clearance could be worked out.   It should be possible to prove the suggested complete removal of all forest in many areas and show to what extent there was a natural regeneration of woodland, or whether most of the waste was pasture. in the economic decline of the later medieval period.[147]   There could also be much information gained about the various cereal crops and their associated weeds, together with evidence for subsidiary sources of fuel, which could all make a great difference to our understanding of the medieval way of life, especially if it was done for whole parishes on a large scale.

   [147] For evidence from Wales see p. 264 below.

CHAPTER THREE

Gazetteer of Excavations at Medieval House and Village Sites (to 1968)

J. G. HURST

I

This gazetteer of excavations comprises work known at those occupation sites in England which are datable to between the end of the Roman period in the early fifth century and the beginning of the Tudor "Great Rebuilding", *c.* 1570.

The list extends beyond D.M.V.s to all rural domestic sites, whether nucleated villages, isolated huts or farms so that archaeological evidence from deserted and undeserted sites may be examined side by side. Urban and monastic sites are not included; nor are palaces, castles and isolated manor houses. I would be glad to be informed of any sites omitted, since it has become clear during the preparation of this gazetteer that there is much more excavation material available for study than had previously been thought. It is often said that there is very little evidence from Anglo-Saxon domestic sites, but in fact there is now firm evidence for at least 108 settlement sites from 115 investigations in different parts of England. There may still be other sites which are known to local workers or about which information is buried in early or obscure publications.

There have been several earlier attempts to list Anglo-Saxon domestic sites. The earliest of these, apart from general remarks (Leeds, 1922), was published in 1932 (Kendrick and Hawkes, 1932) when seven sites were listed. By 1935 Mr. O. G. S. Crawford was able to plot 18 sites on the *Dark Age Map* (Ordnance Survey, 1935), although the sites were not named. In 1936 seven major sites were listed (Leeds, 1936) but the first major attempt both to map and to list Anglo-Saxon domestic sites was by Mr. C. W. Phillips in the second edition of the *Dark Age Map* (Ordnance Survey, 1966), when 64 sites were recorded. This gazetteer indicates work at many more sites, although the *Dark Age Map* did not extend to Late Saxon sites.

As far as I am aware, there was no attempt to list excavations at medieval rural domestic sites until my own interim list (Hurst, 1954). This named 29 sites but was concerned only with D.M.V.s. Since that time many more village sites have been excavated, and some other earlier excavation reports have been brought to light, so that the total is now 209 investigations at 186 sites (see Table XVI).

There have been difficult decisions as to what ranks as an "investigation". The criterion has been the recording of structures either by complete excavation, by trial excavation, or by observation during or soon after destruction (usually the result of gravel-working, bull-dozing or deep ploughing). Scattered finds of loomweights, pottery and building material have not been included.

II

The gazetteer lists 290 sites where excavation or recording has taken place. On 30 of these work has been carried out on more than one occasion so that there have been 320 separate investigations. In Table XVI these figures are further analysed: Part I shows that nearly twice as much work has been done on later medieval as on earlier sites. The increased amount of work accomplished during the last twenty years is demonstrated by the further subdivision into investigations before and after 1939: 261 compared with 59.

In Part II of the Table the evidence is divided into three categories and two periods. It will be seen that in both periods roughly half the investigations (143) consisted of significant excavations from which single or several house-plans were obtained. The remainder of the work comprised either small-scale and not very productive trial excavations, or, especially in the Anglo-Saxon period, the results of the watching briefs, during quarrying and other types of destruction; when it was often possible so recover dating evidence and signs of structures, but rarely any complete house-plans. This lesser work has been included in the gazetteer in order to make it as comprehensive a record as possible. It has not been possible to comment on the evidence from all these investigations in detail in Chapter 2; its references are therefore to the more important.

Part III of the table further divides the periods of occupation at Anglo-Saxon domestic sites into early, middle, and late: from which it will be seen that those of the Pagan period predominate, mainly due to the easy recognition of sunken-huts. Part IV analyses the various types of Anglo-Saxon structures: it will be seen how sunken-huts predominate in the investigations of the Pagan period, while from late Saxon times increasing numbers of more substantial timber buildings have been found.

In Part V of the Table the character of the later medieval sites investigated demonstrates that most of the work has been on D.M.V.s with very little investigation of isolated farm or house-sites. At the same time it is shown that far more work (28%) has been carried out at surviving or shrunken villages than is often realised. Part VI analyses the various types of structure found on later medieval sites, showing the number of sites where complete plans have been obtained of all three house types, and the numbers of churches and chapels investigated.

Part VII of the table shows the progress of publication. Only about one-third of the sites investigated have received adequate publication but there are interim reports or notes in print for over half the sites. Delay in publication is one of the greatest problems of modern archaeology, but it is hoped that full reports will appear in due course for most of the significant work. The D.M.V.R.G. hopes to arrange the re-printing of early excavation reports and salvage some of the unpublished material for editing and printing. For many smaller investigations, such as Mr. Brewster's watching briefs on Yorkshire sites, it is hoped to prepare and publish general syntheses of work in particular areas.

TABLE XVI

Numerical analysis of excavations at medieval house and village sites

I. *Date of investigation of sites of different periods*

Periods	Sites investigated		Total number of sites investigated	Total number of separate sites investigated
	1840–1939	1939–1968		
400–1066	33 (30%)	78 (70%)	111*	104*
1066–1570	26 (13%)	183 (87%)	209	186
Total	59 (19%)	261 (81%)	320	290

II. *Character of work at sites of different periods*

Periods	Trial excavation, or recording only: no complete plans	One building excavated, or recorded	Several buildings excavated, or recorded
400–1066	59	32	20
1066–1570	105	56	35
Total	164	88	55

III. *Periods of occupation at Anglo-Saxon sites investigated*

Periods	Sites investigated
Pagan Saxon 400–650	89
Middle Saxon 650–850	12
Late Saxon 850–1066	18

* Four of the 209 medieval sites also showed Anglo-Saxon structures.

IV. *Number of sites where various types of structures have been found at Anglo-Saxon sites investigated*

Periods	Sunken-huts	Timber buildings at ground level
Pagan Saxon 400–650	22	6
Middle Saxon 650–850	2	7
Late Saxon 850–1066	4	14
Totals	28	27

V. *Character of later medieval (1066–1570) sites investigated*

D.M.V.s	Shrunken or surviving villages	Isolated farms or houses	Total
112 (60%)	52 (28%)*	22 (12%)	186

* Of these, 12 may ultimately be classified as D.M.V.s

VI. *Number of sites where various types of structures have been found at later medieval (1066–1570) sites investigated*

Churches or chapels	Type 1 small house	Type 2 Long-house	Type 3 Farm
23	39	27	22

VII. *Progress of publication of investigations*

Periods	Published		Total published	Interim note or report	Unpublished	Total
	1840–1939	1939–68				
400–1066	12	19	31 (27%)	65 (60%)	15 (13%)	111
1066–1570	15	54	69 (33%)	116 (56%)	24 (11%)	209
Total	27	73	100 (31%)	181 (56%)	39 (13%)	320

III

Sites have been listed alphabetically by modern counties[1] under the usual name of the site. There has been no attempt to list them under their present parishes. The sites are numbered consecutively and these numbers are used in Chapter 2 as short references to excavations there cited. Where more than one excavation has taken place at a site the references continue as A, B, etc.

Each entry has the following categories of information, separated by semi-colons.

1. Site name, six figure National Grid reference and date of excavation or investigation.
2. Name of excavator or recorder if not under (5).
3. Character of finds.
4. Character of work: excavation, recording, etc.
5. Publication, if any. Short titles (e.g. Jope, 1951) refer to the Bibliography, Chapter 6. Items not in this Select Bibliography are given fuller references.

Gazetteer

BEDFORDSHIRE

1   FELMERSHAM (SP 990578) 1940; Saxon and medieval structures; excavated; Jope, 1951.
2   HARROLD (SP 954572) 1953; Miss M. A. Bennett-Clark; pagan Saxon structures; excavated before gravel-working; report in *Beds. Archaeol. Journ.*, forthcoming.
3   PUDDLEHILL (TL 004234) 1951; pagan Saxon sunken-huts; excavated before quarrying; Matthews, 1962.

[1] Soke of Peterborough sites are still shown under Northamptonshire.

BERKSHIRE

4   RADLEY (SU 513982) 1928; pagan Saxon sunken-huts; recorded during gravel-working; not published, listed by Leeds, 1936, 21.

4A —— 1965: M. Avery; 2 sunken-huts; excavated; no report published.

5   SEACOURT (SP 486075) 1937–39; medieval structures; excavated; Bruce-Mitford, 1940.

5A —— 1958–59; several medieval buildings; excavated and recorded before and during roadworks; Biddle, 1961–62.

6   SUTTON COURTENAY (SU 489940) 1921–37; 33 sunken-huts; excavated before and during gravel-working; Leeds, 1923, 1927 and 1947.

7   TULWICK (SP 413904) 1961–67; medieval structures; excavated; no reports published or received.

8   UFTON NERVET (SU 617690) 1962; pagan Saxon sunken-hut; excavated; W. H. Manning, *Berks. Archaeol. Journ.*, LX (1962), 116–17.

9   WINDSOR, OLD (SU 991746) 1953–58; B. Hope-Taylor; middle and late Saxon buildings and sunken-huts; excavated; interim report in *Med. Archaeol.*, II (1958), 183–85.

10   WOODROWS (SU 545792) 1963; medieval structures; recorded after ploughing; P. Wood, *Berks. Archaeol. Journ.*, LXI (1963–64), 105.

BUCKINGHAMSHIRE

11   CALDECOTE (SP 839126) 1964–66; C. N. Gowing; medieval structures; excavated before building; interim notes in *Med. Archaeol.*, IX (1965), 208, and X (1966), 209.

12   CUBLINGTON (SP 834223) before 1908; excavator unknown; 60 graves; found east of motte; not published, noted by Allcroft, 1908, 548.

12A —— 1925; P. Maitland; church site; excavated; no report published cf. Beresford & St. Joseph, 1958, 102.

13   HEDSOR (SP 906983) 1894–95; medieval timber structures; recorded by the river Thames; A. H. Cocks, "Pile Dwellings at Hedsor, Buckinghamshire", *Proc. Soc. Antiq.*, 2nd ser., XVI (1895), 7–15.

14   LATIMER (SU 998986) 1965–66; K. Branigan, pagan Saxon timber building over Roman villa; excavated; interim note in *Med. Archaeol.*, XI (1967), 263, publication in *Med. Archaeol.*, XII (1968), 1–11.

15   OLNEY HYDE (SP 887541) 1967; P. Mayes; medieval pottery kiln and structures; excavated after ploughing; interim note and plan in *Med. Archaeol.*, XII (1968), 206–7, Fig. 57.

16   SHABBINGTON (SP 668067) 1964; C. N. Gowing; medieval structures; recorded during destruction; interim note in *Med. Archaeol.*, IX (1965), 208.

17   STANTONBURY (SP 837428) 1956; G. K. Tull; medieval church; excavated; no report published, results will be incorporated in report on A.

17A —— 1966; D. C. Mynard; medieval structures; recorded during gravel-working; interim note in *Med. Archaeol.*, XI (1967), 305. To be published with 17 in *Rec. of Bucks.*, forthcoming.

18 WALTON (SP 825133) 1905; medieval sunken-hut; excavated; Cocks, 1909, but see *Rec. of Bucks.*, XVIII (1967), 117, for doubts on the interpretation.

CAMBRIDGESHIRE

19 CHILDERLEY (TL 357615) 1961; J. A. Alexander; medieval structures; excavated after ploughing; interim note in *Med. Archaeol.*, VI–VII (1962–63), 341, longer interim in *Annual Report*, IX (1961), 9–11.

20 CLOPTON (TL 302488) 1961–62 and 1964; medieval church, Saxon and medieval structures; excavated; Alexander, 1968.

21 WATERBEACH (TL 489656) 1927; pagan Saxon sunken-hut; excavated; Lethbridge, 1927.

CORNWALL

22 CRANE GODREVY (SW 591425) 1955–58; A. C. Thomas; medieval building; excavated; interim notes and plan in *Med. Archaeol.*, I (1957), 160; II (1958), 201–02 and III (1959), 315–16 and Fig. 105.

23 GARROW (SX 146780) 1959; medieval buildings; excavated; Dudley and Minter, 1962–63.

24 GUNWALLOE (SW 659206) 1930; medieval structures; recorded in cliff face; A. H. A. Hogg, "Kitchen Midden Gunwalloe", *Journ. Royal Inst. Corn.*, XXIII (1930), 325–26.

24A —— 1947; further medieval structures; excavated and recorded; Jope, 1956. For pottery see *Corn. Archaeol.*, II (1963), 60.

25 GWITHIAN (SW 585416) 1953–56; four Dark Age buildings; excavated; A. C. Thomas, "Excavation of a Dark Age Site, Gwithian, Interim Report, 1953–54", *Proc. West Corn. Field Club*, new ser., I (1953–56), 59–72; A. C. Thomas, "Excavations at Gwithian, Cornwall, 1955", *Proc. West Corn. Field Club*, new ser., I (1953–56), appx., 1–17 and A. C. Thomas, "Gwithian, Ten Years Work, 1949–58", *West Corn. Field Club* (1958). For report on the field system see P. J. Fowler and A. C. Thomas, "Arable Fields of the Pre-Norman Period at Gwithian", *Corn. Archaeol.*, I (1962), 61–84.

26 HELLESVEAN (SW 506400) 1929; R. J. Noall; late Saxon building; excavated; A. Guthrie, "Dark Ages Sites at St. Ives", *Proc. West Corn. Field Club*, new ser., I (1953–56), 73–74 and A. Guthrie, "The Hellesvean Dark Age House", *Proc. West Corn. Field Club*, new ser., II (1959–60), 151–53.

26A —— 1957; no further structures found; trial excavation in advance of building; K. J. Barton, "Excavations at Hellesvean, St. Ives, in 1957", *Proc. West Corn. Field Club*, new ser., II (1959–60), 153–55.

27 LANYON (SW 422337) 1964; two medieval buildings; excavated; Mrs. E. M. Minter, "The Medieval Settlement at Lanyon in Madron", *Corn. Archaeol. Soc. Field Guide*, X (1964), 3–7; Mrs. E. M. Minter, "Lanyon in Madron; Interim Report on the Society's 1964 Excavation", *Corn. Archaeol.*, IV (1965), 44–45 and interim note and plan in *Med. Archaeol.*, IX (1965), 208 and Fig. 46.

28 MAWGAN PORTH (SW 852673) 1950–54; several late Saxon buildings; excavated; *Bruce-Mitford*, 1956.

29 SMALLACOMBE (SX 239748) 1866; medieval farm; planned; Blight, 1868–70.

30 TRESMORN (SX 161977) 1964–67; G. Beresford; several medieval buildings; excavated; interim notes with plans in *Med. Archaeol.*, IX (1965), 210; X (1966), 209; XI (1967), 305–06 and Fig. 86; and XII (1968), 199.

31 TREWORLD (SX 123903) 1963; two medieval buildings; excavated before ploughing; Dudley and Minter, 1966.

32 TREWORTHA (SX 239750) 1891–92; nine medieval buildings; excavated; Baring-Gould, 1892–93.

33 VENDOWN (SX 103881) 1956; medieval structures; excavated; Miss D. Dudley, "Vendown Minster", *Proc. West. Corn. Field Club*, new ser., I (1955–56), 147–48.

DERBYSHIRE

34 BARTON BLOUNT (SK 209346) 1968; G. Beresford; several medieval timber buildings; excavated after ploughing; interim note in *Med. Archaeol.*, XIII (1969), forthcoming.

DEVON

35 BEERE, GREAT (SX 690034) 1938–39; medieval building; excavated; Jope and Threlfall, 1958.

36 DEAN MOOR (SX 679654) 1956; medieval farm; excavated before flooding for reservoir; Fox, 1958.

37 DINNA CLERKS (SX 692751) 1966; Mrs. E. M. Minter; medieval farm; excavated before ploughing; interim note in *Med. Archaeol.*, XI (1967), 301.

38 HOUND TOR I (SX 745789) 1960–68; Mrs. E. M. Minter; several late Saxon and medieval buildings; excavated; interim notes with plans in *Med. Archaeol.*, VI–VII (1962–63), 341–43 and Fig. 102; VIII (1964), 282–85 and Figs. 90–91; IX (1965), 210 and X (1966), 210 and Fig. 86.

39 HOUND TOR II (SX 745791) 1964—68; Mrs. E. M. Minter; several medieval buildings; excavated; interim notes in *Med. Archaeol.*, VI–VII (1962–63), 339 and IX (1965), 211.

40 HUTHOLES (SX 702758) 1964–65; Mrs. E. M. Minter; two medieval buildings; excavated; interim notes in *Med. Archaeol.*, IX (1965), 212 and X (1966), 210.

41 LUNDY, WIDOW'S TENEMENT (SS 136468) 1964–66; K. S. Gardner; medieval building; excavated; interim notes and plan in *Med. Archaeol.*, IX (1965), 206 and XI (1967), 301–02 and Fig. 84; *Current Archaeol.*, I (1968), 196–202.

42 THORNE, NORTH (SS 647413) 1959–62; H. J. Brooks; medieval structures; excavated; interim note in *Med. Archaeol.*, VI–VII (1962–63), 343; longer note in *Annual Report*, IX (1961), 12–13.

DORSET

43 COMPTON VALENCE (SY 582943) 1964; medieval structures; recorded after ploughing; J. Radley, "A Deserted Medieval Farmstead at Compton Valence, Dorset", *Proc. Dor. Archaeol. Soc.*, LXXXVII (1965), 88–89.

44 GILLINGHAM (ST 796281) 1966; W. W. Slade; medieval structures; excavated; interim note in *Med. Archaeol.*, XI (1967), 306.

45 HOLWORTH (SY 769833) 1958; medieval building; excavated; Rahtz, 1959.

46 WITCHAMPTON (ST 990063) 1924–25; Mrs. MacGeagh and H. Sumner; medieval structures and chessmen; excavated; interim note on structures in *Journ. Rom. Stud.*, XIV (1924), 235–37 with plan and XV (1925), 238; there are further unpublished plans in the Dorchester Museum; for the chessmen see, O. M. Dalton, "Early Chessmen of Whale's Bone Excavated in Dorset", *Archaeologia*, LXXVII (1928), 77–86; the other medieval finds are in the Poole Museum.

47 WOOLCOMBE (SY 554953) 1966–68; G. Rybot; medieval structures; excavated; interim note in *Med. Archaeol.*, XI (1967), 306, XII (1968), 199 and XIII (1969), forthcoming.

48 YONDOVER (SY 499939) 1956; medieval structures; recorded during building works; R. A. H. Farrar and J. G. Hurst, "Romano-British and Medieval finds at Yondover, Loders", *Proc. Dorset Archaeol. Soc.*, LXXVIII (1956), 85–87.

48A —— 1965; J. Bailey; no structures; excavation during further building; interim note in *Med. Archaeol.*, X (1966), 210.

DURHAM

49 GARMONDSWAY (NZ 346347) 1950; R. Walton; medieval buildings; excavated; no report published.

50 HARTBURN, WEST (NZ 358142) 1961–62; medieval building; excavated, Still and Pallister, 1964.

50A —— 1965; second medieval building; excavated; Still and Pallister, 1967.

50B —— 1968; L. Still and A. Pallister; third medieval building; excavated; interim note in *Med. Archaeol.*, XIII (1969), forthcoming.

51 SWAINSTON (NZ 419294) 1957–60; J. Booth, two medieval buildings; excavated; interim notes in *Med. Archaeol.*, II (1958), 210; III (1959), 321; IV (1960), 160 and V (1961), 334. *Proc. South Shields Archaeol. and Hist. Soc.*, I (1957), 9–15.

52 YODEN (NZ 433418) 1884; Mrs. R. Burdon; medieval structures; excavated; Middleton, 1885.

ESSEX

53 BONHUNT (TL 511335) 1967–68; B. Hooper; medieval structures and burials; excavated after ploughing; interim notes in *Med. Archaeol.*, XII (1968), 201 and XIII (1969), forthcoming.

54 BULMER (TL 834384) 1958; pagan Saxon structures; recorded after ploughing; B. P. Blake, "Anglo-Saxon site at Hole Farm, Bulmer Tye, Essex", *Med. Archaeol.*, III (1959), 282–85.

55 CHADWELL ST. MARY (TQ 657779) 1968; R. Doyle; pagan Saxon sunken-hut; excavated before gravel-working; interim note in *Med. Archaeol.*, XIII (1969), forthcoming.

56 MUCKING (LINFORD) (TQ 672803) 1955; pagan Saxon buildings and sunken-huts; excavated before gravel-working; Barton, 1960.

56A —— 1966–68; Mrs. M. U. Jones; 68 pagan Saxon sunken-huts; excavated before gravel-working; interim report in *Antiq. Journ.*, XLVIII (1968), 217–49.

57 OAKLEY, LITTLE (TM 222292) 1958; R. H. Farrands; pagan Saxon structures over Roman site; excavated; interim note in *Colchester Archaeol. Group Bull.*, I (1958), 43–45.

58 RAINHAM (TQ 542818) 1963; Dr. Isobel Smith; medieval structures; excavated in advance of gravel-working; interim note in *Med. Archaeol.*, VIII (1964), 271.

59 WENDENS AMBO (TL 510365) 1958; G. M. Knocker; late Saxon structures; excavated in advance of development, interim note in *Med. Archaeol.*, III (1959), 295–96.

GLOUCESTERSHIRE

60 BOURTON-ON-THE-WATER (SP 171221) 1931; Miss H. E. Donovan (Mrs. O'Neil); pagan Saxon sunken-hut; excavated; Dunning, 1932.

61 BRIMPSFIELD (SO 921124) 1961; G. Harding; late medieval building; excavated; interim note in *Med. Archaeol.*, VI–VII (1962–63), 339.

62 FROCESTER (SO 770033) 1957–8; Church over Roman site; excavated; H. S. Gracie "St. Peters Church, Frocester", *Trans. Bristol and Gloucs. Archaeol. Soc.*, LXXVII (1958), 23–30.

63 HULLASEY (ST 974993) 1900s; three medieval buildings and chapel; excavated; Baddeley, 1910.

64 MANLESS (SO 928117) 1962; G. Harding; medieval structures; excavated after ploughing; interim note in *Med. Archaeol.*, VIII (1964), 284.

65 SENNINGTON (SP 024219) 1936; Miss H. E. Donovan (Mrs. O'Neil); one medieval building; excavated; no report published, plan, photographs and description in the files of the D.M.V.R.G.

66 TEMPLE GUITING (SP 128263) 1957; medieval farm; excavated; R. C. Baldwyn and Helen E. O'Neil, "A Medieval Site at Chalk Hill, Temple Guiting", *Trans. Bristol and Gloucs. Archaeol. Soc.*, LXXVII (1958), 61–65.

67 UPTON (SP 152344) 1959–64; medieval farm complex; excavated; Hilton and Rahtz, 1966.

67A —— 1965–68; second building; excavated; report in *Trans. Bristol and Gloucs. Archaeol. Soc.*, forthcoming. For interim note and plan see *Med. Archaeol.*, X (1966), 210 and Fig. 87 and *Current Archaeol.*, I (1957), 98–99.

HAMPSHIRE

68 CHALTON (SU 734145) 1960's; B. W. Cunliffe; pagan Saxon sunken-huts; observed during ploughing; excavation to start in 1969.

69 EMSWORTH (SU 746054) 1957; R. Bradley; late Saxon sunken-hut; excavated before development; report in *Proc. Hants. Field Club*, forthcoming.

70 MILTON (SZ 238941) 1956; superimposed late Saxon and medieval timber buildings under moated site; excavated; Hurst and Hurst, 1967.

71 ISLE OF WIGHT: WOLVERTON (SZ 537778) 1952; Maj. G. Fowler; medieval structures; excavated; no report published; interim report in the files of the D.M.V.R.G.

HEREFORDSHIRE

72 HAMPTON WAFER (SO 577570) 1957–58; two medieval buildings; excavated; Stanford, 1955–57.

73 HENTLAND (SO 543267) 1960; N. Bridgewater; medieval structures; excavated; interim note in *Med. Archaeol.*, v (1961), 329.

HERTFORDSHIRE

74 ASHWELL (TL 264394) 1957; medieval timber buildings under moated site; excavated; Hurst and Hurst, 1967.

75 BROADFIELD (TL 325312) 1965; P. A. Rahtz; medieval timber structures and church; excavated before ploughing; interim note and plan in *Med. Archaeol.*, x (1966), 186 and Fig. 77.

HUNTINGDONSHIRE

Sites in the Soke of Peterborough are still listed under Northamptonshire.

76 BUCKDEN (TL 201680) 1961; P. V. Addyman, pagan Saxon sunken-hut; excavated before gravel-working; interim note in *Med. Archaeol.*, vi–vii (1962–63), 307–08.

77 BUCKDEN (TL 191628) 1961; late Saxon boat-shaped building; excavated during roadworks; Tebbutt, 1961.

78 EATON SOCON (formerly in Beds.) (TL 173588) 1962; late Saxon building; excavated before building; Addyman, 1965.

79 EYNESBURY (TL 182599) 1963; C. F. Tebbutt; pagan Saxon sunken-hut recorded during building; no report published. Now (1969) thought to be Iron Age.

80 EYNESBURY (TL 186592) 1960; medieval sunken-hut; excavated; Tebbutt, 1960.

81 HEMINGFORD GREY (TL 302690) 1937; pagan Saxon sunken-hut; recorded during gravel-working; C. M. Coote, "An Early Saxon and Roman Site at Hemingford Grey", *Proc. Cambs. and Hunts. Archaeol. Soc.*, vii (1952), 68.

82 HOUGHTON (TL 287717) 1950; pagan Saxon sunken-hut; excavated; C. M. Coote, "Saxon Hut", *Proc. Cambs. and Hunts. Archaeol. Soc.*, vii (1952), 71.

83 ORTON LONGUEVILLE (TL 170965) 1930's; pagan Saxon sunken-huts; recorded during gravel working; no report published, information G. Wyman Abbott.

84 ORTON WATERVILLE (TL 157963), 1930's; pagan Saxon sunken-huts; recorded during gravel working; no report published, information G. Wyman Abbott.

85 PAXTON, LITTLE (TL 192624), 1961–62; P. V. Addyman, late Saxon structures; excavated before gravel working; interim note and plan in *Med. Archaeol.*, vi–vii (1962–63), 308; viii (1964), 234–36 and Fig. 80.

86 ST. NEOTS (TL 186602) 1929–32; eight late Saxon sunken-huts; excavated before gravel working; Lethbridge and Tebbutt, 1933.

86A —— 1961; P. V. Addyman; late Saxon buildings; excavated before building; interim note and plan in *Med. Archaeol.*, vi–vii (1962–63), 308 and Fig. 96.

87 SALOME (TL 122775) 1930's; medieval timber structures and chapel; excavated; Garrood, 1937. See also J. R. Garrood, "Late Saxon and Early Medieval Pottery in Huntingdonshire", *Trans. Cambs. and Hunts. Archaeol. Soc.*, vi (1947), 107–10, for description of the finds.

88 UPTHORPE (TL 127721) 1958; D. Corbett; remains of medieval structures; excavated before ploughing; interim note in *Med. Archaeol.*, III (1959), 323. Longer note in *Annual Report*, VI (1958), 6–7.

89 WATER NEWTON (TL 108969) 1958; late Saxon structures; excavated before roadworks; Green, 1964.

90 WEALD (TL 230596) 1941; medieval structures and chapel; excavated; Newton, 1947.

91 WOODSTON (TL 182973); pagan Saxon sunken-huts; recorded during gravel working; no report published, information G. Wyman Abbott.

KENT

92 DARTFORD (TR 546746) 1955; pagan Saxon sunken-hut; excavated; P. J. Tester, "An Anglo-Saxon Occupation Site at Dartford", *Archaeol. Cantiana*, LXX (1956), 256–59.

93 LULLINGSTONE (TQ 530650) 1958; Col. G. W. Meates; medieval structures; excavated; no report published.

94 MERSTON (TQ 704723) 1956–57; medieval chapel; excavated; A. F. Allen, "The Lost Village of Merston", *Archaeol. Cantiana*, LXXI (1957), 198–205.

95 SANDTUN (TR 120340) 1930's; J. Birchell and G. Ward; Saxon and medieval structures; excavated; no report published, see *Med. Archaeol.*, III (1959), 21. There are plans and records of the excavation in the British Museum.

LEICESTERSHIRE

96 ALDEBY (SK 552987) 1950's; medieval church; excavated; no report published.

97 BESCABY (SY 823263) 1957; J. G. Hurst; medieval structures; recorded after ploughing; interim note in *Annual Report*, V (1957), 4.

98 GLEN PARVA (SP 577981) 1966; K. Clarke; middle Saxon structures under moated site; excavated; interim note in *Med. Archaeol.*, XI (1967), 267. Thermoluminescent dating has now (1969) shown this site to be Iron Age.

99 HAMILTON (SK 645075) 1948; W. G. Hoskins; medieval structures; excavated; no report published.

100 HARSTON (SK 850314) 1935–36; pagan Saxon sunken-hut; excavated; Dunning, 1952.

101 KIRBY BELLARS (SK 718183); 1960 and 1965; A. E. Grimbley; late Saxon structures; excavated; J. G. Hurst; "Saxon and Medieval Pottery from Kirby Bellars", *Leics. Archaeol. and Hist. Soc.*, XLIII (1967–68), 10–18, and XLI (1966–67), 66 and 72.

102 POTTERS MARSTON (SP 498964) 1945; E. Pochin; medieval pottery kiln; excavated; Haynes, 1952.

103 WELBY (SK 725210) 1968; medieval structures; excavated; no report published.

LINCOLNSHIRE

104 BAGMOOR (SE 893181?) 1928; pagan Saxon finds; recorded during ironstone working; Myres, 1951, 96 and Dudley, 1949, 224. Mr. C. Knowles reports that this may be the same site as 114.

105 BARTON-ON-HUMBER (TA 033220) 1966–68; G. F. Bryant; pagan Saxon structures; excavated before building; interim notes in *Med. Archaeol.*, XIII (1969), forthcoming.

106 CASTHORPE (SK 872351) 1958–60; R. C. Haw; pagan Saxon sunken-huts; observed after ploughing; *East Mid. Archaeol. Bull.*, III (1960), 8.

107 CAYTHORPE (SK 940470) 1920's; pagan Saxon structures; observed during ironstone working; Phillips, 1934, 146–47 and 163.

108 CLAXBY (TF 453712) 1906; medieval structures; excavated; Tatham, 1906.

108A —— 1948; medieval enclosure; sectioned; H. L. Barker, "Excavation of Medieval Enclosure at Claxby, Nr. Alford", *Lincs. Archit. and Archaeol. Soc. Reps. and Paps.*, VI (1955), 14–16.

109 KEAL, EAST (TF 383640) 1959; Mrs. E. H. Rudkin; medieval structures; recorded after ploughing; interim note in *Med. Archaeol.*, IV (1960), 159.

110 KETTLEBY THORPE (TA 042079) 1964; Mr. and Mrs. R. C. Russell; medieval buildings; excavated and planned before and after ploughing; interim note in *Med. Archaeol.*, IX (1965), 213.

111 LANGTON-BY-SPILSBY (TF 391702) 1959; medieval structures; excavated before ploughing; Butler, 1962.

112 MANTON (GREETWELL Farm) (SE 932046); D. N. Riley and G. R. Walshaw; pagan Saxon finds; observed; Myres, 1951, 98 and Dudley, 1949, 143 and 231.

113 MESSINGHAM (MELLS Farm) (SE 910034) 1933; D. N. Riley and G. R. Walshaw; pagan Saxon finds; observed; Myres, 1951, and Dudley, 1949, 143 and 234–5.

114 NORMANBY in BURTON-ON-STATHER (SE 896165); pagan Saxon finds; observed; Dudley, 1949, 233.

115 NORMANBY-LE-WOLD (TF 126941) 1967–68; J. B. Whitwell; middle Saxon structures with stone foundations; excavated before ploughing; interim note in *Med. Archaeol.*, XII (1968), 159, and XIII (1969), forthcoming.

116 RISBY (SE 917129) 1933; late medieval building; excavated; G. R. Walshaw and H. E. Dudley, "Excavation of a Medieval Building", *Scunthorpe and Frodingham Star*, February 10, 1934.

117 RISEHOLME (SK 980753) 1954–55; medieval building; excavated and village planned; Thompson, 1960.

118 SALMONBY (TF 332731) 1954–58; G. V. Taylor; pagan Saxon sunken-huts with stone foundations; excavated; interim notes in *Lincs. Archit. and Archaeol. Soc. Reps. and Paps.*, VI (1955), 10–11 and VIII (1959–60), 20–22.

119 SLEAFORD, OLD (TF 076458) 1961–62; Mrs. M. U. Jones; medieval church and structures; excavated before building; interim note in *Annual Report*, IX (1961), 11.

120 SNARFORD (TF 051825) 1957; S. E. West; medieval structures; excavated before ploughing; report in *Lincs. Hist. and Archaeol.*, forthcoming.

121 SOMERBY-BY-GAINSBOROUGH (SK 846897) 1957; D. Corbett; medieval building; excavated before ploughing; interim note in *Med. Archaeol.*, II (1958), 210–11; full report in *Lincs. Hist. and Archaeol.*, forthcoming.

122 STOKE, NORTH (SK 913285) 1968; D. Kaye; medieval church and structures; excavated; interim note in *Med. Archaeol.*, XIII (1969), forthcoming.

123 WALESBY (TF 134925) 1968; G. F. Bryant; medieval building; excavated before development; interim note in *Med. Archaeol.*, XIII (1969), forthcoming.

124 WELTON-LE-WOLD (TF 270875) 1959; R. J. Smith; medieval structures; excavated; interim note in *Med. Archaeol.*, IV (1960), 160. Interim report with plans and photographs in the files of D.M.V.R.G.

125 WILLOUGHTON (SK 933925) 1932; Mrs. E. H. Rudkin; pagan Saxon sunken-hut; excavated; interim notes in Phillips, 1934, 154; Dudley, 1949, 232 and Myres, 1951, 88 and 99.

126 WOOLSTHORPE (SK 848335) 1882; pagan Saxon structures; observed during ironstone working, "Discovery of the site of an Anglo-Saxon Camp or settlement near Woolsthorpe-by-Belvoir", *Assoc. Archit. Soc. Reps.*, XVIII (1885), 132–4; Phillips, 1934, 147 and 187; *Lincs. Archit. and Archaeol. Soc. Reps. and Paps.*, VI (1955–56), 11.

MIDDLESEX

127 HANWELL (TQ 153800) 1910 and 1915; R. Garraway-Rice; pagan Saxon site; observed during gravel-working; R. E. M. Wheeler, *London and the Saxons*, London Museum Cats., VI (1935), 136–39.

128 NORTHOLT (TQ 133841) 1950–68; several Anglo-Saxon and medieval buildings under moated site; excavated; Hurst 1961; for later work see *Med. Archaeol.*, VI–VII (1962–63), 309–10, Fig. 97; VIII (1964), 272; IX (1965), 213–14; XI (1967), 298 and XII (1968), 201.

NORFOLK

129 BABINGLEY (TF 670263) 1956–57; several late medieval buildings; planned after ploughing; Hurst, 1961A.

130 BUNWELL (TM 129932) 1964; P. Day; pagan Saxon structures; excavated; interim note in *Med. Archaeol.*, IX (1965), 172.

131 CAISTER-ON-SEA (TG 515123), 1951–2; C. Green; pagan Saxon circular huts over Roman site; excavated; interim notes in *Journ. Rom. Stud.*, XLII (1952), 96–97 and XLIII (1953), 122.

132 CALDECOTE (TF 743033) 1960; R. R. Clarke; Saxon structures; recorded after ploughing; interim note in *Med. Archaeol.*, V (1961), 332.

133 ELMHAM, NORTH (TF 987215) 1967–68; P. Wade-Martins; late medieval building; excavated before ploughing; interim note in *Med. Archaeol.*, XII (1968), 201 and XIII (1969), forthcoming; see also *Current Archaeol.*, I (1968), 148–52.

134 GRENSTEIN (TF 906199) 1965–66; P. Wade-Martins; medieval building complex; excavated; interim note and plan in *Med. Archaeol.*, X (1966), 212 and Fig. 88. Longer interim in *Annual Report*, XIII (1965), 23–25 and XIV (1966), 23–24.

135 HEMSBY (TG 494171) 1960 and 1963; pagan Saxon structures; excavated; interim note in *Med. Archaeol.*, VIII (1964), 237.

136 LYNN, NORTH (TF 615215) 1953; J. O. H. Nichols, medieval structures; excavated before ploughing; no report published.

136A —— 1960–68; further structures; excavated before development; interim note in *Med. Archaeol.*, V (1961), 333, and XII (1968), 201.

137   MARKSHALL (TG 235049) 1949; late medieval farm; excavated; Larwood, 1952.

138   POSTWICK (TG 300074) 1935; pagan Saxon sunken-hut; excavated; R. R. Clarke, "An Iron Age Hut at Postwick, Norfolk", *Norf. Archaeol.*, XXVI (1937), 271–77. For re-assessment see *Norf. Archaeol.*, XXXI (1957), 407.

139   SEDGEFORD (TF 711363) 1953; C. H. Lewton-Brain; middle Saxon hut; excavated; interim note in *Norf. Archaeol.*, XXXI (1957), 407.

139A —— 1958; P. A. Jewell; middle Saxon building; excavated; interim note in *Med. Archaeol.*, III (1959), 298.

140   SNETTISHAM (TF 692332) 1950–51; C. H. Lewton-Brain; Anglo-Saxon structures; observed after ploughing; interim note in *Norf. Archaeol.*, XXXI (1957), 407.

141   THUXTON (TG 043080) 1963–65; L. A. S. Butler; several medieval buildings; excavated after ploughing; interim note in *Med. Archaeol.*, VIII (1964), 286 and IX (1965), 214. Longer interim in *Annual Report*, XII (1964), 12–13.

142   WITTON (TG 337322) 1961–64; E. J. Owles and J. E. Turner; several pagan Saxon sunken-huts; excavated; interim notes in *Med. Archaeol.*, VI–VII (1962–63), 309; VIII (1964), 237 and IX (1965), 173.

143   WYUELING (TF 692207) 1962; J. O. H. Nicholls; several late Saxon structures; excavated; interim note in *Med. Archaeol.*, VI–VII (1962–63), 286.

NORTHAMPTONSHIRE

The Northamptonshire entries include sites in the Soke of Peterborough which are now in Huntingdonshire.

144   BRIGSTOCK (SP 945855) 1931; several pagan Saxon sunken-huts; observed; no report published, information from G. Wyman Abbott.

145   CASTOR (TL 125984) 1957–58; C. Green; Anglo-Saxon structures; excavated; no report published.

146   COTTON, MALLOWS (SP 976733) 1909; G. V. Charlton; several medieval structures; excavated; no report published; only record letter to Ordnance Survey dated February 7, 1924.

147   FAXTON (SP 785752) 1965–68; L. A. S. Butler; several medieval buildings; excavated; interim notes and plan in *Med. Archaeol.*, X (1966), 214; XI (1967); 307–79 and Fig. 87 and XII (1968), 203 and XIII (1969), forthcoming. See also *Current Archaeol.*, I (1967), 48–50, and (1968), 163–64.

148   HARROWDEN, GREAT (SP 879708) 1966; Mrs. G. Brown; medieval structures; planned during road-widening; interim note in *Med. Archaeol.*, XI (1967), 308.

149   LYVEDEN (SP 984861) 1965–67; medieval structures; excavated; Steane, 1967.

149A —— 1968; medieval pottery kilns and building; excavated; report in *Journ. Northampton Mus. and Art Gall.*, forthcoming.

150   MAXEY (TF 124081) 1960; seven middle Saxon buildings and five possible sunken-huts; excavated; Addyman, 1964.

151   MUSCOTT (SP 625633) 1958; P. Savage; medieval buildings; excavated; interim note in *Med. Archaeol.*, III (1959), 323.

152   OLNEY (SP 520715) 1949; A. Franey; medieval site planned but no structures found; trial excavation; no report published, see Beresford, 1954–56, 70 and 367.

153 PETERBOROUGH (TL 189974) 1923; G. Wyman Abbott, pagan Saxon sunken-huts; observed; no report published, noted in Kendrick and Hawkes, 1932, 323.

154 SILSWORTH (SD 620707) 1964; Mrs. G. Brown; medieval structures; excavated; interim note in *Med. Archaeol.*, IX (1965), 214. Longer interim in *Annual Report*, XII (1964), 18–19.

155 THORPE WATERVILLE (TL 026817) 1967; Mrs. G. Brown; medieval structures; planned during roadworks; interim note in *Med. Archaeol.*, XII (1968), 203.

156 UPTON (SP 714602) 1965; D. A. Jackson; large pagan Saxon sunken-hut; excavated; interim note in *Med. Archaeol.*, X (1966), 172. Full report *Antiq. Journ.*, forthcoming.

157 WYTHEMAIL (SP 840719), 1954; Mrs. D. G. Hurst; medieval building complex; excavated before ploughing; interim report in *Annual Report*, II (1954), 12; full report in *Med. Archaeol.*, XIII (1969), forthcoming.

NORTHUMBERLAND

158 LILBURN, WEST (NU 022243) 1933; medieval church; excavated; Honeyman, 1933.

159 LINBRIG (NT 893069) 1967; Miss B. Harbottle; medieval building; excavated; interim note in *Med. Archaeol.*, XII (1968), 198.

160 MEMMERKIRK (NT 922123) 1962; medieval building; excavated; Harbottle and Cowper, 1963.

161 OUTCHESTER (NU 147334) 1961; medieval structures; excavated before ploughing; B. Harbottle and N. McCord, "An Excavation at Outchester", *Archaeol. Aeliana*, 4th ser., XLIII (1965), 235–42.

162 WHELPINGTON, WEST (NY 974837) 1958–60; six medieval buildings; excavated in advance of quarrying; Jarrett, 1962.

162A —— 1965–68; M. G. Jarrett; several medieval building complexes; excavated; report in *Archaeol. Aeliana*, forthcoming.

NOTTINGHAMSHIRE

163 ADBOLTON (SK 600384) 1945–60; G. Richardson; three medieval buildings and industrial site; excavation before gravel-working; no report published. Letters about the finds in D.M.V.R.G. files.

164 ANNESLEY (SK 504524) 1949; J. N. Chaworth-Musters; medieval structures; recorded after ploughing; no report published.

165 ATTENBOROUGH (SK 518345) 1967–68; A. MacCormick; medieval structures; excavated after finding of coin hoard of 1420; interim note in *Med. Archaeol.*, XII (1968), 203 and XIII (1969), forthcoming.

166 KEIGHTON (SK 542382) 1953–56; medieval structures; excavated before building; D. H. Kerridge; "University Park in the Middle Ages", *Nott. Univ. Survey*, IV, 3 (1954), 43–48; typed report with plans and photographs in the D.M.V.R.G. files, D. H. Kerridge, "The Report of the Excavations on the Medieval Building Site in University Park, 1955–56".

166A —— 1968; further excavation; to be published with earlier work in *Trans. Thoroton Soc.*, forthcoming.

167 THURGARTON (SK 693489) 1948–53; various late Saxon and medieval structures; excavated; Hodges, 1954.

167A —— 1954–55; further structures; excavated; Gathercole and Wailes, 1959.

168 WHIMPTON (SK 795740) 1906; medieval site planned and structures excavated; Pryce and Dobson, 1907.

168A —— 1960; H. L. Barker; further finds during roadworks; interim note in *Med. Archaeol.*, v (1961), 333.

169 WILLOUGHBY BY NORWELL (SK 478363) 1954–55; H. Burrows; late medieval structures; excavated; no report published, typed report with plans, sections and pottery drawings in the files of the D.M.V.R.G.

OXFORDSHIRE

170 ASTERLEIGH (SP 400224) 1948; S. E. Rigold; medieval structures recorded during quarrying; *Oxoniensia*, XVIII (1948), 67–68.

170A —— 1959; further structures; recorded; interim note in *Med. Archaeol.*, IV (1960), 159.

171 CASSINGTON (TOLLEY Pit) (SP 453103) 1932–39; pagan Saxon sunken-huts; observed during gravel working; interim notes in *Congress Archaeol. Soc.* (1932–33), 28 and (1934), 28; noted by Leeds, 1936, 21; *Oxoniensia*, III (1938), 165 and v (1940), 3, Fig. 1.

172 CASSINGTON (PURWELL Farm) (SP 444121) 1956–59; pagan Saxon sunken-huts; recorded and excavated during gravel working; B. V. Arthur and E. M. Jope, "Early Saxon Pottery Kilns at Purwell Farm, Cassington", *Med. Archaeol.*, VI–VII (1962–63), 1–14.

173 DORNFORD (SP 450206) 1964–65; G. Cowling and E. J. Adnams; medieval building complex, excavated; interim notes in *Med. Archaeol.*, IX (1965), 214 and XI (1967), 310. Longer note in *Annual Report*, XII (1964), 19.

174 EYNSHAM (NEWLAND Street) (SP 436098) 1938; pagan Saxon sunken-huts; recorded during gravel working; interim note in *Oxoniensia*, III (1938), 167.

175 EYNSHAM (NEW WINTLES Farm) (SP 432108) 1967–68; Mrs. S. Hawkes and Mrs. M. Gray; three pagan Saxon buildings and five sunken-huts; excavated before gravel-working; interim note in *Med. Archaeol.*, XIII (1969), forthcoming.

176 LEA (SP 389385) 1958; P. J. Fowler; medieval structures; excavated; interim note in *Med. Archaeol.*, III (1959), 319 and *Oxoniensia*, XXV (1960), 4–5 and Fig. 1C.

177 PINKHILL (SP 436072) 1963–64; Miss H. Sutermeister and D. J. Keene; medieval structures; excavated; interim note in *Med. Archaeol.*, IX (1965), 214; longer interim in *Annual Report*, XII (1964), 19–20.

178 SPELSBURY (SP 339213) 1938; pagan Saxon sunken-hut; recorded during gravel-working; *Oxoniensia*, III (1938), 168.

179 STANDLAKE (SP 385045) 1857; pagan Saxon sunken-huts; recorded during gravel-working; Stone, 1857.

179A —— 1940s; further discoveries; interim note in *Oxoniensia*, VIII–IX (1953–54), 199.

180 STANTON HARCOURT (SP 403055) 1858; pagan Saxon sunken-huts; recorded and excavated during gravel-working; Stone, 1858.

180A —— 1940's; further sunken-huts; recorded; *Oxoniensia*, VII (1942), 104.

181 WILCOTE (SHAKENOAK) (SP 373138) 1960–68; A. Hands; pagan Saxon features over Roman buildings; excavated; interim note in *Med. Archaeol.*, XI (1967), 268.

182 WOODPERRY (SP 575105) 1840's; medieval structures and church; excavated; Wilson, 1846; and J. Wilson, "Roman Antiquities Discovered at Woodpury in Oxfordshire", *Archaeologia*, XXXII (1847), 392.

182A —— 1953; E. M. Jope; medieval church and structures; excavated; no report published; interim report in the files of the D.M.V.R.G.

183 YELFORD (SP 360040) 1858; pagan Saxon sunken-huts; recorded and excavated during gravel-working; Stone, 1858.

RUTLAND

184 BARROW (SK 885155) 1959; medieval building and malt kiln; excavated; E. G. Bolton, "Excavation of a House and Malt Kiln at Barrow", *Med. Archaeol.*, IV (1960), 128–31.

185 EMPINGHAM (SK 944077) 1967; M. Dean; pagan Saxon sunken-hut under cemetery; excavated; interim note in *Med. Archaeol.*, XII (1968), 160.

186 MARTINSTHORPE (SK 865046) 1960; medieval building; excavated; Wacher, 1963–64.

SHROPSHIRE

187 ABDON (SO 865575), 1966; R. T. Rowley; medieval building; excavated; interim note and plan in *Med. Archaeol.*, XI (1967), 310–12 and Fig. 88.

188 BRAGGINGTON (SJ 336140) 1963; medieval building; excavated before ploughing; Barker, 1968.

189 BURY WALLS (SJ 575275) 1930; P. W. Taylor; medieval building; excavated; no report published; plan in Rowley House Museum, Shrewsbury.

190 DETTON (SO 667796) 1960; medieval structures; excavated before ploughing; Stanford, 1965.

191 SUTTON (SJ 503104) 1967–68; W. E. Jenks; several medieval structures; excavated before development; interim notes in *Med. Archaeol.*, XII (1968), and XIII (1969), forthcoming.

SOMERSET

192 BARROW MEAD (ST 729628) 1953–54; medieval structures; excavated before building; Rahtz, 1960–61.

192A —— 1964; P. A. Rahtz; further excavation; interim note in *Med. Archaeol.*, IX (1965), 207.

193 BINEHAM (ST 500250) 1951–52; medieval building; excavated; interim report, H. S. L. Dewar, "Discovery of Lost Medieval Village in Somerset", *Archaeol. News Letter*, IV (1951), 42–43.

194 CAMERTON (ST 686575) 1960; W. J. Wedlake; medieval structures; excavated; no report published.

195 HOLCOMBE (ST 668507) 1911; medieval building; excavated, Wickham, 1912.

195A —— 1956; Rev. A. Watkin; medieval structure; excavated; no report published; interim note in the files of the D.M.V.R.G.

196 MORETON (ST 562592) 1953–55; P. A. Rahtz; several medieval buildings; excavated before flooding for reservoir; report in "Chew Valley Lake", H.M.S.O. publication forthcoming.

197 PICKWICK (ST 595661) 1958; K. J. Barton; medieval building; excavated; interim note in *Med. Archaeol.*, III (1959), 156. Full report in *Proc. Univ. Bristol Spel. Soc.*, XII (1969), forthcoming.

198 WRAXALL (ST 487731) 1958; two medieval buildings; excavated; K. S. Gardner, "Moat House Farm, Medieval Buildings and Earthworks", *Som. and Dorset Notes and Queries*, XXVII (1960), 289–90.

STAFFORDSHIRE

199 SANDON (SJ 953295) 1968; F. Celoria; medieval structures; excavated; no report received.

SUFFOLK

200 ASHBOCKING (TM 175551) 1950; B. J. W. Brown; pagan Saxon sunken-huts; recorded; interim note in *Proc. Suff. Inst. Archaeol.*, XXV (1949–51), 206.

201 BEALINGS LITTLE (TM 228464) 1958; three pagan Saxon sunken-huts; recorded; interim note in *Proc. Suff. Inst. Archaeol.*, XXVIII (1958–60), 90.

202 BRANDON (TL 785865) pagan Saxon structures; recorded; information from Ordnance Survey.

203 BUTLEY (NEUTRAL Farm) (TM 379500) 1949; B. J. W. Brown, several pagan Saxon sunken-huts; recorded; interim note in *Proc. Suff. Inst. Archaeol.*, XXV (1951), 207–08.

204 BUTLEY (CHURCH Site) (TM 374500) 1950; B. J. W. Brown; pagan Saxon structures; recorded; *Proc. Suff. Inst. Archaeol.*, XXV (1951), 207–08.

205 GRIMSTONE END (TL 935690) 1953–54; pagan Saxon structures; excavated before gravel-working; B. J. W. Brown, G. M. Knocker, N. Smedley and S. E. West, "Excavations at Grimstone End, Pakenham", *Proc. Suff. Inst. Archaeol.*, XXVI (1954), 197–207.

206 RENDLESHAM (TM 340510) 1951; W. G. Arnott; late Saxon structures; recorded; interim note in *Proc. Suff. Inst. Archaeol.*, XXV (1949–51), 308.

207 RICKINGHALL INFERIOR (TM 040760) 1964–67; B. J. W. Brown; several pagan Saxon sunken-huts; excavated; interim note in *Proc. Suff. Inst. Archaeol.*, XXX (1964), 122.

208 RICKINGHALL SUPERIOR (TM 042738) 1953; B. J. W. Brown; pagan Saxon sunken-huts; recorded; no report published.

209 RICKINGHALL SUPERIOR (TM 038743) 1958; B. J. W. Brown; pagan Saxon structures; recorded; no report published.

210 STOW, WEST (TL 797714) 1957–60; Miss V. Evison; pagan Saxon sunken-huts; excavated; interim notes in *Med. Archaeol.*, II (1958), 189–90; III (1959), 300; IV (1960), 137 and V (1961), 311.

210A —— 1965–68; S. E. West; three pagan Saxon building and 34 sunken-huts; excavated; interim notes in *Med. Archaeol.*, X (1966), 174; XI (1967), 269–70 and Fig. 75; full interim report in *Med. Archaeol.*, XIII (1969), forthcoming.   See also *Current Archaeol.*, I (1967), 16–17.

211 WATTISFIELD (TM 006741) 1958; B. J. W. Brown: pagan Saxon structures; recorded; no report published.

212 WATTISFIELD (TM 005731) 1955; B. J. W. Brown; pagan Saxon structures; recorded; no report published.

213 WORLINGTON (WEST ROW) (TL 673742) 1933; pagan Saxon sunken-hut; excavated; Lethbridge and Tebbutt, 1933.

SURREY

214 CUDDINGTON (TQ 228631) 1959; M. Biddle; medieval church; excavated; interim note and plan in *Med. Archaeol.*, IV (1960), 143–45 and Fig. 52.

215 FARNHAM (SU 842466) 1924; H. R. Huband; pagan Saxon sunken-hut; excavated before gravel-working; interim note in *Surr. Archaeol. Coll.*, XXXVI (1925), 123.   Fuller report in K. P. Oakley, W. F. Rankine and A. W. G. Lowther, "A Survey of the Prehistory of the Farnham District", *Surr. Archaeol. Soc.*, (1930), 255–59.

216 HAM (TQ 169715) 1950; B. Hope-Taylor and S. S. Frere; sunken-hut; excavated before gravel-working; interim note in *Surr. Archaeol. Coll.*, LII (1952), 101–02.

217 WATENDONE (TQ 321594) 1966; Mrs. M. Saaler; medieval church; excavated; interim note in *Med. Archaeol.*, XI (1967), 283.

SUSSEX

218 BALSDEAN (TQ 378060) 1950; medieval church and structures; excavated; Norris and Hockings, 1953.

219 BARPHAM, UPPER (TQ 067089), 1953–55; complex Anglo-Saxon and medieval church; excavated; Barr-Hamilton, 1961.

220 BISHOPSTONE (TQ 467007) 1967–68; D. Thompson; pagan Saxon sunken-huts; excavated; interim notes in *Med. Archaeol.*, XII (1968), 161 and XIII (1969), forthcoming.

221 BRAMBER (TQ 190106) 1961; E. W. Holden; medieval structures; recorded during drainage works; interim note in *Med. Archaeol.*, VI–VII (1962–63), 339.

222 BRAMBLE BOTTOM (TV 575978) 1953; medieval farm; excavated; Musson, 1955.

223 ERRINGHAM, OLD (TQ 204075) 1964; E. W. Holden; pagan Saxon sunken-hut; excavated; interim note in *Med. Archaeol.*, IX (1965), 175.

224 ERRINGHAM, OLD (TQ 205077) 1957; E. W. Holden; medieval structures; excavated; interim note in *Med. Archaeol.*, II (1958), 194.

225 EXCEAT (TV 522992) 1913; medieval church; excavated; Budgen, 1916.

226 GORING (TQ 106026) 1963; medieval sunken-hut; excavated; Barton, 1965.

227 HANGLETON (TQ 268074) 1952–54; six medieval buildings; excavated; Holden, 1963.

227A —— 1954; four medieval buildings; excavated; Hurst and Hurst, 1964.

228 MEDMERRY (SZ 837937) 1934; late Saxon structures; excavated; White, 1934.

229 NORTHEYE (TQ 68072) 1953; no information; no report published.

230 RACTON (SU 783093) 1962; medieval structures; recorded after ploughing; R. Bradley, "The Deserted Medieval Village of Racton", *Suss. Notes and Queries*, XVI (1967), 328–29.

231 TARRING (TQ 133040) 1964; late Saxon medieval building; excavated; Barton, 1964.

232 TELSCOMBE (TQ 405033) 1964; late Saxon structures; observed; E. W. Holden, "Saxo-Norman Remains at Telscombe", *Sussex. Notes and Queries*, XVI (1965), 154–58.

233 THAKEHAM (TQ 104174) 1934; pagan Saxon sunken-hut; excavated; E. and E. C. Curwen, "A Saxon Hut-site at Thakeham", *Antiq. Journ.*, XIV (1934), 425–26.

WARWICKSHIRE

234 ALVESTON (SP 213554) 1934; Saxon structures; recorded; no report published; material in the Stratford Museum.

235 BAGINTON (SP 342747) 1961–62; Miss G. G. Wilkins; pagan Saxon sunken-hut; excavated; interim note in *West Mid. Ann. Archaeol. News Sheet*, V (1962), 4.

236 BIGGIN (SP 535781) 1950–51; T. Fawcett; medieval road and bank; sectioned; *Rep. Rugby School Nat. Hist. Soc.*, LXXXV (1951), 17–19.

237 RADBOURN (SP 440570) 1959; Miss J. M. Morris, medieval structures; recorded after ploughing; interim note in *Med. Archaeol.*, IV (1960), 159.

238 STRETTON BASKERVILLE (SP 420910) 1947–8; M. W. Beresford; medieval structures; excavated; interim notes in Beresford, 1950, 69–71 and 1954–56, 68 and 70.

239 STRETTON-ON-THE-FOSSE (SP 216383) 1968; W. Ford; pagan Saxon sunken-huts under cemetery; excavated before gravel working; interim note in *Med. Archaeol.*, XIII (1969), forthcoming.

240 WOLFHAMPCOTE (SP 530652) 1955; Mrs. D. G. Hurst; no medieval buildings found only ditches; excavated; interim note in *Annual Report*, III (1955), 11–12.

WESTMORLAND

241 MILLHOUSE (SD 635852) 1964; medieval farm; excavated; Lowndes, 1967.

WILTSHIRE

242 ASHLEY (ST 945315) 1904; late medieval building; excavated; Stallybrass, 1906.

243 BRATTON (ST 914519) 1965; A. L. Foster; possible medieval structures; excavated; interim note in *Med. Archaeol.*, X (1966), 214.

244 GOMELDON (SU 182356) 1963–68; J. W. G. Musty and D. Algar; seven medieval buildings; excavated; interim notes and plans in *Med. Archaeol.*, VIII (1964), 289 and Fig. 94; IX (1965), 214; X (1966), 214; XI (1967), 214 and Fig. 89 and XII (1968), 203 and XIII (1969), forthcoming; fuller interim stencilled reports issued for the first three seasons, J. Musty and D. Algar, "The Excavations at the Deserted Medieval

DESERTED MEDIEVAL VILLAGES

Village Site of Gomeldon, Near Salisbury, Wiltshire", *Salisbury Mus. Res. Com.*, I (1963); II (1964) and III (1965).

245 HUISH (SU 145637) 1967–68; N. P. Thompson; medieval church and buildings; excavated; N. P. Thompson, "Huish Church: Excavation of the Original Foundations and Early Chapel", *Wilts. Archaeol. Mag.*, LXII (1967), 51–66; interim note in *Med. Archaeol.*, XII (1968), 205 and XIII (1969), forthcoming.

246 MANTON DOWN (SU 146717) 1949; medieval enclosure but no structure; excavated; O. Meyrick, "An Early Medieval Site on Manton Down", *Wilts. Archaeol. Mag.*, LIII (1950), 328–31.

247 MORGAN'S HILL (SU 040671) 1909; medieval enclosure but no structure; excavated; Cunnington, 1910.

248 POTTERNE (ST 996585) 1962; late Saxon church; excavated; Davey, 1964.

249 SHAW (SU 135653) 1929; medieval church; excavated; H. C. Brentnall, "Shaw Church", *Marlborough Coll. Nat. Hist. Soc. Rep.*, LXXVIII (1929), 95–96.

250 WARDOUR (ST 925272) 1963; P. J. Fowler; medieval structures; recorded after ploughing; interim note in *Med. Archaeol.*, VIII (1964), 289.

251 WESTBURY (ST 873503) 1963–64; Col. W. D. Shaw, J. W. G. Musty and P. J. Fowler; no definite Anglo-Saxon structures located; interim notes in *Wilts. Archaeol. Mag.*, LIX (1964), 187–88 and LX (1965), 136. Pottery in P. J. Fowler, "Two finds of Saxon Domestic Pottery in Wiltshire", *Wilts. Archaeol. Mag.*, LXI (1966), 31–37.

252 WICK (ST 941287) 1962–63; bank sectioned, no medieval structures located; P. J. Fowler, "A Rectangular Earthwork Enclosure at Tisbury", *Antiquity*, XXXVII (1963), 290–93.

253 WINTERBOURNE GUNNER (SU 180354) 1965; D. J. Algar; medieval structures; excavated; interim note in *Med. Archaeol.*, X (1966), 216.

254 WROUGHTON (SU 139707) 1959–62; medieval farm; excavated; Bowen and Fowler, 1961 and Fowler, 1963.

WORCESTERSHIRE

255 ELMONT (SO 975373) 1938; medieval farm; excavated; Murray-Threipland, 1946–48.

256 FLADBURY (SO 996464) 1967–68; middle Saxon building and sunken-hut; excavated before development; interim notes in *Med. Archaeol.*, XII (1968), 162 and XIII (1969), forthcoming. See also *Current Archaeol.*, I (1968), 123–24.

257 WALTON (SO 946801) 1952; medieval building; excavated; G. S. Taylor, "Walton Hill, Romsley", *Trans. Birm. Archaeol. Soc.*, LXXII (1956), 10–13.

YORKSHIRE E.R.

258 CAYTHORPE (TA 120678) 1963–67; R. Hall; medieval building; excavated; interim note in *Med. Archaeol.*, VI–VII (1962–63), 289.

259 ELMSWELL (TA 000576) 1935–37; pagan Saxon structures; excavated; A. L. Congreve, "A Roman and Saxon Site at Elmswell", *Hull Mus. Pub.* CXCIII (1937), 1–28 and CXCVIII (1938), 1–41.

260   FLIXTON (TA 022806) 1949; medieval structures; excavated; Brewster, 1952.

261   FLOTMANBY (TA 080799) 1955; T. C. M. Brewster; medieval structures; recorded during ploughing; no report published.

262   GRINDALE (TA 131711) 1962–65 and 1968; T. C. M. Brewster; medieval structures; recorded before and after ploughing; *Annual Report*, x (1962), 6; *Med. Archaeol.*, x (1966), 216.

263   HILDERTHORPE (TA 174655) 1954–55; Mrs. D. G. Hurst; medieval structures; recording during cutting of sewer trench; interim note in *Annual Rep.*, II (1954), 11 and III (1955), 7.

264   KEMP HOWE (SE 962662) 1968; T. C. M. Brewster; pagan Saxon sunken-hut excavated close to Anglian burials; interim note in *Med. Archaeol.*, XIII (1969), forthcoming.

265   KNAPTON, EAST (SE 883760) 1964; T. C. M. Brewster; medieval structures; excavated; *Med. Archaeol.*, IX (1965), 217–18.

266   OUSETHORPE (SE 820515) 1963; W. J. Varley; late Saxon structures; excavated; no report published.

267   RAISTHORPE (SE 855617) 1961; T. C. M. Brewster; medieval structures; recorded during ploughing; *Annual Rep.*, x (1962), 7.

268   RIPLINGHAM (SE 963320) 1956–57; two medieval buildings; excavated; Wacher, 1966.

268A   —— 1966; P. T. Norfolk; medieval building; excavated; interim note and plan in *Med. Archaeol.*, XI (1967), 313–14 and Fig. 89.

269   SPEETON (TA 154747) 1960; T. C. M. Brewster; medieval structures; recorded after ploughing; interim note in *Med. Archaeol.*, V (1961), 333.

270   STAXTON (TA 024794) 1947–48; pagan Saxon structures; excavated; T. C. M. Brewster, "Excavations at Newham's Pit, Staxton", *Yorks. Archaeol. Journ.*, XXXIX (1956–58), 193–223.

270A   —— 1948; medieval building; excavated; Brewster, 1951.

271   SWAYTHORPE (TA 038691) 1962; R. Hall; medieval building; excavated; interim note in *Med. Archaeol.*, VI–VII (1962–63), 290.

272   WAULDBY (SE 974297) 1950; J. Hunter; no details; no report published; see *Annual Rep.*, II (1954), 2.

273   WAWNE (TA 093365) 1960–61; H. C. Jones; thirty-four medieval buildings; planned after ploughing; interim note and plan in *Med. Archaeol.*, VI–VII (1962–63), 343–45 and Fig. 103.

274   WHARRAM PERCY (SE 858646) 1950–60; J. G. Hurst; medieval croft and manor; excavated; interim notes in *Annual Reports*, II (1954), 14–15; III (1955), 9–11; IV (1956), 8–9; V (1957), 5–6; VI (1958), 4–5; VII (1959), 7–8; VIII (1960), 8–11; shorter notes and plans from 1956 onwards in *Med. Archaeol.*, I (1957), 66–68, Fig. 34; II (1958), 205–07, Fig. 51; III (1959), 324; IV (1960), 161, 164; V (1961), 335.

274A   —— 1961–68; J. G. Hurst; medieval croft and church; excavated; interim notes in *Annual Reports*, IX (1961), 7–9; X (1962), 9–12; XI (1963), 7–10; XII (1964), 10–11; XIII (1965), 20–22; XIV (1966), 27–28; XV (1967), 11; shorter notes and plans in *Med. Archaeol*; VI–VII (1962–63), 345–46; VIII (1964), 250–91, Fig. 95;

(1965), 187–215; x (1966), 188–89, 216; xi (1967), 314; and *Annual Reports*, xvi (1968) and *Med. Archaeol.*, xii (1968), 205 and xiii (1969), forthcoming. See also *Current Archaeol.*, i (1967), 92–93.

275 WINTHORPE (TA 000453) 1956–62; G. D. Lloyd; medieval structures; excavated; interim notes in *Med. Archaeol.*, i (1957), 164; ii (1958), 206–08; v (1961), 329; vi–vii (1962–63), 336 and viii (1964), 274.

YORKSHIRE N.R.

276 CAWTHORN (TA 773891) 1945–46; R. H. Hayes; medieval structures; no report published.

277 CROSSGATES (TA 032832) 1947–56; pagan Saxon structures; excavated; Rutter and Duke, 1958; for further work, *Yorks. Archaeol. Journ.*, xli (1963–66), 10 and 173.

278 DANBY-IN-CLEVELAND (NZ 700063) 1963; C. V. Bellamy; medieval structures: interim note in *Med. Archaeol.*, viii (1964), 215.

279 HATTERBOARD (TA 017887) 1957–59; five medieval buildings; excavated before development; Rimington, 1961.

279A —— 1968; P. Farmer; further structures; excavated; interim note in *Med. Archaeol.*, xiii (1969), forthcoming.

280 LAZENBY (SE 340986) 1957; Miss J. Telford; medieval structures; excavated; interim note in *Med. Archaeol.*, ii (158), 211.

281 LILLING, EAST (SE 664645) 1948; M. W. Beresford; medieval structures; excavated; see Beresford, 1954C, 29–36 and 70.

282 OSGODBY (TA 057827) 1963–65; five medieval buildings; planned during road-works; P. Farmer, "1963 Excavations at Osgodby", *Trans. Scarborough and Dist. Archaeol. Soc.*, viii (1965), 14–19; "Excavations at the Deserted Medieval Village of Osgodby, near Scarborough, 1956–65", *ibid.*, xi (1968), 29–61.

283 THORNTON RISEBOROUGH (SE 747826) 1945; R. H. Hayes; no medieval structures found; no report published, report and pot drawings in the files of the D.M.V.R.G.

284 WYKEHAM (SE 966837) 1951–52; pagan Saxon sunken-huts; excavated; Moore, 1966.

YORKSHIRE W.R.

285 AISMUNDERBY (SE 306686) 1964–65; C. V. Bellamy; medieval chapel; excavated; interim notes in *Med. Archaeol.*, ix (1965), 187 and x (1966), 216.

286 MALHAM (SD 897675) 1949–60; medieval buildings; excavated; Raistrick and Holmes, 1962.

287 STEETON (SE 532441) 1951–52; medieval structures; excavated; see note in Beresford, 1954C, 59–61.

288 STOCKTON (SE 335456) 1956–57; medieval structures; excavated; C. V. Bellamy, "Excavations at Stockton in the West Riding or Yorkshire", *Yorks. Archaeol. Journ.*, xli (1963–66), 701–08.

289 UNDERBANK (SD 668925) 1955–56; medieval buildings; excavated; Addyman *et al.*, 1963.

290 WILSTROP (SE 484553) 1949; medieval structures; excavated; see notes in Beresford, 1954C, 70.

CHAPTER FOUR

An Historian's Appraisal of Archaeological Research

M. W. BERESFORD

INTRODUCTION

Chapters 1 and 2 were written independently of each other, although the authors had been closely associated in fieldwork over the last twenty years and knew something of each other's views. In this chapter, written after reading Mr. Hurst's contribution, I have attempted an assessment of the evidence produced by archaeological investigations from the viewpoint of a "pure" historian. If it is a critical assessment, that is not in order to usurp the function of the more detached, outside critic.

On many occasions a working historian is brought up against the sad fact that in respect of documentary evidence his Dark Age may extend far beyond whatever point is conventionally taken as the end of the "Dark Ages" and the dawn of medieval light. Faced with a village that has an interesting and provocative name or topography, an historian may have cause to bemoan the paucity or absence of documents which he can summon to his aid. But when he surveys the much more severe restraints on the activities of the research archaeologist he may pause to count his blessings. He sees the work that Mr. Hurst's chapter synthesises, not as a disarray of meagre skirmishes in a campaign where the enemy has yet to be properly engaged, but as a considerable tribute to human resilience.

Yet while the documentary historian has to reconcile himself to evidence long since destroyed, the field archaeologist sees evidence being destroyed before his own eyes, with the State possessing very limited sanctions against unlawful destruction, very limited powers of preservation in the face of agricultural demands, and very limited resources for research excavation ahead of threatened (and lawful) destruction. Thus excavations may have to be undertaken not where the frontier of knowledge is most likely to be profitably extended but where the threat is most imminent. At the frontier of knowledge itself—or where the frontier seems speculatively to lie at any given moment—the archaeologist is faced with far greater problems of access than an historian seeking permission to view documents. There are owners of documents who are secretive and possessive but in general their permission to view is not likely to involve them in physical disturbances, inconvenience, and loss of potential revenue that face and deter a landowner (and his tenant) when permission is requested for an archaeological invasion. There are costs in money and effort for every journey that an historian makes to an archive but an historian who has witnessed the planning, execution and reporting of an excavation must finish with increased respect for the effort, of muscle as well as mind, and for the organisation, of men as well as of spoil-heaps, that lie behind even the curtest excavation report.

The most cursory glance at any of Mr. Hurst's plans is enough to disabuse anyone who imagines that the excavation of a medieval village house is a mere matter of scraping off the accumulated sands of time. Complexity in revealed structures is exposed only at costs in money and time which the inexperienced cannot imagine. The enthusiasm of an amateur labour force, where one can be found, does not negative this assertion. Professional supervision of a particularly skilled and tactful kind is necessary to make effective use of amateurs, and anything complex is unlikely to be completed in those limited number of weeks in the year when amateurs can be collected together. Holding the loyalty of volunteer amateurs for successive seasons is a problem in itself.

The complexity, even of the buildings within a single village croft, is such that any possibility of the total excavation of a deserted medieval village lies beyond the anticipated future. Only the emergence of the most magnanimous patron could make this financially possible, and money might not be able to remove all the impediments. It does seem likely therefore, that the total excavation of a medieval town street (at Winchester) will be achieved long before what might, at first glance, seem so much easier, the total excavation of an English medieval village street.

It is in this context of constraints, not of the archaeologists' chosing or making, that the historian must view the results so far achieved. The absence of a single, completely-excavated village makes it impossible for some important historical questions to be answered yet: and, of course, the variety of English local economies was such that generalisations based on one total excavation would be hazardous and highly vulnerable to criticism. Therefore, an historian has to say that the archaeological supplement to knowledge that is already available in conventional, documentary sources still derives from deserted villages small in number compared with the known total; from villages unevenly distributed over the country; from villages that do not yet represent more than a few of the inter-regional variations in such economic assets as soils or building materials; and from villages where even the largest-scale and continuing excavation has not yet progressed beyond the parish church, a manor house and two crofts, with at least thirty more crofts on the agenda. But he says this in charity and not in criticism.

The economic historian has conventionally been most familiar with the actual products of economic activity at second hand. That is, documentary descriptions of operations in the field, in the workshop, at the counter or on the high seas have been his principal means of reconstructing and interpreting past economies. Some of these products have been available to be seen in museums and some are pictured in contemporary graphics: to this degree, if there is unfamiliarity or mystery, it arises from a simple failure in communication. Much of the nonsense written a generation or two ago about self-sufficiency in the medieval countryside would have been more quickly exposed if its readers had been more familiar with the interior of museum showcases, although it must be acknowledged that the museum curators of the period were not always possessed by the desire to communicate through lively display of objects in their care. Thus even the best of the inter-war studies, such as those of H. S. Bennett[1] and G. C. Homans,[2] were refreshingly realistic about the peasant as a man but reticent about his artifacts and manufactures; the realistic study of the Orwins[3] did not come in from the fields to the village houses. Even the professional historians of architecture had their interests limited to surviving structures and thus came to a village only for the study of its medieval church or manor house features.

The peasant-house was buried from historians' sight. A few romantics may have imagined that medieval England consisted of Anne Hathaway cottages and picturesque houses in Cotswold and other local stones. Their delusion has been for ever laid by Professor Hoskins' and M. W. Barley's work on the "Great Re-building" of the period 1570–1640, which has established the veteran houses of the Old English Village of the travel posters as emphatically post-medieval: and so the peasant-house of the Middle Ages still remains buried from sight.

The principal interest that a village historian finds in Mr. Hurst's chapter is likely, therefore, to be in one area of novelty and one area of re-emphasis. The novelty concerns the peasant-house and its illustration of living standards and changing economic pressures: while the re-emphasis concerns the variety of artifacts produced or consumed within them. Of the fields themselves, beyond the enclosed crofts adjoining the houses, the excavator will naturally have very much less to say, although there is a case for some selected exploration of the sub-soils of medieval ploughland well-preserved in modern grassland, an area annually diminishing at a rate which adds urgency to the application of techniques demonstrated by Mr. H. C. Bowen and Mr. P. J. Fowler in the "Celtic" field systems. I myself am consoled, of course, that the close relation of ridge-and-furrow to the topography of the perimeter of house-crofts and medieval field-roads helps to confirm the medieval date for this land feature which I had deduced from correlations with sixteenth-century estate surveys.

Finally, while some archaeological features within the deserted medieval village cannot be expected in the un-deserted, "normal" village, much of the evidence presented by Mr. Hurst seems relevant to the general history of the medieval village, and thus contributes substantially to that wider study of settlement forms which was anticipated in the closing paragraphs of our *Preface*.

I: DATING

The paragraphs which follow are a gloss on Mr. Hurst's chapter, the main purpose being to emphasise points which seem particularly interesting to an historian (but without repeating his references); to make minor criticisms; and to suggest where the specialist needs of historians might be met by further archaeological inquiries.

[1] H. S. Bennett, *Life on the English Manor* (1937).
[2] G. C. Homans, *English Villagers of the Thirteenth Century* (1941).
[3] C. S. and C. S. Orwin, *The Open Fields* (1938).

The historian notes that archaeologists have now made forays at sites with desertion periods well spread over time. Anglo-Saxon sites apart, there are reports from early medieval desertions, such as Grenstein; from probable Black Death depopulations, such as Upton and Seacourt; from fifteenth-century desertions, such as Martinsthorpe; from sheep depopulations, such as Wharram Percy; from the eighteenth century, as at West Whelpington; the nineteenth, as at Riplingham; and indeed the twentieth at Faxton. However, accurate and confirmatory dating of desertion periods is not yet likely to be the archaeologists' major contribution to the study. I did not at once realise this. Even economic historians have to think of history as being somehow concerned with dates, and in so far as I can recall my own motives for wanting to explore beneath the sod at Stretton Baskerville (Warws.) in 1947 it was to bolster my confidence in the assertions which I was beginning to make, that the greater part of the depopulations were before the reign of Henry VII, i.e. in the 1460's and 1470's; and that the folk myths explaining known village earthworks by the ravages of the Black Death were untenable as history. My pathetic ignorance both of the techniques of archaeological dating and of the complexity of structures would probably have resulted more in the destruction of evidence than of its production, but my translation from Rugby to Leeds fortunately saved the site after only one or two small trenches had been driven across the supposed Stretton Baskerville church. My amateurish expeditions to Wilstrop, Steeton (Yorks., W.R.) and East Lilling (Yorks., N.R.) in 1948 and 1949 were similarly motivated and no better equipped. At Wharram Percy in 1950 I was still groping for desertion dates when Mr. Hurst and Mr. Golson arrived, fresh from the Archaeological Tripos, to professionalise the enquiry, and allow me to take up a more harmless role in the commissariat, recruiting, public relations and welfare sides of that excavation.

At this distance I know that to hope for an excavation to give a completely convincing demonstration of a desertion date was too optimistic. This is not so much because the principal archaeological dating evidence for a peasant house—that is, pottery—cannot yet be dated to within plus or minus three decades, but because it would be necessary to excavate at least the upper layer of all, if not most, of the house sites in a village. Anything less would lay one open to the criticism that the unexcavated houses happened to be those where habitation had continued. If a depopulation date was to hang on one single excavated structure it would indeed be safer—although still hazardous—to hang it on the excavation of the village church. Yet the abandonment of a church should be datable with less effort from ecclesiastical records. Thus, at Seacourt (Berks.) in 1439 the vicar declared in a letter to the Pope:

> the church is collapsed, the houses and habitations in the parish exposed to ruin and uninhabited, with the exception of two only and these distant from the church and from one another; with this exception there are no parishioners.

Seacourt has been fortunate in the way it has attracted the attention of archaeologists. There were trial excavations in 1937–39, and in 1958–59 Mr. Martin Biddle directed excavations ahead of the works for the western sector of the Oxford by-pass that was to traverse the main part of the village site.

Although the five seasons' work did not meet the strictest requirement of totality urged above, yet Mr. Biddle's conclusions on dating, in his excellently produced report, confirm the documentary evidence, that this village had very little life in the post-Black Death period.

> The latest pottery from the village suggests a little activity down to 1400, but these late sherds are so few in number that it is difficult to imagine anything except a reduced population after the Black Death . . . there is only slight evidence for any occupation of the village after c. 1350 and none at all for any continued occupation after 1400.

Similarly, although on the basis of fewer house-sites excavated, Mr. Rahtz concluded at Upton (Glos.):

> there is no reason at present to question the late 14th century date for the desertion suggested by the documentary evidence.

Mr. Wacher's work at Martinsthorpe, on the other hand, illustrated the difficulties of a single season's work on a limited area within a site, all that is usually possible where a site is threatened by development.

> In contrast to the lack of structural information, the excavations did produce some dated pottery. . . . The pottery found is representative of the period from the twelfth to the eighteenth century.

The wide span of time indicated by the pottery is not surprising at a site which was chosen for a new Hall by an earl of Denbigh in the late seventeenth century, but now completely deserted.

The most that can be said, therefore, is that no excavation has yet produced pottery evidence for occupation at a date that contradicts the depopulation date already suggested from documents. This is as true for Hangleton (Sussex), where it is known that there were only two households in 1428, as for West Whelpington (Northumb.) with a much longer known history. The Wharram Percy excavations, probably the most detailed of any at a deserted village site, have produced no pottery incongruous with a desertion c. 1500, as described in the evidence produced to Wolsey's Commissioners for Depopulation in 1517–18.

Again pre-occupied with dating, an innocent historian might perhaps have expected that excavations would easily contribute to the difficult questions of village origins by moving rapidly back from the medieval to the pre-medieval, and from there to the mysteries of discontinuity of settlement or Finbergian continuity à la Withington. Reality has proved more complex and elusive: successive occupation of the same toft area has too often disturbed the flimsier Anglo-Saxon remains; and again, the smaller size of Anglo-Saxon populations would imply that only a portion of the area occupied in medieval times could be expected to yield earlier material: but to locate the earliest area at any settlement brings us up against the magnitude of a total excavation of a village site. It will be noted that Roman material has appeared at Upton and an Iron Age burial at Wharram Percy but neither finds were in quantity or position such as contribute to the debate on continuity of settlement; and that at Hound Tor the occupation has been taken back to the ninth or tenth centuries; and at Wharram Percy the foundations of an Anglo-Saxon church have been found, although houses of that period still elude.

II: CHANGES IN HOUSE STRUCTURE

The historian will gratefully accept the illustrations of the flimsy structures of medieval peasant-houses revealed by excavation, and compare them with those of the upper strata in medieval society.[4]   They can also be compared instructively with the cruder Anglo-Saxon peasant-houses, little better than holes in the ground, and with the improved village houses of the "Rebuilding" encountered in the sixteenth and seventeenth centuries.   These comparisons are non-quantitative measures of changes in rural living standards.   But the medieval economy was not static, and it is natural to ask whether village buildings reflect any of the changes in population, availability of resources, and distribution of wealth, that historians believe they have detected in the medieval centuries; remembering that medieval documentary sources are reticent about houses at the peasant end of the social scale.

It may be convenient to distinguish between those archaeological evidences which square with the conventional wisdom of history teaching and those which raise problems, not all insurmountable.   Firstly, as to the consequences of the long period of expanding population and consequent agricultural colonisation: in its most direct form, the need for more housing, this seems to be clearly visible in the continued addition of houses to the village nucleus, some of the additions looking like acts of seignurial planning akin to new urban developments of the same period; these additions were sometimes set on former arable furlongs, and took their shape from them; and sometimes set in the demesne closes near the manor house which, as the Wharram Percy case shows, could itself be demolished to make room for extra village houses and be replaced by a new structure in a more remote and private quarter.   Exactly the same expansion and revision of plan is seen where village churches have been available for excavation.

Other consequences of population expansion were an increase in the cultivated area, and a steady clearance of woodland.   In terms of village structures it would not be unreasonable to expect building timber then to become more difficult to obtain locally, and stone to be increasingly employed in those areas where it lay at or near the surface.

When one passes to structural features of houses there are more difficult reconciliations to be made between history and archaeology, and it may be useful to set down certain relationships, not without their own contradictions, which might exist between the house-types of a village and the economic environment.   An over-riding consideration for any such discussion must be the simultaneous existence of peasants within the same village who had different status and wealth—and who sometimes practised specialist occupations.   Even in the villages most intimately known to archaeology it has not been possible to use documentary evidence to link a particular house with a particular class of owner: where more than one house has been excavated in a village, and contemporaneous differences of structure appear, one may associate extreme differences of size with differences of status; but that does not take us far beyond the platitudinous.

---

[4] The difference in quality between a manor house and peasant-house can be expressed in terms of working archaeology as I often observed it from the organiser's side-lines. A sixth-form schoolgirl could easily lift into a barrow the chalk stones from the walls of a thirteenth-century peasant-house: while a single dressed stone from the Norman manor house (or the church) needed two husky Borstal lads, at the end of their teens.

1. *Charlecote Park and Old Town, Warwickshire, 1736*
   Old Town, two closes of 7½ and 12½ acres, now lie within the park, and earthworks also testify to a village site here. In 1736 the two closes seem to lie outside the park, across the small tributary which runs into the Avon on the left of the Lucys' manor house, begun in 1558. Charlecote village is seen below *The Park* (where Shakespeare is alleged to have been caught poaching), so that the *Town* may be Hunscote, an adjoining de-populated village. But John Rous described Charlecote as 'almost all imparked', so that the original village may have continued over to *Old Town*. (Map by James Fish in Warws. County Rec. Off., L6/1935).

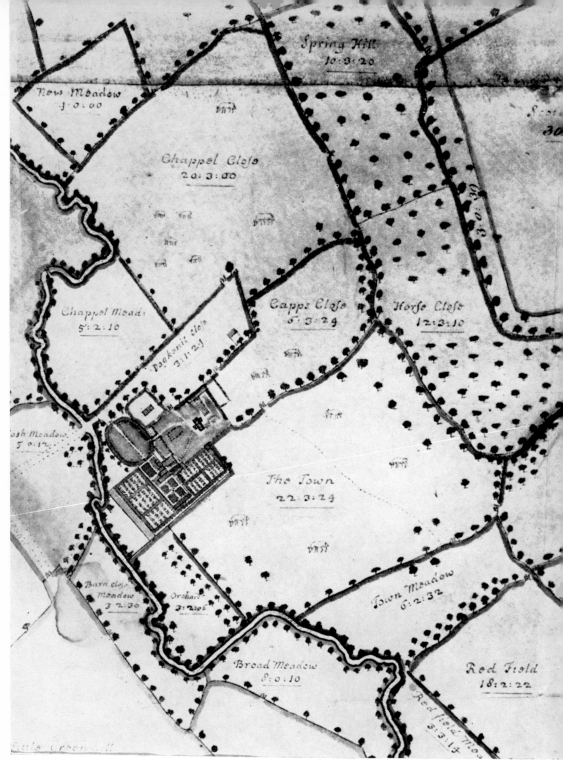

2. *Walton Deyville, Warwickshire: the Town in the park, 1728*
Animals graze the closes within the park: *The Town* of $22\frac{3}{4}$ acres, south-east of the
Hall and *Chappel Close* of $20\frac{3}{4}$ acres to the north-east.   St. James' church had been
incorporated into the gardens immediately north-east of the Hall.   Wolsey's inquiry
of 1517 was told that the whole village was destroyed in 1509.   (Map by James Fish
in Warws. County Rec. Off., CR 750/1.)

3a. *Pudding Norton, Norfolk: ruins of St. Margaret's church*
The west tower and fragments of the nave.   There were at least 15 families in the village in 1329.   For the adjacent village earthworks, see two air photographs in *Lost Villages*, Plate 7.

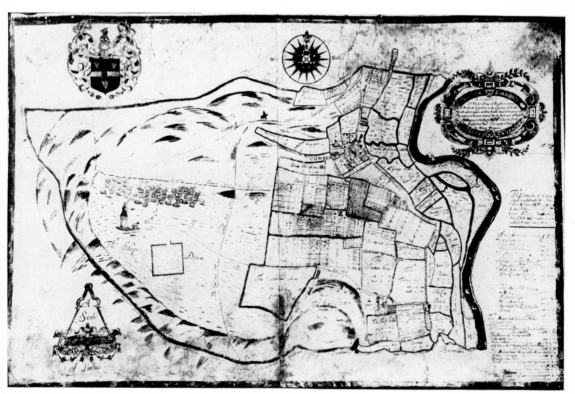

3b. *Coombes, Sussex, in 1677 before its desertion*
Now a church and farm but then still a village with its open fields, riverside meadow and extensive sheepdown.   Applesham, in the south of the township, had at least five houses: it is now one farm. (See also Plate 4.)

4. *Coombes in 1677: the village centre*

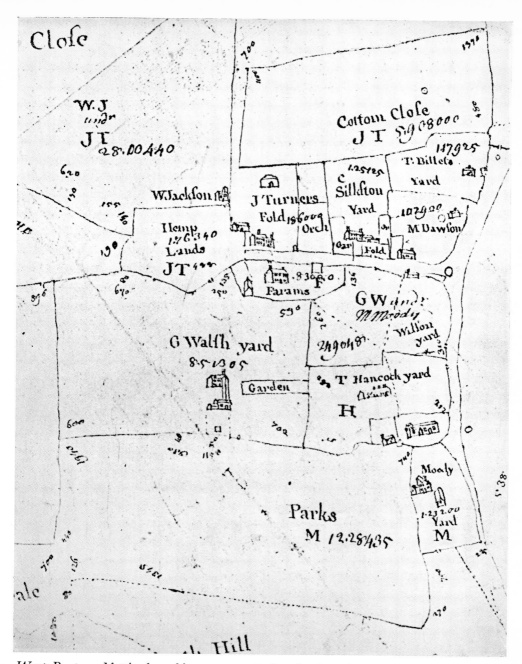

5. *West Burton, Nottinghamshire, c. 1750 before its desertion*
This undated draft plan is from the papers of the surveyor William Fairbank I; it shows houses on the west bank of the Trent and along a street leading west into fields which were already enclosed. Twelve farms and the church are shown. An accompanying survey shows that four of the twelve proprietors lived in adjacent villages. (Sheffield City Libraries, Fairbank Ms. WES 1L and CP/42/67–8.)

6. *Water Eaton, Oxfordshire: ridge and furrow surrounding the deserted village site*
This section of an R.A.F. photograph, taken in January 1947 with a low mid-day
sun, shows the shadows in the grass furrows that delineate the selions and furlongs of
the medieval fields.   No ridging appears in the riverside meadows (right) nor
around the village earthworks (centre left); note the reversed-S shape of the selions.
(See *Sutton, 1964–65,* 99–115 and fig. 38.)   There were still 30 tenants here, mostly
resident, in 1659–70.

7. *Barton Blount, Derbyshire*
View of excavation showing a complex series of post-holes and foundation trenches for superimposed timber buildings, with no change to stone foundations, ranging in date from the eleventh to fourteenth century (see page 96).

8. *Hound Tor I, Devon*
   View of excavation, showing the thirteenth-century stone long-house 1 which overlies earlier turf-walled buildings (see Fig. 14 and page 91).

9. *Garrow, Cornwall*
Photograph of the byre-end of the long-house (see Fig. 19A), showing the manger with tethering holes for the animals (see page 113).

10. *Lower Ditchford, Gloucestershire*
Oblique air photograph looking south-west. A typical clay site with a network of sunken roads and raised rectangular tofts and crofts. Beyond the site can be seen the modern farm built on ridge and furrow which surrounds the site. To the left are the water meadows which were never ploughed (see pages 95 and 117).

11. *Rand, Lincolnshire*

Oblique air photograph looking west. A typical clay site with a network of sunken roads and raised rectangular tofts and crofts. Beyond the site can be seen the present farm and the medieval church with the square moated enclosure beyond, jutting out into the surviving ridge and furrow of the open fields. In the centre of the site is a recent pond (see pages 95 and 117).

12. *Ludborough, Lincolnshire* (*TF 295955*)

Oblique air photograph looking north-west. The earthworks surrounding the present village clearly demonstrate that it was once larger. These form the normal pattern of rectangular tofts common on clay sites. Some ridge and furrow is visible but most of it has been ploughed. In the foreground can be seen a chain of fishponds. The modern road pattern of this shrunk village cuts across the medieval layout suggesting a change in plan (see pages 95 and 117).

13. *West Firsby, Lincolnshire*
Oblique air photograph looking west.   A typical stone site with the tumbled walls
of the medieval peasant-houses showing as rectangular parchmarks in the grass.
The village shows a clear pattern of a planned street green in contrast to Walworth,
Plate 14.   The same complexity of building periods is visible without excavation.
The surrounding fields show ridge and furrow of the open fields (see page 95).

14. *Walworth, County Durham*
Oblique air photograph looking south-east. A typical stone area site with the tumbled walls of the medieval peasant-houses showing as rectangular parchmarks in the grass. The village shows a clear pattern of a planned green with the houses facing on to it and the tofts behind. The complexity of the walls visible suggests several periods of rebuilding. The modern farm has been built in the centre of the green. All the surrounding ridge and furrow is under plough (see page 95).

15. *South Middleton, Northumberland*
Oblique air photograph looking west.   A typical stone area site with the tumbled walls of the medieval peasant-houses showing as rectangular earthworks in rectangular banked tofts.   The limits of the village are clearly defined by the ridge and furrow of the open fields with a modern hedge cutting across them (see page 95).

16. *Holme, Bedfordshire*
Oblique air photograph, looking south-east. The site has recently been ploughed for the first time so that the pattern of roads and tofts is clearly seen as soil-marks (see pages 65 and 135).

17. *Wharram Percy, Yorkshire East Riding*
Area 10: superimposed walls at the east end (Fig. 27, squares LM/2–7) showing the complex rebuilding phases on different alignments (see page 122).

18. *North Elkington, Lincolnshire* (*TF 286904*)
Oblique air photograph looking north, showing a rectangular layout of roads
and tofts. Some foundations of stone houses are visible but other tofts presumably had timber buildings leaving no earthworks (see page 129).

19. *North Elkington, Lincolnshire*

Above, Oblique air photograph showing the valley immediately to the east of the main site, looking west towards the centre of the village seen on Plate 18. This is clearly a regular planned extension of the village.

Below, Oblique air photograph looking west, showing a further arm of the village extending south from the main site. Some ridge and furrow is visible (see page 129).

20. *Wharram Percy, Yorkshire East Riding*
St. Martin's church from the north-east, showing the various rebuildings of the east end of the chancel, with the smaller surviving seventeenth-century chancel in the background and the foundations of the north-east aisle-chapel on the right (see plan, Fig. 30, and page 132).

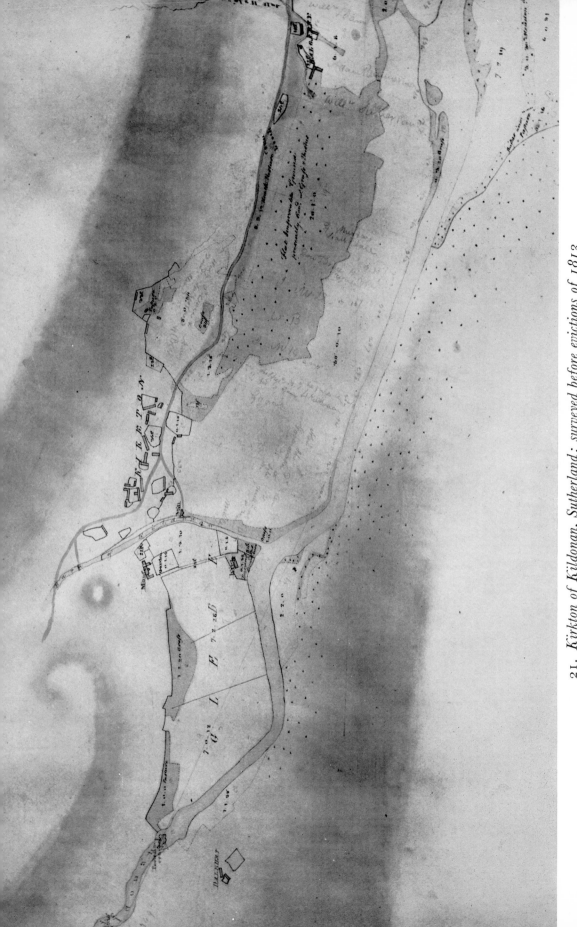

21. *Kirkton of Kildonan, Sutherland: surveyed before evictions of 1813*

22. *Tirai, Glen Lochay, Perthshire: widely-spaced long-houses and outhouses*

23. *Rosal, Sutherland: excavated long-house*
Note the central hearth and the dry-stone wall-base for the former turf superstructure.

24. *Lawers, Perthshire: eighteenth-century long-house and later house*

25. *Loch Duich, Ross and Cromarty: stone-and-wicker-walled houses*

26. *Fettercairn (near), Kincardineshire: clay-walled house*

27. *Dinas Noddfa, Glamorgan*

Lower House from east, looking across valley to Cefn Merthyr. The two central poles mark interior post-holes, the laths mark post-holes of side walls and of two entrance porches. In foreground are stones of 'hood' wall (Fig. 37e and p. 260).

28. *Aber Valley, Caernarvonshire*
Dwelling house, with entrance (centre left), byre (on left under tarpaulin); later dairy and barn beyond; recent sheepfold between house and byre (Fig. 37a and p. 260).

29. *Stonecarthy, Co. Kilkenny: oblique air photograph*
Site with hollow-way, banks, and terraces.   No house-sites visible.

30. *Granardkille, Co. Longford: oblique air photograph*
Deserted settlement; for discussions see Gazetteer, Chapter 12.

31. *Ballyduagh, Co. Tipperary: oblique air photograph*
Deserted settlements; isolated church and graveyard, hollow-ways, field banks, and house-sites.

The importance of this point, however, is seen when one takes into account the partial nature of village excavations so far achieved: unless sufficient houses were excavated to demonstrate that houses of every status in a village were affected by some external influence, it remains impossible to isolate this influence from those arising from changes in wealth and status. With our small repertoire of examples we may also be unwittingly blind to some crucial local peculiarity.

Many external influences might be presumed to bear directly on the changing character of village houses. One is a change in the availability of building materials. This may be positive, like the coming of brick in the sixteenth century, or negative, like the diminution in available building timber with the clearing of woodland and the extension of cultivation in the course of the thirteenth century. The movement to the greater use of stone in these circumstances could not be universal, for since building-stone does not occur at or near the surface in all parts of England, transport costs were high enough to circumscribe the area where villagers could afford stone as a replacement for wood: outside it, timber would have to remain as the main material even though its quality deteriorated. In this light, Mr. Hurst's demonstration of stone houses then being succeeded in the fifteenth century by half-timbered frames set on dwarf stone walls may be related to a renewed availability of immature woodland timber where agricultural land had been abandoned for scrub. Here, historical and archaeological evidence are congruous.

Another external influence is both more complex and more difficult to reconcile with the evidence. It is that of increased or decreased prosperity, and the prosperity relevant to the houses of the class here being considered is generally that of the peasant, and not of his seigneur unless a lord took it upon himself to provide his tenants' houses. Now the conventional wisdom of historical teaching on this subject, deriving largely from Prof. Postan and Prof. Hilton, is that the period of population expansion and colonisation brought a strengthening of the seigneur's bargaining power over his tenants as well as a decrease in the area and quality of land available to the average household. Villagers with special skills, such as millers, millwrights or textile workers, might be an exception to this general depression of income. The release of the pressure of population on land, beginning perhaps as early as the 1290's and unquestionably after the Black Death, reversed the position. Land was abundant, hands were scarce, and those peasants who survived the plagues enjoyed a golden age, shared (as Prof. Phelps Brown and Miss Hopkins have shown)[5] by those who laboured for a wage. As in modern times of labour shortage, the gap between the incomes of the skilled and the unskilled steadily narrowed. It has always been clear that the Hoskins–Barley Tudor rebuilding was undertaken by those who had been lucky in the ups and downs of Tudor economic change: but it has never been quite clear what the prosperous peasants, whom Prof. Postan long ago identified as the beneficiaries of fifteenth-century changes, were actually doing with their extra wealth. Did their spending pattern change to more food? to better-quality textiles? and to better village houses?

In relating late-medieval peasant-houses to economic prosperity of the peasantry it

---

[5] E. H. Phelps Brown and Sheila V. Hopkins, "Seven centuries of the prices of consumables, compared with builders' wage-rates", *Economica* (1956), reprinted in E. M. Carus-Wilson, ed., *Essays in Economic History*, II (1962), 179–96.

would be necessary, of course, always to distinguish two categories. On the poorer soils from which population had retreated after the plagues, it would not be surprising to find fifteenth-century deterioration in the quality of houses that were still occupied, alongside others totally abandoned. (A short-term gain, however, was the supply of ready-quarried building stone if manor houses or church fabrics were in decay: re-used stone from socially superior buildings and from the church walls is a common feature of Wharram peasant-houses.) A second category of experience would have been felt in the fertile areas, where the peasantry were making real gains in bargaining power and standing most to gain by the effort that they put into working their enfranchised land. It would be in such regions that an historian would expect the archaeologist to report the greatest spread of improved village housing.

What, in the context of the opportunities available in the Middle Ages, did "improvement" mean? Its character in the post-medieval centuries, as demonstrated by Prof. Hoskins and Mr. Barley from the descriptions in probate inventories and glebe terriers, is clear: the addition of an upper floor; more interior room divisions on both floors; the separation of working, living and sleeping quarters; the removal of animals from proximity to the humans, usually into detached buildings across a yard; and the replacement of the central floor-hearth by a brick fireplace and chimney set in the wall, thereby reducing both the risk of fire and the amount of smoke circulating in the living room. Hygiene and comfort were as much improved—perhaps more—by the expulsion of smoke as by that of the farm animals. These changes of the period after 1540 do not have to be sought by excavation; they are well-documented and there are surviving houses to be inspected.

Some of these changes, particularly the development of separate complexes of animal buildings, stores and implement sheds, must now be recognised as beginning in the Middle Ages. The additional floor would not be easy to detect archaeologically, but for the time being this improvement is not being claimed as having a medieval origin. As a change in technology, the improvements that Mr. Hurst described did not involve anything inventive. Just as peasants' rubbish pits contain pottery, glazed and decorated, once thought to be the seigneur's prerogative, so the replacement of timber by stone walls, the division of rooms and the multiplication of out-buildings in the yards of the long-houses could all be copied from the houses of the peasants' betters: but the modifications, it will be noted, did not involve any very complicated building skill. Real complications, with a village house aspiring to have walls firm enough to bear a second storey, can be left to the post-medieval "Rebuilding".

The chronology of change in house-forms that Mr. Hurst puts forward does not match these presumed economic changes very well. In so far as his data show any "improvements", they emerge as widespread in the thirteenth century, not the fifteenth. This is true both of the move from wholly-timber buildings and the first elaboration of the long-house into the farmhouse complex. It was in the thirteenth century that he shows stone-walled houses replacing wholly-timber houses, and in the same period that the first elaborations of the long-house into the farmhouse complex are seen. It is not yet clear whether the historian will have to yield to the archaeologist or vice versa, for how exceptional are the early examples of farm complexes? It is certainly plain that the long-house continued in use right up to the Great Rebuilding in some villages, and the difference between it and the farmhouse complex may not be the "improvement" we imagine, but perhaps be connected with some change in agricultural needs—say, the role of the animals?

Finally, some warnings should be given about too close a connection being assumed between "prosperity" and rebuilding observed in medieval villages. If house-holders in a modern economy were observed pulling down and rebuilding their suburban houses or adding second garages, car-ports, and central heating, then it might be a fair deduction that incomes had risen, provided that no startling reduction had taken place in the price of these luxuries while the price of some alternative had soared out of reach. But in the medieval village the archaeologists have shown that the flimsiness of the peasant-house necessitated its rebuilding at least once a generation, so that a rebuilding was not an extra activity, the product of more income or more leisure, but a normal necessity. Modern rebuilding, even in an age of do-it-yourself shops, mortgages, and hire purchase would imply some extra money earned before the new building was contemplated: but for the peasant the building of his house would have involved him very little in money or market matters. The quality of workmanship now seen in the excavated structures, as well as the local sources of the main building materials put the whole operation well inside the do-it-yourself range.

When Mr. Hurst writes of "stone houses" a reader should not picture regular blocks of quarried, chiselled, and faced stones such as he would expect in a medieval church or manor house, every angle a right-angle. House-stones were roughly faced, and not on all faces; and, as the Wharram evidence has revealed, their source was not some distant quarry, implying purchase from the quarry owner and transport costs, but within the toft itself, within stumbling distance of the house, every man his own quarry-owner. Turf for the roof, mud for the wattle-filling and *house-bote* rights to take timber from the wastes: these leave only nails, door-hinges, hooks, and hasps, in the catalogue of purchases, and the prevalence of iron slag that Mr. Hurst reports may put these also into the do-it-yourself category for many villages.

A new house, a newly-patterned house and a larger house all emerge, therefore, as possible without more money in the pocket to hire carpenters, tilers, and masons. It was an investment not of some flush of income but of the peasant family's time and physical effort, and if they were not working at full pressure at all seasons this was not analogous to the disposal of wealth made when a seigneur decided to dip into his pocket for a new manor house, a new castle, a new church, or a new monastery. Seigneurial building must have been connected with the state of seigneurial incomes, but even here there are complexities (which cannot now be elaborated) obstructing a simple inference of prosperity from observed rebuilding.

III: CHANGES IN VILLAGE PLANS

But however oddly the changes in structural characteristics fit in with the assumptions of "pure" history, there are also unexpected geographical elements in what the excavations so far achieved have to report about the positioning of houses; in other words, the village plan. I myself had certainly not bargained for the flux revealed in such plans as those on pages 118–126. Indeed, what I have written in the past as commentary on air photographs discloses that my interest in photographs of deserted sites largely derived from the opportunity I believed they gave to see medieval village plans unaffected by changes in the period of the Tudor "Great Rebuilding" or subsequent developments in brick. I was aware that villages had not been born instantaneously, and therefore that a village plan of the desertion period was made up of successive additions at various earlier periods of population expansion, each of these additions necessarily encroaching on agricultural land. I was also aware that there had been shrinkage on many sites before the final depopulation, and that it was therefore unhistorical to see the earthworks of the deserted sites as representing houses all of which were inhabited in (say) 1450; but I would have accepted them as a valid plan of the village during the century or so of most active colonisation, (say, 1200–1350). Now, it seems, if one were to make animated diagrams of changing village plans, the steady rectangles of the house-earthworks in the air photographs would be replaced by a jerky dance in which the rectangles sometimes spun on their axes and sometimes jumped sideways in a frenzy. Even toft and croft boundaries, that I certainly assumed to be permanent property boundaries, prove not to have been sacred, and manor houses join in the restless movement. Nor does the church site escape the flux. It is known that the church has actually changed its site (Eaton Socon, Hunts., and Potterne, Wilts.) while five other church excavations have shown that older domestic buildings had earlier occupied the site (Salome, Hunts., Weald, Hunts., Clopton, Cambs., Broadfield, Herts. and Balsdean, Sussex).

Mr. Hurst also makes an important point when he criticises the simplicist interpretation of an air photograph—*et peccavi*—that ignores the possibility of post-desertion looting of house-foundations for their ready-worked stones. In such cases there certainly may be visual obliteration of some houses or distortion of house-shapes through the remains of trenches ("robber trenches") that were dug around the walls into order to extract the stonework.

The greatest damage from the advance of knowledge must fall on that part of the history of settlement which has based itself on the shape of a village, that is on the patterns produced by the positioning of houses in relation to each other and to the linking streets. Village morphologists have of course been aware—with a notorious exception—that current large-scale O.S. plans might mislead by including fairly recent additions to a village, but the Tithe Award maps of the early Victorian period have been accepted as a working base for historical deductions, and their alignment of village houses taken as "original". But we now know that even late-sixteenth-century village maps can deceive, for a whole street of houses could be laid out in the thirteenth century where a Norman manor house had previously stood; that a village once arrayed around a green can now be replaced by a single street; and that many existing villages of the "shrunken" class have earthworks that double the area of former occupation and, as at Wawne, quite alter the "shape" of the village if they are taken into account.

If such radical revisions of village plans were possible in the Middle Ages, they suggest some unifying, perhaps seignurial, authority to direct each of them and adjust the property rights involved. One would expect that some regularity in alignment of houses, croft length and croft width would accompany such an organised revision, and excavation of an apparently very "regular" village (perhaps one looking like a "Green Village") would be particularly interesting if it revealed houses at a lower archaeological level that had a quite different formation. Groups of regular crofts in any of the deserted sites would also, on this count, repay excavation: not only for the possibility of older houses below them but for any remains of open field furlongs, furlong boundaries, balks, and field access-ways which the boundary banks of the crofts may seal.

Mr. Hurst notes that deeply-worn village streets would make it progressively more difficult to ignore them in any re-alignment of plan; and that the great house-platforms on clay sites would also impose rigidity. We shall see: but surely, if foundations of manor houses and deep stone quarries could be filled up and built over, why should hollow ways and boundary ditches present obstacles when Necessity drove?

Finally, three small matters may be mentioned. Historians of climatic change will notice with interest Mr. Hurst's suggestion that increasing wetness of the climate may have been a factor producing the characteristic raised house-platforms found on sites all over the clay lowlands, together with encircling ditches that were a microcosm of the non-defensive drainage moats that manor houses were developing at the same period; where (in the stone belts) a timber-framed house on a low wall was replacing a frame set directly on the soil, there may have been a similar motive of preventing timbers rotting too fast.

Agrarian historians will notice the prevalence of horse-bones among the animal re-mains that have been analysed. Ownership of horses by peasants is not incongruous with the horses that appear in late thirteenth-century tax assessments and in heriots; nor with what historians of technology have claimed for the horse-collar in turning the noble animal of chivalry into the mundane servant of agriculture. The analysis of other animal bones, it will be seen, challenges the assumption that animals could generally expect to be killed off in the first autumn of their lives.

Exotic objects, brought by trade, are always of interest to economic historians, and the finds among the rubbish pits, farmyards and house-floors of peasant-houses afford a rare opportunity of seeing how far down the scale of incomes these traded purchases came. There is abundant evidence in what Mr. Hurst reports for the long-distance movement of coal, iron, glazed pottery, and quern-stones. He might have added millstones, had there yet been an excavation of a village windmill or watermill. Documents indicate that these clumsy components of the village's largest piece of capital equipment were carried by parties of villeins owing carrying services to their seigneurs, but the distances involved must have brought the stone within the ambit of specialist trade since millstone grit occurs naturally in only a few areas of England, all of them north of the Trent and few of them well-served by navigable rivers: whereas mills were needed everywhere.

IV: THE SOCIETY FOR MEDIEVAL ARCHAEOLOGY

The inter-action of historical and archaeological studies in recent years does not end with the study of deserted medieval villages. Soon on the heels of the Deserted Village Research Group came the foundation of the Society for Medieval Archaeology, and it is a remarkable comment on the affinity of interests that in 1968 Prof. E. M. Carus-Wilson held the presidency both of the Economic History Society and the Society for Medieval

Archaeology, a conjunction hardly matched since Henry le Waleys, seven centuries ago, found himself in successive years the mayor of London and Bordeaux.

This new Society has provided a forum for the meeting of the various practitioners at its annual residential conference in different parts of Britain (and beyond), and at its annual meeting and lecture in London. By 1968 it also had eleven volumes of the periodical, *Medieval Archaeology*, to its credit. In addition to the usual type of articles expected of a learned journal, *Medieval Archaeology* has a long section (usually of fifty to sixty pages) giving a conspexus of excavation, fieldwork and other major advances made in the previous year. Thus volume XI (1967) summarised the work of *Medieval Britain in 1965* in 57 pages with seventeen figures and four plates. The eleven sub-divisions for the period after the Norman Conquest are:

> monastic; cathedrals and ecclesiastical palaces; churches and chapels; castles; towns; royal palaces; manors and moats; farms and small domestic architecture; villages; other sites; industry.

The range of subject-matter indicates the width of the potential for the illumination of themes in history; especially, but far from exclusively, economic and local history. The arrangement within these eleven sections is by country and then by county, making it easy for an historian concerned with one place or district to see whether archaeological progress has been made in that locality. Indexes have already been published for volumes I–V and VI–X.

V: PERSONAL

This is the place to express, perhaps invidiously, my own appreciation of certain archaeological efforts: those at Hangleton, Seacourt and Upton for the way in which the authors of the reports have been able to marry history and archaeology; Holworth and Martinsthorpe for the usefulness of the total plan of the visible earthworks; West Whelpington for its plan of the fields as well as of the village, and for memories of labouring there within sight of the margin of medieval settlement; Hound Tor for its demonstration of the remote position of the medieval margin in the south-west and for Mrs. Minter and Miss Dudley's list of Cornish sites; and Wharram Percy for its evocation of twenty Julys and its role in bringing together the editors of this volume; all but one of the other contributors have also laboured there.

It has already been explained how little control an English archaeological group has over which particular sites it will next excavate. There is an element of pipe-dreaming as well as presumption, therefore, if an historian makes suggestions for deserted village sites to be excavated in the future, based on his knowledge (from documents) of interesting local features. But there is a place for dreams, and perhaps this concluding paragraph is the appropriate place. Take a site such as Kilpeck (Herefords.), seemingly in such close association with the castle defences as to be virtually a village within a bailey; the Norman church survives, but where is the pre-Norman village? it is unlikely that it obligingly had a conformation that fitted the regular shape of the defensive earthworks; is it sealed below them? Or Weedley (Yorks., E.R.) where one of the two earliest recorded English windmills stood: the site, alas, has been put under the plough, and the air photograph indicates the area of the village by differential scatters of broken chalk house-foundations; but there is a detached, almost circular scatter of white soil, and perhaps the plough has not destroyed more than the surface structures? At Caversfield (Oxon.) there are clear earthworks of fishponds, and Domesday Book records fishponds here: have the retaining banks and the channels been there for 900 years, or were there reconstructions and revisions of fishpond shapes such as Mr. Hurst has shown to be the common lot of churches, peasant-houses, and manor houses in the medieval village?

CHAPTER FIVE

County Gazetteers of Deserted Medieval Villages (known in 1968)

Editor: J. SHEAIL

Scientific Officer, Nature Conservancy

The arrangement of the entries is alphabetical within the present boundaries of present counties.[1]   Six-figure National Grid references locate the site.   Entries with U indicate that no place-name, field-name or other evidence remains to suggest the locality of a site. Sites that can be localised but not precisely identified have six-figure references preceded by *c*.   The form of the village name employed is that of a parish, township, farm, or house appearing on the seventh edition of the one-inch Ordnance Survey map.   Names not on the O.S. map are given their earliest form and printed in italics.

'Known in 1968' indicates the continuing nature of the researches described in Chapter 1.   The basis of the gazetteer is the list of sites published in *Lost Villages*: but with many additions and some subtractions resulting from work in the field and in maps and documents since 1954.   Some of this work has been carried out by the authors; many of the additions derive from Dr. Glasscock's thesis (Glasscock, 1963); and they also derive from many correspondents who have contributed new information.   For reasons set out in Chapter 1, the comprehensiveness of the gazetteer is not uniform for all counties; counties where active work is in progress and supplementation of the gazetteer may be expected are indicated on p. 35 by an asterisk.

[1] Except that the Soke of Peterborough is included within Northamptonshire.

BEDFORDSHIRE

comprising Sheet Numbers 134, 146 and 147 of the one-inch O.S. map (7th edition)

Astwick	TL 213385	Higham Gobion	TL 103327
Cainhoe	TL 100367	Holcot	SP 945388
Chalgrave	TL 010270	Holme	TL 197426
Chellington	SP 961564	Kinwick	c. TL 198473
Colworth	SP 981601	Priestley	TL 020332
Cudessane	U	Segenhoe	SP 980360
Etonbury	TL 195382	Stondon, Upper	TL 150355
Faldo	TL 076326	Stratton	TL 205441
Gravenhurst, Lower	TL 113353	Sudbury	c. TL 183616

BERKSHIRE

comprising one-inch Sheets: 157 and 158

Acenge	U	Maidencourt	SU 373760
Barcote	SU 320979	Marlston	SU 529719
Beckett	SU 246892	*Nachededorne*	U
Betterton	SU 431868	Newton	SU 360980
Bockhampton	SU 334782	Odstone	SU 271862
Burlei	U	Purley Parva	SU 654769
Calcote	c. SU 340698	Seacourt	SU 486075
Carswell	SU 325978	Shalford	SU 569648
Clapcot	SU 605916	Sheffield	SU 653696
Compton, East	SU 525796	Shefford, East	SU 391749
Cruchfield	SU 880740	Shottesbrooke	SU 842771
Draycott	SU 400994	Southcote	SU 375910
Eaton Hastings	SU 260982	Standen, North	SU 313672
Ebrige	U	Stroud	SU 444075
Fulscot	SU 545888	Thrupp	SU 519972
Henwick	SU 498686	Tubney	SP 446010
Hillend	SU 466065	Tulwick	SP 413904
Hodcot	SU 477818	Whatcombe	SU 393789
Holt	SU 401645	Whitley	c. SU 442053
Inglewood	SU 365666	Woolley	SU 410800
Langley	SU 498766	Wyld Court	SU 543760
Liercote	U		

BUCKINGHAMSHIRE

comprising one-inch Sheets: 145, 146 and 159

Ackhampstead	SU 807907	Beachendon	SP 759137
Addingrove	SP 665113	Boarstall	SP 623143
Aston Mullins	SP 769083	Boycott	SP 662372

Burston	SP 842188	Hughenden	SP 865955
Caldecote in Newport Pagnell	SP 879423	Lenborough	SP 705300
		Lillingston Dayrell	SP 706398
Caldecote in Weston Turville	SP 839126	Linslade	SP 910269
		Liscombe	SP 886257
Chetwode	SP 640297	Littlecote	SP 834244
Claydon, Middle	SP 720253	Moreton	SP 792096
Cottesloe	SP 860230	Okeney	SP 920490
Creslow	SP 812218	Olney Hyde	SP 887541
Cublington	SP 834223	Petsoe	SP 919494
Denham	SP 758205	Putlowes	SP 782151
Doddershall	SP 721202	Quarrendon I	SP 800155
Evershaw	SP 636384	Quarrendon II	SP 798158
Eythorpe	SP 770140	Quarrendon III	SP 788177
Fleet Marston	SP 779159	Saunderton	SP 797018
Foxcote	SP 717358	Shipton Lee	SP 728212
Fulbrook	SP 750226	Stantonbury	SP 835428
Gayhurst	SP 847462	Stoke Mandeville	SP 837095
Grove	SP 918225	Stowe	SP 678374
Hallinges	SP 838095	Tattenhoe	SP 829339
Hampden, Great	SP 848024	Tetchwick	SP 679187
Hardmead I	SP 940482	Tyringham	SP 859467
Hardmead II	SP 936470	Tythrop	SP 740070
Hedsor	SP 906983	Waldridge	SP 783073
Helsthorpe	SP 887193	Winchendon, Upper	SP 746145
Hogshaw	SP 739228	Wotton Underwood	SP 688159

CAMBRIDGESHIRE

comprising one-inch Sheets: 134, 135, 147 and 148

Badlingham	TL 678709	Henny	TL 557752
Barham	TL 574461	Landwade	TL 622682
Castle Camps	TL 630425	Malton	TL 373484
Caxton	TL 301582	Nosterfield	*c.* TL 640443
Childerley, Great and Little	*c.* TL 357615	Shingay	TL 310473
		Werateworde	U
Chilford	*c.* TL 567489	Whitwell	TL 403585
Clopton	TL 302488	Wimpole	TL 337510
Croxton	TL 252593		

CHESHIRE

comprising one-inch Sheets: 109 and 110

Brereton	SJ 781648	Shocklach	SJ 432502
Cholmondeley	SJ 545512	*Ulure*	U

CORNWALL

comprising one-inch Sheets: 174, 185, 186 and 189

Avada	U	*Tregrebi*	U
Carwether	SX 102797	*Trenidered*	U
Garrow	SX 146780	Tresibbet	SX 205750
Lanyon	SW 422337	Treworld	SX 121905
Porthillie	SW 932772	Trewortha	SX 239750
Temple	SX 146734		

CUMBERLAND

comprising one-inch Sheet: 76

Brampton, Little	NY 510615	Easby, Little	c. NY 538625
Carlatton	c. NY 530530	Easton	NY 433716
Denton, Nether	NY 595646	Edmond Castle	NY 495585
Easby, Great	c. NY 538625	Liddel	NY 402742

DERBYSHIRE

comprising one-inch Sheets: 111 and 120

Alkmonton	SK 186386	Haddon, Nether	SK 235665
Arleston	SK 335297	Harthill	SK 230246
Ashe	SK 262326	Hazlebadge	SK 171800
Ault Hucknall	SK 466652	Hoon	c. SK 224300
Barton Blount	SK 209346	Hungry Bentley	SK 180388
Birchill	SK 216707	Ireton Parva	SK 313416
Bolun	U	Kedleston	SK 312405
Bupton	c. SK 220370	Kidsley	SK 416459
Callow	SK 257512	Lee	SK 196517
Catton	SK 207155	Mercaston	SK 278424
Chatsworth	SK 260700	Sapperton	SK 186345
Derwent	SK 185885	Sedsall	SK 111376
Drakelow	c. SK 240200	Sinfin	SK 342312
Eaton on Dove	SK 118363	*Tunestalle*	U
Eaton, Cold	SK 148567	Underwood	SK 200482
Foremark	SK 330265	*Welledene*	U
Gratton	SK 209619		

DEVONSHIRE

comprising one-inch Sheets: 163, 175, 187 and 188

Badgworthy	SS 794436	Challacombe	SX 694796
Beere, Great	SX 690034	Corndonford	SX 689745
Blackaton	SX 698783	Cordonford, Little	SX 697745
Bolt Head	SX 715370	Cripdon	SX 735810

Ford	SX 607615	Rowden, South (Hutholes)	SX 702758
Hayne	SX 748805	Thorne, North	SS 646414
Hound Tor	SX 748796	Treable	SX 720928
Rowden, North	SX 701765		

DORSET

comprising one-inch Sheets: 177, 178 and 179

Afflington	SZ 972801	Polingston	SU 667953
Bexington, West	SY 533867	Puddle, Little	SY 710960
Blackmanstone	SY 917806	Ringstead	SY 747815
Brockington	SU 019107	*Selavestune*	U
Bryanston	ST 875070	Shilvinghampton, East	*c.* SY 629844
Frampton	SY 615955	Shilvinghampton, West	*c.* SY 629844
Frome Belet	SY 715895	*Slitlege*	U
Fryer Mayne	SY 735866	Stanton St. Gabriel	SY 402924
Gotowre	SZ 010852	Steepleton Iwerne	ST 862112
Hanford	ST 846112	Stinsford	SY 715914
Hemsworth	SU 970060	Whitcombe	SY 717882
Holnest	ST 656098	Wimborne All Saints	SU 024127
Holworth	SY 770833	Winterbourne Came	SY 705884
Knowlton	SU 024103	Winterbourne	
Lazerton	ST 864106	Farringdon	SY 696885
Lewcombe	ST 559075	Winterbourne	
Mayne, Little	SY 724871	Herringstone	SY 690881
Melcombe, Binham	ST 775021	Witherston	SY 530970
Melcombe Horsey	ST 748024	Wolfeton	SY 679921
Milborne Symondeston	SY 802986	Woodsford	SY 760905
Milton Abbas	ST 799023	Woodyates, West	SU 016196
Orchard	SY 639894	Woolcomb Maltravers	ST 603054

DURHAM

comprising one-inch Sheets: 78 and 85

Burdon, Little	NZ 330164	Garmondsway	NZ 346347
Burdon, Old	NZ 381507	Grindon	NZ 395255
Butterwick	NZ 385298	Hartburn, West	NZ 358143
Castle Eden	NZ 427388	Hulam	NZ 430370
Claxton	*c.* NZ 475280	Hurbuck	NZ 148482
Coxhoe	NZ 331357	Layton	NZ 377270
Dinsdale, Low	NZ 345110	Newbiggin, East	NZ 366189
Elstob	NZ 340238	Newbiggin, West	NZ 355185
Elton	NZ 403174	Newsham	NZ 383113
Embleton	NZ 420298	Shotton	NZ 368254
Foxton	NZ 363248	Slingley	NZ 380480

Sockburn	NZ 349070	Walworth	NZ 231191
Swainston	NZ 419294	Whessoe	NZ 276182
Thrislington	NZ 306333	Yoden	NZ 433418
Ulnaby	NZ 227172		

ESSEX

comprising one-inch Sheets: 148, 149 and 162

Beauchamp St.		*Nortuna*	U
Ethelbert	TL 770420	*Scilcheham*	U
Berewic	U	Snoreham	TQ 885997
Bertuna	U	Stanway	TL 952206
Birch, Little	TL 951209	Thunderley	TL 560360
Braxted, Great	TQ 850155	*Udecheshale*	U
Cheneboltuna	U	*Weneswic*	U
Faulkbourne	TQ 800165	*Westnanetuna*	U
Lega	U	Wickham Bishops	TQ 837120

GLOUCESTERSHIRE

comprising one-inch Sheets: 143, 144, 155, 156 and 157

Abloads Court	SO 827214	*Hundewic*	U
Alkington	ST 693982	*Ildeberga*	U
Ampney St. Mary	SP 088018	Lancaut	ST 533965
Aston	SO 901991	Lark Stoke	SP 197438
Aylworth	SP 110220	Lasborough	ST 821942
Bidfield	SO 908106	*Lega*	U
Boxwell	ST 812927	Lemington, Upper	SP 222341
Brickhampton	SO 870220	Lowsmoor	ST 923997
Castlett Farm	SP 091258	Manless Town	SO 928117
Charlton	c. ST 862917	Naunton	SP 020340
Coberley, Upper	SO 980158	Newington	ST 818947
Combe End	SO 985118	Northwick	SP 168365
Daylesford	SP 243259	Norton, Burnt	SP 145416
Didcot	SP 002356	Norton, Lower	SP 138430
Ditchford, Lower	SP 226367	Oddington	SP 235256
Ditchford, Upper	SP 200368	Oldbury	ST 609919
Elmestree	ST 870918	Owdeswell	SP 024190
Eyford	SP 146246	Oxenhall	SO 711267
Farmcote	SP 061291	Ozleworth	ST 794933
Frampton	SP 011333	Pauntley	SO 749290
Frocester	SO 770033	Pinnock	SP 074281
Gawcombe	SP 212213	*Pontune*	U
Harford	SP 130225	Postlip	SP 000270
Hilcot	SO 998163	Prescott	SO 983292
Hullasey	ST 974993	Roel	SP 074249

Sapletone	U	Taynton Parva	SO 749229
Sennington	SP 024219	*Uletone*	U
Sezincote	SP 170310	Upcote	SP 022169
Shipton Solers	SP 028188	Upton	SP 152344
Slad	SO 919066	Wall	SP 155106
Stockwell	SO 942147	Williamstrip	SP 150050
Stonehouse	SO 799051	Wormington Dastyn	SP 053340
Stowell	SP 087130	Wormington Parva	SP 046346
Sudeley	SP 032276		

HAMPSHIRE AND ISLE OF WIGHT

comprising one-inch Sheets: 168, 169, 179, 180 and 181

Hampshire

Abbotstone	SU 565345	Hartley Mauditt	SU 74236
Allington	SU 480172	Hatch Warren	SU 616488
Aplestede	*c.* SU 610080	Hay, South	SU 773398
Bentley	SU 310295	Highclere	SU 446588
Bieforde	U	Hordle	SZ 27092
Bisterne	SU 149012	Idsworth	SU 74314
Blendworth	SU 712136	Inhurst	SU 575614
Boarhunt	SU 603084	Kempshott	SU 598474
Bossington	SU 335309	Laverstoke	SU 497490
Boyatt	SU 451209	Lee	SU 360179
Broxhead	SU 799369	Lomer	SU 594234
Candover, Brown	SU 576392	Merdon	SU 420264
Candover, Chilton	SU 593401	Minley	SU 825580
Charford, North	SU 170196	Murrell Green	SU 743550
Charford, South	SU 168190	Newtown	SU 471579
Chineham	SU 645540	Northington	SU 501495
Colemore	SU 706307	Nutley	SU 609446
Compton	SU 349291	Oakley, North	SU 53854
Dogmersfield	SU 775515	Otterbourne	SU 46522
Eldon, Upper	SU 365278	Pauncefoot	SU 34320
Ellingham	SU 144084	Pittleworth	SU 32829
Elvetham	SU 782564	Polhampton	SU 52950
Empshott	SU 753312	Popham	SU 55543
Ewhurst	SU 570568	Priors Dean	SU 72829
Farleigh Wallop	SU 623474	Quidhampton	SU 51750
Farley Chamberlaine	SU 395275	Roke	SU 33722
Farlington	SU 686057	Rowner	SU 58401
Finlei	U	St. Anastius by Wyke	SU 30047
Fullerton	SU 376394	Silchester	SU 64362
Gerlie	U	Skidmore	*c.* SU 35618
Godsfield	SU 604371	Snoddington	SU 23844
Harbridge	SU 144101	Somborne, Little	SU 38232

Southwood	SU 852551	Wanstead	SU 642094
Stanbridge	SU 338232	Warblington	SU 729055
Steventon	SU 551472	Wellow, East	SU 303204
Stock	SU 666266	Wellsworth	c. SU 638073
Stoneham, North	SU 440172	Westbury	SU 657239
Stoneham, South	SU 440154	Weston Corbett	SU 688470
Stratfield Saye	SU 695615	Widley	SU 660074
Stratfield Turgis	SU 695593	Winchfield	SU 768538
Swarraton	SU 570371	Winslade	SU 655482
Sydmonton	SU 485580	Wolverton	SU 550585
Tadley	SU 597600	Woodcott	SU 433548
Tidgrove	SU 522544	Worldham, Little	SU 743370
Tidworth	SU 240480	Wymering	SU 650056
Tisted, West	SU 650290		

New Forest

(See *Annual Report*, 1961, Appendix A, for suggested identification of some of these sites.)

Achelie (Boldre)	*Juare*
Achelie (Redbridge	*Lesteorde*
Alwinetune	*Mapleham*
Betramelei	*Nutlei*
Bedecote	*Odetune*
Bile	*Oselei*
Bocolt	*Otreorde*
Bovre	*Oxelei*
Bovreford	*Pisteslei*
Brochelie	*Rowestre*
Cildeest	*Sanhest*
Cocherlei	*Sclive*
Gatingeorde	*Slacham*
Greteham	*Taceberie*
Hardelie	*Truham*
Hariforde	*Wigarestum*
Hincelveslei	

Isle of Wight

Abla	U	Compton	SZ 376851
Afton	SZ 358869	Durton	SZ 522883
Alvington	SZ 475886	Haldley	SZ 494852
Ashey	SZ 584883	Hale	SZ 544846
Atherfield	c. SZ 465795	Hardley	SZ 632866
Bernardsley	SZ 608903	Heasley	SZ 547857
Billingham	SZ 485818	*Heceford*	U
Briddlesford	SZ 547900	Kerne	SZ 578866

Kingston	SZ 478814	Preston	SZ 598914
Knighton	SZ 566867	Scotchells	SZ 582833
Levegarestun	U	Standen	SZ 506874
Luccombe	SZ 583798	Stenbury	SZ 525790
Moor Farm	SZ 533825	Thorley	SZ 367892
Nunwell	SZ 595875	Watchingwell	SZ 447884
Orham	U	Week	SZ 537778
Penna and Fairlie	SZ 506904	Wolverton	SZ 623867

HEREFORDSHIRE

comprising one-inch Sheets: 129, 130, 142 and 143

Chilstone	SO 400394	Hoarwith	SO 544294
Cowarne, Little	SO 601511	Holme Lacy	SO 570350
Deveraux	SO 441313	Kilpeck	SO 445305
Edvin Ralph	SO 645574	Wacton	SO 616575
Hampton Wafer	SO 577570	Wolferlow	SO 667617
Hewland	SO 544264		

HERTFORDSHIRE

comprising one-inch Sheets: 146, 147, 148, 159, 160 and 161

Alswick	TL 376295	Hodenhoe	TL 346334
Ayot St. Lawrence	TL 194169	Ichetone	TL 370300
Ayot St. Peter	TL 218150	*Lewarewiche*	U
Barnet, East	TQ 277946	Libury	TL 345235
Beauchamps	TL 382314	Mimms, North	TL 222045
Berkesden	TL 335276	Minsden	TL 198246
Betlow	SP 897172	Mundon, Great	TL 355243
Boxbury	TL 274266	*Oxewiche*	U
Bozen	TL 412272	Pendley	SP 944117
Bricewolde	U	Stagenhoe	SP 186227
Brickenden	TL 330105	Stanstead Abbots	TL 399110
Broadfield	TL 325310	Stevenage	TL 240262
Burston in St. Stephens	TL 135037	*Stiwicesworde*	U
Caldecote	TL 237385	Thorley	TL 476188
Chesfield	TL 247278	Throcking	TL 337303
Cockenach	TL 396362	Thundridge	TL 368175
Cockhamsted	TL 419253	Tiscott	TL 883178
Corney Bury	TL 358307	Wakeley	TL 342269
Digswell	TL 236149	*Welei*	U
Flaunden	TL 009988	Wickham	TL 475230
Gilston	TL 440135	Windridge	TL 125057
Hainstone	U	*Wlwenewiche*	c. TL 222253

HUNTINGDONSHIRE

comprising one-inch Sheet: 134

Boughton	TL 198646	Overston	TL 123895
Caldecote	TL 142884	Sibson	TL 096977
Catworth, Little	TL 099728	Steeple Gidding	TL 134814
Colne	TL 367762	Upthorpe	TL 125720
Conington	TL 175859	Walton, Wood	TL 209821
Coppingford	TL 166801	Washingley	TL 135890
Gidding, Little	TL 125816	Weald	TL 230596
Hardwick	TL 208567	Wintringham	TL 220594
Midloe	TL 162645	Woolley	TL 150745

ISLE OF WIGHT

see *Hampshire*

KENT

comprising one-inch Sheets: 171, 172, 173 and 184

Acrise	TR 195423	Ham	TR 325547
Afettune	U	*Hertange*	U
Aia	U	Hope	TR 049258
Betteshanger	TR 314527	Horton, Monks	TR 125405
Billerica	TR 090353	*Hougham*	U
Bircholt	TR 075415	*Hucham*	U
Blackmanstone	TR 072296	Hurst	TR 076345
Boardfield	TQ 935523	Hythe, West	TR 125342
Boughton Malherbe	TQ 882496	Kenardington	TQ 974323
Bredhurst	TQ 799621	Knolton	TR 283535
Buckland	TQ 975629	*Lamport*	U
Cildresham	U	Leaveland	TR 005548
Cottington	TR 350534	Leysdown	TR 024704
Darenth	TQ 561713	Lullingstone	TQ 530650
Denton	TQ 660740	Mereworth	TQ 660537
Dowdes	TQ 668638	Merston	TQ 695724
Eastbridge	TR 074322	Midley	TR 031232
Eastenhanger	TR 123372	Mongeham, Little	TR 333509
Ebony	TQ 927297	Monkton	TQ 745555
Eddintone	U	Orgarswick	TR 084307
Elmley	TQ 934680	Oxney	TR 355469
Essella	U	*Pesinges*	U
Estochingesherge	U	Pivington	TQ 919465
Etretone	U	Polton	TR 273413
Fairfield	TQ 965265	Reculver	TR 228694
Fawkham	TQ 585655	Romney St. Lawrence	TR 040255
Gore's End	TR 295694	Romney St. Michael	TR 037257

Ruxley	TQ 486705	*Stanestede*	U
St. John's Sutton	TQ 552704	Stone	TQ 99261:
Selesburne	U	Stonor	TR 33558(
Selinges	U	Waldershare	TR 29748.
Shuart	TR 270678	Warden	TR 02072(
Sidborne	U	Westenhanger	TR 12337:
Sifletone	U	Woodchurch	TR 32968
Snave	TR 014300		

LANCASHIRE

(Work still in progress, see p. 67.)

LEICESTERSHIRE

comprising one-inch Sheets: 121, 122, 132 and 133

Aldeby	SK 552987	Lowesby	SK 72507:
Alton	SK 390148	Lubbesthorpe	SK 54101
Ambion	SK 400003	Marefield, North	SK 75208:
Andreschurch	SK 392222	Misterton	SP 55684(
Atterton	SP 353983	Naneby	SK 43502
Baggrave	SK 697088	*Netone*	U
Belvoir	SK 819342	Newbold Folville	SK 70612(
Bescaby	SK 823263	Newbold Saucy	SK 76509(
Bittesby	SP 500860	Newton, Cold	SK 71606(
Bradgate	SK 535103	Normanton Turville	SP 48999
Brascote	SK 443025	Noseley	SP 73398
Brentingby	SK 784198	Othorpe	SP 77195(
Brooksby	SK 670160	*Plotelei*	U
Cotes de Val	SP 553887	Potters Marston	SP 49896(
Dishley	SK 513212	Poultney	SP 58684(
Elmesthorpe	SP 460965	Prestgrave	SK 81093(
Eye Kettleby	SK 734167	Prestwold	SE 58021
Foston	SP 604950	Quenby	SK 70206(
Frisby	SK 704020	Ringlethorp	SE 77623(
Garendon	SK 502199	Shelthorpe	SK 54518(
Gopsall	SK 353064	Shoby	SK 68320(
Hamilton	SK 645075	Stapleford	SK 81318(
Holt	SP 815937	Starmore	SK 58380(
Holyoaks	SP 845957	Staunton Harold	SK 37920(
Ingarsby	SK 684055	Stretton Magna	SK 65700(
Keythorpe	SP 765995	Sysonby	SK 73919(
Knaptoft	SP 626895	Welby	SK 72521(
Leesthorpe	SK 792136	Wellsborough	SK 36502(
Lilinge	U	Weston	SK 30302(
Lindley	SP 365958	Whatborough	SK 77105(

Whittington	SP 486083	Withcote	SK 797059
Willesley	SK 340146	Woodcote	SK 354187
Willowes	SK 660180	Wyfordby	SK 792189
Wistow	SP 644958		

LINCOLNSHIRE

comprising one-inch Sheets: 104, 105, 113, 114, 122, 123 and 133

Ackthorpe	TF 308894	Casthorpe	SK 863356
Adewelle	*c.* TF 060050	Cauthorpe	*c.* TF 050960
Aisthorpe	SK 947803	Cawkwell	TF 282800
Aleby	TF 438770	Cawthorpe	*c.* TF 335956
Asterby	TF 264794	Claxby Pluckacre	TF 307652
Audby	TF 280971	Cleatham	SE 933010
Audleby	TA 110040	Coates by Stow	SK 914835
Aunby	TF 022147	Coatham	TA 155113
Avethorpe	TF 068296	Cockerington, North	TF 377899
Bacton with Asgarby	TF 124455	Collow	TF 140837
Banthorp	TF 062110	Conesby, Great	SE 894138
Barlings	TF 075749	Conesby, Little	SE 876144
Bassingthorpe	TL 966285	Corringham, Little	SK 870911
Beckering	TF 122807	Cotes	TF 122608
Beckfield	TF 190927	Counthorpe	TF 004202
Beesby	TF 266966	Crofton	TF 055401
Biscathorpe	TF 230849	Crossholme	SK 992917
Bleasby	TF 130847	Dalby	TF 410701
Bonthorpe	TF 482728	Dalderby	TF 249660
Boughton	TF 123455	Darby	TF 478180
Bowthorpe	TF 066154	Dexthorpe	TF 406717
Brackenborough	TF 330906	Draycote	TF 117993
Brauncewell	TF 045523	Driby	TF 390745
Bullington	TF 093780	Dunsby	TF 040515
Burgh	*c.* TF 106465	Dunstall	SK 890936
Burnham	TA 059171	Dunsthorpe, Grantham	*c.* SK 925358
Burreth	TF 152697	Dunsthorpe,	
Burton, Gate	SK 838827	Hameringham	TF 302680
Buslingthorpe	TF 086850	Farforth	TF 318785
Butyate	TF 136718	Fenby	TF 260993
Cadeby, North	TF 270960	Firsby, East	TF 006854
Cadeby, South	TF 244877	Firsby, West	SK 993853
Calceby	TF 386757	Fonaby	TA 109030
Calcethorpe	TF 248888	Fordington	TF 420717
Carlton, Castle	TF 398838	Frunthorpe	TF 202909
Carlton, Middle	SK 950770	Fultnetby	TF 098795
Casewick	TA 078090	Gainsthorpe	SE 956011

Ganthorpe	SK 924291	Marae	SE 850166
Gayton le Wold	TF 237860	Mare	TF 465924
Gilby	SK 864933	Mareham, Cold	TF 085431
Girsby	TF 218870	Mareham on the Hill	TF 286680
Goltho	TF 116774	Mere	TF 010652
Graby	TF 098295	Milthorpe	c. TF 050440
Grebby	TF 438687	Minting, Little	c. TF 160730
Greetham, Little	TF 308708	Newball	TF 073764
Greetwell	TF 014715	Newsham	TA 128133
Grimblethorpe	TF 238865	Newton by Toft	TF 052871
Grimsby, Little	TF 326913	Norcotes	TF 263730
Gunby	TF 468667	Normanby	SK 882830
Gunnerby	TF 215990	Ogarth	SK 990340
Hanby	TF 475698	Orford	TF 204947
Hanbeck	TF 005432	Osgodby	TF 018285
Hardwick	c. TF 175790	Osgodby Bardney	TF 132727
Hardwick, Caistor	TF 122987	Otby	TF 139936
Harrington	TF 367718	Ouseby	TF 104343
Havercroft	c. SK 830930	Oxcombe	TF 311772
Hawerby	TF 262976	Ranby	TF 232786
Haythby	SE 883193	Rand	TF 107791
Holme	SE 908168	Ravendale, West	TF 227997
Holme in Sudbrook	TF 043762	Raventhorpe	SE 937080
Holtham	TA 148168	Revesby	TF 310620
Houflet	c. TA 238130	Riby	TA 186072
Houghton	SK 927742	Riche	TF 260360
Hundon	TA 115025	Rigsby	TF 431754
Hungerton	SK 873302	Ringsthorpe	SK 925415
Ingleby	SK 893778	Ringstone	TF 094268
Ketsby	TF 365768	Risby	TF 145920
Kettleby	TA 034079	Risby, Great	SE 920148
Kettleby Thorpe	TA 042079	Risby, Little	SE 930150
Kingersby	TF 057929	Riseholme	SK 980753
Knaith	SK 830848	Riskenton	TF 300380
Langworth, East	TF 064765	Roxholm	TF 062498
Lavington, Little	c. TF 030310	Roxton	TA 168126
Laythorpe	TF 352630	Saltfleetby	c. TF 477900
Limber, Little	TA 124105	Santon	SE 940129
Linwood	TF 115867	Sawcliff	SE 912145
Lobingham	TA 143183	Scrafield	TF 304688
Lobthorpe	SK 954207	Scremthorpe	c. TF 490645
Luddington	SE 836173	Scrivelsby	TF 270661
Maidenwell	TF 322795	Sempringham	TF 106329
Maltby	TF 314844	Shillingthorpe	TF 073114
Manby	SE 936088	Skinnand	SK 940575

Sleaford	TF 076458	Thoresby	c. TF 310620
Snarford	TF 051825	Thornton le Moor	TF 049964
Somerby by Brigg	TF 061067	Thorpe	c. TF 217690
Somerby by		Thorpe Latimer	TF 132397
Gainsborough	SK 846897	Thorpe Parva	c. SK 850440
Somerton	SK 954586	Thrunscoe	TA 311077
Southorpe	SK 888952	Tothby	TF 445767
Southorpe in Edenham	TF 060220	Tothill	TF 419813
Stain	TF 469848	Towthorpe	SK 925385
Stainfield	TF 113732	Toynton, Low	TF 279711
Stainsby	TF 339716	Waddingworth	TF 186712
Stapleford Parva	c. SK 900560	Walmsgate	TF 360775
Stenigot	TF 255813	Walton	c. SK 910360
Stenning	TF 231400	Waterton	SE 853180
Stenwith	SK 836363	Weelsby	TA 285075
Stichesby	c. TF 310620	Well	TF 444734
Stocking	c. TF 850465	Westhorpe	c. SK 960336
Stoke, North	SK 913285	Westlaby	TF 093812
Stowe	TF 107110	Wilksby	TF 283628
Strubby	TF 159773	Willoughby, West	SK 965435
Sturton, Little	TF 215755	Winceby	TF 321683
Sudtone	TF 197761	Withcall	TF 283837
Sudwelle	c. TF 990230	Woolsthorpe	SK 836338
Swine Haven	TF 395985	Worlaby	TF 340768
Swinhope	TF 215962	Wyham	TF 276951
Tatebi	c. TF 420740	Wykeham	TF 121974
Temple Bruer	TF 008536	Wykeham, East	TF 225882
Thetford	TF 110149	Wykeham, West	TF 215890
Thonock	SK 828928	Wyville	SK 882292

MIDDLESEX

(Work still in progress, see p. 67.)

NORFOLK

comprising one-inch Sheets: 124, 125, 126, 134, 135, 136 and 137

Alethorpe	TF 950312	Ashby	TG 419158
Algamundestuna	U	Babingley	TF 670263
Algarsthorpe	TG 142082	Barwick, Great	TF 807351
~~*Alia Attebura*~~	~~U~~	~~Barwick, Little~~	~~TF 804358~~
Alvington	TG 140255	Bawsey	TF 663207
Appetorp	U	Bayfield	TG 052405
Appleton	TF 705274	Bec	TG 023208
Apton	TG 306010	Beeston	TG 328220

Bickerston	TG 086087	*Ingolosa*	TM 345967
Bixley	TG 260053	Irmingland	TG 123294
Bowthorpe	TG 177091	*Jerpstuna*	U
Boyland	TF 225944	Keburn	TL 795875
Braydeston	TG 341088	*Kekelingetuna*	U
Breckles, Little	TL 960945	Kempstone	TF 886160
Broomsthorpe	U	Kenningham	TM 206999
Buckenham Tofts	TL 838947	Kilverstone	TL 894841
Burgh	TG 046337	Kipton	TF 844235
Bylaugh	TG 036183	Langford	TL 839965
Caldecote	TF 745033	*Letha*	U
Calveston	TL 794955	Letton	TF 970060
Cavelly	TG 015051	Leziate	TF 697202
Choseley	TF 755408	Lynford	TL 819934
Cleythorpe	TF 805044	Maideston	TG 248216
Clipstone	TF 974304	Mannington	TG 146324
Culesthorpe	TF 785148	Mantateston	TG 022032
Didlington	TL 780970	Markshall	TG 228047
Dykebeck	U	Mintlyn	TF 652192
Earlham	TG 190082	*Mora*	U
Eccles	TG 415288	Narford	TF 764138
Egmere	TF 897374	*Neilanda*	U
Essebei	U	Nessa	TG 490220
Flochethor	U	Nettingdon	TF 720392
Foston	TF 654088	Norton	TL 708010
Frense	TM 135804	Oby	TG 415144
Glosthorpe	TF 695183	Oxborough Hithe	TF 738006
Godwick	TF 904222	Palgrave, Great	TF 835121
Gowthorpe	TG 202027	Palgrave, Little	TF 833135
Grenstein	TF 896191	Panworth	TF 898050
Grensvil	U	Pattesley	TF 899241
Gunton	TG 230340	Pensthorpe	TF 949291
Hackford	TG 079221	Petygards	TF 856085
Halas	U	Pudding Norton	TF 924277
Hales	TM 369960	Quarles	TF 884285
Hargham	TM 020914	Rainesthorpe	TM 203971
Harling, West	TL 975852	Ringstead, Little	TF 688399
Harringby	TG 446103	*Risinga*	U
Helmingham	TG 126157	Roudham	TL 956871
Hidichetrop	U	Roxham	TL 638997
Hockham Little	TL 949910	Ryston	TF 625012
Holkham	TF 878436	Santon	TL 829873
Holt	TF 676185	Semer	TM 183843
Houghton	TF 794285	Shipden	TG 220425
Houghton on the Hill	TF 867053	Shotesham St. Mary	TM 237988

Shotford	TM 251821	*Tofftes*	U
Snareshill, Great	TL 892835	Toimere	TL 650070
Snareshill, Little	TL 882829	*Toketorp*	U
Snore	TL 624993	*Torp*	U
Sparham	TF 876114	Wallington	TF 626076
Stanninghall	TG 255174	Walton, Little	TM 181902
Stinton	TG 117256	Washingford	TM 334993
Stow	TF 807108	*Wasincham*	U
Sturston	TL 875949	Waterden	TF 885358
Summerfield	TF 750385	*Watlinsseta*	U
Suttuna	U	Waxham Parva	TG 445265
Swathing	TF 986059	Well	TF 725203
Testerton	TF 937267	Wella	TF 749047
Thorpe	TF 946841	Whimpwell	TG 385285
Thorpe	TL 899906	*Wica*	U
Thorpe Parva	TM 160796	Wicken	TF 837316
Thorpland	TF 938322	Witchington, Little	TG 115212
Threxton	TL 885001	Wolterton	TG 165318
Thurketeliart	U	Wreningham, West	TM 150984
Thurton	TG 103214	Wretham, West	TL 898916
Thuxton	TG 043080	Wyveling	TF 679209

NORTHAMPTONSHIRE

comprising one-inch Sheets: 123, 132, 133, 134, 145 and 146

Achurch	TL 022832	Cotes	SP 890926
Althorp	SP 682650	Cotton, Mallows	SP 977734
Appletree	SP 483497	Cotton, Mill	SP 974746
Armston	TL 060858	Downtown	SP 613801
Ashby Canons	SP 578506	Eaglethorpe	TL 076917
Astwell	SP 615430	Easton Neston	SP 703493
Astwick	SP 570342	Edgcote	SP 505479
Badsaddle	SP 833730	Elkington	SP 620760
Barford	SP 850820	Elmington in Ashton	TL 055884
Boughton	SP 900815	Elmington in Tansor	TL 053909
Braunstonbury	SP 531655	Falcutt	SP 595430
Brime	*c.* SP 527484	Fawsley	SP 566567
Brockhall	SP 633626	Faxton	SP 785752
Burghley	TF 049061	Field Burcote	SP 667508
Calme	SP 714816	Foscote	SP 662473
Caswell	SP 651510	Foxley	SP 640517
Catesby	SP 515596	Furtho	SP 774430
Charwelton Church	SP 545555	Glassthorpe	SP 663617
Chelverdescote	U	Glendon	SP 846814
Churchfield	TL 013876	Hale	*c.* TL 027934

Hantone	U	Perio	TL 040924
Hothorpe	SP 667852	Pipewell	*c.* SP 827856
Kingsthorpe	TL 080856	Potcote	SP 657527
Kirby in Blakesley	SP 636495	Purston, Great	SP 518395
Kirby in Gretton	SP 928926	Seawell	SP 630525
Knuston	SP 938661	Sibberton	TL 064998
Lilford	TL 030840	Silsworth	SP 617706
Lolham	TF 111078	Snorscomb	SP 597561
Mawsley	*c.* SP 801768	Steane	SP 555390
Milton	TL 145995	Stuchbury	SP 569441
Muscott	SP 625633	Sulby	SP 653815
Newbold	SP 517606	Thorpe Lubenham	SP 705866
Newbottle	SP 524368	Thrupp	*c.* SP 603652
Newbottle in Harrington	SP 776814	Torpel	TF 113050
Newton, Little	SP 883833	Trafford	SP 527486
Nobold	SP 698821	Upton	SP 717603
Nunton	TF 120073	Walcot	TF 080042
Onley	SP 520715	Walton	SP 506346
Overstone	*c.* SP 810655	Woodcroft	TF 138045
Oxenden, Little	SP 727840	Wothorpe	TF 030056
Papley	TL 106891	Wythemail	SP 840719

NORTHUMBERLAND

comprising one-inch Sheets: 64, 71, 77, 78, 81 and 86

Abberwick	NU 128132	Brunton, East	NZ 235700
Acomb, East	NZ 044641	Buckenfield	NY 179978
Acton	NU 190030	Budle	NY 159351
Alnham	NT 990110	Bullocks Hall	NY 245982
Alwinton, Low	NT 923056	Burton	NU 180330
Backworth, West	NZ 300723	Buston, Low	NU 224074
Barton	NU 080123	Butterlaw	NZ 183690
Bavington, Great	NY 983804	Bywell	NZ 050612
Bavington, Little	NY 990790	Caistron	NT 996013
Bebside	NZ 270810	Carry Coates	NY 920816
Belsay	NY 085785	Cartington	NU 046038
Benridge	NZ 166872	Catcherside	NY 992877
Biddlestone	NT 955082	Chirmundesdon	NT 950063
Bingfield, East	NY 983725	Chirton, Middle	*c.* NZ 335680
Bitchfield	NZ 090770	Chirton, West	*c.* NZ 335680
Black Headley	NZ 054518	Clarewood	NY 018761
Blagdon	NZ 215572	Clennel	NT 929071
Bolam	NY 092827	Cocklaw	NY 938711
Bradford	NZ 067796	Coldcotes	NZ 144748
Brotherwick	NU 228057	Coldwell	*c.* NZ 200822

Corsenside	NY 890893	Kearsley	NZ 028754
Crookdean	NY 976834	Kepwick	NY 951714
Debden	NU 061045	Kirkharle	NZ 011825
Dissington, North	NZ 118716	Kirkley	c. NZ 150772
Dissington, South	NZ 128704	Learchild	NU 095105
Downham	NT 865340	Learmouth, West	NT 864372
Dukeshagg	NZ 108606	Lemmington	NU 120110
Easington	NU 124347	Lilburn, West	NU 022243
Elford	NU 188310	Littlemill	NU 226182
Elwick	NU 115369	Lorbottle	NU 065033
Elyhaugh	NU 158998	Matfen, East	NZ 040713
Evistones	NZ 830968	Middleton, North	NZ 060850
Falloden	NU 205235	Middleton, South	NZ 053840
Fallowfield	NY 930685	Mitford	c. NZ 170858
Fallowlees	NY 019942	Monkridge	NZ 918912
Felton, Old	NU 180023	Monkseaton	NZ 330720
Fenbother	NZ 170923	Moor, Old	NZ 246897
Fotherley	NY 020572	Mousen, Old	NU 117314
Fulwell	NZ 028754	Nafferton	NZ 065660
Gosforth, North	NZ 250710	Nesbitt	NT 983336
Greenleighton	NZ 025920	Newham in Belsay	NZ 110764
Harle, West	NY 990820	Newham in Ellingham	NU 175285
Harnham	NZ 070812	Newsham	NZ 305790
Hartington	NZ 025885	Ogle	NZ 137799
Hartlaw	NU 203061	Ouston	NZ 073704
Hartley	NZ 342757	Outchester	NU 147335
Hartside	NT 975162	Plessey	NZ 230791
Haughton	NY 920730	Ratchwood	NU 144284
Hawick	NZ 963826	Ray	NZ 967856
Haydon	NY 843654	Reaveley	NU 021170
Hazon	NU 193045	Riplington	NZ 116820
Healey, Mount	NU 071009	Ross	NY 135370
Heatherwick	NY 902924	Rothley	NZ 044880
Heaton	NT 901419	Row	NU 091996
Heddon, Black	NZ 080760	Rugley	NU 164099
Heddon, East	NZ 132686	Ryle, Little	NU 020112
Heddon, West	NZ 125688	Scrainwood	NT 990096
Hedgeley	NU 061177	Seaton Delaval	NZ 320763
Hethpool	NT 895285	Shaftoe, East	NZ 060818
Hetton	NU 040334	Shaftoe, West	NZ 045814
Hollonghill	NZ 040963	Shawdon	NU 095144
Horton Grange	NZ 190757	Shilvington	NZ 158809
Horton, High	NZ 276793	Shoreston, Old	NU 204324
Horton, Low	NZ 279797	Shortflatt	NZ 079810
Humbleton	NT 975284	Shotton	NZ 223780

Spindlestone	NY 151332	Twizel	NT 89043
Spital	NZ 078668	Wallridge	NZ 05576
Stanton	NZ 140906	Warenmouth	NU 16235
Styford	NZ 018621	Warenton	NU 10730
Sweethope	NY 957819	Welton	NZ 06367
Swinburn, Little	NY 939786	Whelpington, West	NY 97583
Swineleas	NU 157067	Whitchester	NZ 10068
Thornborough	NZ 105655	Whitfield	NY 77858
Thornton, West	NZ 097866	Whittington	NY 99069
Throckington	NY 959790	Whittle	NZ 07565
Throphill	NZ 125863	Witton, Long	NZ 07589
Tilmouth	NT 885434	Witton, Nether	NZ 10090
Todburn	NT 120957	Woodhouse	NU 21208
Togston	NU 250027	Woolsington	NZ 20071
Trewhit, Low	NU 003048	Wreighill	NT 97601
Trewick	NZ 112796	Yeavering, Old	NT 92330
Trohope	NY 883915	Yetlington	NU 02409
Tughall	NU 217267		

NOTTINGHAMSHIRE

comprising one-inch Sheets: 112, 113, 121 and 122

Adbolton	SK 600384	Hempshill	SK 52544
Algarthorpe	SK 555425	Hermeston	SK 58988
Annesley	SK 504524	Hesley	SK 61895
Babworth	SK 685809	Holbeck	SK 65850
Besthorpe	SK 730605	Holme Pierrepoint	SK 62439
Bingham	SK 714397	Horsepool	SK 70647
Broxtowe	SK 527427	Keighton	SK 54238
Burton, West	SK 798855	Kilvington	SK 80142
Carburton	SK 611733	Kimberley	SK 50045
Chilwell, East	c. SK 540380	Kinoulton	SK 66230
Clowne	c. SK 580738	Knapthorpe	SK 74058
Clumber	SK 627747	Langford	SK 82259
Colston Basset	SK 695338	Martin	SK 63694
Colwick, Over	SK 602390	Meering	SK 81263
Cratley	SK 682634	Milnthorpe	SK 57571
Dallington	c. SK 778429	Morton in Babworth	c. SK 67780
Danethorpe	SK 842577	Morton in Lenton	SK 54737
Flawford	SK 593332	Nettleworth	SK 54965
Gledthorpe	c. SK 592701	Normanton	SK 65074
Greasley	SK 489471	Osberton	SK 62480
Grimston	SK 682658	Ossington	SK 76065
Habblesthorpe	SK 785820	Plumtree	SK 63392
Haughton	SK 692730	Rayton	SK 61579

Rempstone	SK 575245	Warby	SK 621333
Rufford	SK 657642	Welham	SK 727822
Serlby	SK 635895	Wheatley, South	SK 767856
Steetley	SK 544787	Whimpton	SK 795740
Stoke, East	SK 748501	Willoughby by Norwell	SK 788632
Sutton Passeys	c. SK 530390	Willoughby by Walesby	SK 689708
Swainston	c. SK 810750	Winkerfield	SK 630606
Thoresby	SK 648712	Wiverton	SK 715365
Thorney	SK 860726	Woodcotes	SK 780715
Thorpe in the Glebe	SK 607258	Woolsthorpe	c. SK 655464
Wansley	SK 461525		

OXFORDSHIRE

comprising one-inch Sheets: 144, 145, 146, 157, 158 and 159

Adwell	SU 696996	Coat	SP 355214
Albury	SP 655051	Cogges	SP 361095
Alwoldesberie	c. SP 308003	Cokethorpe	SP 374063
Armstalls	SP 415084	Combe	SP 418150
Ascott	SU 613981	Copcourt	SP 707010
Asterleigh	SP 400224	Coton	SP 491445
Astrop	SP 306081	*Cumbes*	c. SP 637036
Attington	SU 700016	Cutteslowe	SP 507112
Bainton	SP 578269	Ditchley	SP 390211
Baldon, Little	SU 565986	Dornford	SP 450205
Barton, Sesswell's	SP 452252	*Draitone*	c. SP 255188
Barton, Steeple	SP 447250	Draycot	SP 648059
Benneye	SP 273015	Dunthrop	SP 352282
Berrings	SP 418207	*Eggesle*	SP 340074
Bignell	SP 559221	Fifield	SU 631921
Bispedone	U	Fulwell	SP 624348
Broadstone	SP 353252	Godington	SP 642278
Brookend	SP 240310	Golder	SU 665977
Cadwell	SU 644957	Gosford	SP 502136
Caswell	SP 320080	Grove	c. SP 413311
Caversfield	SP 584254	Haddon, Lower	SP 302055
Chalford	SP 720010	Haddon, Marsh	SP 303064
Chalford, Nether	SP 347254	Hampton Gay	SP 486165
Chalford, Over	SP 344257	Hardwick	SP 460430
Chilworth, Great	SP 634038	Hordley	SP 447192
Chilworth, Little	SP 615051	Horspath, Old	SP 589048
Chimney	SP 358008	*Hunesworde*	U
Chippinghurst	SP 599013	Ilbury	SP 435310
Clattercote	SP 457492	Langley	SP 302153
Claywell	SP 351052	Latchford	SP 660015

Lea	SP 389385	Standhill	SP 652003
Ledall	SP 616083	Stowford	SP 560082
Ludwell	SP 433223	Thomley	SP 631090
Middleton Stoney	SP 532233	*Tilgardesle*	U
Mongewell	SU 610878	Topples	*c.* SP 371165
Nash	SP 598133	Tusmore	SP 564306
Nuneham Courtenay	SU 542981	Walcot	SP 347198
Pinkhill	SP 436072	Warpsgrove	SU 651982
Prescote	SP 473468	Water Eaton	SP 515121
Putlesle	*c.* SP 355066	Weaveley	*c.* SP 457185
Puttes	SU 284020	Wheatfield	SU 688993
Radcot	SU 285995	Wheatley, Old	*c.* SP 597052
Rofford	SU 629993	Whitehill	SP 482196
Rollright, Little	SP 293301	Wick	SP 552086
Rycote Magna	SP 667046	Widford	SP 272120
Rycote Parva	*c.* SP 665051	Wilcote	SP 375155
Sexintone	SP 560256	Willaston	SP 602298
Shelswell	SP 611309	Woodperry	SP 577105
Shifford	SP 373020	Wretchwick	SP 597214
Showell	SP 358292	Wykham	SP 441379
Somerforde	SP 455106	Yelford	SP 359047

RUTLAND

comprising one-inch Sheets: 122, 123, 133 and 134

Alstoe	SK 893122	Pickworth	SK 992138
Brook	SK 844059	Sculthorp	SK 930027
Gunthorpe	SK 869057	Snelston	SP 864953
Hardwick	SK 971124	Tixover	SP 971998
Horn	SK 954117	Tolethorpe	TF 021105
Martinsthorpe	SK 865046	Wenton	SK 899146
Normanton	SK 933063		

SHROPSHIRE

comprising one-inch Sheets: 118 and 129

Braggington	SJ 336140	*Humet*	U
Caus	SJ 337078	*Lege*	U
Cesdille	U	*Petelie*	U
Clev	U	*Udeford*	U
Detton	SO 667796		

SOMERSET

comprising one-inch Sheets: 164, 165, 166 and 177

Babington	ST 705510	Bickley	ST 130245
Barrow Mead	ST 729628	Bineham	ST 500250

Bradon, Goose	ST 364200	Holcombe	ST 668507
Bradon, North	ST 364200	Horsley	ST 714375
Bradon, South	ST 365187	*Millescota*	U
Camerton	ST 686575	Moreton	ST 562592
Contitona	U	Sock Dennis	ST 517213
Currypool	ST 327285	Spargrove	ST 671380
Dowlish, West	ST 364134	Standerwick	ST 815512
Dudesham	U	Whitcomb	ST 635238
Earnshill	ST 385216	*Wiftuna*	U
Eastham	ST 457104	Woodwick	ST 776604
Fayroke	ST 800488	Wraxall	ST 495718
Hardington	ST 742527		

STAFFORDSHIRE

comprising one-inch Sheets: 111, 119 and 120

Blithfield	SK 045240	Okeover	SK 158482
Blore	SK 137495	Packington	SK 164063
Chartley	SK 008285	Patshull	SJ 809010
Chillington	SJ 865068	Pillaton	SJ 942130
Cippemore	U	Sandon	SJ 953295
Croxall	SK 198136	Shugborough	SJ 990217
Derneslowe	U	Statfold	SK 238073
Fisherwick	SK 180100	Syerscote	SK 223076
Freeford	SK 135075	Tamhorn	SK 180070
Haselour	SK 205108	Thorpe Constantine	SK 260089
Monteville	U	Wychnor	SK 175160

SUFFOLK

comprising one-inch Sheets: 136, 137, 149 and 150

Aldham	TM 040445	Knettishall	TL 972804
Alteinestuna	TM 275370	Langham	TL 980690
Ashby	TM 489990	Linstead	TM 321761
Badley	TM 062560	Livermere, Little	TL 882718
Braiseworth	TM 138712	Mells	TM 405768
Chilton	TL 890422	Redisham	TM 402864
Easton Bavants	TM 517785	Saxham, Great	TL 798628
Elmham, South	TM 338847	Sotherton	TM 442796
Flixton	TM 518955	Sotterley	TM 458854
Fordley	TM 428668	Willingham	TM 446864
Fornham St. Geneveve	TL 840683	Wordwell	TL 829720
Ickworth	TL 813611		

203

SURREY

comprising one-inch Sheets: 170 and 171

Albury	TQ 065479	Tatsfield	TQ 41756
Cuddington	TQ 234636	Titsey	TQ 40755•
Gatton	TQ 276528		

SUSSEX

comprising one-inch Sheets: 181, 182, 183 and 184

Aldrington	TQ 266053	Hove	TQ 28604⸱
Balmer	TQ 359100	Hydneye	TQ 60902⸱
Balsdean	TQ 378059	Islesham	c. TQ 00000•
Barpham, Upper	TQ 067089	Itchenor, East	c. SU 80100⸱
Binderton	SU 851108	Linch	SU 84918⸱
Binsted	SU 982061	Lordington	SU 78209⸱
Botolphs	TQ 194092	Marden, North	SU 80816⸱
Bracklesham	c. SU 805964	Marden, Up	SU 79614⸱
Broomhill	c. TQ 988183	Muntham	TQ 10510⸱
Bulverhythe	TQ 768082	Newtimber	TQ 27113⸱
Burton	SU 967176	*Nonneminstre*	U
Coombes	TQ 191082	Northeye	TQ 68307⸱
Cudlow	c. TQ 002004	Parham	TQ 05914⸱
Duncton	SU 960170	Perching	TQ 24310⸱
Erringham, Old	TQ 205077	Pyecombe	TQ 29312⸱
Esmerewic	U	Racton	SU 78009⸱
Exceat	TV 522992	*Stochestone*	U
Glatting	SU 972142	*Wildene*	U
Hamsey	TQ 414122	Wiston	TQ 15512⸱
Hangleton	TQ 268074	Woodmancote	TQ 23115⸱
Heene	TQ 138027		

WARWICKSHIRE

comprising one-inch Sheets: 120, 131, 132, 144, 145 and 151

Alscot	SP 210504	Bosworth	c. SP 16790⸱
Arnhale	c. SP 336799	Bradmore	SP 29441•
Ascote, Chapel	SP 416564	Bramcote	SP 41288⸱
Aspley	SP 088537	Brookhampton	SP 31950•
Asthull	c. SP 332778	Broom, Burnell's	SP 08552⸱
Baddesley Clinton	SP 200715	Broughton	SP 20446⸱
Barcheston	SP 264399	Budbrooke	SP 25965•
Bericote	SP 320700	Burmington Parva	c. SP 28238•
Biggin	SP 535780	Calcutt	SP 47165•
Billesley Trussell	SP 146568	Caldecote	SP 34895⸱

204

Caludon	SP 374802	Hydes Pastures	SP 396923
Cawston	SP 475730	Idlicote	SP 285445
Cestersover	SP 504820	Itchington, Lower	SP 393564
Charlecote	SP 263565	Kingston	SP 361575
Chelmscote	SP 315427	Kington	SP 152808
Chesterton	SP 348586	Lawford, Little	SP 470772
Clifford	SP 379806	Lee	SP 280613
Clopton	SP 168452	Marston	SP 419761
Compton Scorpion	SP 213405	Meon	SP 182455
Compton Verney	SP 312530	Milburn	SP 305736
Compton Wynyates	SP 323430	Milcote, Lower	SP 172523
Copston Parva	c. SP 445890	Milcote, Upper	SP 192528
Coton	SP 518788	Morrell	SP 313565
Coundon	SP 314814	Morton	SP 535745
Cryfield	c. SP 296756	Morton Bagot	SP 112648
Dassett, Burton	SP 398512	Myton	SP 301652
Dassett, Southend	SP 390520	Naspis	SP 294630
Ditchford, Friary	SP 200370	Newbold Comyn	c. SP 330660
Dodwell	SP 166541	Newbold Pacey	SP 299573
Dorsington Parva	SP 130505	Newnham Paddox	SP 480837
Drakenage	SP 222952	Norton	U
Edstone	SP 175618	Offord	c. SP 150620
Enscote	SP 304657	Oldberrow	SP 122660
Ettington, Lower	SP 249473	Packington, Great	SP 225835
Finham	SP 334738	Packington, Little	SP 212843
Fletchamstead	SP 300373	Pinley	SP 355775
Foxcote	SP 200418	Radbourn	SP 440570
Fulbrook	SP 253607	Ruin Clifford	c. SP 204526
Goldicote	SP 246513	Rykemersbury	SP 255690
Harborough Parva	SP 480788	Shelford	SP 421890
Hardwick in		Shuckburgh, Upper	SP 490628
Burton Dassett	SP 370515	Smercote	c. SP 328856
Hardwick in Tysoe	SP 342475	Smite, Lower	SP 412808
Hasely	SP 240685	Smite, Upper	SP 430825
Hatton on Avon	c. SP 240565	Sole End	c. SP 327877
Hawkesbury	c. SP 363852	Spernall	c. SP 085622
Heathcote	SP 294589	Stoke	SP 370790
Henley	SP 366814	Stokhull	U
Hillborough	SP 123520	Stoneton	SP 464544
Hodnell	SP 424575	Stoneythorpe	SP 404635
Homburn	U	Stratford	SK 214916
Honiley	SP 245722	Stretton Baskerville	SP 420910
Hopsford	SP 425838	Tachbrook Mallory	SP 320618
Hunscote	SP 250550	Tackley	SP 363846
Hurst	SP 286754	Thornton	SP 274503

Upton	SP 370455	Wike	SP 074607
Walton Deyville	SP 285522	Willicote	SP 182487
Watergall	SP 425588	Wilmcote Parva	SP 167577
Weddington	SP 359935	Wishaw	SP 177945
Weethley	SP 055555	Wolfhampcote	SP 530652
Welcombe	SP 209568	Woodcote, Lower	c. SP 283691
Westcote	SP 360478	Woodcote, Upper	c. SP 283691
Weston	SP 280357	Woodloes	c. SP 278670
Whitchurch	SP 227487	Wormleighton	SP 448540
Whitley	SP 350765		

WESTMORLAND

comprising one-inch Sheets: 83 and 84

Langton	NY 710200	Smardale	NY 734085

WILTSHIRE

comprising one-inch Sheets: 156, 157, 166 and 167

Addeston	SU 067433	Choulston	SU 151485
Alderstone	SU 245245	Cockleberg	ST 928739
Alton	SU 153468	Corton	SU 052757
Anstye	ST 955404	Cowesfield	SU 260240
Asserton	SU 075394	Cumberwell	ST 821631
Avon	SU 130330	Dauntsey	ST 980824
Barford	SU 182225	Draycot Cerne	ST 935786
Bathampton, Great	SU 017380	Easton	SU 049645
Bathampton, Little	SU 023378	Eston	ST 886777
Baycliff	ST 813396	Faulston	SU 074255
Baynton	ST 943537	Forde	SU 275638
Beversbrook	SU 004731	Fowlswick	ST 882757
Bincknoll	SU 107797	Foxley	ST 896860
Blackland	SU 013693	Fresden	SU 226922
Bourton	SU 068435	Gomeldon	SU 182356
Bradfield	ST 895829	Groundwell	SU 151890
Bremelham	ST 904861	Gurston	SU 027252
Bremeridge	ST 849509	Harthem	ST 864715
Bridmore	ST 960220	Hazlebury	ST 835684
Broom	SU 165822	Heale	SU 125365
Bulbridge	SU 094309	Hensat	c. SU 240680
Bupton	SU 056763	Hill Deverill	ST 866402
Chalcot	ST 842490	Homanton	SU 069430
Chalfield, Great	ST 860632	Hurdcott	SU 040310
Charnage	ST 834319	Knighton	SU 052254
Chilhampton	SU 095332	Knighton	SU 153456

Longford	SU 172266	Stanley	ST 958729
Lus Hill	SU 168944	Stock Street	ST 994693
Lydiard Tregoze	SU 103848	Stowell, East	SU 146619
Mannington	SU 128842	Surrendell	ST 874821
Middleton	ST 905438	Syrencot	SU 160460
Midgehall	SU 080840	Thornhill	ST 922865
Milbourne	ST 907530	Thoulstone	ST 838481
Newenham	ST 908415	Throope	SU 088264
Norridge	ST 853470	Tockenham, East	SU 040794
Norington	ST 967238	Ugford, South	SU 088303
Penleigh	ST 854509	Upham	SU 226772
Pensworth	SU 208220	Vastern	SU 049816
Pertwood	ST 889359	Walcote	SU 173843
Poulton	SU 195698	Walton	SU 165215
Preshute	SU 180685	Washerne	SU 098308
Puthall	SU 239681	Westlecote	SU 146830
Rabson	SU 099746	Whelpley	ST 231240
Ratfyn	SU 162424	Whetham	ST 979681
Richardson	SU 097742	Whiteclive	ST 859383
St. Joan A Gore	SU 013504	Whitley	ST 993736
Salthrop	SU 118802	Widhill, North	SU 127912
Sarum, Old	SU 142325	Widhill, West	SU 137906
Shaw	SU 135653	Witcomb	SU 025755
Smithcot	SU 003830	Witherington	SU 182248
Snap	SU 225762	Wittenham	ST 810585
Standlynch	SU 183235	Woodhill	SU 060770

WORCESTERSHIRE

comprising one-inch Sheets: 130, 143 and 144

Bickmarsh	SP 109495	Pendock	SO 817337
Elmley Lovett	SO 865697	Poden	SO 125435
Kenswick	SO 792583	Witley, Great	SO 755661
Naunton, Sheriffs	SO 959525		

YORKSHIRE

East Riding

comprising one-inch Sheets: 92, 93, 97, 98, 99 and 105

Argam	TA 112710	Bartindale	TA 109730
Arram	TA 165490	Battleburn	SE 984556
Arras	SE 923417	Belby	SE 771290
Arras, Old	SE 934423	Belthorpe	SE 780541
Auburn	TA 170628	Benningholme, East	TA 128390
Barthorpe	SE 770595	Benningholme, West	TA 117388

Bewick	TA 233395	Houghton	SE 890390
Birdsall	SE 817649	Hundeburton	c. SE 725557
Bonwick	TA 168534	Hunsley	SE 950350
Bracken	SE 981505	Keeling, Nun	TA 143502
Brackenholme	SE 700300	Kelleythorpe	TA 012565
Buckton	SE 843695	Kettlethorpe	SE 916334
Burdale	SE 871623	Kilnwick Percy	SE 824495
Burstwick, Bond	TA 220290	Kiplingcotes	SE 901479
Burton Constable	TA 190368	Kirkham	SE 735658
Camerton	TA 216262	Linton	SE 909708
Cavil	SE 770305	Linton, East	SE 793280
Caythorpe	TA 120678	Linton, West	SE 800283
Cleaving	SE 851460	Lund Garth	TA 200315
Cleeton	TA 187542	Meaux	TA 096403
Cotness	SE 800240	Menethorpe	SE 770677
Cottam	SE 993648	Metham	SE 810248
Cowden, Little	TA 242420	Monkwith	TA 300328
Cowlam	SE 965655	Moreby	SE 595433
Croom	SE 934658	Mowthorpe	SE 895670
Danthorpe	TA 245326	Neswick	SE 974528
Dowthorpe	TA 154381	Newsham	TA 190719
Drewton	SE 925334	Newsome Mowthorne	TA 205268
Dyke	TA 213335	Newton in Cottingham	TA 043310
Eastburn	SE 990558	Newton in Paull	TA 181270
Easthorpe	SE 881454	Newton, Place	SE 885726
Easton	TA 153680	Nuthill	TA 215300
Eddlethorpe	SE 773661	Octon	TA 032700
Enthorpe	SE 915462	Ousethorpe	SE 820515
Eske	TA 057431	Owsthorpe	SE 810310
Etherdwick	TA 231373	Penisthorpe	c. TA 345210
Flotmanby, East	TA 080799	Pockthorpe	TA 040634
Flotmanby, West	TA 073796	Raisthorpe	SE 855617
Fosham	TA 209388	Ravenserod	c. TA 400100
Gardham	SE 945415	Ravensthorpe	TA 010425
Garrowby	SE 795574	Ringborough	TA 273375
Givendale, Little	SE 823530	Riplingham	SE 960320
Goxhill	TA 185450	Risby	TA 010350
Greenoak	SE 815280	Rotsea	TA 065516
Grimston	TA 290350	Rowley	SE 973326
Grimston, Hanging	SE 800600	Rowton	TA 138402
Grimthorpe	SE 812530	Scorborough	TA 015455
Gunby	SE 709354	Scoreby	SE 698529
Hartburn	TA 170600	Sewerby	TA 202691
Hilderthorpe	TA 175655	Skeckling	TA 220280
Holme Archiepiscopi	SE 879581	Skirlington, High	TA 180525

Sledmere	SE 930648	Totleys	TA 239274
Southorpe	TA 198466	Towthorpe	
Storkhill	TA 050418	in Londesborough	SE 867439
Sunderlandwick	TA 010548	Towthorpe in	
Sutton	SE 795704	Wharram Percy	SE 900630
Swaythorpe	TA 037690	Tranby	TA 025282
Tansterne	TA 223376	Waplington	SE 775465
Thirkleby	SE 920687	Wauldby	SE 974297
Thoralby in Bugthorpe	SE 770585	Weedley	SE 954330
Thoralby in Kirby		Welham	SE 783697
Grindalythe	c. SE 905675	Wharram Percy	SE 858642
Thornthorpe	SE 782672	Willerby	TA 008793
Thorpe in Rudston	TA 110678	Wilsthorpe	TA 170640
Thorpe le Street	SE 837440	Winkton	TA 150590
Thorpe Lidget	SE 765295	Wolfreton	TA 036304

North Riding

comprising one-inch Sheets: 84, 85, 86, 90, 91, 92, 93 and 97

Ainderby Mires	SE 257927	Burton on Ure	SE 227827
Airyholme	SE 673734	Busby, Little	NZ 515042
Akebar	SE 191902	Byland	SE 566868
Allerthorpe	SE 330868	Carlton in Stanwick	c. NZ 193122
Appleton, East	SE 236957	Carlton in Stockton	SE 670566
Appleton, West	SE 218945	Catto	SE 428924
Aske	c. NZ 182034	Cawthorn	TA 773891
Baldersby	SE 355786	Clifton in Ure	SE 218844
Barforth on Tees	NZ 164162	Coatham, West	NZ 565229
Barnaby	NZ 580159	Corburn	SE 590580
Barnby	SE 726610	Cornborough	SE 630670
Barwick	NZ 432146	Coulby	NZ 506138
Baxby	SE 512752	Cowton, South	NZ 294022
Birkby	NZ 330025	Crakehill	SE 430735
Birkhou	c. SE 380760	Crosby	SE 406886
Bolton, East	SE 041909	Crossthwaite	c. NY 930255
Bolton, West	SE 020910	Dalby	SE 636712
Borderlby	SE 449985	Dale Town	SE 535885
Bossall	SE 718608	Dalton, West	c. NZ 115085
Bowforth	SE 689837	Danby in Cleveland	NZ 696062
Brandsby	SE 598719	Danby, Little	SE 340962
Brawith	SE 410875	Danby on Ure	NZ 171869
Breckenbrough	SE 383833	Deepdale	c. SE 040852
Brough	SE 215980	Didderston	SE 108080
Broughton, Little	NZ 560068	Dromonby	NZ 534057
Broughton Lythe	U	Easby in Bladesby	c. SE 380760

Easby in Richmond	NZ 185003	Lazenby	SE 340985
Easthorpe	SE 736713	Leake	SE 433906
Ebberston	SE 892833	Leavington, Castle	NZ 461103
Edstone, Little	SE 710850	Leekby	SE 415745
Eldmire	SE 421747	Lilling, East	SE 664645
Ellenthorpe	SE 412673	Marderby	SE 468839
Ellerton	SE 078972	Marton	SE 767842
Etersthorpe	TA 101820	Marton in the Forest	SE 602683
Fornthorpe	c. SE 640710	Mortham	NZ 086142
Fors	SD 947969	Morton	c. NZ 555145
Girlington	NZ 128138	Mowthorpe	c. SE 685690
Greenberry	SE 295987	Moxby	SE 597669
Griff	SE 587839	Newby on Swale	SE 380760
Grimsby	c. NZ 780154	Newham	TA 517133
Grimston	c. SE 604740	Newsham by	
Gristhwaite	SE 425785	Breckenbrough	c. SE 379848
Halnaby	NZ 262069	Newsham by	
Harlsey, West	SE 415981	Butterwick	c. SE 740760
Hatterboard	TA 017887	Newton Picot	SE 312895
Hauxwell, West	SE 165930	Newton, West	SE 645795
Hessleton	SE 199918	Norton Conyers	SE 317763
Hinderskelfe	SE 719700	Osgodby	SE 490810
Holme, North	c. SE 705807	Otteringham, North	SE 363897
Holtby	SE 268922	Pinchinthorpe	NZ 578142
Hornby	SE 222937	Prestby	NZ 904114
Hoverton	c. SE 675860	Preston	c. SE 975847
Howe	SE 806753	Raventhorpe	SE 481866
Howgrave	SE 315793	Riccal	SE 674806
Howthorpe	SE 675726	Roberthorpe	c. TA 100820
Hutton Bonville	NZ 336002	Rokeby	NZ 084144
Hutton Hill	SE 739681	Rook Barugh	SE 721822
Ingleby	NZ 432132	Rookwith	SE 210872
Irby	NZ 410030	Rotherford	NZ 031119
Islebeck	SE 447775	Roxby by Thornton	
Jolby	NZ 257103	le Dale	SE 826828
Killerby	c. TA 065828	Roxby in Pickhill	SE 328825
Killerby by Catterick	SE 260960	Ruswick	SE 195895
Kilton Thorpe	NE 693177	Sandburn	SE 670590
Kilvington, North	SE 423855	Sawcoch	c. SE 420990
Kingthorpe	c. SE 835858	Scawthorpe	c. TA 090830
Kirkby	SE 281958	Sessay, Little	SE 467748
Kneeton	NZ 213069	Shutterskelfe	c. NZ 483070
Landmoth	SE 425927	Sigston, Kirby	SE 417947
Langton, Little	SE 303958	Smeaton, Little	NZ 346035
Laysthorpe	c. SE 636789	Solberg	SE 355891

Sowerby under Cotcliffe	SE 412936	Thorpe Row	NZ 355045
Stanwick	NZ 185120	Tocketts	NZ 619175
Stittenham	SE 679676	Tollesby	c. NZ 510160
Studdah	SE 145908	Tunstall	NZ 531124
Swainby	SE 337855	Twislebrook	c. SE 215799
Swarthorpe	SE 203832	Ulshaw	SE 145872
Tanfield, East	SE 289779	Upsall	c. NZ 560160
Tanton	NZ 524106	Walmire	c. NZ 280060
Thoralby	c. NZ 492073	Wath	SE 677750
Thoresby	SE 030900	Waupley	c. NZ 726145
Thornton Bridge	SE 430714	Westonby	NZ 794072
Thornton le Street	SE 414862	Whorlton	NZ 484025
Thornton on Hill	SE 532741	Wigganthorpe	SE 663724
Thornton Riseborough	SE 747826	Winton	SE 410966
Thorpe in Wycliffe	NZ 104142	Worsall, High	NZ 387093
Thorpe Perrow	c. SE 262855		

West Riding

comprising one-inch Sheets: 91, 95, 96, 97, 102, 103 and 104

Adel	SE 277403	Hammerton	SE 720537
Aismunderby	SE 305686	Hangthwaite	c. SE 554069
Allerton Mauleverer	SE 415580	Harewood	c. SE 314450
Alwoodley	c. SE 301413	Hazelwood	SE 449398
Azerley	SE 260745	Herleshow	SE 277675
Battersby	SE 665514	Hornington	SE 515418
Bilham	SE 485069	Huddleston	SE 465340
Bolton	SE 155365	Humberton	SE 422686
Brandon	SE 340410	Kirkby Ouseburn	SE 465610
Bustardthorpe	c. SE 600495	Lead	SE 464369
Byram cum Poole	SE 494270	Lofthouse	c. SE 324432
Cayton	SE 286632	Lotherton	SE 440360
Chevet	c. SE 345155	Mulwith	SE 363667
Clareton	SE 395594	Newby	c. SE 347675
Clotherholme	SE 287722	Newsam, Temple	c. SE 355320
Easedike	SE 474452	Newton Waleys	SE 446279
Eavestone	SE 224683	Nunwick	SE 322745
Folifoot, East	SE 457463	Oglethorpe	SE 448441
Frickley	SE 468079	Oulston	SE 500425
Gawthorpe	c. SE 310410	Pallathorpe	SE 514427
Givendale	SE 336692	Parlington	c. SE 422300
Grimston	SE 500415	Ribstone Magna	SE 392536
Haganby	c. SE 480420	Scaggiethorpe	c. SE 540550
Haldenby	c. SE 820170	Scawsby	SE 539051

Skelton	SE 341306	Thorpe Underwood	SE 465595
Skibeden	SE 016526	Tilts	SE 572095
Skinthorpe	c. SE 544036	Timble, Little	c. SE 190525
Sleningford	SE 277776	Toulston	SE 452440
Stancil	SK 607960	Walkingham	c. SE 350620
Stapleton	SE 508192	Wallerthwaite	c. SE 295649
Steeton	SE 532441	Westwick	SE 355664
Stockeld	c. SE 375495	Wharncliffe	c. SK 305957
Stockton	SE 335456	Wheldale	SE 450267
Stotfield	SE 472062	Wildthorpe	c. SE 510010
Stubbs	SE 496112	Wilstrop	SE 484553
Studley Parva	c. SE 280720	Wothersome	c. SE 404425
Thornville, Old	SE 457548	Wrangbrook	SE 494133
Thorpe Stapleton	c. SE 350310		

CHAPTER SIX

Select Bibliography, England

Editor: J. G. HURST

INTRODUCTION

This conspexus of published historical and archaeological work excludes specific references to individual deserted villages in such general works as *The Victoria History of the Counties of England* (1899, continuing, 150 vols.), and the classic county *Histories* of the last three centuries. Smaller archaeological reports and notes can be traced through the Gazetteer (Chapter 3).

The Bibliography, like those in Parts Two, Three and Four, excludes works published after January 1, 1969.

ADDYMAN, 1964 — P. V. Addyman, "A Dark Age Settlement at Maxey, Northamptonshire", *Med. Archaeol.*, VIII (1964), 20–73.

ADDYMAN, 1965 — ——, "Late Saxon Settlements in the St. Neots Area, I, The Saxon Settlement and Norman Castle at Eaton Socon, Bedfordshire", *Proc. Cambs. Antiq. Soc.*, LVIII (1965), 38–73.

ADDYMAN et al., 1963 — P. V. Addyman, W. G. Simpson and P. W. H. Spring, "Two Medieval Sites Near Sedbergh", *Yorks. Archaeol. Journ.*, XLI (1963), 27–42.

ALEXANDER, 1968 — J. A. Alexander, "Clopton: The Life-cycle of a Cambridge-shire Village", in L. M. Munby, ed., *East Anglian Studies* (1968), 48–70.

ALLCROFT, 1908 — A. H. Allcroft, *Earthwork of England* (1908).

ALLISON, 1955 — K. J. Allison, "The Lost Villages of Norfolk", *Norfolk Archaeol.*, XXXI (1955), 116–62.

ALLISON et al., 1965 — K. J. Allison, M. W. Beresford and J. G. Hurst, *The Deserted Villages of Oxfordshire*, Univ. of Leics. Dept. Eng. Local Hist., Occ. Paps., XVII (1965), 1–47.

ALLISON et al., 1966 — ——, —— and ——, *The Deserted Villages of Northamptonshire*, Univ. of Leics. Dept. Eng. Local Hist., Occ. Paps., XVIII (1966), 1–48.

ANNUAL REPORT — Deserted Medieval Village Research Group, *Annual Reports*, I–XV (1953–67).

BADDELEY, 1910 — W. St. Clair Baddeley, "The Manor and Site of Hullasey, Gloucestershire", *Trans. Bristol and Glos. Archaeol. Soc.*, XXXIII (1910), 338–54.

BARING, 1901 — F. Baring, "The Making of the New Forest", *Eng. Hist. Rev.*, XVI (1901), 427–38.

BARING-GOULD, 1892–93 — Rev. S. Baring-Gould, "An Ancient Settlement on Trewortha Marsh", *Journ. Royal Inst. Corn.*, XI (1892–93), 57–70 and 289–90.

BARKER, 1968 — P. A. Barker, "The Deserted Medieval Hamlet of Braggington", *Trans. Shrops. Archaeol. Soc.*, LVIII (1968), 122–39.

BARLEY, 1957 — M. W. Barley, "Cistercian Land Clearances in Nottinghamshire: Three Deserted Villages and their Moated Successor", *Nottingham Med. Stud.*, I (1957), 75–89.

BARLEY, 1961 — ——, *The English Farmhouse and Cottage* (1961).

BARR-HAMILTON, 1961 — A. Barr-Hamilton, "The Excavation of Bargham Church Site, Upper Bargham, Angmering, Sussex", *Sussex Archaeol. Coll.*, XCIX (1961), 38–65.

BARTON, 1960 — K. J. Barton, "Settlements of the Iron Age and Pagan Saxon Periods at Linford, Essex", *Trans. Essex Archaeol. Soc.*, 3rd ser., I (1960), 1–48.

BARTON, 1964 — ——, "Excavations in the Village of Tarring, West Sussex", *Sussex Archaeol. Coll.*, CII (1964), 9–27.

BARTON, 1965 — ——, "A Medieval Site at Goring By Sea", *Sussex Archaeol. Coll.*, CIII (1965), 88–93.

BEAN, 1963 — J. M. W. Bean, "Plague Population and Economic Decline in the Later Middle Ages", *Econ. Hist. Rev.*, 2nd ser., XV (1963), 423–37.

BERESFORD, 1950 — M. W. Beresford, "The Deserted Villages of Warwickshire", *Trans. Birm. and Mid. Archaeol. Soc.*, LXVI, for 1945, (1950), 49–106.

BERESFORD, 1951 — ——, "The Lost Villages of Yorkshire, Part I", *Yorks. Archaeol. Journ.*, XXXVII (1951), 474–91.

BERESFORD, 1951A — M. W. Beresford, "The Lost Villages of Medieval England", *Geog. Journ.*, CXVII (1951), 129–49.

BERESFORD, 1952 — ——, "The Lost Villages of Yorkshire, Part II", *Yorks. Archaeol. Journ.*, XXXVIII (1952), 44–70.

BERESFORD, 1953 — ——, "The Lost Villages of Yorkshire, Part III", *Yorks. Archaeol. Journ.*, XXXVIII (1953), 215–40.

BERESFORD, 1953A   ——, "The Poll Tax and Census of Sheep, 1549", *Ag. Hist. Rev.*, I (1953), 9–15.

BERESFORD, 1953B   ——, "The Deserted Medieval Villages of England", *Trans. Anc. Mons. Soc.*, new ser., I (1953), 100–06.

BERESFORD, 1953–54   ——, "A Summary List of Deserted Villages of the County", *Rec. of Bucks.*, XVI (1953–54), 26–8.

BERESFORD, 1954   ——, "The Lost Villages of Yorkshire, Part IV", *Yorks. Archaeol. Journ.*, XXXVIII (1954), 280–309.

BERESFORD, 1954A   ——, "The Poll Tax and Census of Sheep, 1549", *Ag. Hist. Rev.*, II (1954), 15–29.

BERESFORD, 1954B   ——, "The Lost Villages of Northern England", in W. A. Singleton, ed., *Studies in Architectural History* (1954), 115–138.

BERESFORD, 1954C   ——, *The Lost Villages of England* (1954); fourth impression with corrections (1963).

BERESFORD, 1957   ——, *History on the Ground* (1957), 93–124.

BERESFORD, 1961   M. W. Beresford, "Habitation Versus Improvement: The Debate on Enclosure by Agreement", in F. J. Fisher, ed., *Essays in the Economic and Social History of Tudor and Stuart England* (1961), 40–69.

BERESFORD, 1964   ——, "Dispersed and Grouped Settlement in Medieval Cornwall", *Ag. Hist. Rev.*, XII (1964), 13–27.

BERESFORD, 1965   ——, "Villages Désertés: Bilan de la Recherche Anglaise", in École Pratique des Hautes Études, VIe Section, *Les Hommes et la Terre*, XI, Villages Désertés et Histoire Économique (Paris 1965), 533–80.

BERESFORD, 1966   ——, "Fallowfield, Northumberland: An early Cartographic Representation of a Deserted Village", *Med. Archaeol.*, X (1966), 164–67.

BERESFORD, 1967   ——, "East Layton, Co. Durham, in 1608: Another Cartographic Representation of a Deserted Medieval Village Site", *Med. Archaeol.*, XI (1967), 257–60.

BERESFORD AND HURST, 1962   M. W. Beresford and J. G. Hurst, "Introduction to a First List of Deserted Medieval Village Sites in Berkshire", *Berks. Archaeol. Journ.*, IX (1962), 92–97.

BERESFORD AND ST. JOSEPH, 1958   M. W. Beresford and J. K. St. Joseph, *Medieval England: an Aerial Survey* (1958), 17–20, 100–07, and 109–19.

BERSU, 1949   G. Bersu, "A Promontory Fort on the Shore of Ramsey Bay, Isle of Man", *Antiq. Journ.*, XXIX (1949), 62–79.

BIDDLE, 1961–2   M. Biddle, "The Deserted Medieval Village of Seacourt, Berkshire", *Oxoniensia*, XXVI–VII (1961–62), 70–201.

BLIGHT, 1868   J. T. Blight, "Notice of Enclosures at Smallacombe Near the Cheesewring, Cornwall", *Journ. Royal Inst. Corn.*, III (1868–70), 10–16.

BOWDEN, 1952   P. J. Bowden, "Movements in Wool Prices 1490–1610", *Yorks. Bull. of Econ. and Soc. Research*, IV (1952), 109–24.

BOWDEN, 1967   ——, "Agriculture Prices, Farm Profits, and Rents", in Joan Thirsk, ed., *The Agrarian History of England and Wales*, IV (1967), 593–695, and "Statistical Appendix", *ibid.*, 814–870.

BOWEN AND FOWLER, 1961   H. C. Bowen and P. J. Fowler, "The Archaeology of Fyfield and Overton Downs, Wiltshire", *Wilts. Archaeol. Mag.*, LVIII (1961–63), 98–115.

BRADLEY, 1914   Harriet Bradley, *Enclosures in England* (1914).

BREWSTER, 1952   T. C. M. Brewster, *Two Medieval Habitation Sites in the Vale of Pickering*, Stud. Yorks. Archaeol., I (1952), 1–47.

BRUCE-MITFORD, 1940   R. L. S. Bruce-Mitford, "Excavations at Seacourt", *Oxoniensia*, V, (1940), 31–40.

BRUCE-MITFORD, 1956   ——, "A Dark-Age Settlement at Mawgan Porth, Cornwall", in R. L. S. Bruce-Mitford, ed., *Recent Archaeological Excavations in Britain* (1956), 167–96.

BUDGEN, 1916   W. Budgen, "Excete and its Parish Church", *Sussex Archaeol. Coll.*, LVIII (1916), 138–71.

BUTLER, 1962   L. A. S. Butler, "Church Close, Langton by Spilsby, a Deserted Medieval Village", *Lincs. Archit. and Archaeol. Soc. Reps. and Paps.*, IX (1962), 125–33.

CLIFTON-TAYLOR, 1962   A. Clifton-Taylor, *The Pattern of English Building* (1962).

COCKS, 1909   A. H. Cocks, "A Semi-underground Hut in Walton Road, Aylesbury", *Rec. of Bucks.*, IX (1909), 282–96.

COLVIN, 1952   H. M. Colvin, "Deserted Villages and the Archaeologist", *Archaeol. News Letter*, IV (1952), 129–32.

COLVIN, 1958   ——, "Farmhouses and Cottages", in A. Lane Poole, ed., *Medieval England*, I (1958), 77–97.

COPLEY, 1958   G. J. Copley, *An Archaeology of South-east England* (1958), 195–200.

CRAWFORD, 1925   O. G. S. Crawford, "Air Photograph of Gainstrop, Lincolnshire", *Antiq. Journ.*, V (1925), 432–33.

CUNNINGTON, 1909 — Mrs. M. E. Cunnington, "A Medieval Earthwork near Morgan's Hill", *Wilts. Archaeol. Mag.*, XXXVI (1910), 590–08.

D'ARCHIMBAUD, 1962 — Mlle. G. D. D'Archimbaud, "L'Archeologie du village médiéval: exemple anglais et experience provençale", *Annales* (1962), 477–88.

DAVIES, 1949 — A. Morley Davies, "Abefield and Achamstead, Two Lost Places", *Rec. of Bucks.*, XV (1949), 166–71.

DAVEY, 1964 — N. Davey, "A Pre-Conquest Church and Baptistry at Potterne", *Wilts. Archaeol. Mag.*, LIX (1964), 116–23.

D.M.V.R.G., 1963–64 — Deserted Medieval Village Research Group, "Provisional List of Deserted Medieval Villages in Leicestershire", *Trans. Leics. Archaeol. and Hist. Soc.*, XXXIX (1963–64), 24–33.

DOBSON, 1962 — B. Dobson, "Some Current Archaeological Problems of Medieval Durham", *Trans. Archit. and Archaeol. Soc. Dur. and Northumb.*, XI (1962), 180–87.

DONKIN, 1960 — R. A. Donkin, "Settlement and Depopulation on Cistercian Estates in the Twelfth and Thirteenth Centuries, Especially in Yorkshire", *Bull. Inst. Hist. Res.*, XXXIII (1960), 141–65.

DONKIN, 1962 — R. A. Donkin, "Some Aspects of Cistercian Sheep Farming in England and Wales", *Citeaux*, XIII (1962), 296–310.

DONKIN, 1963 — ——, "The Cistercian Order in England: Some Conclusions", *Trans. Inst. Brit. Geog.*, XXXIII (1963), 181–98.

DONKIN, 1964 — ——, "The Cistercian Grange in England in the Twelfth and Thirteenth Centuries, with special reference to Yorkshire", *Studia Monastica*, VI (1964), 95–144.

DUDLEY, 1949 — H. Dudley, *Early Days in North-west Lincolnshire* (1949).

DUDLEY AND MINTER, 1962–63 — Miss D. Dudley and Mrs. E. M. Minter, "The Medieval Village at Garrow Tor, Bodmin Moor, Cornwall", *Med. Archaeol.*, VI–VIII (1962–63), 272–94.

DUDLEY AND MINTER, 1966 — —— and ——, "The Excavation of a Medieval Settlement at Treworld, Lesnewth, 1963", *Corn Archaeol.*, V (1966), 34–58.

DUNNING, 1932 — G. C. Dunning, "Bronze Age Settlements and a Saxon Hut near Bourton-on-the-Water", *Antiq. Journ.*, XII (1932), 279–93.

DUNNING, 1952 — ——, "Anglo-Saxon Discoveries at Harston", *Trans. Leics. Archaeol. Soc.*, XXVIII (1952), 49–54.

DYER, 1965–67 — C. Dyer, "The Deserted Medieval Village of Woollashill", *Trans. Worcs. Archaeol. Soc.*, 3rd ser., I (1968), 55–61.

DYER, 1968   ——, "Population and Agriculture on a Warwickshire Manor in the late Middle Ages", *Univ. Birm. Hist. Journ.*, XI (1968), 113–27.

ÉCOLE PRATIQUE   École Pratique des Hautes Études, VIe Section, *Les Hommes et la Terre*, XI, Villages Désertés et Histoire Économique (Paris, 1965).

FIELD, 1965   R. K. Field, "Worcestershire Peasant Buildings, household goods and farm equipment in the later Middle Ages", *Med. Archaeol.*, IX (1965), 105–45.

FOSTER, ED., 1920   C. W. Foster, ed., *Final Concords of the County of Lincoln*, Lincs. Rec. Soc., XVII (1920).

FOSTER AND LONGLEY, 1924   C. W. Foster and T. Longley, *Lincolnshire Domesday*, Lincs. Rec. Soc., XIX (1924), xlvii–xc.

FOWLER, 1963   P. J. Fowler, "The Archaeology of Fyfield and Overton Downs, Wiltshire, 2nd Interim Report", *Wilts. Archaeol. Mag.*, LVIII (1961–63), 342–50.

FOX, 1937   Aileen Fox, "Dinas Noddfa, Gelligaer Common, Glamorgan: Excavations in 1936", *Archaeol. Camb.*, XCII (1937), 247–68.

FOX, 1939   ——, "Early Welsh Homesteads on Gelligaer Common, Glamorgan: Excavations in 1938", *Archaeol. Camb.*, XCIV (1939), 163–99.

FOX, 1958   ——, "A Monastic Homestead on Dean Moor, South Devon", *Med. Archaeol.*, II (1958), 141–57.

FOX AND RAGLAN, 1953   Sir Cyril Fox and Lord Raglan, *Monmouthshire Houses, Part II, Sub-Medieval Houses, c. 1550–1610* (1953).

GARROOD, 1937   J. R. Garrood, "A Medieval Chapel at Salome Lodge, Leighton, Huntingdonshire", *Trans. Cambs. and Hunts. Archaeol. Soc.*, V (1937), 385–90.

GATHERCOLE AND WAILES, 1959   P. W. Gathercole and B. Wailes, "Excavations on Castle Hill, Thurgarton, 1954–55", *Trans. Thoroton Soc.*, LXIII (1959), 24–56.

GAY, 1903   E. F. Gay, "Inclosures in England", *Quart. Journ. of Econ.*, XVII (1903).

GAY, 1904   ——, "The Midland Revolt and the Inquisitions of Depopulation of 1607", *Trans. Royal Hist. Soc.*, 2nd ser., XVIII (1904), 195–237.

GELLING, 1952   P. S. Gelling, "Excavation of a Promontory Fort at Port Grenaugh, Santon", *Proc. Isle of Man Nat. Hist. and Antiq. Soc.*, V (1952), 307–15.

GELLING, 1957   ——, "Excavation of a Promontory Fort at Scarlett, Castletown, Isle of Man", *Proc. Isle of Man Nat. Hist. and Antiq. Soc.*, V (1957), 571–75.

GELLING, 1959   ——, "Excavation of a Promontory Fort at Cass ny Hawin, Malew, Isle of Man", *Proc. Isle of Man Nat. Hist. and Antiq. Soc.*, VI (1959), 28–38.

GELLING, 1962–63   ——, "Medieval Shielings in the Isle of Man", *Med. Archaeol.*, VI–VII (1962–63), 156–72.

GLASSCOCK, 1963   R. E. Glasscock, "The Distribution of Lay Wealth in S.E. England in the Early Fourteenth Century", unpublished Ph.D. thesis, University of London (1963).

GOULD, 1952   J. D. Gould, "The Inquest of Depopulation of 1607 in Lincolnshire", *Eng. Hist. Rev.*, LXVII (1952), 392–96.

GOULD, 1955   ——, "Mr. Beresford and the Lost Villages", *Ag. Hist. Rev.*, III (1955), 107–13.

GREEN, 1964   C. Green, "Excavations on a Medieval Site at Water Newton, in the County of Huntingdon, in 1958", *Proc. Cambs. Antiq. Soc.*, LVI–II (1964), 68–87.

GRIMM, 1939   P. Grimm, "Hohenrode, eine mittelalterliche Siedlung im Südharz", *Veröffentlichungen der Landesanftalt für Volheitkunde zu Halle*, II (1939), 1–56.

HARBOTTLE AND COWPER, 1963   Miss B. Harbottle and R. A. S. Cowper, "An Excavation at Memmerkirk, Northumberland", *Archaeol. Aeliana*, 4th ser., XLI (1963), 45–63.

HARRIS, 1958   A. HARRIS, "The Lost Village and the Landscape of the Yorkshire Wolds", *Ag. Hist. Rev.*, VI (1958), 97–100.

HARRIS, 1968   A. Harris, "Some Maps of Deserted Medieval Villages in the East Riding of Yorkshire", *Geographische Zeit.*, LVI (1968), 181–93.

HAYNES, 1952   Joyce Haynes, "A Thirteenth Century-Kiln-Site at Potters Marston", *Trans. Leics. Archaeol. Soc.*, XXVIII (1952), 55–62.

HILTON, 1954   R. H. Hilton, "Medieval Agrarian History of Leics." in *V.H.C. Leics.*, II (1954), 145–98.

HILTON, 1955   ——, "A Study in the Pre-History of English Enclosure in the Fifteenth Century", in *Studi in Onore di Armando Sapori* (1955), 675–85.

HILTON AND RAHTZ, 1966   R. H. Hilton and P. A. Rahtz, "Upton, Gloucestershire, 1959–1964", *Trans. Bristol and Gloucs. Archaeol. Soc.*, LXXXV (1966), 70–146.

HODGES, 1954   H. W. M. Hodges, "Excavations on Castle Hill, Thurgarton", *Trans. Thoroton Soc.*, LVIII (1954), 1–16.

HOLDEN, 1962   E. W. Holden, "Deserted Medieval Villages (of Sussex)", *Sussex Notes and Queries*, XV (1962), 312–15.

HOLDEN, 1963   ——, "Excavations at the Deserted Medieval Village of Hangleton, Part I", *Sussex Archaeol. Coll.*, CI (1963), 54–181.

HOLLAND, 1967   D. Holland, "A Note on the Deserted Village of West Burton", *Trans. Thoroton Soc.*, LXXI (1967), 70–71.

HONEYMAN, 1933   H. L. Honeyman, "West Lilburn Chapel", *Archaeol. Aeliana*, 4th ser., X (1933), 210–23.

HOPE-TAYLOR, 1961   B. Hope-Taylor, "The Boat-shaped House in Northern Europe", *Proc. Cambs. Antiq. Soc.*, LV (1961), 16–22.

HOSKINS, 1946   W. G. Hoskins, "The Deserted Villages of Leicestershire", *Trans. Leics. Archaeol. Soc.*, for 1944–45, XXII (1946), 241–64. Revised in *Essays in Leicestershire History* (1950), 67–107.

HOSKINS, 1953   ——, "The Rebuilding of Rural England, 1570–1640", *Past and Present*, No. 4 (1953), 44–59. Reprinted in *Provincial England* (1963), 131–48.

HOSKINS, 1955   ——, *The Making of the English Landscape* (1955), 92–107.

HOSKINS, 1956   ——, "Seven Deserted Village Sites in Leicestershire", *Trans. Leics. Archaeol. and Hist. Soc.*, XXXII (1956), 36–51. Reprinted in *Provincial England* (1963), 115–30.

HOSKINS, 1963   ——, *Rutland, a Shell Guide* (1963), 49–52.

HURST, 1954   J. G. Hurst, "Excavations at Lost Village Sites in Great Britain", in M. W. Beresford, *The Lost Villages of England* (1954), 415–17.

HURST, 1956   ——, "Deserted Medieval Villages and the Excavations at Wharram Percy", in R. L. S. Bruce-Mitford, ed., *Recent Archaeological Excavations in Britain* (1956), 251–73.

HURST, 1961   ——, "The Kitchen Area of Northolt Manor, Middlesex", *Med. Archaeol.*, V (1961), 211–99.

HURST, 1961A   ——, "Seventeenth Century Cottages at Babingley, Norfolk", *Norf. Archaeol.*, XXXII (1961), 332–42.

HURST, 1965   ——, "The Medieval Peasant House", in A. Small, ed., *The Fourth Viking Congress, York, 1961*, Aberdeen University Stud., CXLIX (1965), 190–96.

HURST AND HURST, 1964   J. G. Hurst and D. Gillian Hurst, "Excavations at the Deserted Medieval Village of Hangleton, Part II", *Sussex Archaeol. Coll.*, CII (1964), 94–142.

HURST AND HURST, 1967   D. Gillian Hurst and J. G. Hurst, "Excavation of Two Moated Sites, Milton Hampshire and Ashwell, Hertfordshire", *Journ. Brit. Archaeol. Assoc.*, XXX (1967), 48–86.

ARRETT, 1962   M. G. Jarrett, "The Deserted Village of West Whelpington, Northumberland", *Archaeol. Aeliana*, 4th ser., XL (1962), 189–225.

OBEY, 1961   G. Jobey, "Further notes on Rectilinear Earthworks in Northumberland: Some Medieval and Later Sites", *Archaeol. Aeliana*, 4th ser., XXXIX (1961), 87–102.

OBEY, 1962   ——, "A Note on Scooped Enclosures in Northumberland", *Archaeol. Aeliana*, 4th ser., XL (1962), 47–58.

OHNSON, 1968   G. D. Johnson, "Pende—a Lost Port", *Sussex Notes and Queries*, XVII (1968), 46–49.

OPE, 1951   E. M. Jope, "Medieval and Saxon Finds from Felmersham, Bedfordshire", *Antiq. Journ.*, XXXI (1951), 45–50.

OPE, 1956   ——, "A Late Dark Ages Site at Gunwalloe", *Proc. West. Corn. Field Club*, new ser., I (1956), 136–46.

OPE AND THRELFALL, 1958   E. M. Jope and R. I. Threlfall, "Excavation of a Medieval Settlement at Beere, North Tawton, Devon", *Med. Archaeol.*, II (1958), 112–40.

KENDRICK AND HAWKES, 1932   T. D. Kendrick and C. F. C. Hawkes, *Archaeology in England and Wales, 1914–1931* (1932), 320–25.

KERRIDGE, 1955   E. Kerridge, "The Returns of the Inquisitions of Depopulation", *Eng. Hist. Rev.*, (1955), 212–28.

LARWOOD, 1952   G. P. Larwood, "A Late Medieval Farmstead at Markshall", *Norf. Archaeol.*, XXX (1952), 358–64.

LEADHAM, 1897   I. S. Leadham, *The Domesday of Inclosures*, 2 vols. (1897), see also *Trans. Royal Hist. Soc.*, 2nd ser., VI–VIII (1892–94) and XIV (1900); *Thoroton Soc. Rec. Ser.*, II (1904).

LEEDS, 1923   E. T. Leeds, "A Saxon Village Near Sutton Courtenay, Berkshire", *Archaeologia*, LXXIII (1923), 147–92.

LEEDS, 1927   ——, "A Saxon Village at Sutton Courtenay, Berkshire (Second Report)", *Archaeologia*, LXXVI (1927), 59–79.

LEEDS, 1936   ——, *Early Anglo-Saxon Art and Archaeology* (1936), 21–28.

LEEDS, 1947   ——, "A Saxon Village at Sutton Courtenay, Berkshire (Third Report)", *Archaeologia*, XCII (1947), 79–93.

LETHBRIDGE, 1927   T. C. Lethbridge, "An Anglo-Saxon Hut on the Car Dyke at Waterbeach, Cambridgeshire", *Antiq. Journ.*, VII (1927), 141–46.

LETHBRIDGE AND TEBBUTT, 1933   T. C. Lethbridge and C. F. Tebbutt, "Huts of the Anglo-Saxon Period", *Proc. Cambs. Antiq. Soc.*, XXXIII (1933), 133–151.

LINEHAN, 1966

Catharine D. Linehan, "Deserted Sites and Rabbit Warrens on Dartmoor, Devon", *Med. Archaeol.*, x (1966) 113–44.

LLOYD, 1964–65

T. H. Lloyd, "Some Documentary Sidelights on the Deserted Oxfordshire Village of Brookend", *Oxoniensia* XXIX–XXX (1964–65), 116–28.

LOBEL, 1935

M. D. Lobel, *A Short History of Dean and Chalford*, Oxon. Rec. Soc., XVII (1935).

LOWNDES, 1967

R. A. C. Lowndes, "A Medieval Site at Millhouse in the Lune Valley, Westmorland", *Trans. Cumb. and West. Antiq. and Archaeol. Soc.*, LXVII (1967), 35–50.

MATTHEWS, 1962

C. L. Matthews, "Saxon Remains on Puddlehill, Dunstable", *Beds. Archaeol. Journ.*, I (1962), 48–57.

MIDDLETON, 1885

R. M. Middleton, "On Yoden, A Medieval Site Between Castle Eden and Easington", *Archaeol. Aeliana*, new ser., x (1885), 186–87.

MOORE, 1966

J. W. Moore, "An Anglo-Saxon Settlement at Wykeham, North Yorkshire", *Yorks. Archaeol. Journ.*, XLI (1963–66), 402–44.

MUNBY, 1961

L. M. Munby, "Deserted Villages in Hertfordshire", *Herts. Past and Present*, II (1961), 11–16.

MURRAY-THREIPLAND, 1946–48

Leslie Murray-Threipland, "Medieval Farmstead on Bredon Hill, Elmont", *Trans. Brist. and Gloucs. Archaeol. Soc.*, LXVII (1946–48), 415–48.

MUSSON, 1955

R. Musson, "A Thirteenth Century Dwelling at Bramble Bottom, Eastbourne", *Sussex Archaeol. Coll.*, XCIII (1955), 157–70.

MYRES, 1951

J. N. L. Myres, "The Anglo-Saxon Pottery of Lincolnshire", *Archaeol. Journ.*, CVIII (1951), 65–99.

NEWTON, 1947

E. F. Newton, "Late Saxon Sites and a Medieval Chapel at Weald, Huntingdonshire", *Trans. Cambs. and Hunts. Archaeol. Soc.*, VI (1947), 166–75.

NORRIS AND HOCKINGS, 1953

N. E. S. Norris and E. F. Hockings, "Excavations at Balsdean Chapel, Rottingdean", *Sussex Archaeol. Coll.*, XCI (1953), 53–68.

ORDNANCE SURVEY, 1935

Ordnance Survey, *Map of Britain in the Dark Ages, South Sheet* (1935).

ORDNANCE SURVEY, 1966

Ordnance Survey, *Map of Britain in the Dark Ages*, 2nd ed. (1966), 15–16 and 48–49.

OWEN, 1957–58   D. M. Owen, "Thornton Abbey and the Lost Village of Audleby", *Lincs. Archit. and Archaeol. Soc. Reps. and Paps.*, VII (1957–58), 113–16.

PALMER, 1933   W. M. Palmer, "A History of Clopton", *Proc. Cambs. Antiq. Soc.*, XXXIII (1933), 3–60.

PARKER, 1947   L. A. Parker, "The Depopulation Returns for Leicestershire in 1607", *Trans. Leics. Archaeol. Soc.*, XXIII (1947), 229–89.

PARKER, 1948   ——, "Enclosure in Leics., 1485–1607". Unpublished Ph.D. thesis, University of London (1948).

PEATE, 1940   I. C. Peate, *The Welsh House, A Study in Folk Culture*, Y Cymmroder, XLVII (1940); 3rd ed., Liverpool (1946).

PHILLIMORE, 1884   W. P. W. Phillimore, "Notes on Some of the Deserted Villages and Churches of Nottinghamshire", in J. P. Briscoe, ed., *In Old Nottingham*, 2nd ser. (1884), 66–88.

PHILLIMORE, 1894   ——, "Deserted Villages of Nottinghamshire", *Notts. and Derbs. Notes and Queries*, II (1894), 128–35, 150–52 and 161–68.

PHILLIPS, 1934   C. W. Phillips, "The Present State of Archaeology in Lincolnshire II", *Archaeol. Journ.*, XCI (1934), 97–187.

PICKERING, 1966–67   J. Pickering, "Ammington, Warwickshire—A Deserted Medieval Village Site", *Lichfield and South Staffs. Archaeol. and Hist. Soc.*, VIII (1966–67), 48.

POSTAN, ED., 1966   M. M. Postan, ed., *Cambridge Economic History of Europe*, I, 2nd ed. (1966).

PRYCE AND DOBSON, 1907   T. D. Pryce and F. W. Dobson, "An Ancient Village Site: Whimpton, Nottinghamshire", *Trans. Thoroton Soc.*, XI (1907), 139–44.

RADFORD, 1957   C. A. R. Radford, "The Saxon House: a Review and Some Parallels", *Med. Archaeol.*, I (1957), 27–38.

RAHTZ, 1959   P. A. Rahtz, "Holworth, Medieval Village Excavation 1958", *Proc. Dorset Nat. Hist. and Archaeol. Soc.*, LXXXI (1959), 127–47.

RAHTZ, 1960–61   ——, "Barrow Mead, Bath, Somerset", *Proc. Som. Archaeol. and Nat. Hist. Soc.*, CV (1960–61), 61–76.

RAISTRICK AND HOLMES, 1962   A. Raistrick and P. F. Holmes, "Archaeology of Malham Moor", *Field Studies*, I (1962), 73–100.

RAMSEY, 1963   P. Ramsey, *Tudor Economic Problems* (1963).

RIMINGTON, 1961   F. C. Rimington, *The Deserted Medieval Village of Hatterboard near Scarborough*, Scar. and Dist. Archaeol. Soc. Res. Rep., II (1961), 1–39.

ROLLINSON, 1963   W. Rollinson, "The Lost Villages and Hamlets of Low Furness", *Trans. Cumb. and West. Antiq. and Archaeol. Soc.*, new ser., LXIII (1963), 160–69.

ROUS, 1716   J. Rous, *Historia Regum Angliae*, ed. T. Hearne, (1716) 2nd ed. (1745).

RUTHERFORD-DAVIES, 1964   K. Rutherford-Davies, "Deserted Medieval Villages in Hertfordshire—A Supplementary List", *Herts. Past and Present*, IV (1964), 11.

RUTTER AND DUKE, 1958   J. G. Rutter and G. Duke, *Excavations at Crossgates near Scarborough 1947–1956*, Scar. and Dist. Archaeol. Soc. Res. Rep., I (1958), 1–68.

ST. JOSEPH, ED., 1966   J. K. S. St. Joseph, ed., *The Uses of Air Photography* (1966).

ST. JOSEPH, 1967   ——, "Air Reconnaisance: Recent Results, II, North Marefield, Leicestershire", *Antiquity*, XLI (1967), 216–18.

SALTMARSH, 1941–43   J. Saltmarsh, "Plague and Economic Decline in England", *Camb. Hist. Journ.*, VII (1941–43), 23–41.

SIMMONDS, 1961   L. P. Simmonds, "Some Remnants of the Medieval Landscape in South Worcestershire", *Trans. Worcs. Archaeol. Soc.*, XXXVII (1961), 1–10.

SMITH, 1960   M. W. Smith, "Snap, a Modern Example of Depopulation", *Wilts. Archaeol. Mag.*, LVII (1960), 386–90.

SPUFFORD, 1965   Margaret Spufford, *A Cambridgeshire Community: Chippenham from Settlement to Enclosure*, Univ. of Leics. Dept. Eng. Local Hist., Occ. Paps., XX (1965).

STALLYBRASS, 1906   B. Stallybrass, "Fifteenth Century Site, Inner Ashley Wood Down", *Wilts. Archaeol. Mag.*, XXXIV (1906), 422–44.

STANFORD, 1955–57   S. C. Stanford, "A Medieval Settlement at Hampton Wafer", *Trans. Woolhope Nat. Field Club*, XXXV (1955–57), 337–44.

STANFORD, 1965   ——, "A Medieval Settlement at Dettonhall, Shropshire", *Trans. Shrop. Archaeol. Soc.*, LVIII (1965), 27–47.

STEANE, 1967   J. M. Steane, "Excavations at Lyveden, 1965–67", *Journ. Northampton Mus. and Art Gall.*, II (1967), 1–37.

STEENSBERG, 1952   A. Steensberg, *Bondehuse og Vandmøller i Danmark gennem 2000 år*, Copenhagen (1952) with English Summary: Farms and Watermills in Denmark during 2000 years.

STILL AND PALLISTER, 1964   L. Still and A. Pallister, "The Excavation of One House Site in the Deserted Village of West Hartburn, County Durham", *Archaeol. Aeliana*, 4th ser., XLIII (1964), 187–206.

STILL AND PALLISTER, 1967   —— and ——, "West Hartburn 1965, Site C", *Archaeol. Aeliana*, 4th ser., XLV (1967), 139–48.

STONE, 1857   S. Stone, "Account of certain (supposed) British and Saxon Remains Recently Discovered at Standlake, in the County of Oxford", *Proc. Soc. Antiq.*, 1st ser., IV (1857), 70–71, 92–100.

STONE, 1858   ——, "Recent Explorations at Standlake, Yelford and Stanton Harcourt, in Oxfordshire", *Proc. Soc. Antiq.*, 1st ser., IV (1858), 213–19.

SUTTON, 1964–65   J. E. G. Sutton, "Ridge and Furrow in Berkshire and Oxfordshire", *Oxoniensia*, XXIX–XXX (1964–65), 99–115.

TATHAM, 1906   H. R. Tatham, "Earthworks at Claxby-by-Alford", *Lincs. Notes and Queries*, IX (1906), 103–10.

TAWNEY, 1912   R. H. Tawney, *The Agrarian Problem in the Sixteenth Century* (1912).

TAYLOR, 1967   C. C. Taylor, "Whiteparish, a study of the development of a forest edge parish", *Wilts. Archaeol. Mag.*, (1967) 79—101.

TEBBUTT, 1960   C. F. Tebbutt, "An Early Twelfth Century Building at Eynesbury, Huntingdonshire", *Proc. Cambs. Antiq. Soc.*, LIV (1960), 85–89.

TEBBUTT, 1961   C. F. Tebbutt, "An Eleventh Century Boat-shaped Building at Buckden, Huntingdonshire", *Proc. Cambs. Antiq. Soc.*, LV (1961), 13–15.

THIRSK, 1954   Joan Thirsk, "Agrarian History of Leics., 1540–1950", in V.C.H. Leics., II (1954), 199–264.

THIRSK, 1959   ——, *Tudor Enclosures* (Hist. Asscn. pamphlet G41, 1959).

THIRSK, 1959A   ——, "Sources of Information on Population", *Amat. Hist.*, IV (1959), 182–85.

THIRSK, ED., 1967   ——, ed., *The Agrarian History of England and Wales* (1967).

THOMAS, 1959–60   A. C. Thomas, "Post-Roman Rectangular House Plans in the South-west", *Proc. West Corn. Field Club*, II (1959–60), 156–62.

THOMPSON, 1960   F. H. Thompson, "The Deserted Medieval Village of Riseholme, near Lincoln", *Med. Archaeol.*, IV (1960), 95–108.

THORPE, 1964   H. Thorpe, "The Lord and the Landscape", in *Volume Jubilaire M.A. Lefevre*, Acta Geographica Lovaniensia, III (Louvain, 1964), 77–126; reprinted in *Trans. Birmingham Archaeol. Soc.*, LXXX (1965), 38–77.

TURNER, 1867   E. Turner, "The Lost Towns of Northeye and Hydneye", *Suss. Archaeol. Coll.*, XIX (1867), 1–35; see also XXI (1869), 220–21.

WACHER, 1963–64   J. S. Wacher, "Excavations at Martinsthorpe, Rutland 1960", *Trans. Leics. Archaeol. Soc.*, XXXIX (1963–64), 1–19.

WACHER, 1966   ——, "Excavations at Riplingham, East Yorkshire, 1956–57", *Yorks. Archaeol. Journ.*, XLI (1963–66), 608–69.

WADE-MARTINS AND WADE, 1967   P. Wade-Martins and K. Wade, "Some Deserted Villages in Norfolk: Notes for Visitors", *Norf. Res. Com. Bull.*, XVII (1967), 2–8.

WAITES, 1962   B. Waites, "The Monastic Grange as a Factor in the Settlement of North-east Yorkshire", *Yorks. Archaeol. Journ.*, XL (1962), 627–56.

WHISTON, 1966–67   J. W. Whiston, "Croxall, Staffordshire, An Air Photograph of a Deserted Medieval Village", *Lichfield and South Staffs. Archaeol. and Hist. Soc.*, VIII (1966–67), 46–47.

WHITE, 1934   Miss G. M. White, "A Settlement of the South Saxons", *Antiq. Journ.*, XIV (1934), 393–400.

WICKHAM, 1912   Rev. J. D. C. Wickham, *Records by Spade and Terrier* (1912).

WIGHTMAN, 1961   W. E. Wightman, "Open Field Agriculture in the Peak District", *Derbys. Archaeol. Journ.*, LXXXI (1961), 111–25.

WILLIAMS-ELLIS *et al.*, 1919   C. Williams-Ellis and J. and Elizabeth Eastwick-Field, *Building in Cob, Pisé and Stabilized Earth* (1919). Rev. ed. 1947.

WILSON, 1846   J. Wilson, "Antiquities found at Woodperry, Oxfordshire", *Archaeol. Journ.*, III (1846), 116–28.

WILSON, 1962   D. M. Wilson, "Anglo-Saxon Rural Economy", *Ag. Hist. Rev.*, X (1962), 65–79.

Part Two

Scotland

CHAPTER SEVEN

The Study of Deserted Medieval Settlements in Scotland (to 1968)

I. RURAL SETTLEMENT

H. FAIRHURST

Department of Archaeology, University of Glasgow

II. THE PEASANT-HOUSE

J. G. DUNBAR

Royal Commission on the Ancient and Historical Monuments of Scotland

I. RURAL SETTLEMENT

As yet, very little has been written on the vernacular architecture and rural settlement of Scotland in periods before the nineteenth century, and for the medieval period strictly speaking, the dearth of information is almost complete. Partly this is a result of lack of interest, partly it is due to the poverty of the country during the centuries between the outbreak of the Wars of Independence and the Act of Union in 1707. Over and above that, however, the nature of the settlement itself, the impermanence of the building materials in use and the lack of documentary evidence, all create difficult problems. The study of medieval rural settlement must develop along specialised lines and rely upon evidence of a different nature from that available for England and Wales.

It must be emphasised from the outset that documentary evidence relating to rural conditions appears to be extremely scarce and any discussion based on this information alone would have to be largely hypothetical. It is true that publication of medieval charters and records has been assiduously carried out by societies such as the Spalding and the Maitland Clubs; we have a concise survey of the history of lands and their owners in *Origines Parochiales Scotiae*[1] where it is possible to follow the various transfers affecting even remote townships in the Highlands. There is, however, strangely little

[1] C. Innes and J. E. Brichan, eds., *Origines Parochiales Scotiae*, Bannantyne Club, (2 vols., 1850 and 1855).

reference to details of farming, settlement and rural conditions generally.   Much of the land remained the property of a relatively few great landowners and the individual tenant farmer acquired no customary rights over the long period of time, comparable with those of the English villagers.

In sharp contrast to the earlier periods, a wealth of material begins to be available from the late seventeenth century onwards.   The information is of the greatest importance, for until this time rural conditions seem to have been stagnant for long periods and all writers imply survivals on a large scale from medieval times.   It is hardly necessary to stress the dangers of projecting this state of affairs, these anachronisms of the eighteenth century, indefinitely backwards into the past, but, *faute de mieux*, the data must be examined before turning to the alternative approach through archaeology.

The literature of the "Age of the Improvements" has been summarised recently (Handley, 1953).   Special mention, however, must be made of *The Statistical Account of Scotland*[2] published in the 1790's in which each minister of every parish wrote a description at a very interesting period of change.   Much of the old still survived and many of the accounts are written with deep insight into rural conditions.   Attention must also be drawn to the numerous large-scale estate surveys which date back to the latter half of the eighteenth century.   Modernisation by many of the larger landowners was literally a planned operation and the first step was often to arrange for a professional survey of the existing state of affairs.   Some of the plans are exquisitely drawn and show the dimensions of houses and the individual rigs; others seem to have been rather casual in this respect as though the surveyor knew that much of the old settlement pattern was soon to be replaced (Third, 1957, and Fairhurst, 1964).

Much regional variation undoubtedly occurred, but broadly speaking there was a degree of uniformity in settlement form in Highlands and Lowlands alike (Grant, 1930). Apart from the large and small burghs, the castles of the great landowners and the houses of the lesser lairds, the recurring settlement unit was not the village in the English sense, but a small cluster of houses and associated buildings forming a group-farm.   In the Lowlands these agrarian units were called *fermtouns* and in the Highlands the Gaelic word *clachan* is often used (Fairhurst, 1960).   These were occupied normally on a yearly basis, by tenants jointly responsible for the rent and maintaining the common plough. Numbers within the group varied but three to eight tenants were usual.   In addition, there might also be several cottars there on sufferance to provide additional labour.

These small clusters of dwellings might also be the site of a church (a *kirkton*) Plate 21, a mill (milton), a smiddy or a school.   Usually, however, each of these institutions would serve several group farms and they were not regular features in any one unit; a settlement with all of them would be an outstanding centre such as would normally have been granted the rights of a burgh.   Conversely, many small burghs in Scotland long continued to attach great importance to their farm lands and were in fact an integral part of the rural settlement pattern.

There is every reason to believe that many of the group farms were in existence in the medieval period though there is so little reference directly to their functions in the documentary record.   The village in Scotland is generally regarded as a very late

[2] Sir John Sinclair, *The Statistical Account of Scotland* (21 vols., 1791–99).

feature for the most part, often associated with industrial or fisheries development and showing a planned lay-out. All the same, in that area south of the Firth of Forth where Anglian influence was strong, some settlements may have approached in size and organization the villages of northern England (Barrow, 1962), but much more study of this question is needed. Moreover, sites of a number of possible medieval villages are known both in the Lothians and in southwest Scotland, but none has yet been subjected to systematic archaeological excavation. In some cases, as for example at the two neighbouring Kirkcudbright villages of Galtway (NX 706487) and Dunrod (NX 699459), considerable surface remains are visible, and it is clear that sites of this nature provide extensive opportunities, not only for field investigation, but also for documentary research.

Returning to the group farm, however, the morphology of this settlement unit must be examined in the light of geographical conditions. The cooler summers and especially the rain and cloud of much of the west and north of Scotland made extensive grain production more difficult that on the English Plain. An emphasis on stock-rearing may well have been characteristic since prehistoric times. Then too, the rugged nature of so much of Scotland, and especially the Highlands, tended towards a relative fragmentation of the arable lands.

Perhaps both this fragmentation and the relative importance of stock-rearing favoured the emergence of a small settlement unit, as compared, for instance, with the village communities of the English Midlands where a three-field system was characteristic. There is no geographical determinism about this, however, as the comparatively small group farm was to be found in the areas where the arable land might be continuous as in Strathmore; ingrained tradition obviously enters into the problem.

Very extensive common grazings were a characteristic feature of the old farms particularly in the upland areas. The practice of sending the cattle away to summer pastures at the shielings must once have been universal, judging by the *shiel* names in the south; in the Highlands, the old habit survived to the end of the last century and a pale reflection of it persisted in the Outer Islands until very recently.

The much restricted arable land of the Scottish group-farm was usually in the form of infield and outfield, but sometimes there was only the one or the other, as is shown, for instance, by the Tayside Survey of 1769.[3] The infield comprised the best land, normally close to the clustered dwellings, which was kept under constant tillage without fallow; this was made possible by the regular application of all the available dung. The outfield was cultivated without dung except perhaps from tethered animals; it was divided into patches each of which was kept under cultivation for several successive years and was then left to recover fertility for as many seasons as possible. The plough on the group farm was jointly maintained and the arable of the tenants was in *run-rig*, i.e. in intermixed strips in the form of narrow, high ridges or *rigs*.

The location of a great many of the fermtouns and clachans in the mid-eighteenth century is known partly through the estate plans and also from the Military Map of Scotland surveyed immediately after the Rising of 1745 (*Roy's Map*). Here the clusters are indicated by a little group of dots, but clearly, from available evidence, these are diagrammatic, not representative of individual houses.

[3] Margaret M. McArthur, ed., *Survey of Lochtayside, 1769*, Scot. Hist. Soc. 3rd. ser., XXVII (1936).

What is going to be very difficult to establish is the precise location of the fermtouns and clachans at earlier periods.   Charters of medieval date may make specific reference to "the lands of" such and such a township where the site of a late cluster of dwellings can be found without difficulty, but continuity of occupation is another matter.   The late literary references make it obvious that the vernacular architecture was in flimsy materials including dry-stone or mud-mortared stone, clay, wattle and daub, turf and probably wood in earlier times (see below).   Particularly under a system of yearly leases, these buildings must often have been abandoned or fallen into disrepair; continual rebuilding may well have allowed some migration of site and little of the older periods has survived.   Fieldwork to date has made it abundantly clear that is is going to be difficult to find even the vaguest traces of medieval settlements, even on known and accessible sites.

In the Lowlands, many of the old fermtouns were modernised out of recognition in the late eighteenth and early nineteenth century.   The rural landscape today is in many ways surprisingly modern.   No great difficulties were experienced by the landowners in the process of enclosure of the common fields; the tenants on the old Scottish group farm rarely held on more than a year's lease, and they had no long-standing customary right to protect them against eviction.   A short series of Acts, passed just before the independent Scottish Parliament ceased to function, was all that was needed for the landlord to abolish the group-farms and run-rig.   So thorough was the obliteration of the old that now it is wellnigh impossible over wide areas to find a site of even a single one of the fermtouns which is at all representative of the old settlement unit.   Sometimes the buildings of the new consolidated farms occupied the old sites, but sometimes not even a modern cottage marks the position of the old cluster.

In the Highlands, change came more slowly but it was apt to be catastrophic.   After 1745, under the peaceful conditions and with the coming of the potato as a new food crop, population at first began to increase very rapidly.   The old clachans swelled in size and overpopulation occurred before improved techniques of farming could provide any solution to the problem.   Then in the earlier decades of the nineteenth century there commenced an era of depopulation.   Often it was a matter of rising standards of living and a harsh environment with a drift away either to the Colonies or to the growing industrial areas of the south.   In many cases, however, widespread and thoroughgoing evictions were initiated by the landlords to provide sheep runs in view of the high prices of wool for the new textile mills.   These clearances have left a very bitter memory.

On some of the old clachan sites of the Highlands, occupation has lingered on into this century; the much modified buildings of the now-deserted settlements date back perhaps a century and a half, but rarely so far back as 1750.   In other areas, as for instance in Sutherland, where whole glens and straths were cleared at one time, the ruins of the old clusters can still be seen in the midst of the sheep walk or grouse moor, little disturbed since they were deserted a century and a half ago.   The dwellings were abandoned before modernisation had had any marked effect on either the lay-out or building technique.

This type of deserted settlement site in the Highlands is almost unique in Europe. Many at least of the place-names can be traced back to medieval times; many must represent perfect examples of the rural settlement of the Highlands in the eighteenth

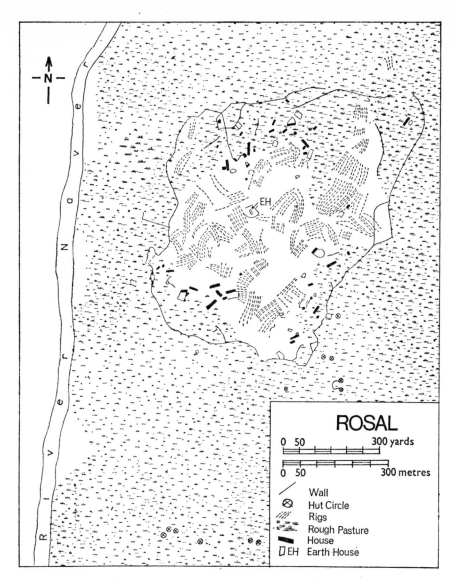

Fig. 31. Rosal, Sutherland
Plan of township

century, bearing in mind, however, that the old clusters had in many cases, grown to unhealthy proportions in the last phase of occupation. Some pioneer investigations with very limited excavation, have been attempted at Rosal, in Strath Naver, and Lix, in West Perthshire, but as yet only a preliminary report has been published (Fairhurst and Petrie, 1964).

Rosal was cleared in 1814–18 and the old arable land now appears like a green island

233

in the surrounding moor (Fig. 31). Temporarily, it has been preserved from planting by the Forestry Commission after its significance was recognised. The rigs of the eighteenth century are clearly traceable, measuring some 3·6 m. to 7·6 m. wide between furrows, and sometimes stretching continuously for over 100 m. mainly at a very slight angle to the contour. Heaps of stones piled into elongated cairns indicate the effort expended on field clearance. The old buildings were of turf on a stone foundation and though the outlines are but little disturbed since the evictions, it is surprisingly difficult without excavation to differentiate between some of the smaller examples of long-houses, and the barns, stables and cottages. A corn-drying kiln was apparently shared by several tenants but each farmer had his own stackyard to keep out grazing animals when the whole township was thrown open after the harvest. About seventeen families seem to have been in occupation latterly, the dwellings being very loosely distributed in three groups around the periphery. The individual structures are so widely separated, however, and the spacing is so haphazard that it is quite difficult to recognise the farm buildings which belonged to any one tenant.

Apart from some very vague traces here and there of older foundations the extant structures clearly belong to the last phase of occupation, though the lands of Rosal are mentioned in a charter as early as 1269.[4] An *earth house* within the arable lands, and a number of hut circles not far away, indicate prehistoric occupation of the same general area, but no direct continuity of settlement can be postulated.

The shielings at Rosal occur in several locations about a mile or so distant from the main settlement. The huts are recognisable as rectangular stone settings about 5 m. by 2·5 m. located within a green patch in the moor, due to the congregation of stock in the locality. Some had become the sites of tiny permanent settlements at the time of the Clearance, presumably due to pressure of population. Place-names elsewhere in Strath Naver show that this hiving-off process had also occurred at earlier periods.

Undoubtedly the details had changed at Rosal since medieval times and indeed the first signs of modernisation of the traditional way of life could be detected, for instance, in the quantity of mass-produced pottery from kilns in southern Scotland. Neverthe-less it is doubtful whether the general pattern of the settlement had changed radically for centuries. Such sites as Rosal are of exceptional interest when continuity of occupa-tion over a very long period is apparent from the documentary record. With more developed techniques of excavation, much might be learned of earlier settlement phases which at present seem to have left no superficial trace.

Investigations at Lix illustrate different phenomena. The first documentary records appear to go no further back than the mid-sixteenth century, but the little barony of Lix was by then a defined entity and may well be much older. A relatively full description can be compiled of the three group farms of West, Mid and East Lix for the years just before 1745 from the Breadalbane papers, and there is a small-scale plan for 1755 when the lands were under the administration of the Commissioners for the Forfeited Estates. Sometime shortly after 1790 the whole settlement was reorganised and the old clustered dwellings were broken up. The position of some of the old buildings of 1755 at Mid and East Lix can be fixed with some accuracy on what is quite open ground, but no trace can now be detected of the foundations. Subsequently a

4 *Op. cit.* in fn. 1, 1, 175.

second reorganisation, to give the three modern sheep farms, took place between 1828 and 1845, and the ruined and deserted settlements now visible belong to the short intermediate period.   Excavation showed that even in these dwellings of the early nineteenth century very primitive features occurred within what were indubitably long-houses.   One suspects that Lix is far from unique in having two reorganisations in this way and clearly illustrates the difficulty of penetrating backwards towards medieval times.

Summarising the position of Scotland with regard to the survival of medieval settlements as a whole, as distinct from house types, it must be emphasised that only a relatively few sites comparable to the deserted villages of England can be expected.   These must be looked for primarily in the Border counties and the Lothians where Anglian and later English influence was at its strongest.   Elsewhere the medieval fermtoun and clachan can have left only slight traces, especially in view of the flimsy building materials which appear to have been employed and of the short term leases of the tenant farmer each of whom maintained the fabric of his own dwelling.

The many hundreds of surviving examples of deserted clachans in the Highlands often stand in open sheep walk.   Excavation is perfectly feasible, unlike the English village today, and might prove very rewarding on carefully chosen sites where long continuity of occupation can be proved from the records.   From personal experience, it must be emphasised that some of the contemporary documentation for the last phase of occupation is of the utmost importance in excavation.

Some of the ruinous clusters provide very impressive memorials of the Highland group farms such as they existed, as anachronisms, just before desertion.   Tirai in Glen Lochay, West Perthshire, with its widely spaced, well preserved long-houses, standing in green pastureland, is a remarkable museum piece by any standards (Plate 22).   Auchindrain near Inveraray in Mid-Argyll, which was occupied until the last few years, still keeps to a surprising extent the pattern of the old group farm (Dunbar, 1965): attempts are being made to create here a museum of the countryside for Argyll.   Rosal and Grummore in upper Strath Naver are two rather contrasting types of Clearance settlements; at the moment, both have some degree of protection.   A good example for the south eastern Highlands occurs at Dalforth in Glen Esk, Angus, near the small folk museum; it seems to have been preceded by shieling huts, traces of which still remain, and the clachan may not be very old.   In the island of Rhum the Nature Conservancy have under their protection the two settlements at Harris and Kilmory, deserted early last century.   All round the latter two are the distinctive narrow ridges produced by foot plough cultivation.[5]

No doubt more extensive survey will yield other excellent examples, but meanwhile some degree of preservation of selected sites is abundantly necessary (see Appendix II). With adequate plans and notice boards, a number of these, including shieling sites, could be made attractive to the student and tourist alike.   So many foreign visitors to Scotland are of Highland descent and come with a desire to see the old home district, often remembered over several generations; these ruined deserted settlements require no embellishment to tell their story.

[5] Detailed plans, as yet unpublished, have been drawn of both settlements under the supervision of Mr. G. Petrie, Dept. of Topographic Science, Glasgow University.

II. THE PEASANT-HOUSE

Architectural characteristics

Little is known as yet about the layout and structural characteristics of the medieval peasant-house in Scotland. There are virtually no standing remains of a date earlier than about the second half of the eighteenth century, and it is only within the past few years that attempts have been made to investigate buildings of this type by means of archaeological excavation. There is a good reason to believe, however, that because of the comparative backwardness of the Scottish economy, the pattern of rural building remained fundamentally medieval in character long after improved standards of housing had been generally adopted in more favoured areas of Britain. Indeed, there were few parts of Scotland where agricultural improvements made much impression before the last quarter of the eighteenth century, while in more remote areas of the Highlands their impact was not felt until almost a century later.

Fortunately, a good deal of documentary evidence is available concerning the farmhouses and cottages of the period immediately prior to the agricultural revolution, while numbers of buildings erected at this time survive in varying states of completeness. By taking this comparatively recent material into account, therefore, it is possible to make at least one or two tentative deductions as to the character of the medieval peasant-house.

Plan-form

Turning firstly to varieties of plan-form, there is no doubt that the long-house was formerly widely distributed throughout Scotland, and it is probable that at one time the dwellings of the more substantial joint-tenants, both of Lowland and of Highland farms, were typically of this form. One of the earliest known literary references to the Scottish long-house relates to Orkney, where a visitor observed in 1577: "their houses are verie simply builded with pibble stone, without any chimneys, the fire being in the middest thereof. The good man, wife, children, and other of their familie eate and sleepe on the one side of the house and their catell on the other, very beastlie and rudely in respect of civilitie".[6] There are numerous references to the existence, or recent disappearance, of long-houses in the writings of the agrarian reformers of the late eighteenth and early nineteenth centuries, and it is noticeable that these are not confined to works dealing only with Highland districts, but occur also, although less commonly, in descriptions of conditions in the Southern Lowlands.[7]

The former widespread distribution of the long-house has been confirmed by a number of excavation reports, although the evidence so far available relates only to buildings of early medieval, or of post-medieval date. Some Norse houses of ninth to thirteenth century date at Jarlshof and Underhoull, Shetland (Fig. 36) (Hamilton, 1956) and at Birsay, Orkney (Radford, 1959) were of this type, and a seventeenth-century dwelling at Muirkirk, Ayrshire, excavated some forty years ago, was found to conform to the same

---

[6] D. Settle, *A true Reporte of the laste voyage into the West and North-West regions*, quoted in *Proc. Soc. Antiq. Scot.*, xxxv (1900–01), 463.

[7] P. Graham, *General View of the Agriculture of Stirlingshire* (1812), 77; W. Aiton, *General View of the Agriculture of the County of Ayr* (1811), 114 sqq.

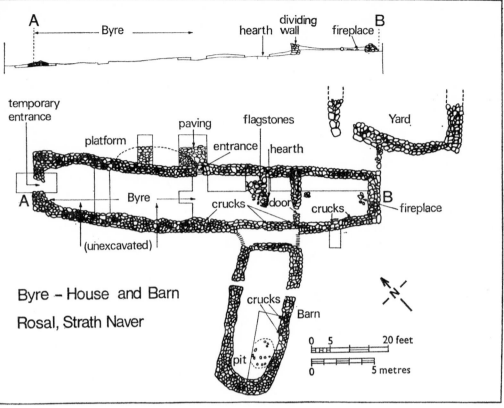

A ———— Byre ————→ hearth dividing wall fireplace B

temporary entrance
platform
paving
flagstones
entrance
hearth
Yard
A
Byre ————→
crucks
door
crucks
B
fireplace
(unexcavated)

Byre – House and Barn
Rosal, Strath Naver

crucks
Barn

pit

0 5   20 feet

0   5 metres

Fig. 32. Rosal, Sutherland

Plan of long-house (byre-house) and barn

general pattern (Fairbairn, 1926–27). A similar conclusion has been drawn from the recent examination of another building of this latter period at Hawick, Roxburghshire (Wood and Scott, 1965), while investigations at the site of the Clearance village of Rosal, Sutherland (Plate 23), and at the group-farm of Lix, Perthshire, have shown that farmhouses of long-house type were still being erected in the Highlands at the turn of the eighteenth and nineteenth centuries (Fairhurst and Petrie, 1964, and Fairhurst, 1964).

It is in these Highland areas that there are to be found all the known surviving examples of long-houses. The majority of these that are still inhabited have been remodelled so as to exclude either their human or their animal occupants, but it is still possible to find long-houses fulfilling their original function in parts of the Outer Hebrides, and instances are not unknown in the western mainland. Most of these buildings appear to be of late eighteenth or nineteenth century date, and none is likely to have been erected before the Forty-five.

Scottish long-houses were similar in lay-out to those built in other parts of Britain (see p. 107, Fig. 32, above). Most of the recorded examples have been found to measure at least 15 m. in length, however, and in some cases, as, for example, at Rosal, they attained a length of more than 30 m.   The houses of the period immediately prior to the agricultural revolution usually contained two main dwelling-apartments, of which the outer and larger one served as the kitchen and living-room, while the inner, invariably a room of quite modest dimensions, was utilised as the householder's bedroom and parlour.   At an earlier period, however, it may have been the practice to have a single living-room, and the existing long-house at Camserney, Perthshire, seems originally to have been of this type (Dunbar, 1956–57).   All these buildings were single-storeyed although some, no doubt, contained lofts or half-lofts.

When the house stood upon sloping ground the byre usually, but not always, occupied the lower part of the building.   There is some evidence to suggest that before the end of the eighteenth century it was customary for the cattle and the family to enter the building by a common doorway,[8] but most surviving long-houses have separate byre-doorways placed either midway along one of the side walls or centrally in a gable end. In the same way, an early and primitive arrangement whereby the dwelling area was shut off from the byre only by a low wall, or stone kerb and timber screen, seems gradually to have given way to one in which these two divisions were separated by a stone partition-wall containing a communicating doorway.   The Scottish long-house rarely appears to have been provided with a cross passage, but this type of arrangement has been recorded in one of the early Norse houses at Birsay (Radford, 1959) and is known also to have been found in the Southern Lowlands during the eighteenth century.[9]

The fire was invariably placed within the kitchen, in some cases being kindled upon a stone hearth in the middle of the earthen floor, and in others, as, for example, in the traditional Orkney farmhouse, being set against a partition wall.   Fireplaces were often provided with large canopied chimneys of wattle-and-daub supported on cross-spars or brackets (an excellent example of this type of construction survives at Camserney Farmhouse, Perthshire), but in some parts of the country, such as the Hebrides, it was customary to allow the smoke to swirl freely upwards within the roof space before escaping through small smoke-holes, or gradually finding its own way through the thatch.   Built-in fireplaces with stone chimney-flues were not found in houses of this class before the time of the agrarian revolution.

Passing now to a consideration of buildings other than those of orthodox long-house type, some mention must first be made of the Hebridean *black house*, whose plan-form appears to be unique in Britain.   In its most primitive known form (modified examples of which still remain in occupation in the Island of Lewis) the Hebridean farmhouse comprised an irregular cluster of three separately roofed but intercommunicating buildings constructed alongside each other (Fig. 33).   The central building was of typical long-house plan, while the flanking units incorporated a combined porch and stable, a barn, and, in some cases, a storeroom; it was not uncommon for one or more bed-recesses to be contrived within the thickness of the walls, which measured up to 2·5 m. in width.   The whole complex was served by a single entrance-doorway, and

---

[8] Aiton, *op. cit.* in fn. 7, 114; *Dunbar, 1956–57,* 89; *Dunbar, 1965.*
[9] Aiton, *op. cit.* in fn. 7, 115; Royal Comm. on Anc. Mons., *Inventory of Stirlingshire* (1963), no. 360.

there were no windows apart from a few small unglazed openings formed in the lower part of the roof. The origins and antiquity of this type of plan are alike uncertain, the closest analogies being found among the traditional *beehive* shieling huts of the same area, and in the medieval and later passage-houses of Greenland and Iceland, where climatic conditions are similar.

Byre-houses in which intercommunicating apartments were ranged alongside each other have also been recorded in the Northern Isles (Roussell, 1934), while the more

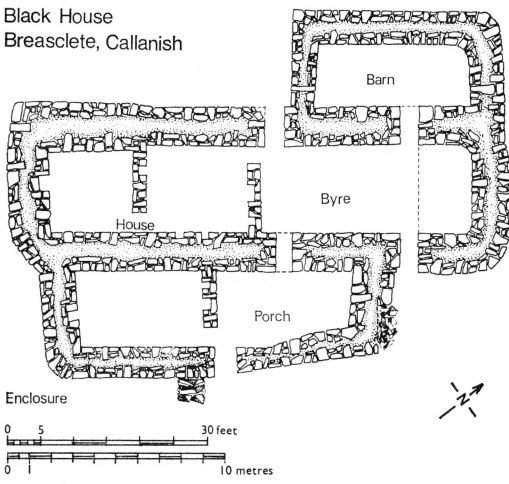

Black House
Breasclete, Callanish

Barn

House

Byre

Porch

Enclosure

0   5   30 feet

0   1   10 metres

Fig. 33. Callanish, Lewis

Plan of Hebridean black house

orthodox long-houses that are characteristic of these areas frequently incorporate ancillary chambers, such as bed-alcoves and storerooms, projecting at right angles to the main axis of the building. Some of the larger Orkney farmhouses comprised two main ranges of buildings running parallel to one another and separated by a narrow passage

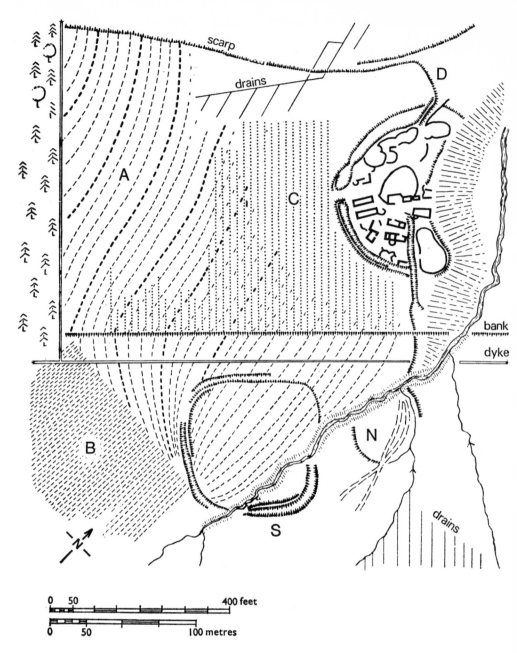

scarp

drains

A

C

D

B

N

S

bank

dyke

drains

0 50   400 feet

0   50   100 metres

Fig. 34. Lour, Peeblesshire: plan of township

r *close*, while others again were partly two-storeyed (Clouston, 1923). In general, however, farmhouses of more than one storey were rare before the latter part of the eighteenth century and nearly all the existing two-storeyed farmhouses that antedate this period were originally erected for small lairds or tacksmen, rather than for ordinary tenant-farmers.

Farm labourers and the poorer tradesmen usually seem to have lived in small single-roomed cottages such as John Ray described in an account of a journey through East Lothian in 1662: "the ordinary country houses are pitiful cots, built of stone, and covered with turves, having in them but one room, many of them no chimneys, the windows very small holes, and not glazed".[10] A dwelling of this type recorded during excavations at the seventeenth-century Border township of Lour, Peeblesshire (Fig. 34)

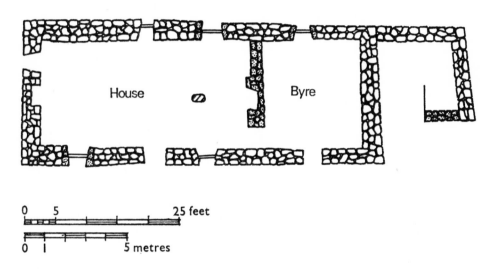

House Byre

0 5   25 feet

0 1   5 metres

Fig. 35. Auchindrain, Argyll

Plan of long-house D: period I cruck roof, open hearth with wattle chimney; periods II–III
stone chimneys inserted (stippled); also three windows and addition to east end

(Dunbar and Hay, 1960–61), measured about 6 m. by 4 m. internally and contained an open hearth; other examples of more recent date have been noted at the Highland group-farms of Lix, Perthshire (Fairhurst and Petrie, 1964) and Auchindrain, Argyll (Dunbar, 1965).

Materials and methods of construction

It is likely that in many parts of Scotland the typical medieval peasant house was of primitive timber-framed construction. So much at least may be inferred from the

[10] P. Hume Brown, *Early Travellers in Scotland* (1891), 231.

widespread distribution of structures of this type as late as the beginning of the nineteenth century, when improved standards of rural housing had already begun to be adopted in more advanced areas of the country. Numerous descriptions of these unimproved dwellings are to be found in travellers' accounts of the period and in the writings of agrarian reformers, while a number of actual examples survive—albeit much altered—to the present day. The most common type of construction was one in which a cruck frame-work was employed in conjunction with walls of turf, wattle, clay or drystone masonry. Techniques varied a good deal from one district to another but, to judge from surviving examples, standards of construction were generally poor, the cruck bays being closely spaced, and the blades themselves being irregular in form and of modest height and span.

Most surviving examples of cruck-framed houses are stone-walled (Plate 24). The literary evidence suggests, however, that in the Highlands turf and wattle-walled buildings predominated up to the middle of the eighteenth century and a similar state of affairs may well have prevailed in other parts of the country at a somewhat earlier period. There is, for example, a casual reference to a "great house constructed of wattles" at Kilpatrick, Dunbartonshire, in a document of the early thirteenth century,[11] while there is ample evidence to show that turf-walled buildings were still being erected in some parts of the Lowlands on the eve of the agrarian revolution.

The wattled buildings erected in the Scottish Highlands during the eighteenth century were sometimes known as *creel-houses* or *basket-houses* (Plate 25). One particular variety was constructed with inner walls of stake and wattle and outer walls of turf, to which divots were pinned like slates; the main weight of the thatched roof was carried by a primitive cruck framework.[12]

While the majority of turf-walled and wattle-walled houses were probably timber-framed, many buildings of clay and dry-stone construction incorporated load-bearing walls and coupled roofs. *Clay biggins*, as they were frequently termed, were constructed of local clay, mixed with straw, or some other binding materials, and laid in courses a few centimetres in thickness.[13] The walls had an average width of about 0·6 m. and were commonly founded upon a rough plinth of boulders (Plate 26). The good insulating qualities of the material made these buildings warm and comfortable to live in, and they were also fairly durable so long as steps were taken to protect the external wall-surfaces from the elements by means of harling. It is probable that structures of this type were found wherever supplies of clay lay ready to hand, and numbers still survive in the Solway district of Dumfriesshire, and in certain areas of Berwickshire, Angus, Aberdeenshire and Morayshire.

It is difficult to assess the distribution of stone-built peasant-houses in Scotland before the time of the agrarian revolution. So far as the Lowlands are concerned, there is a certain amount of evidence to indicate that buildings of stone laid in clay mortar were not uncommon in the post-medieval period.[14] On the other hand it has already been suggested that in most parts of the Highlands there was a predominance of turf and

[11] *Registrum Monasterii de Passelet* (1832), 166.
[12] A. J. Warden, *The Linen Trade* (1864), 453.
[13] Sir John Sinclair, *The Statistical Account of Scotland*, II (1792), 22 sqq.
[14] *Wood and Scott, 1965*, 6; *Fairburn, 1926–27*, 286; *Dunbar and Hay, 1960–61*, 201.

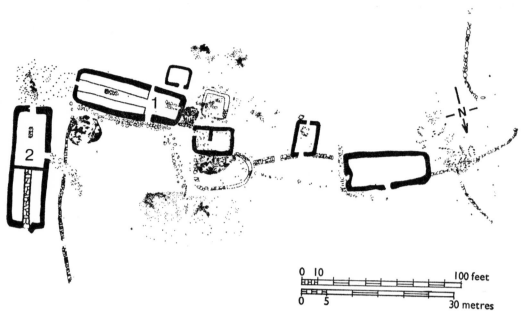

Fig. 36. Jarlshof, Shetland

Plan of Viking settlement in phase II (c. 850–900)

wattle-walled buildings of timber-framed construction. Structures of this latter type could not be readily erected in treeless localities such as the Western and Northern Isles, however, and there can be little doubt that in these areas buildings were traditionally constructed with loadbearing walls of stone and turf. The internal wall-faces of stone-built houses were often pointed with clay in an attempt to exclude draughts.

In the majority of the Norse houses excavated at Jarlshof (Fig. 36), the walls measured some 1 m. or so in width and comprised a turf core compressed between facework composed of alternate courses of stone and turf (Hamilton, 1956, 102). The medieval houses recently investigated at Little Dunagoil, Bute, and ascribed to the thirteenth century, were constructed of similar materials, but in this case the walls attained a thickness of up to 1·5 m. (Marshall, 1964), and the lower courses, at least, were composed almost entirely of stone.

The most remarkable type of thick-walled stone building, and the only one of which habitable examples survive, is the Hebridean *black house* of which some mention has already been made. The walls of these structures measured up to 2·4 m. in thickness and, since the roof is set upon the inner edge of the wall, the wall-head is exposed as a broad scarcement, allowing the rainwater to percolate the turf corework (Fig. 33).

The external corners of the Hebridean black house are noticeably rounded; a method of construction which invites the adoption of a hipped roof. But although most surviving buildings of Hebridean type have roofs of this form, the round-cornered houses of Jarlshof are thought to have been gable-ended (Hamilton, 1956, 103), a feature perhaps

243

best explained by the necessity of supplying end-bearings for purlins carried on the double rows of internal timber posts of which traces were revealed by excavation. Knowledge of early methods of roofing is inevitably hard to come by, however, and so far as timber-framed buildings of the types described above are concerned, it is impossible to do more than to suggest that where a stout well-braced cruck framework was employed, gable-ended roofs may have been customary, but that in other cases the hipped form was preferred. The roof covering itself was generally of thatch, but turf was also widely used, while in Orkney the local flag-stone was often employed.

CHAPTER EIGHT

Select Bibliography, Scotland

J. G. DUNBAR AND H. FAIRHURST

BARROW, 1962

G. W. S. Barrow, "Rural Settlement in central and eastern Scotland: the medieval evidence", *Scot. Stud.*, VI (1962), 121–44.

CLOUSTON, 1923

J. Clouston, "Old Orkney Houses", *Proc. Orkney Antiq. Soc.*, I (1923), 11–19 and 39–47.

DUNBAR, 1956–57

J. G. Dunbar, "Some cruck-framed buildings in the Aberfeldy district of Perthshire", *Proc. Soc. Antiq. Scot.*, XC (1956–57), 85–92.

DUNBAR, 1965

——, "Auchindrain: a mid-Argyll township", *Folk-life*, III (1965), 61–67.

DUNBAR AND HAY, 1960–61

J. G. Dunbar and G. D. Hay, "Excavations at Lour, Stobo, 1959–60", *Proc. Soc. Antiq. Scot.*, XCIV (1960–61), 196–210.

FAIRBAIRN, 1926–27

A. Fairbairn, "Notes on excavations of prehistoric and later sites at Muirkirk, Ayrshire, 1913–27", *Proc. Soc. Antiq. Scot.*, LXI (1926–27), 287–90.

FAIRHURST, 1960

H. Fairhurst, "Scottish Clachans", *Scot. Geog. Mag.*, LXXVI (1960), 67–76.

FAIRHURST, 1964

——, "The Surveys for the Sutherland Clearances, 1813–20", *Scot. Stud.*, VIII (1964), 1–18.

FAIRHURST AND PETRIE, 1964

H. Fairhurst and G. Petrie, "Scottish Clachans, II: Lix and Rosal", *Scot. Geog. Mag.*, LXXX (1964), 150–63.

GRANT, 1930

I. F. Grant, *The Social and Economic Development of Scotland before 1603* (1930).

HAMILTON, 1956

J. R. C. Hamilton, *Excavations at Jarlshof, Shetland* (1956).

HANDLEY, 1953

J. E. Handley, *Scottish Farming in the Eighteenth Century* (1953).

MARSHALL, 1964

D. N. Marshall, "Report of Excavations at Little Dunagoil", *Trans. Bute. Nat. Hist. Soc.*, XVI (1964), 1–69.

RADFORD, 1959

C. A. R. Radford, *The Early Christian and Norse Settlements at Birsay, Orkney* (1959).

ROUSSELL, 1934   A. Roussell, *Norse Building Customs in the Scottish Isles* (1934).

SMALL, 1964–66   A. Small, "Excavations at Underhoull, Unst, Shetland", *Proc. Soc. Antiq. Scot.* (1964–66), 225–48.

THIRD, 1957   B. M. W. Third, "The significance of Scottish estate plans and associated documents", *Scot. Stud.*, 1 (1957), 1–64.

WOOD AND SCOTT, 1965   G. O. Wood and F. T. Scott, "Crumhaugh Tower excavation", *Trans. Hawick Archaeol. Soc. 1965* (1965), 3–26.

Postscript

A comprehensive *Bibliography of Books and Articles relating to Vernacular Architecture in Scotland* was issued by the Vernacular Architecture Group in 1964, and is currently being revised prior to re-issue in printed form.

Part Three
Wales

CHAPTER NINE

The Study of Deserted Medieval Settlements in Wales (to 1968)

L. A. S. BUTLER

Lecturer in Medieval Archaeology, University of Leeds

I. HISTORICAL INTRODUCTION

Deserted medieval villages in England have left evidence of their existence in historical documents and on the ground. The pioneer work of Prof. M. W. Beresford in stimulating and co-ordinating research into this twofold aspect of medieval economic and agrarian history and of medieval archaeology is well known. In Wales the problems are different because the historical development of settlement did not necessarily follow the same course as in England; even when the Principality shared in an appearance of political unity after the Edwardian conquest this did not produce the same conditions as the fourteenth- and fifteenth-century developments did in England.

The Lost Villages of Wales cannot be written until the great difference between lowland England and Wales in its political development, in land-use, especially of the Welsh heartland, and in the social structure influencing settlement patterns has been understood. The fieldwork needed to identify and record deserted medieval settlement has been tackled unevenly from county to county, and the differing phenomena of desertion are only now being recognised. However, between the uplands of Wales and the untamed areas of Devon and Cornwall, the Pennines and Cumbria there is considerable similarity in the challenge offered by natural forces and the response of man in meeting this challenge. The similarity extends to types of settlement and to techniques of building.

The desertion of villages in England implies the recognition and isolation of the village as a unit of settlement. In pre-Norman England this was the unit initiated at the *ham*, *tun*, *thorp* or *by*, and expanding at or from this nucleus. In pre-Norman Wales the basic unit was the *tref*, a township or hamlet of infinitely variable size and composition. Work in recent years has concentrated on refining this broad term *tref* and on placing it and the lands to which it referred in an historical context. Mr. G. R. J. Jones in rejecting the tribal nomadic pastoralism of medieval Wales has stressed the importance of the bond hamlet. "For several centuries before 1100, bond hamlets had been granted to individual freemen as well as to the church. . . . Bond hamlets were, therefore, more numerous before 1100 than after: indeed almost every Celtic church appears to have been established in a bond hamlet, the only exceptions being occasional lonely hermitages" (Jones, 1959, 340). Thus the basic unit is seen as the bond settlement with the super-imposition of princely and free families, both elements bond and free using in conjunction the winter pastures of the lowlands and the summer pastures of an upland devoid of permanent settlement. Prof. T. Jones-Pierce had given more prominence to the *gwely* as the explosive force fashioning settlement from the twelfth century onwards (Jones-Pierce, 1959). "In origin the *gwely* (literally a bed or resting-place) is seen simply as an area of cleared land in association with a single enclosed homestead marking the first permanent settlement within a recently delimited *tref* (the sites of these primary settlements can be easily recognised at the present day in large consolidated farms bearing the name *hendref* or ancient settlement) and occupied by one family—the precursor of several clans whose component families would eventually clear other suitable sites and create fresh hamlets out of the waste. . . . The *gwely* expressed, in terms of the legal and personal relations imposed upon it, an attempt to harmonise traditional notions of proprietorship and kinship with a movement from semi-nomadism to selective settlement. This movement began in the early twelfth century in the north-eastern borderland on territory recovered by the Welsh from former Saxon and Norman proprietors, and gradually spread westwards, pinpointing the sites of permanent rural occupation down to our own day; fixing the spheres of tribal influence permanently marked in modern parochial and township boundaries creating new elements in the topographical nomenclature of the Welsh countryside in short creating the framework of an abiding landscape the details of which have been elaborated and recast in later generations" (Jones-Pierce, 1959, 333–4). The bond vill, once the basic unit, now becomes the cohesive factor wherever the princes' or the chieftains' households establish or retain nucleated groups of servile tenants incapable of further division and dispersion. It is still under discussion (see p. 264, below) whether the tenurial character of a vill, bond or free, produces a distinctive settlement type recognisable on the ground.

Whereas the settlement names in England often provide the place-name scholar with a clear distinction between village names and field names and minor natural features, in Wales there is seldom any comparable aid to the date and personal origin of the pre-Norman settlement. Indeed it has been suggested that the various settlements within the *cantref* and the commote were of little significance and it was the genealogy of their inhabitants that was far more meticulously recorded. However, in the centuries following the Norman Conquest the *tref* and the *cantref* (hundred townships) were increasingly used as the units of English administration. In similar fashion the twelfth-century reorganisation of the four dioceses by Norman bishops caused the churches and chapels to be listed systematically, especially in the taxations of 1254 and 1291. One attempt at mapping desertion could start by examining all the parishes and determining whether they had a complement of dependant townships, appropriate to the size of the church and appropriate to the tax assessment bearing in mind the soil qualities. Areas of depopulation and desertion could then be detected by the absence of townships.   Evidence of church decay, destruction or migration could indicate other cases of deserted settlement.

Attempts to study desertion will be an incomplete exercise until the framework of the historical growth of settlement has been constructed.   Four approaches providing such a framework have been made, based on geography, continuity, Christianity and place-names.

A geographical approach considering the factors of soil, rainfall, drainage, water supply, and the natural resources of timber and minerals has enabled the settlement pattern in Anglesey to be established both for prehistoric (Grimes, 1945) and for medieval centuries (Jones, 1955).   By this careful analysis, Mr. Jones shows that only nine out of 209 medieval vills or hamlets had disappeared so completely that they could not be traced, but over a quarter are now represented by a single farm.   By a similar approach medieval settlement in east Caernarvonshire has been discussed (Hughes, 1940; Jones-Pierce, 1942, 162–177).

The emphasis on soils as a major determinant in settlement has been used (Jones, 1960 and 1963) to illustrate theories of continuity between native occupation in the Roman Iron Age and the early medieval period.   However to Mr. L. Alcock the gap to be bridged has seemed to be too great (Alcock, 1962); the population of the oppida cannot be shown to have transferred to the *Llan*-settlements sheltering below their defences.   Where the occupation of hill forts such as Coygan (Carms.) and of Roman camps such as Llystin and Caerhun (Caerns.) can be shown to continue after the removal of the legions, then the gap in time betweeen the *heroic* society and that recorded in the Welsh Laws is lessened, though Mr. Alcock has emphasised the limited character of the evidence for the period 400–700 (Alcock, 1963 and 1964).

Even if continuity within the immediately post-Roman period still remains obscure, can the arrival of Christianity be used to pierce the darkness? The settlements of the Celtic saints around the coasts of Wales and penetrating the westward-flowing river valleys may provide an historical yardstick to measure the gradual spread of missionary activity (Bowen, 1954).   This rests on two premises: that the churches dedicated to the popular saints such as Cybi, David, Deiniol and Dyfrig received those dedications from the saint in his lifetime or from his disciples soon after his death; and that there has been no extensive rededication of churches to more popular saints, such as Michael or Mary.   The evidence of church siting is still an imprecise historical aid to the location of the settlements which the missionary churches served.

The use of place-names as an indicator of settlement history has only recently been tackled with regard to Welsh place-names, although river names (Thomas, 1938) and non-Celtic elements (Charles, 1938) have long been isolated and evaluated.   The Irish elements in west Wales have recently received attention (Richards, 1960 and 1962) and the area names and commote names have been used to point to historical origins and the sequence of political development, though not necessarily of settlement (Richards, 1964).   With the broad framework now being sketched in, there is hope that the far more numerous but often poorly documented parish and township names can be arranged in historical order.

This paucity of documents is a constant problem in medieval Welsh economic history.   The Chronicles provide a narrative of national events, often bare and seldom well-clothed. The Laws have with difficulty been used as an indicator of social and economic change on the pre-Norman *maenor* (Jones-Pierce, 1961, 187–88). The Domesday Survey entered five counties, but hardly any land west of Offa's Dyke was examined in detail. From Atiscross hundred (Flints.) at least ten village names have disappeared from the present map, though there may have been renaming after the Welsh regained the area. These border lands also suffered from the punitive campaigns of Gruffyd ap Llywelyn into England and Harold into Wales, precursors of the harrying expeditions of William in the north and west of England, but in a land long acquainted with such campaigning the lasting effects of this devastation are likely to be slight.

The Norman settlement in Wales, accomplished within the half-century after the Domesday Survey, extended along the littoral of South Wales to the mouth of the Teifi at Cardigan and along that of North Wales to the mouth of the Clwyd at Rhuddlan. It was on the coastal strip, especially beside the Severn and generally below the 100 m. contour, that an English pattern of nucleated villages was established; many bore the surnames or forenames of Norman founders or owners, such as Bonvilston, Simondston, Flemingston, Herbrandston and Wizton; others retained the church name in Norman form, as Cadoxton, St. Hilary and Wonastow. A Flemish settlement in Rhos (Pembs.) and the Gower coast was quickly assimilated with the other invaders. The much earlier Scandinavian settlement was confined to the islands, with a possible exception of the Cardiff district, and was short-lived. The question is still disputed as to how far these invaders introduced or imposed an alien pattern and how far they adapted existing institutions. One extreme view is that "the lowland pattern in South Wales—the ground-plan of the *maenor* or Norman manor in South Wales—was basically of Celtic origin with its scattered hamlets and core of Welsh customary tenants in so many ways indistinguishable from the survivors of ancient servitude in Welsh Wales" (Jones-Pierce, 1961, 188). Whether this would make the distinction between Coity Anglia and Coity Wallia, between Gower Anglia and Gower Wallia solely tenurial is doubtful. Certainly it was these lowland villages which were later subject to the same economic pressures as were felt in lowland England (Rees, 1924).

The Norman penetration of the valleys of mid-Wales by way of the rivers Severn, Wye and Dee enabled a chain of lordships to be consolidated, the conquest being strengthened by a network of mottes. The creation of vills at these mottes as a matter of policy and profit would suggest that some mottes which do not possess attendant vills are the sites of positive desertions or of abortive settlements. Alexanderston (Brecs.), Trefilan, Llanfair Treligon and Adpar, a failed borough (south Cards.), may be suggested as examples of such vills. In North Wales the spread of Norman control beyond Flintshire was a gradual process, though it has already been suggested (p. 250, above) that it hastened the introduction of the *gwely*.

The military invaders were followed closely by religious invaders. Benedictine houses were founded by the Normans, usually as dependencies of large abbeys in England or Normandy. They accepted gifts of land from donors of both races with equal gratitude; until the fourteenth century, however, there is little evidence of deliberate depopulation or of attempts made to improve the lands given to the monks. The Cistercian abbeys, founded from the 1130's onwards, were more numerous and more richly endowed whether established in Norman territory by the invaders or placed on Welsh territory at the invitation of Welsh princes. The majority of the Cistercian houses were situated in previously unoccupied or lightly occupied land (Turner, 1964); they also seem to have been in a situation favourable to the creation of granges on their low-lying lands. However the evidence is slight and has not been examined closely (Williams, 1965, 12–24; Cowley, 1967, 13–15). Examples of this process may be the establishment of Rhydllan Teifi (Cards.) as a grange of Whitland, the reduction of Sturmeston (Glam.) to grange status and the displacement of free tenants from arable holdings at Llangewydd and (the lost vill) Bradington both by Margam and the diminution of the vill of Maenan (Caerns.) to allow for the refoundation of Aberconway. The verdict of Gerald of Wales, a close if biased observer, and the frequent unrest on monastic lands may be seen as the turbulent harvest reaped through the forcible conversion of townships to granges. However, much of the recorded opposition to Cistercian houses came not from the laity whose pasture rights were infringed, but rather from other religious houses defending their ill-defined upland territories and ambiguous estaurine claims. In the secular field it would be unwise to place too much reliance upon the ecclesiastical taxations of 1254 and 1291 because all churches valued at less than six marks were excluded, and because local warfare and bad harvests might reflect unevenly on the health of the churches and, therefore, on the prosperity of their contributory vills. The inclusion of dependent chapelries in these lists can be taken as a sign of expanding settlement, but the converse, the disappearance of chapels, need not indicate depopulation.

In contrast to the general ecclesiastical records, there are the seigneurial land surveys of the thirteenth and fourteenth centuries which provide an imperfect overall picture. There are no comparative surveys for the Marcher lands of Wales such as those provided by the *Nomina Villarum* taken in conjunction with the lay Tax of 1334 and subsequent years. Instead there is for the royal lands the *Record of Caernarvon* which was prepared in the second quarter of the fourteenth century for Edward the Black Prince, and surveyed the rents and services due from the recently conquered lands in Anglesey, Caernarvonshire and Merioneth: the former principality of Lywelyn ap Gruffydd. From this survey the changes over the succeeding decades can with difficulty be traced, usually in conjunction with a rather different class of document. The *Record* does provide adequate insight into tenurial arrangements and indeed was used for this purpose by Prof. Jones-Pierce (Jones-Pierce, 1941). It can only give a hesitant answer to questions of desertion and depopulation. Similarly the Bolde rental (Bangor MS. 1939) rests on the basis of townships then existing and only provides the names and locations of single homesteads (*tyddynau*) deserted shortly before the rental was prepared in the late fifteenth century (Jones-Pierce, 1942; Gresham, 1965). Other seigneurial documents such as those detailing the lordships of Chirk, of Oswestry, of Bromfield and Yale, of Chepstow, and of the Knights Hospitallers, do indicate townships which have not survived under their medieval name, but without further research there is insufficient indication whether it is the name that has changed or whether a more drastic removal has occurred. The manorial documents of the chapters of St. Asaph and St. Davids and of the abbeys of Brecon, Tewkesbury, Margam and Tintern provide similar slight information. Only when the pattern of land holding, indeed of land terminology, is fully understood, can appropriate attention be given to the phenomena of desertion, which is the modification of a regional settlement pattern. The work of Prof. Jones-Pierce (Jones-Pierce, 1939; 1949; 1951; 1951A; 1959A and 1963) in elucidating this pattern in Gwynedd and Ceredigion, and the work of Prof. W. Rees in South Wales and the March (Rees, 1924) has provided a starting-point, but only the survey of Anglesey (Jones, 1955) has been sufficiently thorough to enable the degree of desertion to be determined.

The effects of the Black Death on the economic life of Wales have been examined (Evans, 1929; Rees, 1924, esp. 241–52); but the continued unrest of a people chafing under alien domination and the petty raiding which culminated in the revolt of Glyndwr have prevented the effects of plague from being isolated from the other factors in late fourteenth-century Wales. This legacy of opposition to an imposed authority persisted throughout the fifteenth century and the many claims to be released from taxation whether royal, seigneurial or episcopal cannot often be used as an indicator of villages fading into oblivion, but only as an overall condition of poverty in a subsistence economy of a society, precarious but also tenacious.

One factor in desertion can be isolated. This was the overwhelming of coastal villages by sand-dunes at various points along the coast of Glamorgan and Gower, at Halkin (Hawton) on the Towy, at Llandanwg below Harlech, and at Llanddwyn on the edge of Newborough Warren. This movement started in the mid-thirteenth century and continued for nearly two centuries. In Glamorgan the villagers migrated inland to the safety of higher ground as from Kenfig to Pyle, and in Gower there were new foundations at Penmaen, Penard, Rhosili and, possibly, Nicholaston (Higgins, 1933). More gradual erosion has affected Sudbrook and Lavernock now perched on cliffs above the Severn.

The stimulus to enclose arable and so facilitate the production of wool in the decades after 1450 had far less effect in Wales than it had in midland England (Jenkins, 1969). A partial explanation may be that the sheep pastures were already fully stocked by the Cistercian houses grazing in common with all others who enjoyed the rights to the mountain land. The pressure was not to enclose arable land, a rare enough commodity in Wales, but to overstock pastures and to insist on exclusive grazing rights. Cases illustrating this process may be cited both within the last century of the monasteries' existence (Williams, 1965, 34) and in the next half-century (Gresham, 1960). Sheep were not the only beasts ranging the Welsh hills; goats also cropped the craggy heights and cattle were pastured on the middle ground (Emery, 1967, 125–29). The need to milk the cows daily and to herd the sheep and goats protecting them from wolves and other wild beasts led to the establishment of huts or farms (*hafodau, lluestau*) on the summer pastures. The practice of transhumance is still operated on a minor scale today. Some of these temporary settlements blossomed into permanent farms or even into hamlets in the late Middle Ages (Sayce, 1956 and 1957; Richards, 1959 and 1960A). The rich marshland grazing in the Dee estuary and on the Wentlwg levels must also be stressed, but this seldom produced further new settlement (Sylvester, 1958; Davies, 1958).

A drastic transition from an arable to a pastoral economy was present only on a much reduced scale and the marketing outlets were proportionately meagre (though the practice of cattle droving over very long distances may be a compensatory factor). Evidence for depopulation attributable to this cause is negligible when compared with John Rous's lamentations in Warwickshire. Instead the pressure came early in the sixteenth century from the new landed gentry rising to power through their manipulation of monastic finances such as the Herberts or Mansells or through their service to the Tudor dynasty at Westminster and Ludlow such as Sir Rhys ap Thomas. A third class were the English settlers in the boroughs who through their business acumen could break the web of petty holdings divided into non-viable units by inheritance and reconstruct the holdings in their own interest, such as the Boldes of Conway, the Bulkeleys of Beaumaris and the Stedmans of Cilcennin (Jones-Pierce, 1940 and 1968). Though their emparking was not on the scale of Knole or Holdenby, it seems probable that some townships disappeared as at Penrhyn (Caerns.), Clemenston (Glam.), Maesllwch and Llangoed (Brecs.) or St. Pierre (Monm.). It is certain that granges also were converted into lesser mansions as at Sker and Cwrt-y-carnau on the lands of Neath (Glam.). This process of territorial aggrandizement commencing early in the sixteenth century has been illustrated in Cardiganshire with the Vaughans of Trawscoed (Howells, 1956), but it is uncertain whether the creation of lesser houses such as Madryn, Llandudwen (Caerns.) involved the displacement of neighbouring landowners or merely ensured the permanent depression in status and possession of those nearby. Enclosing, emparking and estate-building gave added importance to the preparation of extents and rentals, and those which have been published, such as the Bolde rental, can be used both to illustrate the progress of redrawing the landscape in a new fashion and also to recapture the earlier pattern before all trace of it was lost (Jones-Pierce, 1940A and 1942).

Estate-building broke the tenurial pattern and often undermined the agrarian system of open-field or of communal enterprise. Work is still proceeding on disentangling the strip field system of *tir cyfrif* (reckoned land) associated with the bond communities set in a nucleated settlement and, in contrast, the more irregular open and quilleted arable associated with the *rhandir* (shareland) of the free communities whose homesteads set in small enclosures were ranged in girdle pattern around their arable land (Jones, 1959A and 1960). Attention has been drawn to the survival of quillets in various parts of Wales (Jones, 1964; also Davies, 1923, Thomas, 1957 and Grove, 1962). The anglicised pattern of open field at Rhosili (Glam.) has been discussed by Dr. Margaret Davies (Davies, 1956) and early seventeenth-century parish plans showing open field systems succumbing to enclosure have been published and discussed (Davies, 1957; Davies, 1958 and Sylvester, 1958). The broader pattern of landscape and settlement has been admirably summarised (Emery, 1967) supported by the evidence from local studies (Sylvester, 1954 and 1956, and Pryce, 1961). Throughout the sixteenth century changes were taking place in agrarian practice and tenurial organisation which effectively weakened the communal farming practices, but there is no clear evidence that this movement accelerated depopulation in the countryside or enforced a migration to the towns.

Those changes during the seventeenth and eighteenth centuries which created deserted settlements must be touched upon briefly. The parks of the gentry as at Rug (Mer.) or Llansannor (Glam.) did incorporate earlier arable; their expansion caused

the removal of the isolated farm and a few cottages.   Generally in Wales the enforce
migration of an established village does not occur, even in parks of the size of Wynnstay
Kinmel and Bodelwyddan.   Instead it is the abandonment of large-scale transhumanc
towards the end of the eighteenth century which caused the decay of so many of th
summer dwellings—the shielings or *hafodau*.   Their overgrown ruins can be seen dotte
over many mountain-sides in the heartland of Wales, often in a sheltered situatio
chosen through long familiarity with the area in contrast to the boldly placed squatte
cottages of the early nineteenth century.   Even the squatter cottages, the *tai unos*, ar
decaying in the quarry districts, as at Garn Dolbenmaen or Waunfawr (Caerns.) : ther
the moss-grown ruins of igneous rock still protrude from their hastily seized sites on th
edge of the commons, while in the vale of Aeron (Cards.) the mud walled cottages, thei
thatch fallen in, revert to earth as mounds of grass and thistle.   Except where moder
industry ensured their survival, the newly founded agrarian settlements and the outpos
on marginal land were the first to suffer in the mid-nineteenth century agricultura
depression and to feel the effects of the exodus to the coal-mines, to the towns and to th
New World.   The long established settlements, the medieval *trefi*, survived this on
slaught and only now are succumbing to forestry, to water boards and other publi
institutions.   Throughout Wales it is the nearness to marginal subsistence that ha
made the settlement particularly sensitive to economic changes, but it is also th
resilience in adversity which has carried the agrarian settlements through the lean years

II. EXCAVATION

Fieldwork and excavation on deserted rural settlement in Wales have proceeded slowly
lacking until well into this century the stimuli of museums, university colleges an
archaeological societies in all parts of the country.   The significant starting-point wa
in 1934 with the publication by Sir Cyril and Lady Fox of their work on Margan
Mountain, Glamorgan.   There they identified rectangular houses set on platform sites
stating that "the majority of the domestic sites are unrecorded; they seem to represen
types new to archaeological science" (Fox and Fox, 1934, 396).   An immediate out
come of the survey was the excavation on Gelligaer Common (site 10)[1] by Lady Fo
and the fieldwork in Gwynedd by Hemp and Gresham, while Peate's valuable stud
of *The Welsh House* was a by-product of this same quest for post-Roman domesti
structures.

The work of the Foxes concentrated on the upland pastoral region, the Welshry c
Glamorgan or *blaenau Morgannwg*, and although it is in this terrain that earthworks ca
more readily be detected by ground survey and are less likely to have been destroye
by intensive arable clearance, it has resulted in far less attention being paid to the low
lying mixed farming regions where villages were established on an anglicised pattern
This concentration on the hill districts was continued in *Monmouthshire Houses* (Fox an
Raglan, 1951) in which Gwent Iscoed was less thoroughly searched and in which th
Wentlwg levels are most cursorily treated.   The recent work of the Royal Commissio
on Ancient Monuments and the excavations conducted by Mr. H. Thomas have partl
redressed the balance in favour of lowland sites.

[1] Such references lead a reader to the gazetteer of excavated sites, pp. 270–271.

Rural settlement in the pastoral uplands was predominantly a dispersed pattern of single farmsteads, seasonally supplemented by the summer dairy houses (*hafodau* or *lluestau*) and occasionally interspersed with nucleated hamlets. These three elements will be considered separately.

Single farmsteads could exhibit a wide range of personal wealth and architectural pretension. At one end of the scale are the abandoned hall-houses of the chieftains' families, proud of their pedigrees and jealous of their social rank. The two houses which have been excavated are Cefn-y-fan (site 3) (Hogg, 1954) and Siambr Wen (site 7) (Beste, 1911; Cochrane, 1912). These two sites suggest that English influence generally produced a three-fold division of hall (with solar above or beyond), screens passage and kitchen (with buttery) below the screens. Architectural survey upon surviving buildings (Smith, 1967; Smith and Lloyd, 1964) has shown that these general conclusions are valid. At the lower end of the scale there is more regional variation (Fig. 39a), and the only excavated house must be regarded as atypical. This was a twin-cell homestead on the Penmaenmawr uplands (site 4), measuring 9 m. by 3·5 m. with a long central entrance passage dividing a living room lined by benches and a smaller paved store-room or dairy; it was suggested (Griffiths, 1954) that this house belonged to the sixteenth-century expansion onto the upland plateaux described in Sir John Wynn's *An Ancient Survey of Pen Maen Mawr*.

Fieldwork has tended to be concentrated on the two geographical extremes of Glamorgan in the south-east and of Caernarvonshire in the north-west. Since the isolated medieval settlement has left the clearest evidence of its former position by the platforms scooped into sloping ground, the platform house has tended to be equated with medieval hut groups; it should, however, be noted that long huts do occur on level ground and that buildings continued to be set on artificially levelled platforms well into the eighteenth century. In Glamorgan the wide variety of platform house plans, their position in relation to altitude and ground slope, and their location with reference to known medieval structures has been noted in a series of articles (Fox and Fox, 1934; Fox, 1937 and 1939; Green, 1956; Morris, 1956). This work has extended the distribution of this house type from Machen in the east to Pontardulais in the west. Recent fieldwork has investigated similar sites in southern Breconshire. One anomalous site has been published from Radnorshire (Fox, 1939A), but other more typical sites occur in Radnor Forest, at Llanbadarn Fynydd and on the hills south and west of Rhayader. In North Wales the Royal Commission on Ancient Monuments' *Inventory of Caernarvonshire* and the work by Mr. C. A. Gresham in the *History of Merioneth* (Vol. II—forthcoming) have led to the discovery of numerous sites indicating a wide variety of plans but with platform sites predominating. The characteristics of these sites have been described (Gresham, 1954) and the Caernarvonshire evidence summarised (R.C.A.M., 1964, CLXXVIII). In both North and South Wales there is a common uniformity of rectangular building, seldom exceeding 18 m. in length and 6·5 m. in width, and usually smaller in the north.

Attempts at dating these surface remains without excavation have to rely upon such imprecise factors as the tenurial history of the locality, the association of the site with an adjacent medieval chapel, the chance finds of pottery or the date *ante quem* assigned because of a subsequent building on the site. Similar attempts at correlating literary

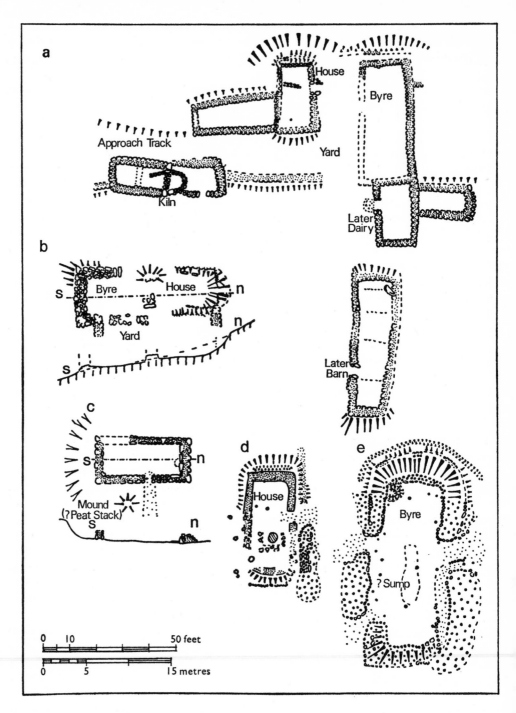

Fig. 37. Plans of upland farms and hafodau: key, p. 259

a. Aber valley (*Nant-yr-cadrat*), Aber, Caerns.; an upland hafod originating in a house and byre (after Butler, 1962).
b. Nant-y-moch, Ystradfellte, Brecknock; an isolated house-and-byre homestead (after Fox, 1940).
c. Bwlch-yr-hendre, Pont Erwyd, Cards.; an isolated long hut (after Butler, 1963).
d. Dinas Noddfa, Gelligaer, Glam.; "Upper House".
e. Dinas Noddfa, Gelligaer, Glam.; "Lower House".
an upland farm group with possible distinction between the dwelling house (d) and the cattle house (e) (after Fox, 1937).

descriptions with surface remains have not been totally convincing: the use of the description in the medieval Welsh romance *Breuddwyd Rhonabwy* as an accurate account of a house-and-byre dwelling combined under a single roof has been queried. The continuity between the houses described in *The Welsh Laws* and the houses of the nucleated hamlets has also been questioned.[2] The evidence of The Laws on constructional practice depends on the interpretation of *Fforch* (Latin *furca*) and no satisfactory decision has yet been reached whether it means a cruck truss or whether it describes a vertical post with a forked top carrying a ridge pole. A less disputed comment on the character of native housing is the observation by Giraldus Cambrensis, writing in the end of the twelfth century, that "the Welsh content themselves with small huts made of boughs of trees twisted together, constructed with little labour and expense and sufficient to endure throughout the year". It is generally assumed that Giraldus was describing rectangular huts, though the possibility that round huts were still built in the twelfth century cannot be completely ruled out.

The poverty in material objects possessed by the upland farmers is reflected in the disappointing results from the excavation of single farmsteads or hut groups. The farmsteads on Bodafon Mountain (site 1, Griffiths, 1955) and House A at Beili Bedw (site 15, Alcock, 1961) produced no evidence of settlement earlier than the eighteenth century despite the promising surface indications. The single huts beside Nant-y-moch (site 2, Fox, 1940) and near Bwlch-yr-hendre (site 6, Butler, 1963) also had no satisfactory dating evidence. The former hut (Fig. 37b) was dated on typological grounds to a date later than the thirteenth century and earlier than the seventeenth century; it measured approximately 16·6 m. by 6·3 m., and showed a difference in construction between the upper half of the platform (living accommodation) and the lower half (stable or byre). There was a cross-wall dividing the two halves of the house and it is probable that there were opposed entrances at this point. Houses B and C at Beili Bedw (Alcock, 1962A), were of this general type with probably fourteenth-to-fifteenth-century occupation. At Bwlch-yr-hendre (Fig. 37c) an initial occupation in the late sixteenth or early seventeenth century continuing until its replacement in the mid-eighteenth century was suggested on land use considerations; it measured 9 m. by 3·5 m., with a hearth at one end and a single doorway placed centrally in a side wall.

---

[2] Insufficient work has been done on the etymology of the names given to the various rooms within a house or to the various structures comprising a farmstead in the medieval period.

Excavation at the summer dairy houses, the *hafodau*, has produced similarly tentative results. A long hut group in the Aber valley (site 5, Butler, 1962) could well have been the *hafotry* of Nanteracadrat mentioned in the mid-fourteenth-century *Record of Caernarvon*. The probable arrangement (Fig. 37a, Plate 28), was of two separate buildings, house and byre (*beudy*), facing each other across a small yard; each building was set on a platform and had a single doorway midway along the side wall. Evidence from fieldwork, as at the neighbouring Meuryn and Maes-y-gaer (Fig. 39b), suggests that this was the normal arrangement in North Wales, and that the interconnecting house-and-byre was confined to South Wales. Recent fieldwork in Breconshire has recorded some *hafodau* sites and has suggested an origin in the fourteenth century for transhumance in the Brecon Beacons, though the illustrated site appears to be eighteenth century (Crampton, 1966; also Miller, 1967).

Nucleated settlements, whether they originated as bond vills or as groups of free tenants settled in a loose agrarian association, are seldom found on the uplands. In North Wales recent fieldwork has suggested three sites and at present one is being excavated: the township of Ardda above the Conway valley was of late medieval origin and was not deserted until the eighteenth century: the settlement of fourteen huts at Nant Gwrtheyrn, Pistyll (Fig. 38a) is not documented. Another settlement of fifteen or more long-huts, now known as Hen Caerwys (site 8), is under excavation. Two houses so far excavated are on platform sites, with stone walls, evidence of central postholes and traces of domestic occupation in the fourteenth century. Annexes to the main structures are associated with metal working and had central ridge posts. Elsewhere in North Wales the even looser grouping of long-huts and farmsteads at Rhiw, Pennant Dolbenmaen and Llanaber in Ardudwy may approximate to the girdle pattern described by Mr. Jones (Jones, 1960). In South Wales the semi-nucleated settlement is more often found. Groupings of long-huts, many of them on the southern ridges dividing the tributaries of the Taf, may well be termed linear hamlets (Fig. 41b), and despite their altitude of 430 m. above sea level they were considered by Lady Fox to be permanent dwellings (though this identification has been doubted by Dr. Peate). The two excavated sites are situated among the six sites comprising ten huts on Gelligaer Common East (site 10, Fox, 1939) (Fig. 38b) and the smaller group at Dinas Noddfa (site 9, Fox, 1937). In so far as these settlements and others, as at Cefn Brithdir, seem to be linked by a single trackway running along the ridge, they may each be considered as a single hamlet. However their importance lies not in the pattern of settlement but in the internal arrangements of the houses. At Dinas Noddfa (Fig. 37d–e, Plate 27) the two houses differed in their construction: the upper house measured 12·5 m. by 5·8 m. and was turf-walled; the lower house was 18 m. by 6·6 m. with dry-stone walling. In each the entrances were in the centre of the long side: in the upper house a single doorway was placed on the side away from the prevailing wind; in the lower house there were opposed entrances and a paved cross passage with cobbled exterior approach. The upper house had no sign of fire or hearth and only slight paving inside it. The lower house had a central flagged area, and the irregularities of the side walls were interpreted as the provision for sleeping quarters. Lady Fox noted that "the centre and west (lower) end were the superior part of the house". The postholes indicated a central row of posts supporting a ridge, and a second row of minor

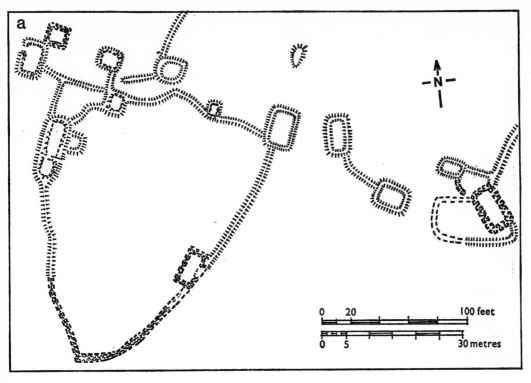

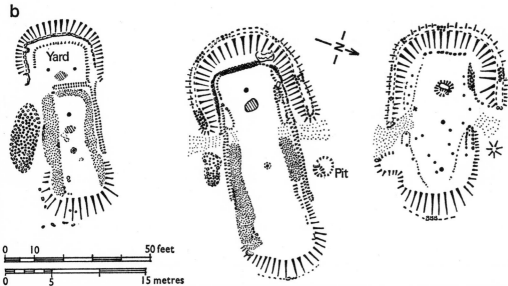

Fig. 38. Plans of hamlets in the uplands

a. Nant Gwrtheyrn, Pistyll, Caerns.; an upland hamlet (after R.C.A.M.).
b. Gelligaer Common East, Glam.; an upland farm group in a linear hamlet (after Fox, 1939).

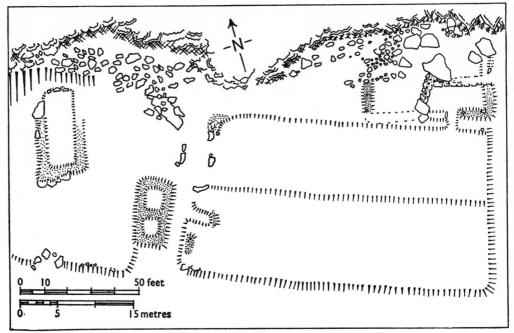

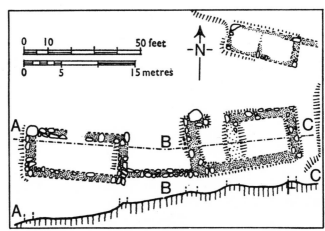

Fig. 39. Plans of isolated farms in the uplands

a. Cil Drygwr, Dolbenmaen, Caerns.; an upland hut group (after R.C.A.M.).
b. Maes-y-gaer, Aber, Caerns.; an upland farm group (after R.C.A.M.).

posts along both sides and at the upper end. In this pair of huts there is a suggestion that the differences in construction and extent of paving reflected different but related functions in a pastoral economy. There was no evidence of a house-and-byre combined under one roof, and the absence of such provision would strengthen the case

262

for regarding this pair as a summer dwelling. The absence of finds would also lend support to this suggestion.

The three platform houses excavated at Gelligaer Common East (Fig. 38b) were considered to be components of a single farmstead. They were similar in construction with turf walling on a low stone base, but varied in size: the centre house was 18·6 m. by 6 m., the south house was 16·3 m. by 6 m. (limits of platform), the north house was 14 m. by 7 m. In each there were opposed entrances at the centre of the long side; in the north house one entrance was sheltered from the prevailing wind by a screen wall; in the south house the entrances were less clearly defined and the upper part of the platform was regarded as an open yard. There was a clearly marked fireplace at the upper end of the centre house; there was an external fireplace in the upper end of the south platform and some hearth material at two points close to the long axis of the south house. There was no fireplace in the north house, and numerous shallow post-holes at the lower end suggested a raised floor and a storage function. Only the centre house was extensively paved and here the upper end was dirty with occupation debris while the paved lower end was clean, suggesting to Lady Fox that it was probably kept swept and sanded. At the upper end of this house was an internal drainage gutter carrying off the rainwater seeping down the hillside through the end wall out through the entrances. In no house was there a gutter or drain at the lower end.

There was satisfactory evidence of roof construction in two of the houses: the centre house had two post-holes remaining from a series of posts supporting a central ridge-line; the north house had similar evidence of a central ridge line and two lines of minor post-holes close to the side walls, thereby lessening the outward thrust on lightly constructed walls. The south house (Fig. 38b) was seen as a roofed structure (12 m. by 3 m.) at the lower end of the platform with two central posts supporting a ridge line; the upper end was an open yard and two post-holes there were interpreted as uprights which held the wind break for the fire. The last interpretation prompts three observations. Firstly that reliance for classification of house types upon surface indications can often be misleading; when only the earthwork platform has survived, and the turf or timber structure set upon it has disappeared, this may give an exaggerated idea of the building's size, especially if there was a yard or a walk-round. Secondly that the interpretation offered by Lady Fox has been questioned by Mr. Hurst who saw in the arrangement of post-holes an aisled construction in the house part (the upper end) and a central row of posts in the cattle end (the lower part) and could cite the medieval Danish example of Åsa, House D (Hurst, 1965, 195). Thirdly that the placing of the hearth or kitchen outside the thatched structures was a common practice in Wales and continued into the seventeenth century (Smith, 1967, 774).

The importance of the houses on Gelligaer Common is not that these are house-and-byre homesteads, an identification neither claimed for them by Lady Fox nor by Peate (1940, 147–48),[3] but that they produced clear dating evidence. The cooking pots

---

[3] The term long-house (*ty hir*) has been used (Peate, 1940) to describe the rectangular house with opposed entrances and with both men and cattle using these entrances to gain access to a combined house-and-byre homestead. It is not certain that the medieval term *longa domus* always refers to the

were dated to the late thirteenth or early fourteenth century. The evidence of iron smelting and of fine metal work (indicated by a stone mould for casting a pendant) supported this dating. No other house with such a quantity of undisputed medieval material has been found in the pastoral uplands; yet the variety of house plans on other upland sites is not an argument against their medieval date but an argument for examining the structure of society which made such gradations of wealth possible and for examining the range of soils which made such variations in husbandry practice necessary. In particular the association of barns, corn-drying kilns, flax-drying hearths, lazy beds and pens should be noted because it is these minor structures which give an individual character to the apparently uniform pastoral pattern.

In the virtual absence of incontrovertible archaeological evidence for dating these upland huts, various attempts have been made to set these excavated huts in a chronological sequence. A thorough understanding of the tenurial history was used (Jones-Pierce, 1962) to assist the author's excavation in the Aber valley. Mr. Gresham's detailed study of the townships in Isdwyfor in Eifionydd, Caerns. (Gresham, 1954) led him to propose that the long-huts on platform sites should be seen as *tyddynod* of the *priodorion* (homesteads of free Welsh tribesmen), but this assumption has been questioned (R.C.A.M., 1964, CLXXVIII) and Mr. Gresham has also modified his views though still stressing the importance of tenurial status (Gresham, 1963, 276). Indeed the fluid state of tenurial conditions throughout the Middle Ages does cast doubt on any attempt to equate a particular type of site with a distinct class of land-holder, unless there is an exact coincidence of archaeological and documentary evidence. The use of geographical conditions and soil suites so convincingly advanced in Anglesey and Arllechwedd has been followed both in excavation and fieldwork. Only by placing the excavated hut at Bwlch-yr-hendre (site 6) in the context of later (eighteenth century) land use could a satisfactory date be suggested. The work of Dr. R. E. Hughes in using patterns of flora colonisation to place in sequence abandoned field systems and their associated farms and huts on the heights west of the Conway (Hughes, 1953) could have much wider application in the poorly documented upland regions. However the work of Dr. C. B. Crampton in using the survival of linear patterns of gorse and hawthorn to reconstruct earlier field and settlement patterns in north-west Breconshire must be treated with extreme caution (Crampton, 1967). The use of soil samples to determine ancient land-use is still in a preliminary stage in Wales and should at present be seen as playing a confirmatory role rather than as being the sole determinant.

Fieldwork and excavation on <u>lowland</u> settlement is less advanced and has so far

same type of structure. Although the combined house-and-byre is found in England (for discussion see p. 112, above), it was apparently a localised form in South Wales and this is born out by the limited archaeological evidence. Only at Nant-y-moch (site 2, Fox, 1940) is there satisfactory evidence of a house-and-byre homestead; the upland Glamorgan sites excavated by Lady Fox and at Beili Bedw (Site 15, Alcock, 1962) are capable of this interpretation, but in each case there are ambiguous elements, which militate against accepting this identification uncritically. More excavation is needed on *hendre* sites in South Wales to confirm the ubiquity of the combined house-and-byre homestead; similarly more excavation in North Wales, perhaps at Rhiw or Pistyll, would show whether the two separate structures of house and byre are normal in the medieval period. Until such excavation has been undertaken, the vexed problem of the origins of the long-house and the continuity between the post-Roman Iron Age and the medieval period in domestic structures will remain obscure.

yielded less satisfactory results. The various types of village form in the mixed farming lowland region have often been described (e.g. Thomas, 1957; Davies, 1958A; Bowen, 1964; Emery, 1967, 147–57), but only Dr. Margaret Davies has made extensive use of pre-nineteenth-century estate surveys (Davies, 1957). Although large villages do occur on a pattern known in lowland England, hamlets and single farms were also present and each of these three categories will be considered in turn.

The deserted sites of single farms have been noted in many parts of South Wales, but in the absence of excavation the date of sites such as Cae Corrwg and East Flemingston must remain uncertain, though both are possibly seventeenth century. Those single farms placed within the protection of a moated enclosure may be assumed to be medieval, though not certainly so except when documentary evidence supports this assumption. The excavated Hen Gwrt, Llantilio Crossenny, showed occupation in the thirteenth and fourteenth centuries, while a similar date may be anticipated for the few moats in Glamorgan and Pembrokeshire and the more frequent sites in Maelor and the broad valleys of the Severn and the Wye close to the English border. Another specialised form of a single farm was the monastic grange: the characteristics of the upland granges are only now being recognised, as at Hen Denbych, Dinas y Prif and perhaps Llys Arthur. The lowland farms, such as Broughton and Llantwit Major, Glamorgan, can be recognised from surface remains, and the latter when excavated 30 years ago produced evidence of a high standard of material occupation and a complex provision for varied farming processes.

Little excavation has taken place on lowland villages and at only three sites, all in the Vale of Glamorgan close to Barry, have houses within a village complex been examined, all by Mr. Thomas. At Barry (site 12) (Fig. 40b) in the centre of an existing village a three-roomed stone-built house of thirteenth-mid-fourteenth century date was cleared; it measured 15 m. by 6·5 m. with opposed doorways into the large central room, 7·2 m. long. This large room contained a hearth. An elaborate system of slabbed drains inside the building was considered necessary to counteract the dampness of the sloping site. The character of the metal finds, the presence of querns and the discovery of a chamfered window jamb suggested a dwelling well above peasant status (Thomas, 1962). At Lower Porthkerry (site 13) one house out of a small hamlet group was excavated and it produced similar evidence about the status of the occupants (Thomas, 1963). This was a two-roomed house with a thirteenth-fourteenth century phase and a fifteenth century phase; there was also evidence of an earlier occupation on the site. The larger room contained a hearth and was entered by opposing doorways in the long walls. Between the entrances was a slabbed drain, presumably to carry away surface water entering through the doorways. At Highlight (site 14) (Fig. 40c) a stone-built (?) priest's house of two rooms was found within the churchyard at a deserted village (Thomas, 1966). At these three sites the house plans bear a strong resemblance to the lateral entry house (regional Type A of Smith, 1967).

A different type of house plan was found at Mynydd Bychan (site 11) (Fig. 40a). Here, at a distance from the nucleated village, a single peasant's croft was set within a small Iron Age hill fort, the one hectare contained within the defences being used as a yard and garden (Savory, 1955 and 1956). Throughout its history the house was an oblong structure with a ridge roof supported on a central line of small timber uprights

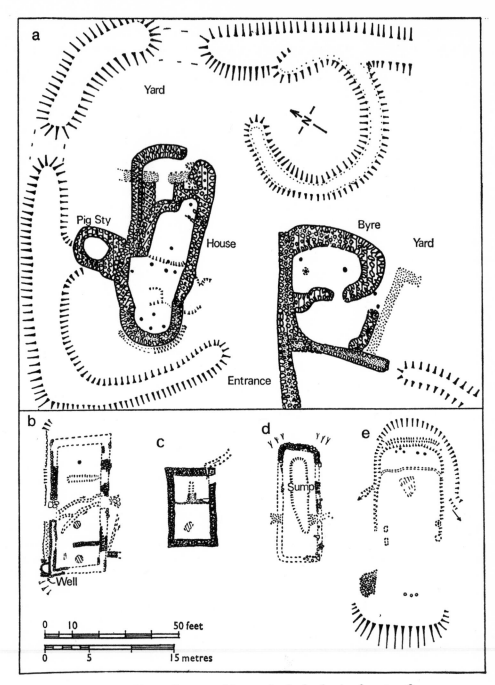

Labels within the figure:

a

Yard

Pig Sty

House

Byre

Yard

Entrance

b

Well

c

d

Sump

e

0 10 50 feet

0 5 15 metres

Fig. 40. Plans of excavated houses in the lowlands: key, p. 267

a. Mynydd Bychan, Llysworney, Glam.; a lowland farm in the Vale of Glamorgan (after Savory, 1955).
b. Barry, Glam.; an excavated three-roomed house within an existing village (after Thomas).
c. Highlight, Glam.; a two-roomed (? priest's) house north-east of the church (Fig. 41a) (after Thomas).
d. Beili Bedw, St. Harmon, Radnors.; House B.
e. Beili Bedw, St. Harmon, Radnors.; House C;
   an upland farm group with possible distinction between dwelling house (e) and cattle house (d) (after Alcock).

and a few side-posts. Originally, perhaps in the late eleventh century or early twelfth century, the house measured 10·3 m. by 3·5 m. with one central entrance, but two subsequent enlargements extended the building to 16 m. by 4·6 m. and gave it an end entry (Smith, Type B). Close to the house in its later phases were a roughly oval pigsty and a second roughly oval building divided into two compartments or stalls. It should not be thought surprising that such variations in plan should occur within the same region during the same centuries, but far more work of excavation will be required before the origins and distribution of these two main types can be determined.

Other work on known village and hamlet sites has followed two directions: there has been the collection of pottery and the recording of masonry at villages deserted because of blown sand, such as Halkin on the Taf, Penmaen in Gower, Candleston and Merthyr Mawr, Glamorgan; there has also been the collection of pottery during building development within existing villages in Glamorgan. The distribution of Ham Green ware, of "Ogmore rim" cooking pots and of flat-based pans has been extended and intensified from besanded sites such as Burrows Well, Rhosili, Halkin and Laugharne Burrows. The occurrence of pottery only indicates a broad date range from the first half of the twelfth century to the mid-fourteenth century, and should be regarded merely as a useful preliminary to excavation.

Fieldwork in identifying village sites is still at an early stage; only one provisional county list has been prepared (Hurst and Butler, 1964). In a few cases toft and croft earthworks, as are commonly found in midland England, are visible though not strongly accentuated. Highlight near Barry (Fig. 41a) and Runston near Chepstow also are good examples, both with a ruined church, sunken village street and six or eight crofts. Penterry, north of Chepstow and Llandewi in Gower have traces of toft and croft less regularly spaced alongside a green close to a surviving church; a compact group of four square enclosures with rectangular platforms for houses and barns may be seen at Gwenddwr in central Breconshire, one kilometre north-west of the present village centre and on the opposite side of a steep stream valley. Examples of house sites placed on the fringes of existing villages occur at West Aberthaw and Cosmeston, while one lowland Glamorgan village which provides evidence of transference is Llanbethery in the Thaw basin. Further fieldwork is needed to determine whether desertion, shrinkage and transference occur in the other lowland counties of mixed farming practice. Such sites that have been investigated in Carmarthenshire and Pembrokeshire have not provided satisfactory evidence. Similarly more work is needed to determine whether

267

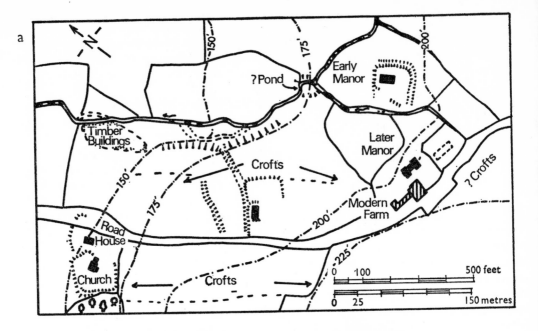

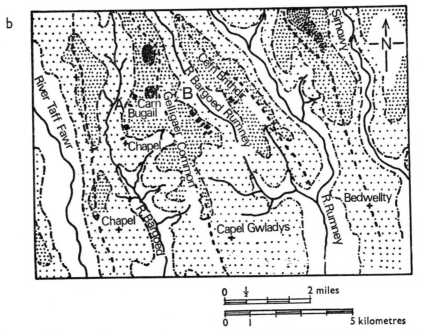

Fig. 41. Plans of villages in Glamorgan

a. Highlight, Glamorgan: a deserted linear village in the Vale of Glamorgan
(after Thomas). House N.E. of church is shown on Fig. 40c.

b. Gelligaer and Bedwellty in *Blaenau Morgannwg* to show upland locations of
linear farmlets comprising platform farm groups and long huts. A is Dinas
Noddfa (Fig. 37d, e); B is Gelligaer Common East (Fig. 38b) (after Fox,
1939).

the village set within a circular enclosure is an isolated phenomenon in Wales; one example can be seen at St. Mary Hill, Glamorgan, and another possibility is Mathry, Pembs., where there is no surviving earthwork.

The direction in which future research must turn is clear. On the one hand a village of apparent Norman foundation in the coastal strip of South Wales or of Flintshire should be excavated in sufficient detail to show the variety or similarity of croft arrangements. On the other hand the several elements within the dispersed Celtic settlement (maerdref, bond vill and tir cyfrif hamlet) should be examined, preferably within the same commote. In both projects there must be an integrated survey of historical, architectural and geographical evidence of the settlement and the land which supported the settlement. Only by such an approach can deserted medieval settlement in Wales be tackled successfully.

CHAPTER TEN

I. Gazetteer of Excavated Sites in Wales

II. Select Bibliography, Wales

L. A. S. BUTLER

Lecturer in Medieval Archaeology, University of Leeds

I. GAZETTEER OF EXCAVATED SITES

ANGLESEY

1   BODAFON MOUNTAIN (SH 471846) Lowland farm; platform type; eighteenth century; Griffiths, 1955.

BRECKNOCK

2   NANT-Y-MOCH, YSTRADFELLTE (SN 904160) Upland farm; platform type; (?) sixteenth century; Fox, 1940.

CAERNARVONSHIRE

3   CEFN-Y-FAN, DOLBENMAEN (SH 506421) Upland farm; fourteenth century; Hogg, 1954.

4   PENMAENMAWR (SH 704752) Upland farm; (?) sixteenth century; Griffiths, 1954.

5   ABER VALLEY (SH 668706) Upland *hafod*; platform type; fourteenth and eighteenth century; Butler, 1962.

CARDIGANSHIRE

6   BWLCH-YR-HENDRE (SN 743878) Upland farm; (? *hafod*); (?) sixteenth-seventeenth century; Butler, 1963.

FLINTSHIRE

7   SIAMBR WEN, DYSERTH (SJ 062797) Upland farm; fourteenth century; Beste, 1911 and Cochrane, 1912.

8   HEN CAERWYS (SJ 137742) Upland hamlet; platform type; fourteenth-fifteenth century; interim note by Leach and Pennant-Williams in *Archaeol. in Wales*, II (1962), 14.

GLAMORGAN

9 DINAS NODDFA (SO 093033) Hamlet; upland farm; platform type; fourteenth century; Fox, 1937.

10 GELLIGAER COMMON (SO 112029) Hamlet; upland farm; platform type; thirteenth-fourteenth century; Fox, 1939.

11 MYNYDD BYCHAN, LLYSWORNEY (SS 960756) Lowland farm; twelfth-fifteenth century; Savory, 1955 and 1956.

12 BARRY (ST 102672) Lowland village; thirteenth-fourteenth century; interim note only, Thomas, 1962.

13 LOWER PORTHKERRY (ST 078669) Lowland hamlet; twelfth-fifteenth century; interim note only, Thomas, 1963.

14 HIGHLIGHT (UCHELOLAU) (ST 096690) Lowland village; thirteenth-fifteenth century; interim note only, Thomas, 1966.

RADNORSHIRE

15 BEILI BEDW, ST. HARMON (SN 966734) Upland farm; platform type; fourteenth-fifteenth century and eighteenth century; interim notes only, Alcock, 1961 and 1962A.

II. SELECT BIBLIOGRAPHY

ALCOCK, 1961 — L. Alcock, "Beili Bedw, St. Harmon", *Archaeol. in Wales*, I (1961), 14–15 (interim note).

ALCOCK, 1962 — ——, "Settlement Patterns in Celtic Britain", *Antiquity*, XXXVI (1962), 36, 51–55.

ALCOCK, 1962A — ——, "Beili Bedw, St. Harmon", *Archaeol. in Wales*, II (1962), 18 (interim note).

ALCOCK, 1963 — ——, "Pottery and Settlements in Wales and the March, A.D. 400–700", in I. Ll. Foster and L. Alcock, eds., *Culture and Environment: Essays in Honour of Sir Cyril Fox* (1963), 281–302, esp. 294 ff.

ALCOCK, 1964 — ——, "Some Reflections on Early Welsh Society and Economy", *Welsh Hist. Rev.*, II (1964–65), 1–8.

BESTE, 1911 — K. D. Beste, "Recent Excavations at Siamber Wen, near Dyserth, Flintshire", *Archaeol. Camb.*, LXVI (1911), 54–77.

BOWEN, 1954 — E. G. Bowen, *The Settlements of the Celtic Saints in Wales* (1954), esp. 140–60.

BOWEN, 1964 — ——, "The Settlement Pattern of Wales", in J. A. Steers, ed., *Field Studies in the British Isles* (1964), 279–93, esp. 279–86.

BUTLER, 1962 — L. A. S. Butler, "A Long Hut Group in the Aber Valley", *Trans. Caerns. Hist. Soc.*, XXIII (1962), 25–36.

BUTLER, 1963 ——, "The Excavation of a Long Hut near Bwlch-yr-Hendre", *Ceredigion*, IV (1963), 450–57.

CHARLES, 1938 B. G. Charles, *Non-Celtic Place Names in Wales* (1938), esp. XXI–XXXV.

COCHRANE, 1912 R. Cochrane, "Medieval House, Dyserth, Flintshire", *Archaeol. Camb.*, LXVII (1912), 33–38.

COWLEY, 1967 F. G. Cowley, "The Cistercian Economy in Glamorgan, 1130–1349", *Morgannwg*, XI (1967), 5–26.

CRAMPTON, 1966 C. B. Crampton, "Hafotai Platforms on the North Front of the Brecon Beacons", *Archaeol. Camb.*, CXV (1966), 99–107.

CRAMPTON, 1967 ——, "Ancient Settlement Patterns in Mid-Wales", *Archaeol. Camb.*, CXVI (1967), 57–70.

DAVIES, 1923 I. E. Davies, "The Tithe Map of Dwygyfylchi", *Archaeol. Camb.*, LXXVIII (1923), 327–33.

DAVIES, 1956 M. Davies, "Rhosili Open Field and Related South Wales Field Patterns", *Ag. Hist. Rev.*, IV (1956), 80–96.

DAVIES, 1957 ——, "Field Patterns in the Vale of Glamorgan", *Trans. Cardiff Nat. Soc.*, LXXXIV (1954–55), 5–14.

DAVIES, 1958 ——, "Common Lands in South-East Monmouthshire", *Trans. Cardiff Nat. Soc.*, LXXXV (1955–56), 5–15.

DAVIES, 1958A ——, *Wales in Maps* (1958), 54–55.

EMERY, 1967 F. V. Emery, "The Farming Regions of Wales", in Joan Thirsk, ed., *The Agrarian History of England and Wales*, IV (1967), 113–60.

EVANS, 1929 D. L. Evans, *Flintshire Ministers' Accounts 1328–1353*, Flintshire Historical Society, Record Series, II (1929), LXXII–LXXV.

FOX, 1937 A. Fox, "Dinas Noddfa, Gelligaer Common, Glamorgan: Excavations in 1936", *Archaeol. Camb.*, XCII (1937), 247–68.

FOX, 1939 ——, "Early Welsh Homesteads on Gelligaer Common, Glamorgan: Excavations in 1938", *Archaeol. Camb.*, XCIV (1939), 163–99.

FOX, 1939A C. Fox, "A Settlement of Platform Houses, Dyrysgol, St. Harmon, Radnorshire", *Archaeol. Camb.*, XCIV (1939), 220–23.

FOX, 1940 ——, "A Croft in the Upper Nedd Valley, Ystradfellte, Brecknockshire", *Antiquity*, XIV (1940), 363–76.

FOX AND FOX, 1934 C. and A. Fox, "Forts and Farms on Margam Mountain, Glamorgan", *Antiquity*, VIII (1934), 395–413, esp. 402ff.

FOX AND RAGLAN, 1951   C. Fox and Lord Raglan, *Monmouthshire Houses, Part I— Medieval* (1951).

GREEN, 1956   H. Green, "Medieval Platform Sites in the Neath Uplands", *Trans. Cardiff Nat. Soc.*, LXXXIII (1953–54), 9–17.

GRESHAM, 1954   C. A. Gresham, "Platform Houses in North-West Wales", *Archaeol. Camb.*, CIII (1954), 18–53.

GRESHAM, 1960   ——, "The Forest of Snowdon in its Relationship to Eifionydd", *Trans. Caerns. Hist. Soc.*, XXI (1960), 53–62.

GRESHAM, 1963   ——, "The Interpretation of Settlement Patterns in North-West Wales, in I. Ll. Foster and L. Alcock, eds., *Culture and Environment* (1963), 263–79.

GRESHAM, 1965   ——, "The Bolde Rental (Bangor MS. 1939)", *Trans. Caerns. Hist. Soc.*, XXVI (1965), 31–49.

GRIFFITHS, 1954   W. E. Griffiths, "Excavations on Penmaenmawr, 1950", *Archaeol. Camb.*, CIII (1954), 66–84, esp. 74–77, 82–83.

GRIFFITHS, 1955   ——, "Excavations on Bodafon Mountain, 1954", *Trans. Anglesey Antiq. Soc.* (1955), 12–26.

GRIMES, 1945   W. F. Grimes, "Early Man and the Soils of Anglesey", *Antiquity*, XIX (1945), 169–74.

GROVE, 1962   J. C. Grove, "Eighteenth-Century Land Use Records in Breconshire", *Brycheiniog*, VIII (1962), 83–94.

HIGGINS, 1933   L. S. Higgins, "An Investigation into the Problem of the Sand-Dune Area on the South Wales Coast", *Archaeol. Camb.*, LXXXVIII (1933), 26–67, esp. 34–35.

HOGG, 1954   A. H. A. Hogg, "A Fourteenth Century House-Site at Cefn-y-Fan, near Dolbenmaen, Caernarvonshire", *Trans. Caerns. Hist. Soc.*, XV (1954), 1–7.

HOWELLS, 1956   J. M. Howells, "The Crosswood Estate, 1547–1947", *Ceredigion*, III (1956), 70–88.

HUGHES, 1940   R. E. Hughes, "Environment and Human Settlement in the Commote of Arllechwedd Isaf", *Trans. Caerns. Hist. Soc.*, II (1940), 1–25.

HUGHES, 1953   ——, "Possible Human Historical Factors Determining the Distribution of *Eriophorum latifolium* in the North-West Conway Valley", in J. E. Lousley, ed., *The Changing Flora of Britain* (1953), 40–45.

HURST, 1965   J. G. Hurst, "The Medieval Peasant House", in A. Small, ed., *The Fourth Viking Congress* (1965), 190–96.

HURST AND BUTLER, 1964   J. G. Hurst and L. A. S. Butler, "Glamorgan D.M.V. List", *Deserted Medieval Village Research Group, 12th Annual Report* (1964), Appendix F.

JENKINS, 1969 — J. G. Jenkins, *The Welsh Woollen Industry* (1969).

JONES, 1955 — G. R. J. Jones, "The Distribution of Medieval Settlement in Anglesey", *Trans. Anglesey Antiq. Soc.* (1955), 27–96.

JONES, 1959 — ——, "Rural Settlement in Ireland and Western Britain: Wales", *Advancement of Science*, xv (1959), 338—42.

JONES, 1959A — ——, "Medieval Open Fields and Associated Settlement Patterns in North-West Wales", *Geographie et Histoire Agraires, Annales de l'Est, Memoire no. 21* (Nancy, 1959), 313–28.

JONES, 1960 — ——, "The Pattern of Settlement on the Welsh Border", *Ag. Hist. Rev.*, VIII (1960), 66–81, esp. 78–81.

JONES, 1963 — ——, "Early Settlement in Arfon: The Setting of Tre'r Ceiri", *Trans. Caerns. Hist. Soc.*, XXIV (1963), 1–20.

JONES, 1964 — ——, "The Llanynys Quillets: a Measure of Landscape Transformation in North Wales", *Trans. Denbigh. Hist. Soc.*, XIII (1964), 133–58.

JONES-PIERCE, 1939 — T. Jones-Pierce, "Some Tendencies in the Agrarian History of Caernarvonshire in the Later Middle Ages", *Trans. Caerns. Hist. Soc.*, I (1939), 20–27.

JONES-PIERCE, 1940 — ——, "Notes on the History of Rural Caernarvonshire in the reign of Elizabeth", *Trans. Caerns. Hist. Soc.*, II (1940), 35–57.

JONES-PIERCE, 1940A — ——, "An Anglesey Crown Rental of the Sixteenth Century", *Bull. Board of Celtic Stud.*, x (1940), 156—76.

JONES-PIERCE, 1941 — ——, "The Growth of Commutation in Gwynedd in the Thirteenth Century", *Bull. Board of Celtic Stud.*, x (1941), 309–32.

JONES-PIERCE, 1942 — ——, "The *Gafael* in Bangor MS 1939", *Trans. Hon. Soc. Cymmrodorion* (1942), 158–88, esp. 162–77.

JONES-PIERCE, 1949 — ——, "Ancient Meirionydd", *Journ. Merioneth Hist. and Rec. Soc.*, I (1949), 12–20.

JONES-PIERCE, 1951 — ——, "Medieval Settlement in Anglesey", *Trans. Ang. Antiq. Soc.* (1951), 1–33.

JONES-PIERCE, 1951A — ——, Foreword to W. J. Slack, *The Lordship of Oswestry, 1393–1607* (1951).

JONES-PIERCE, 1959 — ——, "Agrarian Aspects of the Tribal System in Wales", *Geographie et Histoire Agraires, Annales de l'Est, Memoire no. 21* (Nancy, 1959), 329–37.

JONES-PIERCE, 1959A — ——, "Medieval Cardiganshire—a Study in Social Origins", *Ceredigion*, III (1959), 265–79.

JONES-PIERCE, 1961 ——, "Pastoral and Agricultural Settlements in Early Wales", *Geografiska Annaler*, XLIII (1961), 182–89.

JONES-PIERCE, 1962 ——, "Aber Gwyn Gregin", *Trans. Caerns. Hist. Soc.*, XXIII (1962), 37–43.

JONES-PIERCE, 1963 ——, "Social and Historical Aspects of the Welsh Laws", *Welsh Hist. Rev.*, Welsh Laws Special Number (1963), 33–49.

JONES-PIERCE, 1967 ——, "Landlords in Wales: the Nobility and Gentry", in Joan Thirsk, ed., *The Agrarian History of England and Wales*, IV (1967), 357–81, esp. 366 ff.

MILLER, 1967 R. Miller, "Shiels in the Brecon Beacons", *Folk Life*, V (1967), 107–10.

MORRIS, 1956 B. Morris, "Medieval Platform Sites in East Gower", *Gower*, VII (1956), 40.

PEATE, 1940 I. C. Peate, *The Welsh House, A Study in Folk Culture*, Y Cymmrodor, XLVII, 1940; 3rd ed., Liverpool, 1946.

PRYCE, 1961 W. T. R. Pryce, "Enclosure and Field Patterns in the Banwy Valley", *Montgomery Coll.*, LVII (1961), 23–32.

R.C.A.M., 1964 Royal Commission on Ancient Monuments (Wales and Monmouthshire), *Inventory of Caernarvonshire*, III (1964), CLXXVIII–CLXXX.

REES, 1924 W. Rees, *South Wales and the March, 1284–1415* (1924).

RICHARDS, 1959 M. Richards, "*Hafod* and *hafoty* in Welsh Place Names", *Montgomery Coll.*, LVI (1959), 13–20.

RICHARDS, 1960 ——, "The Irish Settlements in South-West Wales: a Topographical Approach", *Journ. Royal Soc. of Antiq. Ireland*, XC (1960), 133–62, esp. 145–52.

RICHARDS, 1960A ——, "*Meifod, Lluest, Cynhaeafdy* and *Hendre* in Welsh Place Names", *Montgomery Coll.*, LVI (1960), 177–87.

RICHARDS, 1962 ——, "Welsh *Meid(i)r, Moydir*, Irish *Bothar*, 'Lane, Road'", *Lochlann*, II (1962), 128–34.

RICHARDS, 1964 ——, "The Significance of *Is* and *Uwch* in Welsh Commote and Cantref Names", *Welsh Hist. Rev.*, II (1964–65), 9–18.

SAVORY, 1955 H. N. Savory, "Excavations of an Early Iron Age Fortified Settlement on Mynydd Bychan, Llysworney, Glamorgan, 1949–50, part I", *Archaeol. Camb.*, CIII (1955), 85–108, esp. 100–101.

SAVORY, 1956 ——, art. cit., part 2, *Archaeol. Camb.*, CIV (1956), 14–51, esp. 31–34.

SAYCE, 1956   R. U. Sayce, "The Old Summer Pastures, I: a Comparative Study", *Montgomery Coll.*, LIV (1956), 117–45.

SAYCE, 1957   ——, "The Old Summer Pastures, II: Life at the *hafodydd*", *Montgomery Coll.*, LV (1957), 37–86.

SMITH, 1967   P. Smith, "Rural Housing in Wales", in Joan Thirsk, ed., *The Agrarian History of England and Wales*, IV (1967), 767–813, esp. 767–76.

SMITH AND LLOYD, 1964   P. Smith and F. Lloyd, "Plas-ucha, Llangar, Corwen", *Trans. Anc. Mon. Soc.*, XII (1964), 97–112.

SYLVESTER, 1954   D. Sylvester, "Settlement Patterns in Rural Flintshire", *Flint. Hist. Soc. Pub.*, XV (1954), 6–42, esp. 18–26.

SYLVESTER, 1956   ——, "The Rural Landscape of Eastern Montgomeryshire", *Montgomery Coll.*, LIV (1956), 3–26.

SYLVESTER, 1958   ——, "The Common Fields of the Coastlands of Gwent", *Ag. Hist. Rev.*, VI (1958), 9–26.

THOMAS, 1938   R. J. Thomas, *Enwau Afonydd a Nentydd Cymru* (1938).

THOMAS, 1957   J. G. Thomas, "Rural Settlement", in E. G. Bowen, ed., *Wales: A Physical, Historical and Regional Geography* (1957), 141–57, esp. 141–51.

THOMAS, 1957A   W. S. Thomas, "Land Occupation, Ownership and Utilisation in the Parish of Llansantffraid", *Ceredigion*, III (1957), 124–155, esp. 124–129.

THOMAS, 1962   H. J. Thomas, "Recent Excavations in Glamorgan: Barry", *Morgannwg*, VI (1962), 97–98 (interim report).

THOMAS, 1963   ——, "Recent Excavations in Glamorgan: Lower Porthkerry", *Morgannwg*, VII (1963), 127 (interim report).

THOMAS, 1966   H. J. Thomas, "Recent Excavations in Glamorgan: *Uchelolau* (Highlight)", *Morgannwg*, X (1966), 63–66 (interim report).

TURNER, 1964   J. Turner, "The Anthropogenic Factor in Vegetational History: I, Tregaron and Wixall Mosses", *New Phytologist*, LXIII (1964), 73–90, esp. 81–84.

WILLIAMS, 1965   D. Williams, "The Cistercians in Wales", *Archaeol. Camb.*, CXIV (1965), 2–47.

Part Four
Ireland

CHAPTER ELEVEN

The Study of Deserted Medieval Settlements in Ireland (to 1968)

R. E. GLASSCOCK

Lecturer in Geography, The Queen's University, Belfast

I. RURAL SETTLEMENT

Introduction

In the last 30 years there has been a great deal of progress in the study of Irish rural settlement, but there is still very little to show for the medieval period. Most work has been concerned with settlement survivals of one form or another, either with those that have come right through to the present day, for example, the study of rundale communities in Donegal (Evans, 1939), or with those features that were recorded on the first Ordnance Survey maps and have since disappeared, for example, clachans (Proudfoot, 1959). The approach has been very much from the present to the past and on the medieval period there has been little specific work.

There is a number of reasons why the medieval period (here defined as the period between the coming of the Anglo-Normans in 1170 and *c.* 1600) has received so little attention. In the first place relatively few medieval structures survive in the landscape save for churches, monastic buildings, castles and tower houses, most of them now ruinous. Over much of the country the field monuments of the prehistoric and Early Christian periods are not only thicker on the ground, but, on account of their greater antiquity, are more impressive and have attracted far more attention. Medieval archaeology in Ireland is still in its infancy. So far as we know, no small dwellings of the medieval period survive and the "traditional" single-storey whitewashed houses of the Irish countryside may be assigned, for the most part, to the period after 1700. Alongside this paucity of material remains there is the better-known scarcity of medieval documentary material. Admittedly there is much more than has often been presumed but from the settlement viewpoint Ireland has no sources comparable in coverage to the comprehensive lists of settlements that are available for England, say in the Domesday Book of 1086 or the Lay Subsidy of 1334. We therefore lack a point in time or "baseline" in the medieval period when we can see which settlements were already in existence and from which we might measure later changes such as the disappearance of medieval settlements or the arrival of new ones.

A further reason for the neglect of the period is that, understandably, the events of Ireland in the nineteenth century, especially the Famine and its effects, have attracted a great deal of attention. Not only this, but until recently Irish historians have been preoccupied with political and ecclesiastical history at the expense of the social and economic branches. Even now among historians, archaeologists and geographers very few are working on the medieval period. This does not detract from the outstanding contributions of many individuals past and present on specialised aspects of the medieval period: indeed the work of such scholars as Mills, Orpen, Curtis, Gwynn, Leask and Otway-Ruthven stand out the more for being in a difficult and neglected field.

Yet despite their work we still know very little about medieval settlement. Scholars working on settlement survivals and seeking the origins of modern forms have in most cases come up against a blank wall for the period before 1600, and often it has been easier to see prehistoric origins and parallels than medieval ones.

For these reasons the study of medieval settlement in Ireland is at quite a different stage from that in England. But there is every reason for optimism; more attention is now being given to the period and the next twenty years should see considerable advances in our knowledge. But at this stage we are certainly not in a position to say much about "deserted medieval villages", strictly the subject of this book. In Ireland work on this subject has only just begun and of necessity therefore this chapter must concern itself in the main with some of the problems of medieval settlement and the work that lies ahead.

Irish medieval settlement

The forces that created the towns and nucleated villages of the English lowlands were never at work in Ireland. The Romans contemplated invasion but never came; the country was beyond the reach of the Anglo-Saxons and contact with the Scandinavians was limited to the seafarers and traders and not with the settling agricultural peoples. The village as it is known in England is, therefore, absent from most of Ireland. Leaving aside estate-villages of the eighteenth and nineteenth centuries, it is only in the south and east of the country that we have any settlements which in form and function resemble English lowland villages; these were founded by the Anglo-Normans in the twelfth and thirteenth centuries. Therefore the term "village" must be used with care in the Irish context; much more so the term "deserted medieval village" of which we have as yet recognised so few true examples.

We have to face the fact that we still do not know the nature of settlement in Ireland between 1100 and the Tudor plantations. At this stage all we can do is to discuss the various types of settlement and speculate about their roles in the medieval period. To this end we will consider raths, possible associated clustered settlements, clachans and Anglo-Norman settlements (including deserted sites).

Raths

For the pre-Norman period the most abundant evidence of settlement comes from the raths or ring-forts[1] of which 30,000 or so still survive.   Excavation of some 60 of these sites over the last 40 years has shown that these were small circular homesteads containing flimsy timber dwellings and associated buildings (Proudfoot, 1961, 101–04). Their occupation may be dated in broad terms to the first millennium A.D. with some showing signs of earlier occupation and some later.

Although the distribution of raths in Ireland is widespread (see McCourt's map in Evans, 1964, Fig. 3) the density varies from place to place.   We must remind ourselves that this is a map of survivals and that many had no doubt disappeared by the time of the first edition of the Ordnance Survey six-inch map of the period 1830–42.   There are many examples of the sites of raths being marked on these maps.   Even so, we can still ask questions about the medieval period from the nineteenth-century distribution. In some areas, such as parts of Munster and Connacht, raths are so thick on the ground that it is tempting to suggest that no other type of settlement was ever a serious competitor.   Nucleated or clustered settlements may well have been limited to monastic communities in the Early Christian period and to planted towns in the later period.

In other parts of the country, such as Leinster, where raths are much thinner on the ground the likelihood of alternative forms of settlement is much stronger.   Or were raths just as thick on the ground in this area before the spread of Anglo-Norman settlement over the south-east of the country?   The distribution of raths raises many questions so far unanswered, indeed many so far unasked.   Does the varying density of raths reflect fundamental differences in rate of survival, in density of population, in social organisation, or in local economies?   Is it a combination of these?   Did the settlement of the south-east take a different form from elsewhere in the pre-Norman period or were the raths gradually destroyed by the process of Anglo-Norman settlement and later agricultural improvement?   Or again, were raths built and occupied until much later in the west, thus making them thicker on the ground?   In discussing medieval settlement a crucial question is how much were raths in use in the medieval period?

Clearly the terminal dating of the occupation of the raths is a critical problem. Dr. V. B. Proudfoot has pointed out the difficulties and says that the range of dates of occupation can be assessed adequately on fewer than half the excavated rath sites (Proudfoot, 1961, 99).   Despite this he could say that raths were farmsteads belonging in general terms to the first millennium A.D. and that they remained in use "until the coming of the Anglo-Normans in the twelfth century" (p. 94).   Yet in the same paper he states that on some sites in Antrim, Down and Armagh "terminal datings have been fixed within close limits by medieval pottery occurring in late occupation-levels" (p. 99) (having previously defined "medieval" as the period following the Anglo-Norman invasions, p. 94).   He also quotes the example of a rath at Ballingarry Down, Co. Limerick, where there was final occupation in the medieval period.

There is obviously some confusion here.   It would be more true to say that while raths belong primarily to the first millennium A.D. the occupation of many, and perhaps

---

[1] There is a problem of terminology here that has gone on far too long.   Raths/ring-forts are simple circular enclosures surrounded by one or more ditches; the commonest have a bank inside and a single ditch (see O'Riordain, 1942 and later editions).   Archaeologists in the south of Ireland call these *ring-forts* while in the north they are called *raths*.   (For conflicting views on these terms see O'Kelly, 1950, 321, and Proudfoot, 1961, 94.)   For the sake of uniformity the term rath is used in this chapter.

even the building of some, continued well after the late-twelfth century. While we know that the Anglo-Normans raised many raths for their own use as mottes and as the sites for the stone castles, there is nothing to suggest a widespread desertion of raths at the time. Moreover, the lack of datable material, especially pottery, in the upper levels of raths need not necessarily mean that they were not occupied in the medieval period. It is very likely that pottery was not in general use on such sites, and for this reason we should leave open the possibility of much later occupation of the raths than has hitherto been thought.

In a more recent paper on two raths in Co. Clare, Mr. E. Rynne has tentatively suggested a date for the construction of "Thady's Fort" of 1600, and a similar one for the nearby rath at Garrynamona (Rynne, 1962–64, 257 and 266). While he finds it difficult to back up his suggested dates of construction with evidence from other sites, there is more to support at least the late occupation of raths both in Clare and elsewhere, though one of the examples he gives, Tullahoge, Co. Tyrone, the crowning place of the O Neills, must be considered a special case (Illustrated in Hayes–McCoy, 1964, Plate V and 8–9). My feeling, however, is that the survival of such a large number of raths, even allowing for their protection by local folklore, suggests that many were occupied until the end of the medieval period and that they formed an important element in the settlement of medieval Ireland. Only continued excavation is likely to strengthen or refute what at best could be described as a hunch.

Associated clustered settlement

We must now turn from the raths or single homesteads to ideas about associated clustered settlement. In a detailed examination of Co. Down, Dr. Proudfoot showed that raths were thicker on the ground in the west of the county and that there were very few on areas of good land in the east, especially on the Ards peninsula (Proudfoot, 1959, Fig. 1). He concluded that other forms of settlement may have co-existed and suggested that perhaps these were clustered, undefended settlements, occupied by people of inferior social status to the free farmers of the raths. In suggesting this he follows Prof. E. E. Evans (Evans, 1956, 231) who, drawing an analogy from the settlements of north Wales (Jones, 1953) suggested that raths were the homes of freemen and that bondmen lived in nucleated settlements, an idea hinted at by earlier workers (including Duignan, 1944, 128). Prof. Evans has recently asserted this in more definite terms: . . . "Unlike the freemen in their enclosed homesteads, they [the bondmen] must have lived in undefended settlements which have left no mark on the landscape and which archaeology has so far failed almost entirely to discover" (Evans, 1964, 236).

The idea of associated clustered settlements has also been backed from other branches of study. It has the support of the linguistic evidence of the late Mr. S. MacAirt (Proudfoot, 1959, 113) who thought that the term baile (Anglicised form bally) must be pre-Goidelic in origin and that it referred to clustered settlements in which lived cultivators of the lower strata of society. In addition, Prof. Otway-Ruthven in her studies of medieval agriculture (Otway-Ruthven, 1951, 3), states that where betaghs, or unfree tenants, are found in any number they seem to exist separately from other members of the agricultural community living in family groups and holding definite townlands.

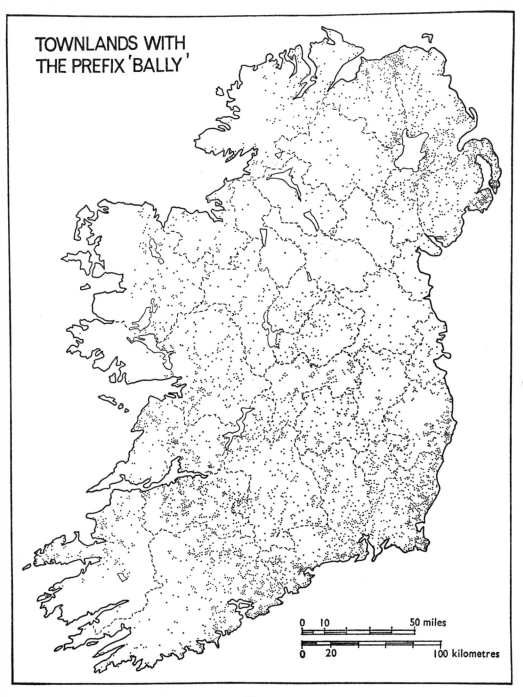

TOWNLANDS WITH
THE PREFIX 'BALLY'

0 10   50 miles

0   20   100 kilometres

Fig. 42

In medieval documents the term *baile* is equated with *ton* and *villa*, both terms implying, in the English sense, some form of nucleated settlement. Following up this line of enquiry by plotting those townlands in Co. Down whose names contain the element *bally*, Dr. Proudfoot was able to show fairly convincingly how the rath and *baile* settlements occupied complementary areas and therefore might have co-existed (Proudfoot, 1959, 113–15). And in broad terms this is true of the country as a whole. A map of the townlands with the prefix *bally* (Fig. 42) shows a broadly complementary picture to the raths. Names are thicker in the south and east where raths are fewer; there are particular concentrations of *bally* names in the coastal areas of Wicklow, Wexford, Waterford and Cork (? suggesting a Viking or Norman origin). Conversely *bally* names are rare in a great slab of country where raths are thick on the ground, i.e. in Tyrone, Fermanagh, Leitrim, Sligo, Monaghan, Cavan, Roscommon and Longford. On the other hand, taken county by county almost every kind of relationship could be demonstrated! Some counties have many of one element and few of the other, and vice versa; Dublin and Meath have hardly any of either. A thorough comparison and analysis of the two maps (and one of clachans) is nevertheless something that ought to be done.

If the so-called associated clustered settlements did not exist then we are wasting our time. If, on the other hand, they did, and it is hard to sweep aside the assertions of several scholars, why cannot we find them? When and why did they disappear? and why do they leave no trace? A number of possibilities exist. The first, is that the clustered settlements disappeared leaving no trace. If they were undefended and had no need of banks or enclosures for cattle (which is hard to believe) there are not likely to be surviving earthworks. Timber or mud buildings leave no surface expression, as has been shown many times by the clear archaeological evidence of wooden structures in raths that had no topographic expression before excavation. Our best hope, therefore, is that such settlements would show up from the air in soil- or crop-marks but to date this has not happened.

A second possibility is that clustered settlements of earlier periods dwindled to single farms. There is, as yet, no archaeological or other evidence to support such a hypothesis; there are no obvious signs of shrinkage indicated by earthworks such as on English "shrunk" village sites. But again, if the buildings were of wood or mud they could have gone without trace. The single farm is the dominant settlement form over much of rural Ireland today. While this form may be of some antiquity as the successor to the enclosed rath homesteads, Prof. Evans has shown that in Donegal at least, the single farm is a recent type of settlement that developed with the break-up of common-field systems (Evans, 1939 and 1939A). Whether this is true for other parts of the country we do not yet know, but we may presume that the many single farms of eastern Ireland were a logical outcome of the enclosure that went on piecemeal and unrecorded in the seventeenth and eighteenth centuries. There is certainly nothing to suggest that the single farm represents a degenerate stage of medieval or earlier clustered settlement.

Clachans

A third possibility is that the clustered settlements did *not* disappear, but that they were limited to certain areas and they were the forerunners of the farm-clusters or clachans that existed side-by-side with single farms at the beginning of the nineteenth century when they were first comprehensively recorded by the Ordnance Survey. These "clachans", as they are now known in geographical literature (Proudfoot, 1959) were locally called "towns" or "villages". Many clachans carried such place-names on the map; for example, on Wexford six-inch Sheet 15, there is Newtown, Barrack Village and Glen Village. But clachans, although nucleated, cannot be called villages in the English sense; their typical form in the early-nineteenth century was an irregular cluster of farmhouses and outbuildings, small by comparison with English villages and usually having less than a dozen dwellings, though some had as many as forty houses or more, for example, Rathlackan, Co. Mayo, still with 56 families in 1918 (Evans, 1957, 24–25). Clachans rarely had a planned geographical centre nor did they focus on a central space or church as is common in English villages, the implication being that they were not planned at the outset but grew sporadically in a haphazard way. The only resemblance that clachans must have had to English medieval villages (and do have even now in a few cases) was in appearance which was often remarkably medieval. All buildings were dwellings or out-buildings, single storey and usually thatched; even now there are seldom shops or retail services in such farm-clusters. Inhabitants were tied to the land and the land was farmed in partnership from the clachan.

The distribution of clachans in the early-nineteenth century has been recorded by Mr. T. W. Freeman (Freeman, 1957, Fig. 5, 32), and by Dr. D. McCourt who has kindly allowed me to refer to his more detailed unpublished map of clachans, 1832–40 (McCourt, 1950). These maps show the distribution of clachans at one point in time; one hundred years earlier the pattern may have been very different, for as Dr. McCourt has shown, this was a very flexible form of settlement. A clachan could grow in the course of two generations and it could disappear just as rapidly. In broad terms their distribution in the early-nineteenth century was peripheral. They were much thicker on the ground in the north and west with particular concentrations in the lowlands of north Antrim and north Derry, coastal Donegal, Mayo, Galway, Clare and the peninsulas of Kerry. In the south and east there were concentrations in east Down, the western fringes of the Wicklows, south Wexford, south Kilkenny and Waterford. Over much of inland Munster and Leinster there were only isolated examples.

The explanation of the distribution of clachans is a subject in itself and one on which Dr. McCourt is working. Here we can only ask questions of relevance to the medieval period. Why, for example, are there so few clachans over large parts of the south and east, an area which broadly corresponds to the Anglo-Norman territory of the thirteenth century? It is tempting to suggest that in some areas clachans existed but disappeared under the influences of the Anglo-Normans, but the existence of clachans in such large numbers in such Norman strongholds as south-east Down and south-east Wexford puts a damper on this idea. Dr. McCourt has shown how the clachans coincide with the important arable areas of the eighteenth and nineteenth centuries, and that their distribution may reflect differences in regional economies. They existed in the tillage areas but less so in the grassland; thus they were absent from much of the midland belt from Monaghan to Cork, including the grazing counties of Meath and Westmeath, Kildare, Leix and Offaly, Tipperary and Limerick. But these counties had not always been in such extensive grassland.   While we know of the conversion of land to pasture in the eighteenth century, grassland must have replaced more extensive tillage some time in the later Middle Ages, although unfortunately we have not got the documentary evidence for such a change-over as that for the swing from arable to pasture in midland England.   Perhaps clachans were formerly more widespread in Munster and Leinster but disappeared early as a result of changes in land use?

From the point of view of this paper the most important question is whether clachans existed in the medieval period.   Frankly we are no nearer an answer now than we were ten years ago when the search for origins led to the excavation of a clachan at Murphystown, Co. Down (Buchanan *et al.*, 1958).   The results were inconclusive; while occupation of the site dated back to Early Christian or medieval times it was impossible to say what form the settlement took at that time.   As there has been no follow-up to this excavation we are still no nearer saying whether or not clachans were a feature of the medieval landscape of Ireland.   The farthest we can push them back with confidence is the seventeenth century (McCourt, 1954–55).

Having been side-tracked on to the clachan we must now return to the possibility that the clustered settlements of the earlier period, referred to by Prof. Evans and others, did not in fact disappear but were the forerunners of the later clachans.   If this is so we would expect to find some correlation over the country as a whole between the distribution of the *bally* element in place-names and the distribution of clachans.   When the maps are compared we do get a striking similarity in some areas, for example, in east Down, the north-west corner of Antrim, south-east Wexford, south Kilkenny and the Dingle peninsula.   In these areas one might legitimately suggest that earlier betagh settlements were the forerunners of the later clachans.   On the other hand, in some areas there is no correlation; some places with clachans have very few *bally* names, for example, north Derry, north Donegal, north Armagh, Galway and Mayo.   Similarly some areas of *bally* names are those where few clachans were recorded in the nineteenth century, e.g. Westmeath, Leix, Offaly, Kildare, Tipperary, Kilkenny, Limerick and east Cork, or in other words, exactly those areas where we have already speculated that nucleated settlement might have existed but disappeared before the end of the eighteenth century.

At this stage it would be honest to say that one could use the maps to prove anything. No hypothesis could or should be advanced before we have made detailed county-by-county comparisons of the distribution of these various elements taking into account regional differences of economy and social organisation.   In short we must first know what our maps mean; in this field there is a great deal to be done at a local level.

In passing, however, it is worth noting that most clachans disappeared in the nineteenth century, part-and-parcel of the upheaval and depopulation caused by the Famine, the disappearance of rundale, and the enclosure and reallocation of land. Some survive today on the Atlantic seaboard and locally in other parts of the country. The desertion of clachans in the nineteenth century is a topic special to Ireland, and it is one that should be tackled now while hundreds of deserted examples may be identified and while material remains are still visible on the surface.   Indeed it is time that some of the better sites were taken into State charge.

Summarising, therefore, this long and tortuous discussion, it is suggested that many raths were occupied in the medieval period and that there is a strong likelihood that small clustered settlements co-existed with them in certain areas both in the pre-Norman and post-Norman periods. Whether or not these were clachans in the later sense must be left wide open. Into this settlement pattern were intruded the "new" settlements of the Anglo-Normans.

Anglo-Norman settlement

The Anglo-Normans under Robert fitz Stephen landed at Bannow Bay, Co. Wexford in 1169, and by 1200 most of the south and east of the country was in their hands. The first stage in the Norman occupation of land was the establishment of local strongpoints, usually earth-built mottes. In some cases raths in prominent positions were raised and adapted for the purpose; even the great passage grave of Knowth in the Boyne valley was apparently adapted to a Norman motte. Between 1200 and 1220 stone castles were being built at crucial positions at the centre of lordships and at strategic river crossings (e.g. Trim, Carlow, Athlone), and around the coast (e.g. Dundrum, Carrickfergus, Limerick, Carlingford). But the Norman conquest of Ireland was not only a military conquest; it was accompanied by new settlers from England and Wales, and as Prof. Otway-Ruthven has suggested (Otway-Ruthven, 1968, 109) the settlement of Ireland at this period was part of the wider European movement of population growth, expansion and colonisation of the twelfth and thirteenth centuries. Although little work has been done on the economic and social history of the period it is likely that Ireland's development at this period followed the broad European pattern of expansion and prosperity in the thirteenth century followed by stagnation and recession in the fourteenth. Certainly, if town foundation is an index of commercial prosperity, Ireland was doing well in the thirteenth century and the decline of Anglo-Norman power in the fourteenth must surely be seen as part of a common European experience and certainly not as the result of the Bruce invasions, the traditional explanation for the wane of Anglo-Norman power.

Settlers moved into Ireland between 1170 and 1300 but there is no means of telling their numbers. Prof. Otway-Ruthven, working on the limited number of manorial documents of the period, has shown the high percentage of English and Welsh surnames on many manors, and infers, with some qualifications, a foreign origin (Otway-Ruthven, 1965), although we do not know the number of settlers involved. The Anglo-Norman territory, which covered roughly two-thirds of the country by the mid-thirteenth century, was divided into manors under tenants-in-chief. The Anglo-Normans developed the coastal trading centres such as Dublin, Cork and Limerick already selected by the Scandinavians, and founded numerous inland towns. Manors were created on English lines and a large number of settlements were created; many were given borough status yet could have been no more than large villages in the English sense. Thus for the first time in Ireland we have true towns, and settlements related in form and function to the villages of the English lowlands. Many such villages have survived especially around Dublin; in some the common-field systems were still detectable in the eighteenth century, for example, at Rathcoole, Dalkey, Saggart and Clondalkin (Otway-Ruthven, 1951, 6). Others did not survive and in the study of deserted medieval villages in Ireland the Norman foundations are the true starting point. Our first job must be to list all such Norman settlements from documentary evidence followed by their identification and field survey. Where later desertion is definitely established, terminology is a problem. A nomenclature for such sites is therefore suggested here for the first time, and that is that where there is definite evidence of burghal status such settlements should be called "deserted Norman rural-boroughs" to distinguish them clearly from true chartered towns and from other villages.

An excellent example of a deserted Norman rural-borough is Kilmaclenine, Co. Cork (for location and details see Appendix), established as a borough by the Bishop of Cloyne c. 1238 (Otway-Ruthven, 1968, 117). Although it had 27 burgesses in the middle of the fourteenth century it must have been primarily an agricultural settlement. This site was kindly brought to my notice in 1967 by Mr. C. J. F. MacCarthy of Cork who has worked on its history. Nothing is to be seen today of the medieval rural-borough save for the curtain wall of a small rectangular castle perched high and dramatically on a Cashel-like outcrop overlooking green fields. The church is ruinous two fields away; there are no visible earthworks nor has air photography given any clue, so far, as to the exact location of the dwellings of the borough. If the site can be pin-pointed, as I hope it will be, Kilmaclenine could be a most important site for archaeo-logical investigation. It is one of the few deserted Norman rural-boroughs for which there is documentary evidence of its burgess population at one point in time in the medieval period, and while the date of desertion is not known it is a site that offers great possibilities for the archaeological study of the dwellings of Norman settlers. Some other important sites are listed in the Appendix.

It is in the Anglo-Norman villages and rural-boroughs that our best hopes lie for the identification and investigation of true deserted medieval villages in Ireland. In this respect air photography has a particularly important role to play and it is con-sidered briefly at this point.

Air photography and progress to date

Air photography is far more important in the study of medieval settlement in Ireland than it is in England for the simple reason that we have not got a good documentary coverage to give us a lead in tracing medieval sites. In England the main role of air photography is to back up the evidence of documents and field survey; only occasionally does the air photograph reveal a site for the first time. In Ireland, as in Scotland, where there are fewer documents and where field survey has only just begun the air photograph has a primary role to play. The greatest strides in the study of deserted medieval settlements will come in the first place from systematic and regular air survey of the Irish landscape. In some ways this will be more difficult than in lowland England. Weather conditions are generally less favourable and as there is less arable land there is less chance of soil- and crop-marks showing up. But thanks to Dr. J. K. S. St. Joseph we are already beginning to see the fruits of air reconnaissance (see, for example, Plates 29, 30 and 31). In the last six years he has built up an impressive collec-tion of air photographs of the country, available for inspection by arrangement both at Cambridge and the National Museum, Dublin. But Dr. St. Joseph's limited pro-gramme per year in Ireland has only scratched the surface, so to speak. We are now dependent upon his annual visits and if for any reason these should be discontinued it will be a serious blow to progress. We can only hope that he will continue to come or that he will find his Irish counterpart based in this country who can devote more time to much-needed survey. Certainly all efforts to promote air survey by different institutions or organisations should be welcomed.

The next steps are identification, ground survey, and wherever possible, excavation. At present work is being concentrated on Co. Tipperary where field survey and air photography are revealing many sites with earthworks, although it must be admitted that in many cases we have no proof that such sites were flourishing settlements in the medieval period. Some of the sites are just as likely to be Early Christian in date. Earthworks of house-sites are for the most part conspicuous by their absence and the most prominent features on many sites are puzzling sinuous banks which may be pre-Norman in origin. What is certain is that fieldwork focused on ruined medieval castles and churches is now producing many sites with earthworks. They represent clustered settlements of some kind: whether they are pre-Norman monastic settlements, Norman villages or rural-boroughs, deserted clachans or the elusive clustered settlements of the betaghs we are not yet in a position to say. But a start has been made and although the work is at an early stage I think we can already say that Anglo-Norman nucleated settlement was more extensive than was formerly thought, even in an area as far from the Pale as Tipperary.

II. THE PEASANT-HOUSE

The study of the peasant-house in Ireland has been a very active branch of study since Mr. A. Campbell laid the foundations of the scientific approach just before the war (Campbell, 1935 and 1937). There is no doubt that the rapid disappearance of traditional houses over the last thirty years (hastened on of late in the west by government subsidies for new houses) has brought a sense of urgency to recording, classification and the search for origins. Following Dr. Campbell, Prof. Evans and Prof. Danaher have been recording and writing for thirty years, and others such as Dr. Lucas, Dr. McCourt, Mr. Gailey, and Mr. Buchanan have added much information on specific house types and methods of building, but, as with settlement, almost all this study is based on survivals. The search for origins comes up against a similar blank wall about 1600 and the few papers which have been devoted specifically to origins (e.g. Aalen, 1966) have been forced entirely into speculation.

We know more about prehistoric and Dark Age structures than we do about those of the period 1100–1600. This is largely the result of more archaeological work on these periods and in particular the large amount done over the last twenty years on raths. There are general summaries on house-types and other buildings found in the raths (O'Kelly, 1950 and Proudfoot, 1961). The only important excavation of a medieval peasant-house *per se* was that at Caherguillamore, Co. Limerick, in the autumn of 1940 (O'Riordain and Hunt, 1942). It is interesting to note that this excavation came about the same time as Prof. Jope was doing pioneer work on medieval houses at Great Beere in Devon, but whereas in England this line of enquiry has been taken up with tremendous results by the Deserted Medieval Village Research Group and others, in Ireland there has been no follow-up to this early work.

At Caherguillamore two houses of the dozen or so clearly visible on the surface were excavated; both were of the rectangular, central hearth type, with clay-bonded stone wall-foundations. The walls of the earlier and larger of the two, House I (externally 43 ft. × 20 ft.) had a wattle lining, an internal partition, and a doorway on the long side slightly towards one end. There was another doorway, blocked, on the opposite side at the opposite end. Although it is not suggested in the report, this may have been blocked up when House II was built so close to it. The external corners of the walls were very rounded giving the plan "almost the form of an 'oval rectangle'". House II was a smaller structure (externally 32 ft. 3 in × 18 ft. 3 in.); curiously, although the walls were straighter and had squared corners, their construction was inferior to those of House I. Finds included coarse and glazed medieval pottery and generally suggested a span of occupation between the fourteenth and sixteenth centuries. There were no earlier structures beneath. Although the report describes these two houses as of the long-house type this is only in the sense of the plans, where the length is approximately twice the width. There is nothing to suggest that these dwellings were of a byre-house type, as they lacked opposite doors and a cross passage.

This was a most important excavation considering its date; the site is still among the most important for the investigation of medieval houses. There are more houses there to be dug. There is a certain amount of documentary evidence for the site, its medieval date is already known, and it has pottery, which is hard to come by on many other sites. We can only hope it is a matter of time before someone takes on where O'Riordain and Hunt left off.

Liathmore-Mochoemog, Co. Tipperary, is another site where excavation in the 1930's produced rectangular peasant-houses, but these were of seventeenth-century date (Leask and Macalister, 1945–48, 3). (Recent identification of the rim sherd from Site A, Fig. 5.1, as North Devon gravel-tempered ware confirms the excavators' tentative dating.) We are currently excavating new areas of this site but in the first season (1968) medieval houses have not shown up. We also have seventeenth- and eighteenth-century structures but none of their medieval predecessors. Another rectangular house, probably of the seventeenth century, and very similar in construction to those at Caherguillamore was excavated in a quadrant of a rath at Shannon airport (Rynne, 1962–64, 256).

In Ireland we are lucky in that we can draw on the findings of our colleagues in England and we should be able to test our sites against some of the general hypotheses that they are now able to put forward, based on the experience of a large number of sites. As yet we have no evidence on changing building techniques, the life-expectancy of the peasant-house, the associated property boundaries, nor in fact on any of the general issues raised by twenty years of excavation on medieval houses in England. For example, we cannot yet say whether houses of the Caherguillamore type evolved from earlier types here or whether they are an Anglo-Norman introduction. Superficially the Caherguillamore houses might appear to be in the middle of a continuum beginning with the rectangular neolithic house at Lough Gur and coming right through to surviving old houses in Co. Limerick (Danaher, 1945). But this cannot be said until some of the gaps are filled. At the moment we must infer from the lack of remains that all domestic houses of the Early Christian and Viking periods were of timber, mud or wattle (as those being excavated at High Street, Dublin). The timber or mud tradition may have carried on unbroken in many parts of the country, hence the conspicuous lack of stone houses on deserted settlements. In other areas timber and mud was replaced by stone. But when and why? In the thirteenth century as in much of England?

Looking ahead, the choice of sites for excavation is going to be difficult. In England the sites which have been naturally attractive for excavation are those where the house foundations are most obvious; the excavator at least knows where to start even if he does not know where it will lead! Here we have as yet only a few sites where a number of houses are obvious; Caherguillamore and Newtown Jerpoint, Co. Kilkenny, are examples. My feeling is that such clear indications of houses probably means late desertion, sixteenth and seventeenth centuries, and that it is a matter of luck whether medieval houses turn up below. In England the effort is now beginning to swing away from the sites with clear foundations to the more problematic Midland and East Anglian sites where there is little surface expression, or even to the "apparently featureless areas" on sites with strong earthworks. The majority of the Irish sites look as if they will be like this; everything suggests that most houses were of timber and or clay and that they will be hard to locate and even harder to excavate. Sites with hollow ways and banks must have had houses and we must find them; four places to try would be Newtown Earls, Co. Kilkenny, and Moyaliff, Kilconnell, and Kiltinan, all in Co. Tipperary.

CHAPTER TWELVE

I. Gazetteer of Deserted Towns, Rural-Boroughs, and Nucleated Settlements in Ireland

II. Select Bibliography, Ireland

R. E. GLASSCOCK

Lecturer in Geography, The Queen's University, Belfast

I. GAZETTEER OF DESERTED TOWNS, RURAL-BOROUGHS AND NUCLEATED SETTLEMENTS

The following is a preliminary list of deserted towns, deserted rural-boroughs, and deserted sites where there is some evidence (from maps, documents or earthworks) to suggest that they were formerly medieval nucleated settlements. A list of Norman rural-boroughs which are now very small is included for their possible value for archaeological investigation. Many sites with earthworks that we know of from air photographs are not included here, either because we cannot be certain that they are of medieval date or because they may be something other than a settlement, such as a monastic site or a large fortification.

After each place-name details are given in the following order: number of the O.S. (Ireland) half-inch sheet, National Grid (Ireland) reference (sub-zone letter followed by co-ordinates); number of the six-inch O.S. sheet (these are numbered by county, e.g. Co. Wexford 45 or Co. Limerick 16, etc.) and whether the site is on the W. or E. half of the sheet, e.g. 45E; Cambridge University (St. Joseph) air photograph number and year, if available.

Deserted Anglo-Norman towns

Co. Kilkenny, NEWTOWN JERPOINT; 19 S 570403; 28W; AJQ 5–7 (1964)
2 m. SW. of Thomastown on the opposite side of the Little Arrigle river from Jerpoint abbey. Town founded *c.* 1200 (Nova Villa de Jeriponte) and probably deserted finally in the seventeenth century. See W. J. Pilsworth, "Newtown Jerpoint", *Old Kilkenny Review*, X (1958), 31–35, which includes an enlarged version of the detailed plan of the town as recorded on the first edition of the O.S. six-inch, where about 25 houses are shown. The ruined church is still standing and there is a circular cross-base (perhaps

the market cross) lying in the graveyard. An improving farmer about 1840 gathered up the stone foundations of the houses into large heaps, some of which completely obscure the position of the houses as shown on the O.S. plan. Many foundations are nevertheless clearly visible with their accompanying burgage plots. No proper excavation has yet been done here. The site is unique and should be put in State charge.

Co. Roscommon, RINDOWN; 12 N 004541; 46W
11 m. SE. of Roscommon, on a peninsula jutting out into Lough Rea. Said to be the site of a town fortified in 1251 (for description see *Shell Guide*, 2nd ed., 346). The site comprises the ruins of a thirteenth-century castle, a medieval church nearby, and a remarkable fortified wall with central gate and towers across the neck of the peninsula. Nothing remains of other buildings within the area of the town but there are heaps of stones as at Newtown Jerpoint which may represent the gathering-up of stone foundations by an improving farmer when the present fields were laid out.

Co. Tipperary, ATHASSEL; 18 S 011365; 68W; ATA 52–56 (1967)
1½ m. S. of Golden on the W. bank of the Suir. Site dominated by the magnificent ruin of the Augustinian priory of St. Edmund founded about 1200. A town which grew up around the priory was burned in 1319 and again in 1329–30. (See Lewis, 1837, I, 81 and *Shell Guide*, 2nd ed., 297; original sources not known to me.) Dr. St. Joseph confirms from recent air photography that there are extensive signs of the site in adjacent fields to the priory but these are hard to distinguish on the ground.

Co. Westmeath, KILBIXY; 12 N 320615; 11W; APH 6–9 (1966) and ATF 79–82 (1967)
9 m. NW. of Mullingar. 1838 six-inch O.S. marks "Site of Kilbixy town" in Baronstown demesne, with ruined structures named. Baronstown church and Kilbixy motte to N. According to Lewis, 1837, II, 52, a medieval town that was in ruins before the end of the eighteenth century. Earthworks confirmed by air photographs; site not yet visited at time of writing.

Co. Wexford, BANNOW; 23 S 823072; 45E
5 m. SSW. of Wellington Bridge. Landing place of the Anglo-Normans in 1169; said to be the first Norman corporate town in Ireland. No evidence of a charter but later refs. to burgage rents, etc. (Lewis, 1837, I, 183). Small church is all that remains, the rest overwhelmed by drifting sand before the end of the seventeenth century, although it continued to send two members to the Irish Parliament up to 1800.

Co. Wexford, CLONMINES; 23 S 843129; 45E
1½ m. S. of Wellington Bridge at head of Bannow Bay. A medieval port; like Bannow it appears not to have had a charter but there are later refs. to burgages (Lewis, 1837, I, 372), and like Bannow it was in ruins before the end of the seventeenth century. The ruins are extensive and very impressive and include four small castles and three churches. Fields around are ploughed but many foundations are visible. Incredible that it is not yet in State charge.

Deserted Anglo-Norman rural-boroughs

Co. Cork, KILMACLENINE; 21 R 505062; 24E; ATD 75–78 (1967)
3 m. SW. of Buttevant. Founded as a borough by the Bishop of Cloyne *c.* 1238.
Twenty-seven burgesses in the middle of the fourteenth century (Otway-Ruthven, 1968,
117). Ruined castle and church, and seventeenth-century fortified house. No earthworks visible. Important site considering available documentary material.

Co. Down, GREENCASTLE; 9 J 247117; 57W
5 m. SW. of Kilkeel. Thirteenth-century borough already in decline by 1333 (E. M.
Jope, ed. (1966), 103 and 106–07). Exact site not known; presumed to be in vicinity
of the castle or the mound (? motte) 400 yards W.

Co. Kildare, ARDSCULL; 16 S 726977; 35E
4 m. NE. of Athy. Burgess settlement (160 burgages, *C.I.P.M.*, II, 251 quoted in
Russell, 1948, 352: also Otway-Ruthven, 1965, 79). Motte remains, skirted by Naas
to Athy road, Silbury-fashion. 1837 six-inch O.S. shows a few houses along the road
and Ardscull House 1 m. SE. with graveyard nearby.

Co. Kildare, DUNFIERTH; 16 N 777381; 4W
2 m. S. of Innfield, Co. Meath. Burgesses at Dunfert (Russell, 1948, 353 and Otway-
Ruthven, 1965, 79). 1838 six-inch O.S. shows Dunfierth church and site of castle with
Dunfierth House ⅓ m. N.

Co. Kildare, DUNMANOGE; 19 S 729831; 39E
(Formerly Mounmohennok.) 7 m. S. of Athy. Burgess settlement (Otway-Ruthven,
1959, 182 and map). 1837 six-inch O.S. shows isolated church and graveyard; town-
land empty except for four scattered farms.

Co. Kilkenny, NEWTOWN (EARLS); 18 S 463438; 27W
2½ m. W. of Kells on N. bank of King's river. No proof yet of burgesses here, but
earthworks suggest a more extensive settlement than that at cross-roads. 1839 six-inch
O.S. shows isolated church (medieval and now a ball court!) and castle ¼ m. away from
modern settlement. Fine hollow-way leads from the church down to the river, with
possible house-sites on both sides.

Co. Limerick, GLENOGRA; 17 R 595149; 31E; ATD 31–32 (1967)
4 m. NW. of Bruff on E. bank of Camoge river. About 120 burgages here in 1298
(Otway-Ruthven, 1965, 82). Remains of a stone castle and medieval church of St.
Nicholas. 1840 six-inch O.S. shows Fair Green. Ground survey shows only slight
indications of earthworks, mostly in large field S. of church.

Co. Tipperary, MOYALIFF; 18 S 042560; 46E
6 m. SW. of Thurles on E. bank of Clodiagh river. 62 burgesses named in *c.* 1305;
settlement precarious under Irish pressure by 1338 (Otway-Ruthven, 1965, 81). One
large house today with ruined castle in yard; isolated ruined church in field to N. No

visible earthworks; land improved.   Potentially a very important site considering documentary evidence and hint of fourteenth-century partial desertion.

Co. Wicklow, BALLINACLOGH (formerly Weyporous); 16/T 278920; 31W
3 m. W. of Wicklow.   Burgesses here (Otway-Ruthven, 1965, 84, footnote 49) but size not known.   1838 six-inch O.S. shows no sign of a settlement.   Ruined castle only.

Anglo-Norman rural-boroughs now very small

Co. Kildare, ARDREE; 16/S 687925; 35W
1 m. S. of the Norman town of Athy on E. side of Barrow river.   Shown as a burgage settlement on Otway-Ruthven's map of Kildare, c. 1300 (1959).   Motte and few houses.

Co. Kildare, GLASSELY; 16/S 756982; 32W
5 m. NE. of Athy.   Burgage settlement on map of Kildare, c. 1300 (supra).   1837 six-inch O.S. shows demesne, corn-mill and few houses.

Co. Kildare, TIPPER; 16/N 918185; 19E
2 m. E. of Norman town of Naas.   Burgage settlement on map of Kildare, c. 1300 (supra).   1837 six-inch OS. shows a few houses, church in ruins.

Co. Tipperary, ARDMAYLE; 18/S 058457; 52E
A small settlement 4 m. NNW. of Cashel on E. side of the Suir.   Perfect river-side site for Norman burgage settlement.   (Burgesses mentioned in *C.I.P.M.*, VIII, 119, listed by Russell, 1948, 352).   Remains of a motte and medieval church.

Co. Tipperary, LISRONAGH; 18/S 201295; 77W
Now a small cross-roads settlement, 4 m. S. of Norman walled town of Fethard. Castle in ruins.   About 48 burgesses in 1333 (Otway-Ruthven, 1965, 81–82).   Ref., E. Curtis (1935–37), 41–76.

Co. Tipperary, MOYCARKY; 18/S 140530; 47E; APD 36–37 (1966)
Very small village 4 m. S. of Thurles.   No proof of burgesses as yet.   Ruins of castle and medieval church: field SE. of castle has earthworks.   39 English tenants and 9 Irish in 1304: for extent of manor see Otway-Ruthven, 1965, 81.

Co. Wicklow, DONAGHMORE; 16/S 923941; 21E
Small settlement 3 m. S. of Donard.   Burgage settlement on map of Kildare, c. 1300 (supra), and stated to be a settlement that had already failed by c. 1303 (Otway-Ruthven, 1959, 183).

Deserted sites where there is some evidence to suggest that places were formerly medieval nucleated settlements (? villages)

Co. Kilkenny, STONECARTHY (Plate 29); 19/S 522414; 27E; AIF 43–44 (1963)
4 m. W. of Thomastown.   Discovered by air photography, 1963.   On ground a hollow

way with a herring-bone pattern of banks and flat terraces. No house sites visible. Ruined medieval church nearby but fields all around are ploughed.

Co. Leix, DUNAMASE; 16/S 530980; 13E; AJQ 60–64 (1964) (castle)
3 m. WNW. of Stradbally. 1839 six-inch O.S. shows "Site of Ancient Village" and some earthworks are shown 700 yards W. of Rock of Dunamase. Ground survey shows field with bumps but no identifiable structures. Dunamase was a great Norman manor: was this the site of the New Town of Leix with its burgesses? (Otway-Ruthven, 1968, 252).

Co. Limerick, CAHERGUILLAMORE; 17/R 612397; 31E; ATD 34 (1967)
3 m. NW. of Bruff. For details see excavation report (O Riordain and Hunt, 1942).

Co. Longford, GRANARDKILLE (Plate 30); 12/N 322803; 10E; AJO 58–60 (1964), AJR 72–78 (1964), ASY 92–93 (1967)
1 m. S. of Granard. This is a special case and it is included here on account of the superb earthworks of the site. Locally it is thought to be the site of the old town of Granard burned by Edward Bruce in 1315. It is labelled "Site of Old Town of Granard" on 1836 six-inch O.S., where the earthworks are shown. But this seems unlikely as the early motte is 1 m. NE. and dominates the present town of Granard, suggesting that if the town was destroyed it was rebuilt on the same site. There is no evidence for the migration of the town. The field of earthworks (which are among the finest in the country) has a main hollow way along the former line of the road, various semi-circular and rectangular structures, enclosure banks and house-sites. It is not known what it represents.

Co. Tipperary, BALLYDUAGH (Plate 31); 18/S 115380; 61W; AIE 1–2, 6–7 (1963), AIF 16 (1963), APD 26–32 (1966)
3 m. SE. of Cashel. Discovered from the air, 1963. Isolated graveyard with foundations of medieval church surrounded by a complex of hollow ways and field banks. Some house-sites visible; one, especially prominent, seems to be that of a small, rectangular mud-walled house.

Co. Tipperary, BALLYNAHINCH; 18/S 036405; 60E; ATA 44–47 (1967)
3 m. W. of Cashel. 1840–41 six-inch O.S. shows earthworks around castle and isolated church. Earthworks confirmed by air photography in 1967; ground survey since. Complex of massive stone-cored banks and structures especially S. and E. of the castle.

Co. Tipperary, BAPTISTGRANGE; 18/S 210301; 77W; APG 50 (1966)
4 m. S. of Fethard. 1840 six-inch O.S. shows church, castle in ruins, graveyard and earthworks labelled "Site of Old Village". Stone structures are still there: ground survey shows bumps but definite features not identified.

Co. Tipperary, KILCONNELL; 18/S 138395; 61E
4 m. E. of Cashel. One farm with ruined castle in yard; isolated graveyard and site of

church. Extensive earthworks including very long hollow way in the field W. of farm. No house-sites visible but house platforms adjacent to hollow way? Some confusing former hedge lines and puzzling sinuous ridges.

Co. Tipperary, KILTINAN; 18/S 230319; 70E
3 m. SE. of Fethard. 1840 six-inch O.S. shows extensive earthworks to N. of isolated Kiltinan church, ruined, and castle. Ground survey shows very extensive site with rectangular layout. Certainly a borough or village. Intersecting hollow ways with house platforms flanking the main N–S hollow way. The most "planned" layout of any site found so far. Should be in State charge.

Co. Tipperary, LEIGHMORE (Liathmore-Mochoemog); 18/S 225577; 42E; ALV 65–67 (1965), APD 46–50 (1966)
6 m. E. of Thurles. For details see excavation report (Leask and Macalister, 1945–48). Currently under further excavation by R. E. Glasscock, 1968.

Co. Tipperary, PIPERSTOWN; 15/M 925037; 4E; ATA 34–35 (1967)
7 m. W. of Birr. 1840 six-inch O.S. shows "Site of Piperstown Village" in Gorta-pheepra Deer Park, south of Lackeen castle (in ruins). Ground survey shows much stonework but it is hard to distinguish features from quarrying and outcrop. All under trees and bushes. Air photo since visit suggests that there are trace of the settlement S. of site marked by O.S.

II. SELECT BIBLIOGRAPHY

AALEN, 1966

F. H. A. Aalen, "The evolution of the traditional house in Western Ireland", *Journ. Roy. Soc. Antiq. Irel.*, XCVI (1966), 47–58.

AALEN, 1965

——, (compiler), "Enclosures in Eastern Ireland: report of a symposium", *Irish Geog.*, v (1965), 29–39.

BRADY, 1961

Rev. J. Brady, "Anglo-Norman Meath", *Riocht na Midhe*, II (1961), 38–45.

BROOKS, 1950

E. St. J. Brooks, *Knights' fees in counties Wexford, Carlow and Kilkenny*, Irish Manuscripts Commission, S.O. (Dublin, 1950).

BUCHANAN, *et al.*, 1958

R. H. Buchanan, J. H. Johnson, and V. B. Proudfoot, "Preliminary report on the excavations at Murphystown", *Ulster Journ. Archaeol.*, 3rd ser., XXI (1958), 115–26.

CAHILL, 1936

Rev. E. Cahill, "Ireland in the Anglo-Norman period (1170–1540)", *Irish Ecclesiastical Rec.*, 5th ser., XLVIII (1936), 142–60.

CAMPBELL, 1935

Å. Campbell, "Irish fields and houses", *Bealoideas*, v (1935), 57–74.

CAMPBELL, 1937–38   ——, "Notes on the Irish house", *Folkliv*, I (1937), 205–34 and II (1938), 173–96.

CURTIS, 1938   E. Curtis, *A History of medieval Ireland, from 1086 to 1513* (1923), 2nd ed., (1938).

CURTIS, 1932–43   ——, *Calendar of Ormonde deeds, 1172–1603*, 6 vols., Irish Manuscripts Commission, S.O., Dublin (1932–43).

CURTIS, 1935–37   ——, "Rental of the manor of Lisronagh, 1333, and notes on 'Betagh' tenure in medieval Ireland", *Proc. Roy. Irish Acad.*, XLIII C (1935–37), 41–76.

DANAHER, 1938   K. Danaher, "Old house types in Oighreacht Ui Conchubhair (Iraghticonnor, Co. Kerry)", *Journ. Roy. Soc. Antiq. Irel.*, LXVIII (1938), 226–40.

DANAHER, 1945   ——, O Danachair, Caomhin, "The traditional houses of County Limerick", *N. Munster Antiq. Journ.*, V (1945), 18–32.

DANAHER, 1946   ——, O Danachair, Caomhin, "Hearth and chimney in the Irish house", *Bealoideas*, XVI (1946), 91–104.

DANAHER, 1957   ——, O Danachair, Caomhin, "Materials and methods in Irish traditional building", *Journ. Roy. Soc. Antiq. Irel.*, LXXXVII (1957), 61–74.

DUIGNAN, 1944   M. Duignan, "Irish agriculture in early historic times", *Journ. Roy. Soc. Antiq. Irel.*, LXXIV (1944), 124–45.

EDWARDS, 1938–39   R. D. Edwards, "Anglo-Norman relations with Connacht, 1169–1224", *Irish Hist. Stud.*, I (1938–39), 135–53.

EVANS, 1939   E. E. Evans, "Donegal survivals", *Antiquity*, XIII (1939), 207–22.

EVANS, 1939A   ——, "Some survivals of the Irish openfield system", *Geography*, XXIV (1939), 24–36.

EVANS, 1942   ——, *Irish Heritage* (1942).

EVANS, 1956   ——, "The ecology of peasant life in Western Europe", in W. L. Thomas, jr., ed., *Man's role in changing the face of the earth* (Chicago, 1956), 217–39.

EVANS, 1957   ——, *Irish Folk Ways* (1957).

EVANS, 1958–59   ——, and others, "Rural settlement in Ireland and Western Britain", *Advance. Science*, XV (1958–59), 333–45.

EVANS, 1964   ——, "Ireland and Atlantic Europe", *Geog. Zeit.*, LII (1964), 224–41.

FLATRÈS, 1957   P. Flatrès, *Géographie rurale de quatre contrées Celtiques, Irelande, Galles, Cornwall et Man*, Rennes (1957).

FREEMAN, 1957   T. W. Freeman, *Pre-Famine Ireland* (1957).

FREEMAN, 1965   ——, *Ireland: a general and regional geography* (1950), 3rd ed. (1965).

GWYNN, 1935   A. Gwynn, "The Black Death in Ireland", *Studies*, XXIV (1935), 25–42.

HAYES-MCCOY, 1964   G. A. Hayes-McCoy, *Ulster and other Irish maps, circa 1600* (1964).

JOHNSON, 1958   J. H. Johnson, "Studies of Irish rural settlement", *Geog. Rev.*, XLVIII (1958), 554–66.

JOHNSON, 1963   ——, "The disappearance of clachans from County Derry in the nineteenth century", *Irish Geog.*, IV (1963), 404–14.

JONES, 1953   G. R. J. Jones, "Some medieval rural settlements in north Wales", *Trans. Inst. Brit. Geog.*, XIX (1953), 51–72.

JOPE, ed., 1966   E. M. Jope, ed., Northern Ireland; Archaeological Survey, *An archaeological survey of County Down*, H.M.S.O., (1966).

KILLANIN AND DUIGNAN, 1967   Lord Killanin and M. V. Duignan, *Shell Guide to Ireland* (1962), 2nd ed. (1967).

LEASK, 1936   H. G. Leask "Irish castles: 1180–1310", *Archaeol. Journ.*, XCIII (1936), 143–99.

LEASK, 1941   ——, *Irish castles and castellated houses* (1941), new ed. (1951).

LEASK, 1955–60   ——, *Irish churches and monastic buildings*, 3 vols. (1955–60).

LEASK AND MACALISTER, 1945–48   H. G. Leask and R. A. S. Macalister, "Liathmore-Mochoemog (Leigh), County Tipperary", *Proc. Roy. Irish Acad.*, LI C (1945–48), 1–14.

LEWIS, 1837   S. Lewis, *A topographical dictionary of Ireland*, 2 vols. (1837).

MACAODHA, 1965   B. S. MacAodha, "Clachan settlement in Iar-Connacht", *Irish Geog.*, V (1965), 20–28.

MCCOURT, 1950   D. McCourt, "The rundale system in Ireland: a study of its geographical distribution and social relations", unpublished Ph.D. thesis, The Queen's University of Belfast, 1950.

MCCOURT, 1954–55   ——, "Infield and outfield in Ireland", *Econ. Hist. Rev.*, 2nd ser., VII (1954–55), 369–76.

MCCOURT, 1964–65   ——, "The cruck truss in Ireland and its West European connections", *Folkliv*, XXVIII–XXIX (1964–65), 64–78.

MACIVOR, 1957–60   Rev. D. MacIvor, "Ardee manor in A.D. 1336", *Journ. Co. Louth Archaeol. Soc.*, XIV (1957–60), 160–64.

MACNIOCAILL, 1964   G. MacNiocaill, *Na buirgeisi XII–XV aois*, 2 vols. (1964).

MILLS, 1891   J. Mills, "Tenants and agriculture near Dublin in the fifteenth century", *Journ. Roy. Soc. Antiq. Irel.*, XXI (1891), 54–56.

MILLS, 1894 ——, "The Norman settlement in Leinster", *Journ. Roy. Soc. Antiq. Irel.*, XXIV (1894), 161–75.

N.M.I., 1964 *National Monuments of Ireland*, Bord Failte Eireann (1964).

O'KELLY, 1950 M. J. O'Kelly, "Ring-fort house-types in the south of Ireland", *Congres Internationale des Sciences Prehistoriques et Protohistoriques*, Zurich, (1950), 317–21.

O'LOAN, 1961 J. O'Loan, "The manor of Cloncurry, Co. Kildare, and the feudal system of land tenure in Ireland", *Journ. Dept. Agric.* (Dublin), LVIII (1961), 14–36.

O'RIORDAIN, 1942 S. P. O'Riordain, *Antiquities of the Irish Countryside* (1942), 4th ed. (1964).

O'RIORDAIN, 1953–54 ——, "Lough Gur excavations: Neolithic and Bronze Age houses in Knockadoon", *Proc. Roy. Irish Acad.*, LVI C (1953–54), 297–459.

O'RIORDAIN AND HUNT, 1942 S. P. O'Riordain and J. Hunt, "Medieval dwellings at Caherguillamore, Co. Limerick", *Journ. Roy. Soc. Antiq. Irel.*, LXXII (1942), 37–63.

O'RIORDAIN AND O'KELLY, 1940 S. P. O'Riordain and M. J. O'Kelly, "Old house types near Lough Gur, Co. Limerick", in J. Ryan, ed., *Essays and studies presented to Professor E. MacNeill* (1940).

ORPEN, 1911–20 G. H. Orpen, *Ireland under the Normans, 1169–1333*, 4 vols. (1911–20).

ORPEN, 1932 AND 1936 ——, "Ireland to 1315, and Ireland 1315–c. 1485", being chapters in *Cambridge Medieval History*, VII and VIII (1932 and 1936).

O'SULLIVAN, 1962 Mary D. O'Sullivan, *Italian merchant bankers in Ireland in the thirteenth century: a study in the social and economic history of medieval Ireland* (1962).

OTWAY-RUTHVEN, 1946–47 Jocelyn Otway-Ruthven, "Anglo-Irish shire government in the thirteenth century", *Irish Hist. Stud.*, V (1946–47), 1–28.

OTWAY-RUTHVEN, 1950–51 ——, "The native Irish and English law in medieval Ireland", *Irish Hist. Stud.*, VII (1950–51), 1–16.

OTWAY-RUTHVEN, 1951 ——, "The organisation of Anglo-Irish agriculture in the Middle Ages", *Journ. Roy. Soc. Antiq. Irel.*, LXXXI (1951), 1–13.

OTWAY-RUTHVEN, 1958–59 ——, "The medieval county of Kildare", *Irish Hist. Stud.*, XI (1958–59), 181–99.

OTWAY-RUTHVEN, 1959 ——, "Knight service in Ireland", *Journ. Roy. Soc. Antiq. Irel.*, LXXXIX (1959), 1–15.

OTWAY-RUTHVEN, 1961 ——, "Knights fees in Kildare, Leix and Offaly", *Journ. Roy. Soc. Antiq. Irel.*, XCI (1961), 163–81.

OTWAY-RUTHVEN, 1965 ——, "The character of Norman settlement in Ireland", *Hist. Stud.*, v (1965), 75–84.

OTWAY-RUTHVEN, 1968 ——, *A history of medieval Ireland* (1968).

PRICE, 1963 L. Price, "A note on the use of the word 'Baile' in place-names", *Celtica*, vi (1963), 119–26.

PROUDFOOT, 1955 V. B. Proudfoot, "The people of the forths", *Ulster Folklife*, i (1955), 19–26.

PROUDFOOT, 1959 ——, "Clachans in Ireland", *Gwerin*, ii (1959), 110–22.

PROUDFOOT, 1961 ——, "The economy of the Irish rath", *Med. Archaeol.*, v (1961), 94–122.

RUSSELL, 1948 J. C. Russell, *British Medieval population* (1948), especially the section on Irish boroughs (351–56).

RYNNE, 1962–64 E. Rynne, "Some destroyed sites at Shannon airport, Co. Clare", *Proc. Roy. Irish Acad.*, LXIII C (1962–64), 245–77.

SHELL GUIDE (See under Killanin.)

UHLIG, 1961 H. Uhlig, "Old hamlets with infield and outfield systems in Western and Central Europe", *Geografiska Annaler*, XLIII (1961), 285–312.

WATT, *et al.*, 1961 J. A. Watt, J. B. Morrall and F. X. Martin, eds., *Medieval studies presented to Aubrey Gwynn, S.J.* (1961).

WESTROPP, 1896–1901 T. J. Westropp, "The Ancient Forts of Ireland", *Proc. Roy. Irish Acad.*, XXXI (1896–1901), 579–730.

Memoranda on the Preservation of Deserted Medieval Village Sites

THE TWO Memoranda were submitted on behalf of the D.M.V.R.G. The first, composed in 1965, was considered by the Ancient Monuments Board for England in the following terms: "A research report prepared by the Group, under the chairmanship of our member, Prof. Grimes, much impressed us, and we commended the proposals therein submitted to the Ministry as being both reasonable and practicable. We considered that the Ministry should take into guardianship such of those of six 'best sites' recommended as might prove to be available, without waiting for the report of the Field Monuments Committee. It is apparent to us that analogous problems will arise in respect of prehistoric and Romano-British settlements, and we hope that similar constructive research may be undertaken in regard to them".[1]

Difficult problems of finance and staffing did not enable the Ministry of Public Building and Works to implement the Board's recommendation for the guardianship of the six sites in Appendix A of the Memorandum until 1969. The Committee of Enquiry into the Arrangements for the Protection of Field Monuments, under the chairmanship of Sir David Walsh, reported in February, 1969.[2] If its recommendations are accepted it will be easier to preserve the scheduled sites in Appendix B–D of the Memorandum.

The second Memorandum was submitted in 1969 to the Ancient Monuments Board for Scotland, who are now considering it.

1. *Memorandum to the Chief Inspector of Ancient Monuments, Ministry of Public Building and Works, prepared by the Deserted Medieval Village Research Group, 1965*

SUMMARY

Two thousand deserted medieval villages have so far been identified in England. Of these nearly 500 have been totally destroyed in past centuries. 1,250 of the other sites have only poor or medium quality earthworks, mainly through partial destruction in the past centuries. This leaves only about 250 sites of the first quality. Since the last war there has been a great increase in the processes of destruction by the bulldozing of marginal land for agriculture, building, new roads, etc. As a result there are now in many areas only one or two good

---

[1] Ancient Monuments Boards for England, Scotland and Wales, *Annual Reports, XIII, 1966* (1967), 5, para. 13.

[2] *Report of the Committee of Enquiry into the Arrangements for the Protection of Field Monuments, 1966–68*, Chairman Sir David Walsh (1969), Cmnd. 3904

quality deserted villages left. It is, therefore, essential that the best sites are preserved before it is too late.

For the purpose of this survey the country has been divided into 54 regions, each displaying a combination of soils, relief, climate and agrarian history not encountered in another area of the country. This system of division into regions of widely differing size, inevitably gives equal attention to areas that are dense with sites and those with few, but it must be remembered that the historical and geographical factors causing desertion did not apply equally in all parts of the country, i.e. no desertion in the Fens or on the Yorkshire Moors.

It is recommended that one site from each of these regions should be preserved for posterity together with two shrunken sites and four sites each representing a typical period of desertion. The six best deserted villages should be taken into Guardianship immediately. Eight other sites should be considered for eventual Guardianship; and the other 46 sites should be scheduled and preserved in the best way possible. In addition one site in Wales and one in Scotland should be preserved now, and other sites considered for preservation.

The sites suggested by the D.M.V.R.G., together with notes of explanation, are listed below. In view of the possible difficulties in preserving specific sites, alternatives are given wherever this is possible.

SITES DESTROYED BEFORE 1939

Out of 2,000 D.M.V.s 134 sites cannot be located and a further 112 are flat grass where the sites should be. It is assumed that most of these 246 sites have been destroyed by ploughing, building and other activities during the 500 years since the main period of desertion.

SITES DESTROYED 1939–52

A further 36 sites were under the plough when visits were first made to them during the 1950's. In many cases these sites had been destroyed during the intensive ploughing during World War II.

SITES DESTROYED SINCE 1952

Since 1952, however, there has been a remarkable increase in the tempo of destruction and 201 threats have been reported in these 13 years. If one adds to these the 36 sites destroyed during the 1940's, it will be seen that as many sites have been threatened during the past 25 years as during the previous 500 years.

PREVIOUS ACTION TAKEN

The Ministry of Public Building and Works have, under very difficult conditions due to the problems of compensation, tried to preserve some of these threatened sites. They have been able to negotiate with the owners in 27 cases, and these sites have been saved and in most cases scheduled under the Ancient Monuments Acts. In a further 30 cases only part of the site was threatened, or it was possible to negotiate for parts of the earthworks to be left intact. 144 of the 201 sites threatened have therefore been completely destroyed.

The Ministry of Public Building and Works have carried out excavations on about 25 of these threatened villages, ranging from major excavations, such as those at Hangleton in Sussex, to smaller watching briefs to recover some of the evidence after destruction, as at Babingley, Norfolk. Further work has been impossible owing to the high cost of excavation and the limited funds available. On the recommendation of the D.M.V.R.G., sites for excavation have been chosen, where possible in those areas where little previous work had been done. For example, between 1964 and 1966 the major excavations of the Ministry were in Norfolk (at Thuxton and Grenstein), an area without previous excavation of D.M.V. sites.

RECOMMENDATIONS FOR FUTURE PRESERVATION

Despite this wholesale destruction of deserted village sites there are still between 200 and 250 sites of A or A* quality which are important enough to be preserved. The country has been divided for selection of recommendations into 54 regions, and it is suggested that one site in each area should be preserved at all costs. In some regions there are still up to six good sites intact, so that here a gradual selection can be made: but in other areas only one good site remains, and here urgent action is required to ensure preservation. In addition six other sites should be preserved, irrespective of area, to preserve a typical shrunk village and sites illustrating the different periods of desertion. This list only applies to England: sites should also be preserved in different regions of Scotland and Wales.

It is proposed that, as a first step, six sites in England, one in Scotland and one in Wales should be taken into Guardianship by the Ministry of Public Building and Works immediately, and that over the next few years an additional eight sites in England (making 14 in all) should be taken into Guardianship, so that at least one deserted village is preserved for posterity in each major region of the country. Forty-six other sites should be scheduled where this has not already been done and their future watched carefully. If any threat develops to them they should be preserved, if necessary by Guardianship, unless another similar site in the area can be preserved. For this reason alternative sites have been given where possible for each of these additional areas.

There are eighteen regions where insufficient work has taken place for a site to be named for preservation. It is hoped that these gaps will be filled as the work of the D.M.V.R.G. progresses and before all sites in these areas are destroyed. There are several areas where only one site still survives of sufficient quality for Guardianship but not of the quality of the first 14, so it must wait for the third stage of preservation. It is suggested that in these cases the owners should be informed of the special importance of these sites and the hope expressed that they will be able to keep them intact. If unfavourable replies are received it may be necessary to bring some of these sites forward in the programme.

A list of our sixty sites recommended for preservation is given in Appendices A–D. Where possible, alternative names are given so that there can be some room for manoeuvre in the case of difficult landowners.

Appendix A. *The six best sites in England for Guardianship*

Four of these (Wharram Percy, Gainsthorpe, Broadstone and Hound Tor) are so important, and the earthworks so impressive, with all the houses clearly visible as earthworks, that they should be taken into Guardianship without any further discussion. The owners of Wharram Percy and Hound Tor are sympathetic and may offer the sites to the Ministry. The D.M.V.R.G. have not been in touch with the owners of Broadstone or Gainsthorpe. For the two other sites in the six it is essential that Midland Clay sites should be included. There are many choices, and if the Ministry does not get a favourable reply to the first choice another could be suggested. Ingarsby (Leicestershire) should be tried first, on the grounds both of the quality of its earthworks and of the documentary evidence (the actual day the village was destroyed is known). There are two possible sites in East Anglia, Godwick and Pudding

Norton. Both have strong reasons to be put first so it is suggested that approaches should be made to both owners: the replies received might tip the balance.

There is no doubt that the first choice for Wales should be Runston not only because of its excellent earthworks but because the Ministry already have the church in Guardianship. In Scotland it is suggested that one of the Sutherland clearance villages, such as Rosal, should be included first.

The most urgent need is to preserve these sites, so although it is hoped that, as funds become available, some of the sites might be excavated and selected houses laid out, there should in the first instance be no heavy charge on the Ministry for consolidation and maintenance. After the sites are fenced, if required, it should be possible for the farmers to graze them, and in this case maintenance charges should be nil.

The parish church is an integral part of a medieval village. In most cases the building has been destroyed but there are several sites where the church, or the ruins of the church, survive. It is recommended that two of the first six sites should be villages containing churches. Runston, the Welsh recommendation, has a church also. Godwick and Pudding Norton have ruins of churches which will require consolidation but in either case the sum required should not be large. The case of Wharram Percy is different as here, except for the fallen tower, the church is intact, so that the roof could be removed and the walls consolidated with the remains of the tower. Though the cost would be considerable, it would be of the greatest importance as the church fabric epitomises the expansion and contraction of the village. The Church authorities are sympathetic to giving the church to the Ministry as they have not the funds to preserve it. Although the Ecclesiastical authorities suggested 10 years ago that the Ministry should take it over, there seem to be legal difficulties at the moment which might mean a delay. If this is the case it is hoped that it may be possible to carry out urgent repairs to avoid any further collapse of the fabric. At Runston the church is already consolidated and in good order.

APPENDIX A

	Site name	County	County division	Topographical division
North England	1 Wharram Percy	Yorks E.R.	East	Wolds
East Midlands	2 Gainsthorpe	Lincs. Lindsey	North	Limestone Heath
East Midlands	3 Ingarsby	Leics.	East	Heights
South Central	4 Broadstone	Oxon.	North	Cotswolds
East Anglia	5 Godwick or Pudding Norton	Norfolk	West	Loams
South-west England	6 Hound Tor	Devon	Central	Dartmoor
Wales	Runston	Monmouth		
Scotland	Rosal	Sutherland		

Appendix B. The second group of 8 sites for eventual Guardianship

Sites are suggested for six of eight regions. Work in Kent and north-west England has not yet progressed far enough for sites to be suggested but places should be kept open on the list for suitable sites to be decided upon. Thus at the moment the second list, like the first, contains six sites. It is suggested that owners of these 12 possible sites should be approached over the next few years with a view to seeing which are the most suitable for Guardianship and whether any of the owners might offer their sites to the Ministry.

APPENDIX B

	Site name	County	County division	Topographical division
North England	7 South Middle-ton or Welton	Northumberland	South	Fells
	8 —	Cumberland or Westmorland	—	Fells
West Midlands	9 Abdon or Heath	Shrops.	South	Upland
East Midlands	10 Hungry Bentley or Alkmonton	Derbyshire	South	Lowlands
	11 Wolfhampcote or Braunston-bury	Warwks. Northants.	Central West	Feldon
South Central	12 Quarrendon or Burston	Bucks.	North	Clayland
	13 Gomeldon	Wilts.	South	Downland
South East	14 (Northeye)	Sussex	South	Coastal Plain

Appendix C. The third group of 40 sites for preservation

Sites are suggested for 27 of the regions. Names for the other 13 will be given as the work of the D.M.V.R.G. progresses. As in Appendix B, alternative sites are given in each area. The first thing to be done is to ensure that all these sites are scheduled and that the owners are aware of their importance. If threats develop, some of these sites may have to be brought forward in the preservation programme especially in those areas where there are no alternative good quality sites known.

APPENDIX C

	Site name	County	County division	Topographical division
North England	15 Old Mousen or Tughall	Northumberland	North	Coastal Plain
	16 Barton	Northumberland	Central	Fells
	17 Yoden or Garmondsway	Durham	Central	Coastal Plain

Appendix D. The fourth group: periods of desertion together with examples of shrinkage for preservation

The same remarks apply as for Appendix C.

	Site name	County	County division	Topographical division
North England	18 West Hartburn or Walworth	Durham	South	Tees Valley
	19 South Cowton or Lazenby	Yorks. N.R.	Central	Vale of York
	20 Newton Mulgrave	Yorks. N.R.	North	Cleveland
	21 East Lilling or Marton	Yorks. N.R.	South	Vale of York
	22 East Tanfield or Humberton	Yorks. N.R. Yorks. W.R.	North	Vale of York
	23 Toulston or Steeton	Yorks. W.R.	North	Vale of York
	24 Eske or Southorpe	Yorks. E.R.	East	Holderness
	25 —	Yorks. Notts.	South North	Vale of York
	26 —	Cheshire Lancs.		
	27 —	Westmorland Cumberland		Fells
West Midlands	28 Wychnor	Staffs.	Central	Lowland
	29 Stretton Baskerville	Warwks.	Central	Feldon
	30 —	Heref.		Vale of Evesham
	31 Sheriffs Naunton	Worcs.	South	Vale of Evesham
	32 Lower Ditchford or Lower Norton	Gloucs.	North	Vale of Evesham
South Central England	33 Hampton Gay or Wretchwick	Oxon.	Central	Clayland
East Midlands	34 Sulby or Starmore	Northants. Leics.	East East	Heights Heights
	35 Mallows Cotton or Boughton	Northants. Hunts.	East North	Lowland Lowland
	36 Clopton	Cambs.	South	Upland
	37 Bingham or East Stoke	Notts.	East	Trent Valley
	—	Lincs., Kesteven Rutland		Limestone Heath
	38 or Horn			
	39 Rand	Lincs., Lindsey	South	Clay Lowland
	40 Calcethorpe or South Cadeby	Lincs., Lindsey	South	Wolds

		Site name	County	County division	Topographical division
East Anglia	41	—	Norfolk Suffolk		Clays
	42	—	Essex		Clays
South West	43	—	Cornwall	West	
	44	Trewortha or Garrow	Cornwall	East	Bodmin Moor
	45	Badgworthy	Devon	North	Exmoor
	46	—	Somerset	Central	
	47	—	Somerset	South	
West Midlands	48	—	Gloucs.	South	
	49	Sennington	Gloucs.	Central	Cotswolds
South Central	50	—	Wilts.	North	Downland
	51	Holworth or a Winterbourne	Dorset	North	Downland
	52	Abbotstone	Hants.	Central	Downland
	53	—	Bucks. Berks.	South East	
	54	—	Kent		

APPENDIX D

Category	County	Site Name	
Shrunk	Lincolnshire	55	Broxholme
Shrunk	Warwickshire	56	Cosford
Domesday Desertion		57	—
Monastic Desertion		58	—
Black Death Desertion	Oxfordshire	59	Tusmore
Eighteenth-Century Emparking	Leicestershire	60	Stapleford

2. *Memorandum to the Inspector of Ancient Monuments for Scotland, prepared by the Deserted Medieval Village Research Group, 1969*

Although there were undoubtedly regional variations, there was a degree of uniformity in medieval settlement form in the Scottish Highlands and Lowlands alike. Apart from the burghs, the castles of the great landowners, and the houses of the lesser lairds, the recurring settlement was not the village in the English sense, but a small cluster of houses and associated buildings forming a group-farm or fermtoun. Numbers within the group varied, but three to eight tenants were usual. In addition there might also be several cottars to provide additional labour.   After 1745 many of the Highland townships swelled in size, and then in the early nineteenth century there commenced an era of depopulation.   This type of deserted settlement site in the Highlands is almost unique in Europe and many of the place-names can be traced back to medieval times.   Such sites are of exceptional interest since much might be learned of earlier settlement phases which at present have left no superficial trace, because of the flimsy building materials employed.

Some of these ruinous clusters provide very impressive memorials of the Highland group-farms as they existed as anachronisms just before desertion.   No doubt more extensive survey will yield other excellent examples but meanwhile some degree of preservation of selected sites is abundantly necessary.   With adequate plans and notice-boards a number of these could be made attractive to the student and tourist alike.   So many foreign visitors to Scotland are of Highland descent and come with a desire to see the old home district, often remembered over several generations: these ruined deserted settlements require no embellishment to tell their story.   In the Lowlands, where Anglian influence was strong, some settlements may have approached in size and organisation the villages of northern England but much more study of this question is needed.   Meanwhile selected sites may be suggested for Scheduling.

It is realized that the preservation of the standing remains on many of these sites could be a very costly business if they were taken into Guardianship by the Ministry of Public Building and Works.   This is made more difficult by the fact that many of the walls are bonded together only with clay mortar, or are of dry-stone construction.   It is suggested that sites 2, 3A, 4, 5, 6, 8 should be Scheduled as Ancient Monuments in the hope that a representative series of sites may be preserved in different parts of Scotland.   Site 1 at Arrol is already in Guardianship and Site 3B is already being preserved and restored by local initiative.   It is hoped that over a period of time it will be possible for all the other sites to be taken into Guardianship by the Ministry but for the present it is strongly recommended that a single site should be chosen as soon as possible for Guardianship, consolidation and preservation of the standing remains.   There is little doubt on our present information, and as a result of the tour of sites made by members of the D.M.V.R.G. in 1964 and 1966 that the best site would be Tirai in Perthshire.   This site is easy of access, lying close to a main tourist route along Loch Tay and is in a perfect setting in pasture.   Consolidation would be expensive but urgent work where walls are falling could be carried out in the first instance with further consolidation over a number of years.   With this experience it might then be possible to move on to other sites.

This initial programme would preserve a representative series of settlements of different types in different regions.

Roofed Buildings in (1) Lewis by the Ministry, and in (3B) Argyll by local effort.

Ruins in (2) Rhum, (3A) Kintyre, (5) Angus, (6) Perthshire, and (7B) Kirkcudbright.

Earthworks in (4) Sutherland, (7A) Kirkcudbright and (8) Peeblesshire.

There is no doubt that as well as the impressive remains of castles and abbeys in Guardianship there should be preserved typical village sites so that future generations can get a better idea of how the ordinary people lived before the fundamental changes of the twentieth century.

List of Scottish Deserted Settlements Recommended for Preservation

(1)   OUTER HEBRIDES

LEWIS—BARVAS, ARROL (NB 3148)

Hebridean House No. 42 is already in Ministry Guardianship.   This is a good example of a typical black house, still roofed and habitable.   It stands in one of the Lewis townships listed in Category B by the Scottish Development Department under the 1947 Planning Acts.

310

(2) INNER HEBRIDES
RHUM—KILMORY (NG 3603) AND HARRIS (NM 3395)

These sites deserted in the early nineteenth century are under the protection of the Nature Conservancy and they have round them the distinctive narrow ridges produced by foot plough cultivation. The whole agrarian unit could therefore here be preserved without difficulty since in most other cases modern agricultural needs will prevent the sterilization of such large areas.

Kilmory is the more interesting site of the two. It comprises a compact group of round-cornered dry-stone houses and outbuildings, with walls up to 4 ft. 6 in. thick and sharply battered, clustered round a medieval burial-ground. There is no evidence on the ground for the medieval chapel described in the Hebridean *Inventory*, but this may lie beneath the township. The remains are exceptionally well-preserved and sand clearance would probably reveal further buildings.

The Topographic Science sub-section of the Geography Department of Glasgow University, under Mr. G. Petrie, have recently mapped Rhum for the Nature Conservancy. With the aid of air photographs, detailed plots have been made of the deserted settlements in such detail that each individual ridge made with the foot plough is portrayed.

(3) WEST
(A) ARGYLL—KINTYRE—BALMCVICAR (NR 5909)

A site with extensive remains of buildings including a horizontal mill and a corn-drying kiln impressively situated on the coast but difficult of access.

(B) MID-ARGYLL—AUCHINDRAIN (NN 032033)

This village is being preserved as a Folk Museum. It shows a later stage in the desertion of multiple-tenancy farms since it was not finally abandoned till 1954. The buildings, probably of eighteenth and nineteenth century date, are mostly cruck-framed, some including gable crucks to carry hipped roofs. One shows evidence of a central hearth for which the smoke-hole still exists in the thatched roof. The evolution of the byre-dwelling into the typical two-roomed peasant-dwelling of the nineteenth century, is reflected in the development of some of the buildings. See J. G. Dunbar, "Auchindrain: A Mid-Argyll Township", *Folklife*, III (1965), 61–67.

Preservation and restoration work is now under way, but financial difficulties are likely to make this a long task. Nevertheless it is hoped that in this case this unique site will be preserved by local effort.

(4) NORTH
SUTHERLAND—STRATH NAVER—ROSAL (NC 688416).

The settlement was cleared in 1814–18 and is now preserved in a 45-acre enclosure surrounded by Forestry Commission plantations. Seventeen families were loosely distributed in three groups of houses around the periphery. There is documentary evidence as far back as 1269. There has been limited excavation by Mr. H. Fairhurst. This is a very important site because of its long historical documentation but there are many problems of preservation and it may not be possible to preserve it in perpetuity.

An alternative might be Grummore which lacks such good documentation but has impressive remains including a Broch and remains of cultivation ridges between scattered remains of buildings.

(5) EAST

ANGUS—GLEN ESK—DALFORTH (NO 573775)

An important site with upstanding remains situated not far from the Tarfside Folk Museum. There seems to be a sequence from early grassed-over structures, which may have been *shielings*, through dry-stone walled buildings to later clay-bonded walls.

(6) CENTRAL

PERTHSHIRE—GLEN LOCHAY—TIRAI (NN 528367)

A very impressive assemblage of scattered upstanding buildings on either side of a burn. Unlike other sites which are confined by trees, or obscured by rough moorland, this site stands in open pasture which makes an appreciation of its site very clear. Mr. A. Morrison, who is at present working on the Tayside and Assynt Surveys of 1769–1772, reports that he has not located any better examples in the area. There are very many sites in Upper Strathtay which are being studied by the Breadalbane Society, Aberfeldy, but none of these are as impressive as Tirai, except perhaps Tomtayewen which is at present much obscured by vegetation and is rather difficult of access being some way from the road.

(7) SOUTH-WEST

(A) KIRKCUDBRIGHT—GALTWAY (NX 707487)

An impressive site more like English examples with grass-covered foundations of buildings and associated cultivation ridges. It is thought that this site was deserted in the mid-eighteenth century.

(B) KIRKCUDBRIGHT—POLMADDIE (NX 590878)

A site on higher ground with scattered groups of dry-stone walled buildings like the main Highland sites. Both villages should be preserved, if possible, to show the contrast of site.

(8) THE BORDERS

PEEBLESSHIRE—LOUR (NT 179357)

A *fermtoun* occupied from the sixteenth to the eighteenth century with good quality earthworks. One building has been excavated by Mr. J. G. Dunbar, see *Proc. Soc. Antiq. Scot.*, XCIV (1960–61), 195–210.

There are very few other outstanding sites in the region so far identified.

Fieldwork Questionnaire

DESERTED MEDIEVAL VILLAGE RESEARCH GROUP (D.M.V.R.G.)
67 GLOUCESTER CRESCENT, LONDON, N.W.1

Introduction to Fieldwork Questionnaire

THE PURPOSE of this questionnaire is to offer guidance to people interested in carrying out fieldwork on deserted medieval village (D.M.V.) sites and to provide them with an opportunity to make a permanent record of their work in a form which can be filed at the D.M.V.R.G.'s London office and there be available to other workers.

As well as answering this questionnaire, measured plans and sketches should be made of the village site wherever possible. Every opportunity should be taken to use a camera both for any interesting standing buildings and for the site itself, although you will find that earthworks are difficult to photograph effectively from ground level. If possible try to find a high point which overlooks the site. Shadows from a low sun usually show earthworks at their best. From autumn to early spring is the best time of year for fieldwork. During the winter months the grass is short and the earthworks are then much clearer. The arable fields will be ploughed and it should be possible to search for pottery which may at times be the only surviving indication at ground level of the location of a site. (It is usually easier to find pottery on a weathered soil surface than on a freshly ploughed field.) Prints of en-print size should accompany your report. Colour slides are not essential but gifts would be welcome.

The site of the medieval church is often the best starting-point in the search for a village or, failing that, any farms in the area. The name of the village often survives as the name of a modern farm. Many sites have already been discovered and county lists of these are available from the D.M.V.R.G. at 2s. 6d. each. However, for some counties the lists' map references refer often to the church or farmhouse, and one should always check on the ground whether the given map reference really does in fact pinpoint the site.

With the ever-increasing rate of destruction of D.M.V. sites, particularly from bulldozing and ploughing for farm improvement schemes, there is a very urgent need for accurate information about sites. The details collected in this questionnaire may for some sites in fact be their only record before destruction. With this rate of destruction, please keep a subsequent eye on the best sites and report to the D.M.V.R.G. any threat from agriculture, building, quarrying, roadworks, etc. The D.M.V.R.G. all too often hears about a threat when it is already too late.

Remember: Do not walk on land or enter buildings without asking permission first. As well as avoiding a possibly embarrassing scene, you will often gain helpful information about the site.

Farmers

When visiting the farmer try to interest him in his site. Many sites are destroyed by ignorance, and with a little patience and tact many farmers can be interested in their sites. Please report the reaction of the farmer if you have a conversation with him.

Certain information about ownership and tenantry is very useful in anticipating threats to the preservation of the site by ploughing, although its personal nature demands considerable tact in gathering data. Not all the information may be readily obtainable. A threat is most likely to arise with a change of ownership bringing in a tenant with different ideas of farm management or a new landlord intending to make heavy investment in new buildings or extensive improvement of the land. Information on such changes (i.e. bulldozing of earthworks and ploughing of a site) which comes to your knowledge after sending in the report should also be passed on.

The size of the farm has an important bearing on future preservation: for example, it will be very difficult to preserve a 20 acre site on a 100 acre farm. If the grass is rough pasture with thistles etc., this should be reported as such land might soon be improved by ploughing and threaten the earthworks.

Equipment

The basic equipment needed by a fieldworker includes: *Ordnance Survey maps* (no fieldwork can be done without a 2½-inch map; a 25-inch map will be necessary for any detailed survey of a particular site); at least one *100-ft. tape* for measuring earthworks and possibly standing buildings if they are of particular interest; *drawing paper and board* for sketching or planning a site; a *note book*; and *polythene bags* for collecting pottery (the bottom will quickly fall out of a paper bag on a damp day!)

Planning

Obviously, the more accurate the plan the more useful it is, but even simple sketches showing the earthworks corresponding to street, house-sites and field-boundaries can be a very useful beginning. Making this type of sketch is probably what most fieldworkers will prefer and spaces for these drawings have been left in the questionnaire. However, those people who would like to make more accurate plans would find a scale of 1:500 the best and one-foot scale rules for this scale are obtainable from good drawing-equipment shops. Final plans should be drawn on tracing paper so that copies can be made either by the dyeline or TTS processes. This detailed work should not be attempted without first consulting good-quality plans already made of D.M.V. sites. Specimen copies of the plan of Wharram Percy village on this scale can be obtained from the D.M.V.R.G. at a charge of 7s. 6d. each, including postage. A useful guide to surveying can be found in R. J. C. Atkinson, *Field Archaeology* (Methuen, 1953, second edition), 85–137.

Excavating

No fieldworker should take on excavations unless he has already spent several seasons working on medieval excavations to gain the necessary experience. Gaining a good understanding of a site from fieldwork can often be far more rewarding than digging a few trenches because peasant-houses were usually very lightly-built structures, and it is often difficult to understand a single structure without excavating a large area. Those wishing to gain excavation experience may always join the D.M.V.R.G.'s excavations at Wharram Percy near Malton in Yorkshire each July; details from Prof. M. W. Beresford, The University, Leeds,

LS2 9JT. Details of other major D.M.V. excavations by private bodies, or the Ministry of Public Building, may be obtained from the D.M.V.R.G.

COMPLETED QUESTIONNAIRES SHOULD BE SENT TO THE SECRETARY, DESERTED MEDIEVAL VILLAGE RESEARCH GROUP, 67 GLOUCESTER CRESCENT, LONDON, N.W.1. IF ANY QUESTION CANNOT BE ANSWERED, PLEASE STRIKE IT OUT.

DESERTED MEDIEVAL VILLAGE RESEARCH GROUP

Fieldwork Questionnaire

Completed by................................. Date...............19....

1. Name of county:
2. Name of site (if known):
3. Name of present parish:
4. National Grid Reference:

    (a) of site:
    (N.B. Many of these on the D.M.V.R.G. lists at present relate to a modern farm while they should show the exact location of the D.M.V.)
    (b) of medieval church or chapel of village (if any)

5. Name and address of owner/s
6. Name and address of tenant/s farming the site
7. Name and address of nearest inhabited house to the site, if not the same as (6)
8. Remarks and prospects for future preservation of site

THE SITE

9. At what height above sea level does the site lie, and how does this relate to the surrounding landscape?
10. On what kind of soil does the site lie and what is the geology? (you may find published geology maps helpful for the latter)
11. If the village is on a slope, in which direction is it facing?
12. Is there a stream or spring nearby?
13. Is the site ill-drained? (if not, could this be the result of recent field drainage?)
14. Is there a well on the site, and what material is it lined with?
15. What is the relation of the site to the church? (if any)

The earthworks

16. Are there any earthworks, and if so, over what area do they extend? (Very often they are to be found in several adjacent fields. Mark on the first plan the fields in which earthworks of the village can be seen)
17. Is the site sloping, terraced or all on one level?
18. Do the earthworks form a recognisable pattern or are they indistinct and vague?

19. Are the lines of the *roads* visible? (These usually show as sunken ways)
20. Can you pick out any distinct *house-sites*? These are not always seen as buried wall foundations but may be represented by raised platforms; and the positions of hearths may at times be indicated by patches of nettles)
21. Are the house platforms contained within *property enclosures*? (These are either banks, buried stone walls or ditches, depending on the geology)
22. How do these house-sites and boundaries relate to the streets?
23. Is the village site defined by a boundary bank and ditch?
24. Are there any castle or moated sites or particularly extensive or prominent house-sites in the village, and could they represent the site(s) of the *manor house(s)*?
25. How does the site(s) of the castle or manor house(s) relate to the village?
26. Is there a village green? (This is usually a relatively level clear area in the village site, sometimes bounded by streets)
27. Are there any ponds? (There may be a pond on the village green. They will probably have silted up too much today to contain water)
28. Is there any evidence for post-medieval disturbance of the site, by quarrying or modern ponds, for example?
29. Are there any fishponds, millponds or mill leats nearby?

Ploughed sites

30. If the site is partly or wholly ploughed, how long has this been done and was the site levelled first by a bulldozer?
31. Are earthworks still visible in the ploughed field?
32. Are there any signs of soil marks in the ploughsoil representing ploughed up buildings, yards and boundaries?
    Can you make a plan of them?
33. Are there any pieces of worked stone lying in the ploughsoil?
34. Can you collect pottery and other surface finds, bagging them by areas or fields? (If you have a 25-inch map record the field number. If pottery is collected by area, this should give a useful date-range for the different parts of the site and make it possible to suggest expansion and contraction within the site, if you can collect enough)
35. If you visit the site when it is under crop, are there any signs of crop-marks?

Ridge and Furrow

36. Is there any ridge and furrow visible near the village? If so, how is it related to the village?
37. Is it straight or curved?
38. What is the width between the tops of the ridges?
39. How high are the tops of the ridges from the bottoms of the furrows?
40. If possible try to include the outline of any ridge and furrow on your plans.

PLANS

Plan 1.

Show the extent and outlines of the site in the modern field system.

Plan(s) 2.

Detailed plans or sketches or earthworks, etc.

316

STANDING BUILDINGS

41. List the standing buildings on or near the site and give if possible an approximate estimate of their date.   (There may be a church, rectory, manor, farms, cottages)
42. What are the building materials?
    (a) in the church
    (b) in other buildings
    Is it local?

The church or chapel

43. Does the church occupy the highest point on the site?
44. Is the church ruined?   If so, how much of it still survives?
45. If it is intact, how often is it used?
46. What is the earliest architectural style, e.g. Norman?
47. What is the dominant style?   Does this or the size of the church indicate a period of prosperity?
48. Is there evidence of a contraction of the size of the church, e.g. blocked up aisles?
49. To what style does the final period of alteration belong?
50. If the church is a modern building, does it contain any older features such as a font from an earlier church?
51. To what period do the interior ornaments and monuments belong?
52. What are the latest dates for the tombstones in the churchyard?
53. What shape is the churchyard and what is the churchyard boundary made of?

Other buildings of particular interest

54. Are any other buildings of particular interest or of an early date?   (The best clue to the age of a house is in the roof timbering)

Documentation

55. Do you know of any documents mentioning the site?
56. Name and address of compiler

. . . .

. . . .

. . . .

. . . .

. . . .

Index

Place names in the archaeological and county gazetteers are self-indexed but sites referred to only by numbers in the footnotes of Chapter Two are included here.

Sites named here are, unless otherwise stated, deserted villages or settlements. The abbreviation *d.m.vs.* is used. Grid references are given to sites that do not appear in the gazetteers.

Monaghan, co., few clach-
ans, 285; place-names
with *bally*, 284
monasteries, in England,
145, 177, in Ireland,
281, 289, 292; animal
bones, 139–40; granges,
63, 265, and sheep-
farming as factors in
depopulation, 4–6, 73,
252–5, 309; iron-work-
ing, 140; population,
135
Mongewell (Oxon.), 24–5
Monmouthshire, houses, 256
Morayshire, clay houses, 242
Moreton, site 196 (Somer-
set), 83 fn.
Morgan's Hill (Wilts.), enclosure, 82
Morris, B., 257
Morrison, A., 312
mortar, clay (clay-bonding),
94, 290, 310, 312; lime,
94
mortars, 143
mottes, Anglo-Norman, in
Ireland, 282, 287; Nor-
man, in Wales, 252
mould, stone, 264
Mousen, Old (Northumber-
land), 307
Mowthorpe (Yorks. E.R.),
44
Moyaliff (Tipperary),
?houses, 291
Mucking, site 56 (Essex),
Saxon village, 84, 100–
104, 143 fn.
mud, *see* earth, unbaked
Muirkirk (Ayrshire), long-
house, 236–7
Munby, L. M., 68
Munster, isolated clachans,
285–6; raths, 281
Murphystown (Down), cla-
chan, 286
Muscott, site 151 (North-
ants.), 77 fn., 83 fn.,

98 fn., 99 and fn., 137,
Fig. 21
Musty, J. W. G., 78, 84
Mynydd Bychan (Llyswor-
ney, Glam.), farm, 265,
267, Fig. 40

Naneby (Leics.), 32–3
Nant Gwrtheyrn (Pistyll,
Caerns.), 260, 264 fn.,
Fig. 38
Nant-y-moch (Ystradfellte,
Brecs.), farm, 259, 264
fn., Fig. 37
Naunton, Sheriffs (Worcs.),
308
needles, 143
Newbold (Northants.), 74
Newbold Folville (Leics.),
32–3
Newbold Saucy (Leics.), 10,
32–3
New Forest (Hants.),
d.m.vs., 5, 35, 68
Newton, Cold (Leics.), 10,
32–3
Newton, James, rector of
Nuneham Courtenay,
55
Newton Mulgrave (NZ
786156, Yorks. N.R.),
308
Newtown (Wexford), cla-
chan, 285
Newtown Earls (Kilkenny),
?houses, 291
Newtown Jerpoint (Kil-
kenny), houses, 291
Nichols, John, on popula-
tion of Leicestershire,
32–4
Nicholaston (Glam.), ?new
foundation, 254
Nobold (Northants.), 49–50
Nonsuch, palace of (Ewell,
Surrey), built over Cud-
dington Church, 134
Norfolk, ruined churches,
31; d.m.vs., 7, 10, 21–2,

24, 31, 34–5, 39, 67–8,
116; erosion of coastal
villages, 21; field-sys-
tems, 31
Normanby-le-Wold, site 115
(Lincs.), Saxon struc-
tures, 89
Normanton (Rutland), 46
Normanton Turville
(Leics.), 10, 32–3
Northampton, houses
cleared for castle, 128
fn.
Northamptonshire, d.m.vs.,
12, 23, 25, 29, 34–6, 39,
50, 57–9, 65, 67–70,
Fig. 4; shrunken vil-
lages, 20
Northeye (Sussex), 307
Northolt (Mddx.), manor
house and underlying
village, 78, 128, Fig. 23
Northumberland, d.m.vs.,
31, 35, 38–9, 59, 68
Norton, Lower (Gloucs.),
60, 308
Norwich, houses cleared for
castle, 128 fn.; early
settlement, 128 fn.
Noseley (Leics.), 10, 32–3
Nottinghamshire, d.m.vs., 6,
23, 35, 39, 59, 69
Nuneham Courtenay
(Oxon.), 27, 46, 54–6,
Figs. 10–11

Offaly, co., few clachans,
285–6; place-names
with *bally*, 286
Ogle (Northumberland), 60
O'Kelly, M. J., 281 fn., 289
Olney Hyde (Bucks.), 142
O'Neil, H. E., 83
O'Neill family, crowning
place, 282
Onley, site 152 (Northants.),
83 fn.
Ordnance Survey, d.m.vs.
on maps, 31, 41, 46,